Contents

access to history

Britain

1783–1885

BEN ARMSTRONG

HODDER
EDUCATION
AN HACHETTE UK COMPANY

The Publishers would like to thank the following for permission to reproduce copyright material.

Photo credits: p4 Chronicle/Alamy Stock Photo; **p7** Archive.org; **p25** agefotostock/Alamy Stock Photo; **p55** Wikimedia Commons; **p102** Pictorial Press Ltd/Alamy Stock Photo; **p104** Robert Owen within a frame decorated with tools used for gardening and writing. Engraving after W.T. Fry. Credit: Wellcome Collection. CC BY 4.0 (detail); **p113** Llyfrgell Genedlaethol Cymru – The National Library of Wales/Public Domain Mark 1.0; **p125** Baker Street Scans/Alamy Stock Photo; **p132** Pictorial Press Ltd/Alamy Stock Photo; **p150** William Ewart Gladstone. Photograph. Credit: Wellcome Collection. CC BY 4.0; **p151** Portrait of Benjamin Disraeli commission or a Select Committee. Credit: Wellcome Collection. CC BY 4.0; **p158** The Print Collector/Alamy Stock Photo; **p201** Hulton-Deutsch Collection/CORBIS/Corbis via Getty Images.

Acknowledgements: Abacus, *The Age of Revolution 1789–1848* by Eric Hobsbawm, 1962. Cambridge University Press, *Abstract of British Historical Statistics* by B.R. Mitchell and R. Deane, 1962; *British Economic Growth 1688–1959* by P. Deane and W.A. Cole, 1969; *Lord Liverpool and Liberal Toryism 1820–27* by W.R. Brock, 1941. Collins Educational, *Britain 1815–1918* by Derek Murphy *et al.*, 1998. *Economic History Review*, 'English Workers' Living Standards During the Industrial Revolution: A New Look' by Peter Lindhart and Jeffrey Linderson, 1983; 'Urbanization, Mortality, and the Standard of Living Debate: New Estimates of the Expectation of Life at Birth in Nineteenth-century British Cities' by Simon Szreter and Graham Mooney, 1998. Edward Arnold, *Wars and Revolutions, Britain 1760–1815* by Ian R. Christie, 1982. Her Majesty's Stationery Office, *The History of Parliament: The House of Commons 1754–1790* edited by L. Namier and J. Brooke, 1964. Hodder Education, *Labour and Reform: Working-class Movements 1815–1914* by Clive Behagg, 2000; *The Growth of Democracy in Britain* by Annette Mayer, 1999. *Journal of Economic History*, 'Shrinking in a Growing Economy? The Mystery of Physical Stature during the Industrial Revolution' by John Komlos, 1998. Longman, *The Longman Handbook of Modern British History 1714–2001* by C. Cook and J. Stevenson, 2001. Oxford University Press, *The Oxford Illustrated History of Britain* edited by Kenneth O. Morgan, 1984. Pearson, *The Forging of the Modern State, Early Industrial Britain 1783–1870* by Eric Evans, 2001. Shoe String Press, *Anti-Slavery, Religion and Reform* edited by Christine Bolt *et al.*, 1980. Taylor & Francis, *William Pitt the Younger* by Eric Evans, 1999. University of North Carolina Press, *Moral Capital, Foundations of British Abolitionism* by Christopher Brown, 2006. Wiley-Blackwell, *Black Ivory* by James Walvin, 1993.

Every effort has been made to trace all copyright holders, but if any have been inadvertently overlooked, the Publishers will be pleased to make the necessary arrangements at the first opportunity.

Although every effort has been made to ensure that website addresses are correct at time of going to press, Hodder Education cannot be held responsible for the content of any website mentioned in this book. It is sometimes possible to find a relocated web page by typing in the address of the home page for a website in the URL window of your browser.

Hachette UK's policy is to use papers that are natural, renewable and recyclable products and made from wood grown in well-managed forests and other controlled sources. The logging and manufacturing processes are expected to conform to the environmental regulations of the country of origin.

Orders: please contact Bookpoint Ltd, 130 Park Drive, Milton Park, Abingdon, Oxon OX14 4SE. Telephone: +44 (0)1235 827827. Fax: +44 (0)1235 400401. Email education@bookpoint.co.uk Lines are open from 9 a.m. to 5 p.m., Monday to Saturday, with a 24-hour message answering service. You can also order through our website: www.hoddereducation.co.uk

ISBN: 978 1 5104 5915 1

© Ben Armstrong 2020

First published in 2020 by
Hodder Education,
An Hachette UK Company
Carmelite House
50 Victoria Embankment
London EC4Y 0DZ

www.hoddereducation.co.uk

Impression number   10   9   8   7   6   5   4   3   2   1
Year   2024   2023   2022   2021   2020

Cover photo © World History Archive/Alamy Stock Photo
Typeset by Gray Publishing
Printed in the UK by CPI Group Ltd

A catalogue record for this title is available from the British Library.

MIX
Paper from responsible sources
FSC™ C104740
www.fsc.org

Dedication

Keith Randell (1943–2002)

The *Access to History* series was conceived and developed by Keith, who created a series to 'cater for students as they are, not as we might wish them to be'. He leaves a living legacy of a series that for over 20 years has provided a trusted, stimulating and well-loved accompaniment to post-16 study. Our aim with these new editions is to continue to offer students the best possible support for their studies.

Introduction: about this book

This book has been written primarily to support the study of the following courses:

- AQA Component 1: Breadth Study: 1F Industrialisation and the people: Britain, c1783–1885
- OCR Unit Y110: From Pitt to Peel 1783–1853
- Pearson Edexcel Paper 1, Option 1D: Britain, c1785–c1870: democracy, protest and reform.

The specification grid on pages ix–x will help you understand how this book's content relates to the course that you are studying.

The writer hopes that student readers will regard the book not simply as an aid to better exam results, but as a study which is enjoyable in itself as an analysis of a very important theme in history.

The following explains the different features of this book and how they will help your study of the course.

Beginning of the book

Context

Starting a new course can be daunting if you are not familiar with the period or topic. This section will give you an overview of the history and will set up some of the key themes. Reading this section will help you get up to speed on the content of the course.

Throughout the book

Key terms

You need to know these to gain an understanding of the period. The appropriate use of specific historical language in your essays will also help you improve the quality of your writing. Key terms are in boldface type the first time they appear in the book. They are defined in the margin and appear in the glossary.

Profiles

Some chapters contain profiles of important individuals. These include a brief biography and information about the importance and impact of the individual. This information can be very useful in understanding certain events and providing supporting evidence to your arguments.

Sources

Historical sources are important in understanding why specific decisions were taken or on what contemporary writers and politicians based their actions. The questions accompanying each source will help you to understand and analyse the source.

Interpretations

These extracts from historians will help bring awareness of the debates and issues that surround this fascinating history topic.

Chapter summaries

These written summaries are intended to help you revise and consolidate your knowledge and understanding of the content.

Summary diagrams

These visual summaries at the end of each section are useful for revision.

Refresher questions

The refresher questions are quick knowledge checks to make sure you have understood and remembered the material that is covered in the chapter.

Question practice

There are opportunities at the end of each chapter to practise exam-style questions arranged by exam board. The exam hint below each question will help you if you get stuck.

End of the book

Timeline

Understanding chronology (the order in which events took place) is an essential part of history. Knowing the order of events is one thing, but it is also important to know how events relate to each other. This timeline will help you put events into context and will be helpful for quick reference or as a revision tool.

Exam focus

This section gives advice on how to answer questions in your exam, focusing on the different requirements of your exam paper. The guidance in this book has been based on detailed examiner reports since 2017. It models best practice in terms of answering exam questions and shows the most common pitfalls to help ensure you get the best grade possible.

Glossary

All key terms in the book are defined in the glossary.

Further reading

To achieve top marks in history, you will need to read beyond this textbook. This section contains a list of books and articles for you to explore. The list may also be helpful for an extended essay or piece of coursework.

Online extras

This new edition is accompanied by online material to support you in your study. Throughout the book you will find the online extras icon to prompt you to make use of the relevant online resources for your course. By going to www.hoddereducation.co.uk/accesstohistory/extras you will find the following:

Activity worksheets

These activities will help you develop the skills you need for the exam. The thinking that you do to complete the activities, and the notes you make from answering the questions, will prove valuable in your learning journey and helping you get the best grade possible. Your teacher may decide to print the entire series of worksheets to create an activity booklet to accompany the course. Alternatively they may be used as standalone activities for class work or homework. However, don't hesitate to go online and print off a worksheet yourself to get the most from this book.

Who's who

A level history covers a lot of key figures so it's perfectly understandable if you find yourself confused by all the different names. This document organises the individuals mentioned throughout the book by categories so you know your Pitt from your Peel!

Further research

While further reading of books and articles is helpful to achieve your best, there's a wealth of material online, including useful websites, digital archives and documentaries on YouTube. This page lists resources that may help further your understanding of the topic. It may also prove a valuable reference for research if you decide to choose this period for the coursework element of your course.

Specification grid

Chapter	AQA	OCR	Pearson Edexcel
Chapter 1 Context			
Chapter 2 Pitt's Britain and the abolition of the slave trade 1783–1807			
1 William Pitt the Younger as prime minister	✓	✓	
2 Pitt's reforms	✓	✓	
3 Pressures faced by Pitt's government	✓	✓	✓
4 Opposition to reform	✓	✓	✓
5 The abolition of the slave trade			✓
6 Key debate: Which factors were most important in the abolition of slavery?			✓
7 Key debate: How effective were Pitt's domestic policies 1783–1806?	✓	✓	
Chapter 3 Government and a changing society 1812–32			
1 The government of Lord Liverpool	✓	✓	✓
2 Tory governments under Canning, Goderich and Wellington	✓	✓	✓
3 The re-emergence of demands for popular reform	✓	✓	✓
4 The passing of the Reform Act	✓	✓	✓
5 The 'Great Reform Act'?	✓	✓	✓
6 Key debate: What was the nature of Liverpool's government?	✓	✓	
Chapter 4 Foreign policy 1783–1830			
1 Pitt's pre-war foreign policy: ending isolation		✓	
2 Foreign policy during war 1793–1814		✓	
3 Foreign policy after war 1814–30		✓	
Chapter 5 The industrialisation of Britain 1783–1832			
1 The Industrial Revolution	✓		✓
2 The economic impact of the Industrial Revolution	✓		✓
3 The make-up of society	✓		✓
4 Changes to living conditions	✓		✓
Chapter 6 Government and democracy 1832–68			
1 Whig and Tory politics in the 1830s	✓	✓	
2 Peel as prime minister from 1841	✓	✓	
3 Peel's fall from power	✓	✓	
4 Chartism	✓	✓	✓
5 Changes to party political structures by 1866	✓		✓
6 The 1867 Reform Act	✓		✓
Chapter 7 Gladstone and Disraeli's rival ministries 1868–85			
1 Rival statesmen	✓		
2 The competing ministries of Gladstone and Disraeli	✓		✓

Chapter	AQA	OCR	Pearson Edexcel
3 Changes to the democratic process	✓		✓
Chapter 8 Industrialisation and the economy 1832–85			
1 Economic developments of the 1830s and 1840s	✓	✓	✓
2 Economic legislation in the 1840s	✓	✓	✓
3 Mid-Victorian boom to 1873; Great Depression from 1873	✓		✓
Chapter 9 Dealing with the poor: social developments 1832–85			
1 The problem of poverty	✓	✓	✓
2 Social reform 1832–53	✓	✓	✓
3 Social reform 1853–85	✓		✓
4 Cooperative organisations and self-help	✓		✓
Chapter 10 Changes to the workplace 1832–85			
1 Changes to working conditions after 1832	✓	✓	✓
2 The development of trade unions	✓	✓	✓
3 Trade union activity 1866–85	✓		✓
4 Key debate: Had living conditions improved between 1783 and 1885?	✓		✓

CHAPTER 1

Context

Britain in 1783 was a growing country on the verge of great developments. Yet, it had recently lost a challenge to its empire, in the form of the American War of Independence, and was about to face further problems abroad and at home that would lead to significant political, economic and social impacts. By 1885, Britain had vastly changed, as had the lives of most of its population.

Politics

There was no single part of the government which held power. The British constitution was mainly unwritten – not written in laws. Rather, the parts of the constitution acted to provide an executive (the government), legislature (law-making body, or parliament) and judiciary (court system).

The head of state in 1783 was King George III (reigned 1760–1820). He was not an especially inspirational king, largely out of touch with both his population and his government. Unlike many other monarchs of the time, George III was not an absolute monarch (able to rule by decree). While the king could exercise considerable power to influence political decisions, especially through wealth and **patronage**, he needed to cooperate with parliament to rule the country successfully.

The executive

The king formed a government by selecting ministers from within parliament who acted as his supporters and advisers. Chief among these was the prime minister. The government took the lead in proposing legislation in parliament. Although the government did not answer to parliament, without parliamentary support it was difficult for them to be effective at governing.

The legislature

Parliament was responsible for passing new legislation. It consisted of two houses, the House of Lords and the House of Commons:

- The House of Lords was the more powerful of the two houses. It was an unelected body consisting of members of the Church of England clergy, such as bishops, and members of the nobility, such as dukes and earls. The number of members of the House of Lords varied over time. In the eighteenth century, there were 220 members. The House of Lords had the power to veto **bills** passed by the House of Commons.

- The House of Commons proposed and debated new laws. A bill passed in the Commons was sent to the House of Lords to vote on. Members of parliament (MPs) were elected in **constituencies**. Each one sent one or two representatives as MPs. However, the rules for who could vote varied

> **KEY TERMS**
>
> **Patronage** Offering positions, salaries, pensions or honours to supporters.
>
> **Bills** A proposal for a law is a bill. When it is passed, it becomes an Act.
>
> **Constituencies** Voting areas in Britain. In 1783–1870, each one had one or two MPs.

between constituencies, and there was no consistent standard. Southern England was particularly well represented, but the north was not. Since MPs were not paid a salary, it was effectively impossible for anyone without a private income to be involved in politics. Therefore, although the Commons was elected, it was not democratic in the sense that we would understand in modern Britain.

The judiciary

■ Senior judges were appointed by the Crown and given a salary. They had a measure of independence, guaranteed since 1701, that they could not be removed without both the House of Lords and Commons requesting the monarch to do so.

■ Local law and order was maintained by local landlords and justices of the peace (JPs) who oversaw local court cases. Without a police force, they relied on the local militia or **yeomanry**, volunteer paramilitary forces, on which they could call if necessary.

Society

Society in Britain was very clearly stratified. Power and wealth were connected to land:

■ The wealthiest, the nobility, owned huge areas of land. The landed nobility, about 400 families in the 1780s (who provided most of the 220 peers in the Houses of Lords), earned at least £5000 per year; approximately a dozen of the very wealthiest earned £40,000–50,000.

■ The **gentry** had land and money but lacked the titles of the nobility. About 700 families of the gentry earned £3000–4000 annually, while another 4000 earned up to £3000.

■ The yeomanry, less wealthy than the gentry, lived on £300–700 annually.

■ The average British family of the time had an annual income of £20–30 a year.

There was a clear social distinction between those with money and those without. To stand as a member of parliament (MP) in 1783 required property worth £600 if in the country, or £300 if in a town. One could not be a JP with land worth less than £100, and game animals could not be shot, even on one's own farm, by those with land worth less than £100. This meant that there were legal as well as lifestyle differences for those with wealth.

Economy

By the late eighteenth century, new technologies in textiles production and steam power had led to broad changes, collectively referred to by historians as the Industrial Revolution. In turn, this led to changes in communication, banking and the population. Because of industrialisation and **urbanisation**, the social structures of 1783 were starting to face pressure for change. The numbers of rural yeoman and gentry were in decline while the wealth of industrialists was growing.

KEY TERMS

Yeomanry A yeoman was a man owning a small rural area of land, and the yeomanry was a military group made up of these men.

Gentry Wealthy people below the nobility in social class.

Urbanisation The process of towns and cities growing in size and population.

Status quo The existing situation.

Establishment The group of people with power.

As well as challenging social structures, the urbanisation created new centres of industry, especially in the north of England. In the 1780s, Manchester had 40,000 residents but by the 1801 census, this had already grown to over 70,000. These urban areas simultaneously reduced the direct control of landed elites over the working classes who were no longer on their land, and created dangerous, unhygienic areas of growing poverty in which radical ideas against the *status quo* could begin to form and spread. It is no coincidence that much of the political and social protest between 1783 and 1885 has strong links to northern urban areas.

Religion

Britain was fundamentally a Christian country in 1783, represented principally by the established Church of England. Crucially, this was the religion of the king and of the government. The existence of God was a widely accepted belief, with only a minority of radical thinkers open to the possibility of atheism.

Alongside the Anglican Church, there were several other Christian denominations. One was Catholicism, a religion that was viewed with suspicion by the **establishment**. A Catholic, for example, could not stand for election as a MP or hold a position in local government. Until 1778, Catholics had paid an extra tax and been banned from joining the army or purchasing land.

Other Protestant, Nonconformist sects were growing in 1783. They were accepted by Anglicans but seen as overzealous and a potential social threat. Examples include the Christian denominations of **Methodism** and **Quakerism**. These groups encouraged more **evangelical** ideas and sparked a renewed interest in religion and spirituality.

Britain in the wider world

Britain in 1783 was a powerful country, with a growing empire and commercial interests worldwide. However, in 1783, Britain had just lost the American War of Independence, surrendering control of its American colonies to the newly formed United States of America. Also, in 1789, the **French Revolution** challenged the international *status quo* and threatened traditional institutions in Europe. This dragged Britain into the **Revolutionary and Napoleonic Wars**. These conflicts not only stretched Britain's labour and financial reserves, but also opened Britain up to radical protests and demand for domestic reform.

In the eighteenth century, Britain was heavily involved in the trans-Atlantic or '**triangle trade**'. This was a significant economic interest; British merchants controlled a large proportion of the shipping which transported enslaved Africans to the Americas for sale. Although this trade was fundamental to the industrialisation of Britain, especially in the cotton mills of northern England which relied on the cotton brought by merchants on the return leg of the slave journeys, the late eighteenth century also saw a growth in opposition which would result in the abolition of the slave trade by 1807.

KEY TERMS

Methodists A group of Protestant Churches, separate from the Church of England, with fundamentalist beliefs based on a strict reading of the Bible.

Quakers Also known as the Religious Society of Friends. A Christian denomination which emphasises personal spiritual experience over ritual and tradition.

Evangelical A term used collectively to describe fundamentalist Christians who adhere to the Gospels in the Bible and have an enthusiasm to spread their beliefs.

French Revolution Event in 1789 when French radicals overthrew the monarchy and formed a new government. The revolutionary government was based on the radical idea of equal rights for all citizens.

Revolutionary and Napoleonic Wars Conflict broke out between France and other European nations in 1792, called the Revolutionary War. Britain became involved in 1793. After a brief peace in 1802–3, the war resumed until 1815. This second phase is known as the Napoleonic Wars.

Triangle trade Refers to the British slave trade, a reference to the three stages of the journey (Britain to Africa, to the Americas, to Britain).

SOURCE QUESTION

How useful is the picture in Source A for learning about the lives of black people in Britain?

SOURCE A

An engraving of Ignatius Sancho (1729–80), a black writer, composer and shopkeeper in eighteenth-century Britain. He was known for supporting campaigns to abolish slavery. This engraving was made in 1802 as a copy of a painting made in 1768. The very fact that we have two surviving images of him when we have so little evidence of the lives of the majority of the population of Britain at this time is evidence of the prestige that he gained.

Were there black people in Britain?

As well as the wider African cultural history, which is not reflected in the story of the slave trade, there was a small but significant population of black people in England in the eighteenth century, most of whom were not slaves:

- In 1764, the journal *Gentleman's Magazine* estimated that there were 20,000 black servants in London.
- During the American Revolutionary War, thousands of black families had fled to British territories to escape slavery, and over 1000 had ended up in London, Dublin and Liverpool.
- Many black people living in Britain were servants; there were also small communities of black sailors in port towns such as Southampton.
- Some individuals, often ex-soldiers, faced poverty, and it was not uncommon in cities to see black ex-servicemen begging.
- There were a small number of wealthy, successful black individuals who rose from being servants. When John Rippon, a black servant to the Earl of Powis, died in 1800 he left over £130 in his will. Ignatius Sancho was born on a slave ship but died a noted composer and writer (see Source A, above).

This book will address the themes of continuity and change in Britain over these turbulent and changing years from 1783 to 1885. Some of the changes happened because of social pressure; others were due to the leadership and decisions of key individuals, while still others were driven by economic need and changing technology. Remember that in dividing this book into sections, such as political change or international policy, we are using artificial divisions imposed with hindsight. In reality, events rarely divide so cleanly, and you should cross-reference and consider the implications of one area of change on others.

CHAPTER 2

Pitt's Britain and the abolition of the slave trade 1783–1807

When William Pitt the Younger was appointed prime minister in 1783 at 24 years of age, he became the youngest man ever to hold that office. Between 1783 and 1801, he spent seventeen years as prime minister, with a further twenty months between 1804 and 1806. He oversaw reforms to finance, trade and administration, as well as much of Britain's conflict with Revolutionary France. During the same period, Pitt faced challenges from Nationalist groups in Ireland, as well as a growing radical demand for reform to the political system. Additionally, Britain was a leading nation in the trade of slaves. This trade had played a key role in the development of the British economy and empire. Yet in 1807, an Act was passed which abolished the trading of slaves between British colonies.

This chapter examines Pitt's time in office, and the abolition of the slave trade, through the following themes:

◆ William Pitt the Younger as prime minister
◆ Pitt's reforms
◆ Pressures faced by Pitt's government
◆ Opposition to reform
◆ The abolition of the slave trade

The key debate on page 35 asks the question: Which factors were most important in the abolition of slavery? The key debate on page 37 asks the question: How effective were Pitt's domestic policies 1783–1806? (Note: if you are studying the Pearson Edexcel course, the interpretations at the end of the chapter will help you to answer the following question: Which factors were most important in the abolition of slavery?)

KEY DATES

1783	Pitt appointed prime minister
1784	General election called by Pitt
1786	Sinking fund introduced
	Sierra Leone established as a colony for freed black slaves
1787	Society for the Abolition of the Slave Trade, with its London-based Abolition Committee, formed
1788–9	Regency Crisis
1789	French Revolution began
1791	Wilberforce presented first annual anti-slavery bill to the Commons
1793	France declared war on Britain
1797	Fox ended parliamentary opposition to Pitt
1799	Slave Trade Act passed, limiting numbers of slaves on British ships
1799–1800	Combination Acts passed, preventing workers forming trade unions
1800	Pitt's government passed the Act of Union, joining Ireland and Britain, effective from 1801
1801	Pitt resigned as prime minister
1804	Pitt appointed as prime minister for second time
1805	Abolition bill passed in the Commons, although rejected in the Lords
1806	Parliament passed an intercolonial trade ban on slaves outside the British Empire
	Pitt's death
1807	Abolition of the Slave Trade Act passed

1 William Pitt the Younger as prime minister

■ *How did William Pitt the Younger become prime minister?*

William Pitt the Younger became prime minister after a political crisis. Lord North, King George III's friend, had been a popular prime minister since 1770. However, in 1776, the **American War of Independence** had broken out. North and George III were blamed for the defeat, losing popularity and support. The king eventually accepted the Marquess of Rockingham as prime minister, only for Rockingham to die unexpectedly only fourteen weeks later, in July 1782. He was then replaced by Lord Shelburne as prime minister.

In March 1783, North formed a **coalition** with **Charles James Fox**, an outspoken **Whig** and reformist. Together, they supported the Duke of Portland to replace Shelburne as prime minister. This was surprising, since not only were the three from different parts of the political spectrum, but also Fox and North had been political opponents for years. But North needed Fox's popular support in the Commons and Fox needed to work with a politician who was acceptable to the king. Reluctantly, George III appointed Portland as prime minister, with Fox as foreign secretary and North as home secretary.

Portland's government failed mainly because North had lost credibility through association with Fox, whereas Fox looked hypocritical for working with North. Further, they lacked royal support – the king refused to use his patronage by creating peerages to reward their supporters.

The crucial factor in the coalition's weakness was the attempt to pass the 1783 India bill, a law designed to reorganise the power of the **East India Company**. The bill proposed appointing seven of Fox and North's supporters, including North's son, as commissioners to manage the company for four years. It was passed by the Commons, but defeated by the Lords. The failure gave George III the excuse he needed to replace Portland, Fox and North with Pitt the Younger.

The 1784 election

Pitt was a surprising choice for prime minister:

■ He was only 24 years old, with three years' experience in the Commons and nine months as chancellor of the exchequer.

■ He did not have strong popular support; he had lost the 1779 election and used a **rotten borough** to become a member of parliament (MP).

■ The rest of the cabinet were from the House of Lords, not the Commons.

■ Pitt led a **minority government** and could only rely on about 149 votes, while Fox and North controlled about 230 votes.

■ Pitt was socially awkward and so lacked easy charm and charisma.

William Pitt (the Younger)

1759	Born in Hayes, Kent, the second son of former prime minister, William Pitt the Elder
1773	Admitted to Cambridge University
1780	Stood for parliamentary election and lost
1781	Became MP with patronage of Sir James Lowther
1782	Became chancellor of the exchequer
1783	Appointed as prime minister
1784	General election strengthened Pitt's position
1801	Resigned as prime minister
1804	Appointed as prime minister
1806	Died of poor health

Background

Pitt was born to William Pitt the Elder, Earl of Chatham from 1866. His mother's family, the Grenvilles, were an influential Whig family (they opposed royal power and sought reform). This made the family nobility, although as a second son he would not inherit the title of earl. His title 'Younger' was to distinguish him from his father, who was prime minister in the 1750s and 1760s.

Election as a member of parliament

Although Pitt believed in limited democratic reform, he owed his start in politics to the old, corrupt system. Sir James Lowther was a wealthy man who owned the voting rights in several 'rotten boroughs' (where there were very few voters, and the landlord could essentially pick the MP he wanted). After Pitt failed to win the election in 1779, Lowther used one such borough, Appleby, to have Pitt elected to the House of Commons.

Political leadership

Pitt built a reputation as a capable, honest and hardworking minister while serving as chancellor of the exchequer. He had a good relationship with George III, who appointed him prime minister in 1783 in the hopes of creating a strong Tory leadership (one that would support the king and oppose reform). Pitt served as prime minister until he resigned in 1801 in protest at the king's refusal to sign a Catholic Emancipation Act. He served again in 1804 until his death in 1806.

In other ways, Pitt was a good choice:

- His family was politically influential.
- He had a good relationship with the king.
- He had given articulate speeches against electoral corruption.
- He had shown that he was intelligent and thoughtful as chancellor of the exchequer.
- He was popular with independent MPs.
- He had a reputation for honesty, which contrasted with the apparent hypocrisy of North and Fox.

The king wrote to Pitt in January 1784, encouraging him to call an election. He was concerned that the prime minister was reliant on royal patronage. Pitt insisted on delaying the vote, since an election would risk losing his support. He was gambling that the Whig opposition would try to obstruct him, but not force a new election. He hoped that a delay would allow the king's agents to build support for him, and that he could demonstrate his potential as a statesman.

King George III agreed to wait, which shows his confidence in Pitt. By March, Pitt's position was more secure. He had spoken well in the Commons, and many independent MPs warmed to him. He had also made wise ministerial

KEY TERMS

Rotten borough
A constituency with very few voters, often fewer than 30, where the landlord could essentially pick the MP they wanted.

Minority government
When the government controls fewer votes in the Commons than their opponents, making it hard to pass laws that they propose.

appointments, avoiding politicians associated with the previous eighteen months, for example, Fox, who refused to support Pitt, or North, whom the king no longer favoured. Consequently, he was not associated with failure.

Many expected Pitt to offer political office to Charles Jenkinson, a politician favoured by the king, to keep royal favour; Pitt refused, showing that while loyal to the king, he was not simply a mouthpiece. He also rejected royal **sinecures**. The fact that he was clearly independent of royal control encouraged support.

Pitt demonstrated his growing support by passing the mutiny bill. While this was only a formality that was regularly passed to maintain the armed forces, it showed that he was overcoming opposition. In March 1784, he asked George III to call a new election. This was only three and a half years since the previous election; generally elections were held at the seven-year limit.

The new election swung control of the Commons to Pitt. Approximately 160 of Fox's supporters became known as 'Fox's Martyrs' since their loyalty to Fox cost them their seats. Of the 558 MPs elected, nine per cent were Pitt's supporters, whereas 25 per cent were Fox's supporters. The majority of MPs were independent gentlemen, who tended to support Pitt, or MPs who relied on royal patronage and would support the king's prime minister.

The main reasons for Pitt's victory in 1784 were:

- Pitt's leadership. He was intelligent, calm and logical.
- The king's support. George III offered pensions and **peerages** to supporters of Pitt. There were four peerages created in the month leading up to the election, and reports of a promise of thirteen or fourteen more. Several peerages were created among London industrialists.

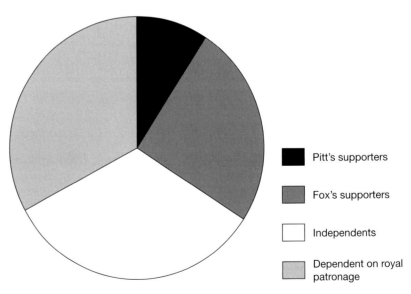

Figure 2.1 The political loyalty of MPs elected in 1784. Data based on L. Namier and J. Brooke, editors, *The History of Parliament: The House of Commons 1754–1790*, Her Majesty's Stationery Office, 1964.

- Popular support. Pitt did particularly well in larger constituencies, where it was harder for opponents to bribe the electorate.
- Pitt's reputation. He had shown himself to be loyal, honest and independent from Crown control.
- The support of notable landowners. Several key landholders supported Pitt. This was important, as many MPs were returned by nomination. Only 75 contested elections occurred in England and Wales, and eight in Scotland.
- A swing against Fox in London. The London metropolitan area returned ten Pitt supporters and only two Fox supporters, including Fox himself – even Fox's victory in Westminster was hard-fought, in contrast to Pitt's formality of an election for Cambridge University. This was probably because of the lack of patrons controlling voters in London, so voters were freer to express their genuine political views.

Yet, since his appointment was based on royal support and the failure of three governments in two years, it was not expected that he would last until Christmas. Consequently, Pitt's government was initially nicknamed 'the mince-pie ministry', and political opponents referred to Pitt as a 'school-boy'.

The significance of the 1784 election

The 1784 election consolidated Pitt's power. It has been said that the election marked the first step in **Tory** politicians beginning to form a party. This is not entirely accurate; the MPs who supported Pitt were not unified, and Pitt did not act as a party leader. There was no expectation of party loyalty, for example. Lowther's nine MPs switched to support Pitt's opposition over the 1789 regency bill.

However, the 1784 election contributed to the idea of the government and opposition as two distinct sides. For example, John Robinson, an election agent, carried out pre-election survey predictions on the basis of whether a pro-Pitt, pro-Fox or neutral MP would return. The concept of belonging to either the government or the opposition would contribute to the solidifying of distinct parties in the first half of the nineteenth century.

KEY TERM

Tories Politicians who supported the king and opposed reform.

ONLINE EXTRAS AQA WWW

Test your understanding of Pitt's policies by completing Worksheet 1 at **www.hoddereducation.co.uk/accesstohistory/extras**

ONLINE EXTRAS OCR WWW

Develop your analysis of Pitt's government by completing Worksheet 1 at **www.hoddereducation.co.uk/accesstohistory/extras**

SUMMARY DIAGRAM

PITT THE YOUNGER AS PRIME MINISTER

1782 North resigned and Shelburne died suddenly → 1783 Portland became prime minister, supported by Fox and North. Portland's ministry collapsed over the India bill → Pitt chosen by George III to replace Portland → Pitt used the 1784 election to strengthen his power

2 Pitt's reforms

■ *How successful were Pitt's reforms?*

While Pitt was in power, he aimed to improve government efficiency, especially in financial matters. From 1783 to 1801, and again from 1804 to 1806, Pitt combined the offices of chancellor of the exchequer and first lord of the treasury with being prime minister. He had significant impact on financial and administrative reform, although he was less successful with political reform and managing the East India Company.

Financial challenges

Pitt faced three financial challenges:

■ The loss of thirteen American colonies by 1783 had deprived Britain of one of its largest markets for manufactured goods.

■ **National debt** had almost doubled from £127 million (1775) to £243 million (1784). This was almost twenty times the national revenue. It cost over half the annual national income to make the annual interest payments alone.

■ There were concerns over corruption. Some investors were making up to six per cent profit on government loans. Much of the rest of government spending was on contracts that were often awarded to the wealthy minority.

Trade

Pitt was a supporter of the contemporary economic thinker Adam Smith, who had published his *Inquiry into the Nature and Causes of the Wealth of Nations* in 1776. Smith argued against the commonly accepted theory that economic strength came through **protectionism**, saying that this held back economic development and reduced the quality of life for all. Instead, he proposed **free trade**, suggesting that trade without control or tariffs was universally beneficial. Countries would offer the best prices to increase trade and would maintain peaceful relationships to protect trade. This would, he insisted, ensure more efficient production, lower prices and an overall improvement in the standard of living.

The radical idea of free trade

Pitt sent representatives to the courts of the principal rulers in Europe to negotiate reduced tariff duties. Very few of the ambassadors achieved their goal. Even the foreign secretary spoke dismissively of the 'present rage for commercial treaties', which he neither liked nor comprehended. When Pitt tried to agree a trade deal with Ireland, it was opposed by the **Dublin Parliament** and industrialists in the north of England who felt threatened by the prospect of competing with cheaper Irish labour. The only notable success was with France, with the Eden trade treaty that lasted from 1786 until the war in 1793.

KEY TERMS

National debt
The amount of money that the government of a country has borrowed from banks and money lenders.

Protectionism
An economic system for safeguarding domestic production by imposing tariffs and levies on imported goods from foreign countries.

Free trade The belief that the economy should be left alone by the government, without tariffs or restrictions.

Dublin Parliament From 1264 until 1800, Ireland had its own parliament. From 1692, it met in Dublin.

Britain accepted the import of French wines at the lower tariff rate granted to the Portuguese. In return, French tariffs on imported British manufactured goods were reduced by ten to fifteen per cent. Northern industrialists took advantage of this, so that by 1792, the value of British trade to the Europe had almost doubled from 1783, and the trade deficit of £2.5 million had become a surplus of almost £2 million. Pitt's government also invested in new ships. In 1760, Britain had 600,000 tonnes of shipping; by 1792, 1.5 million tonnes.

Free trade was not immediately opened to the Americas due to national resentment of the British defeat by American republicans in 1785. Instead, trade in the West Indies was controlled by the Navigation Act (1786), which limited colonial trade to British ships. The aim was to avoid trade with American merchants. A year later, some ports in the British West Indies were opened to small American vessels, which caused British exports to the West Indies to treble. Britain opened more of the West Indian markets to America for free trade by agreeing to the Jay Treaty of 1794. Between 1793 and 1799, British exports to America more than doubled. By 1800, the USA was importing a quarter of British exports, with another quarter of British goods to the rest of the Americas.

However, smuggling was a major problem. It was estimated that twenty per cent of imports overall and 50 per cent of tea leaves were illegally smuggled into Britain. Pitt responded by:

- reducing tariffs and import duties on goods such as wines, spirits and tobacco
- reducing tea duties from 119 per cent to 25 per cent
- introducing a Book of Rates to simplify the tariff system
- passing the 1787 Hovering Act to extend the authority of customs officials to twelve miles off the coast, and allow them to board and seize any ships loitering there.

By 1789, legally imported tea had doubled in quantity. The **Exchequer** reported an extra £200,000 in taxes during 1784–5. By 1793, the British government had increased its revenue by about £3 million.

The sinking fund 1786

In 1786, the government attempted to reduce national debt with a **sinking fund**. This involved the government putting surplus money into a separate fund. The money was used to buy government shares on the stock market at an improved price. Profits were reinvested into the fund, which could be used to pay off the balance of the national debt and reduce the interest payments. To prevent the money being spent on other projects, Pitt established legislation to prevent the money being redistributed, raised taxes to generate £1 million per year, and appointed commissioners to control the fund.

From 1786 to 1793, the fund raised £10 million to reduce the national debt. A second sinking fund was established in 1793, financed by a levy on all new loans to the State. While the sinking fund had worked pre-war, it was not successful

> **KEY TERMS**
>
> **Exchequer** The British government's economic department.
>
> **Sinking fund** A method of government investment to reduce national debt.

during the war years (1793–1815). The war increased government spending and borrowing significantly, so that the national debt was rising faster than the sinking fund could cover. The government had to borrow money to fund the sinking fund, which cost more in interest than was gained by using the sinking fund. By 1801, despite the sinking fund, national debt had increased by 87 per cent to £456 million. Historian Eric Evans (2001) argues that the government had been 'disarmed by the seductive logic of compound interest' and ignored the fact that the fund relied on reducing, not increasing, spending.

The sinking fund only became effective again in 1815, with the end of the Napoleonic Wars, until it was ended in 1829.

Taxation

Pitt reformed the tax system to create revenue, deliberately choosing to affect the wealthy:

- 1784: new taxes on bricks, men's hats, horses and carriages.
- 1785: duties on keeping servants were increased, and new duties introduced for keeping female servants. Bachelors had to pay double. The existing window tax was increased, with a tax of up to £20 for houses with over 180 windows. A shop tax was introduced based on premises size. Tax was added on gloves.
- 1786: new taxes on hair powder for wigs, perfume and cosmetics.
- 1789: increased duties on newspapers, advertisements, playing cards and dice.
- 1796: introduction of inheritance tax.
- 1797: tax on owning watches and clocks. Pitt also introduced a so-called triple assessment payment – a tax on luxury goods that would rise by three to five times as an extra tax, or people could choose to pay ten per cent of their wage instead, unless they earned less than £60 per year.
- 1798: income tax introduced at ten per cent for those with an income of between £60 and £200, and twenty per cent for those over £200. The tax was widely evaded at first, but opposition decreased as the war dragged on and the tax was seen as a patriotic duty. This was Pitt's most effective economic policy.

Pitt's economic policies had mixed success:

- By 1792, Pitt's economic policies had increased government income by £6 million annually, and during the Revolutionary War, a further £1 million annually. However, this was not enough to limit spiralling national debt once war had broken out.
- Some policies were abandoned, such as the shop tax, which was repealed in 1789 following protests in London, and the tax on watches, which was replaced by a tax on using coats of arms after the guild of watchmakers protested against the loss of trade.

- Some policies caused financial strain, for example the window tax. In 1792, Pitt had to exempt houses with fewer than seven windows.
- Pitt's triple assessment collected £3 million, but he had expected £7 million. This was because many people declared their income as just below £60 to avoid paying.
- The system was imprecise. Many tax assessors were local tradesmen, who deliberately undervalued their customers' liability.

Governmental and administrative reform

Pitt reformed the government by focusing on creating a small number of trained, professional employees, rather than many ever-changing amateurs:

- He reduced the number of government employees by combining departments, amalgamating similar jobs and transferring staff into the most important departments. For example, the Board of Taxes grew by 35 per cent, mainly through staff transferred from the treasury and the excise board.
- The customs and excise departments grew to have a combined staff of 600 and contributed two-thirds of government revenue.
- A department was even created to purchase stationery in large quantities, preventing officials from privately purchasing luxury stationery from government funds.

While not substantially reducing the overall costs, the changes ensured that the money was used more efficiently.

To ensure greater control of funds, Pitt created a single consolidated fund at the Bank of England, from which all government salaries were paid, and organised audits of public money to minimise corruption. He also reduced government sinecures. He rejected the honorary title of clerkship of the pells (with a salary of £3000), and public accounts commissioners identified 180 other positions to abolish. Pitt removed 28 of these, and as the remaining post-holders died over subsequent years, they were not replaced. By 1806, almost all sinecures had vanished. Pitt had all but destroyed the patronage system.

Pitt also streamlined military spending, which was two and a half times greater than civilian spending. Again, Pitt did not significantly reduce spending, but ensured that money was spent more wisely to strengthen the military, especially the navy. By 1790, the Royal Navy had 33 new ships. It seems likely that Pitt intended to extend his reforms of the navy to include promotion by merit and seniority rather than patronage, salaries instead of fees, and a stronger navy board, but the **Regency Crisis** of 1788–9 (see page 18) distracted him from completing his reforms.

The East India Company

In 1784, Pitt challenged the power of the East India Company, a behemoth of an institution that controlled trade to Britain from Asia. By the early nineteenth century, 11,000 tonnes of tea were being imported annually into Britain from

Development of cabinet government

A key reform under Pitt was the establishment of the importance of the prime minister and his cabinet in running the country. In modern terms, it seems normal to see the prime minister as the key figure, but this had not always been the case. The role of the prime minister had been developing since the early 1700s. By Pitt's careful construction of a cabinet made of political allies to overcome parliamentary opposition, combined with maintaining a measure of independence from royal influence, he cemented the central role of the prime minister in political governance. This model of political leadership was followed by many prime ministers of the 1800s through to the modern day.

KEY TERM

Regency Crisis When George III took ill, Pitt's opponents tried to appoint Prince George as regent to rule in his father's place.

China via the company. It controlled British territories abroad with managers and a military force on the ground, and company directors back in London, even making diplomatic agreements with other states.

Pitt introduced the India Act 1784, which essentially separated political and economic control. The company kept financial control, but military and political leadership passed to government representatives Lord Cornwallis and Henry Dundas. From 1786 to 1793, the governor-general's powers were increased substantially, thus ensuring governmental control. Diplomatic relations between India and nearby states subsequently improved.

The reform was limited. Cornwallis was unable to control company troops, meaning that the company still effectively had a private army in Asia which wore British uniforms, yet was beyond government control. The company also retained control of its revenue in return for an annual payment to the government of £500,000.

Parliamentary reform

Although Britain had an elected parliament, the unreformed system bore little resemblance to a modern democracy. Between 1790 and 1801, there were 558 MPs elected from 314 constituencies (245 English, 24 Welsh, 45 Scottish). With the 1801 Act of Union, 66 Irish constituencies with 100 MPs were added. There were borough and county constituencies. Borough constituencies were urban areas, generally small towns, while county constituencies were rural areas. In addition, Oxford and Cambridge universities had two MPs each. There were fundamental differences between the voting qualifications across counties and boroughs.

Counties had a voting qualification of owning property worth at least 40 shillings (£2) per year, which effectively disqualified the working poor. Historian R. Thorne (1976) estimated that in this period, voter numbers in all 40 English counties were only about 190,000: an average of 4750 per constituency.

There was greater variety among the 203 boroughs in England, which can be seen in Table 2.1 (see page 15).

Across constituencies, there was huge variety:

- All counties had two MPs, yet the largest (Yorkshire) had 20,000 voters for a population of 660,000 while the smallest (Rutland) had 800 for a population of 18,000.
- Northampton had 1000 voters, while St Germans had twenty. Both were potwalloper boroughs with two MPs.
- There were rotten boroughs such as Old Sarum, an extreme example, which was a burgage borough with two MPs. By the late eighteenth century, seven voters owned all the voting properties yet none lived in Old Sarum. By 1800, no one lived there at all. In 1820, two brothers bought Old Sarum and sat as MPs until 1832.

- Forty per cent of MPs were elected from ten counties south of Bristol and London.
- Cornwall (population *c*.300,000) had 42 MPs, while Lancashire (population over 1 million) had fourteen.
- The English cities of Manchester (1830 population *c*.144,000) and Birmingham (1830 population *c*.182,000) had no MPs at all.

Corruption

Corruption was rife. Landowners dominated the voting, and therefore parliament, through corporation voting, where the vote was limited to those with wealth and power on the corporation, or through owning the freehold and burgage property. Consistently, from 1783 until at least 1867, 70 per cent or more of MPs were landowners. In the counties, landowners could pressure their tenants to vote for their chosen candidates. Lord Lowther, for example, spent £100,000 on land, which meant that by 1784 he controlled nine seats in the House of Commons; in 1780, when voters threatened not to support his candidate, he threatened to cut off their coal. Before 1832, landowner dominance meant that few elections were ever actually contested. In some boroughs, nicknamed 'venal boroughs', voters sold their votes to those willing to pay. Although illegal, this was quite normal.

Table 2.1 The different types of constituency boroughs in England

Type of borough	Number in England in 1790	Average number of voters per constituency	Qualification to vote
Potwalloper	13	550	Meeting the qualification of having a hearth large enough to boil a cauldron
Freeman	91	870	Having the legal status of being a freeman of the borough
Scot and lot	37	650	Paying local taxes, called rates
Corporation	25	30	Being a member of the local corporation, a form of council
Burgage	30	30	Owning certain properties in the borough
Freeholder	7	30	Owning freehold of land; if enough was owned by one person it acted like a burgage borough

Data based on L. Namier and J. Brooke, editors, *The History of Parliament: The House of Commons 1754–1790*, Her Majesty's Stationery Office, 1964.

Pitt's proposal

Ironically, having gained political office through a rotten borough, Pitt attempted to achieve limited constitutional reform to the voting system. In 1785, he proposed that:

- Thirty-six small boroughs should be removed, with the 72 seats distributed among county and city constituencies.

- £1 million should be put aside by the government to compensate borough property owners for their loss in influence.

- The 40-shilling franchise qualification should be extended to long-term renters in the counties to increase voter numbers.

This bill was opposed by landowners and King George III, and defeated in the Commons by 248 votes to 174.

The success of Pitt's reforms

Historians have differing opinions about the success of Pitt's reforms. Table 2.2 (see below) gives a summary of some key points for each side of the argument (also see the key debate on page 37).

Table 2.2 A comparison of the successes and failures of Pitt's policies

Evidence of success	Evidence of limited success
• Government revenue increased by about £4 million per year • Trade with the USA and Europe increased • Britain's international economic dominance was protected • Radical reformers respected the tax system as it targeted the rich • The government became more economically and administratively efficient • Financial corruption was reduced • Britain was strong enough to face France in a long war • Pitt established greater governmental control in India by reducing the East India Company's power	• The sinking fund had a limited impact on national debt • The outbreak of war increased national debt • In 1797, Pitt had to suspend all government payments in an attempt to avoid bankruptcy • Income tax was unpopular • Reforms to the Royal Navy were incomplete • Attempts to reduce tariffs with other European powers were largely unsuccessful • The trade deal with Ireland failed • Pitt's policies were not original. They had been tried or proposed by previous Whig prime ministers • The removal of sinecures was a slow process as he waited for most holders to die • Overall governmental costs did not decrease • The East India Company retained its own troops and control of trade • Reform to the constitution was blocked by opposition, including George III

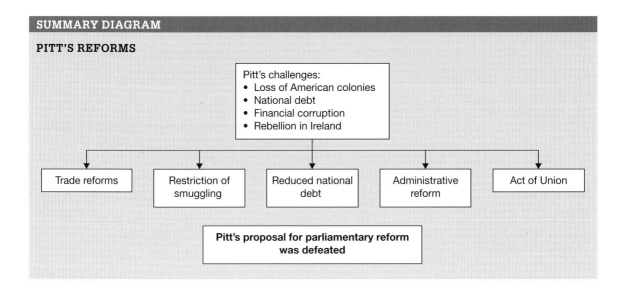

SUMMARY DIAGRAM

PITT'S REFORMS

Pitt's challenges:
- Loss of American colonies
- National debt
- Financial corruption
- Rebellion in Ireland

Trade reforms | Restriction of smuggling | Reduced national debt | Administrative reform | Act of Union

Pitt's proposal for parliamentary reform was defeated

3 Pressures faced by Pitt's government

■ *What were the pressures faced by Pitt's government in the 1790s?*

Pitt's government faced challenges, both externally from the international impact of the French Revolution, and internally from Whig opposition and tensions in Ireland.

The impact of the French Revolution on Pitt's government

The British government was slow to realise the significance of the French Revolution. In 1792, Pitt announced in the Commons that there would be a reduction in spending on defence because 'there never was a time in the history of this country when … we might more reasonably expect fifteen years of peace than at the present moment'. France declared war on Britain in 1793.

Tory MPs and members of the nobility were concerned about the violence against the nobility in France, while the Whigs were divided:

■ Whig MP **Edmund Burke** was critical of the French Revolution in his work *Reflections on the Revolution in France* (1790). While he accepted some of the liberal goals, he was concerned that the revolution was too poorly planned to lead to stability.

■ By contrast, Charles James Fox, the Whig opposition leader, declared the formation of a new constitution based on principles of equality to be 'the greatest event … that ever happened in the world'.

KEY FIGURE

Edmund Burke (1729–97)

Burke was an Anglo-Irish Whig politician and critical of British policy in America as well as of uncontrolled royal patronage. However, he was particularly concerned by the threat of mob rule following the French Revolution, and was an outspoken opponent of what he saw as a threat to British values of tradition, rank and position.

Burke was more influential than Fox, who had destroyed his political reputation during the Fox–North coalition. This contributed to a hardening of opinions against the revolutionary ideals, even among Whigs who favoured reform, and opposition to any bill that sounded vaguely revolutionary.

The challenge of Whig opposition

In the 1780s, the Whigs posed a strong challenge to Pitt. Key examples are the 1784 election and the Regency Crisis.

Regency Crisis 1788–9

In 1788, King George III suffered a mental breakdown. To Pitt and the king's medical attendants, the king had simply gone mad, leading to his nickname in history as 'Mad King George who lost America'.

The heir to the throne, George, Prince of Wales, 'Prinny' to his Whig friends, was a drinking partner of Fox, the opposition leader. He resented his father and formed an 'anti-court' of opposition politicians and courtiers in which drinking and partying were commonplace. This Whig opposition tried to organise the 200 Fox-supporting MPs to unite for 'Prinny' to rule as prince regent in place of George III. This would have ended Pitt's royal support and almost certainly led to a Whig government. The threat failed because:

- The titular leader of the Whigs, the Duke of Portland, considered 'Prinny' irresponsible.
- Instead of working with the Whig leaders, the headstrong Prince of Wales chose to work with the outspoken Whig MP Richard Brinsley Sheridan, a playwright who loved vulgar showmanship and backstage deals and who grossly overestimated his own potential. Working with Sheridan alienated the Prince from many more conservatively minded Whigs like Portland and Burke.
- In January 1789, Pitt's strong arguments in the Commons succeeded in persuading MPs to vote only for limited powers for the prince regent.
- King George III recovered unexpectedly in February 1789, which ended the crisis. Pitt once again had royal support.

The decline of Whig opposition

With their existing divisions and their mixed response to the French Revolution, the Whigs offered little real opposition to Pitt's government in the 1790s. Fox tried to maintain the middle ground to keep the support of the still influential Duke of Portland. But any efforts were soon crushed:

- When the September Massacres (1792) occurred in France, Fox foolishly allowed his own **republican** feelings to overwhelm political judgement and refused to condemn the deaths caused by the revolutionary chaos.
- When war broke out between France and Britain in 1793, Fox's Whigs were tainted by having liberal ideas. In contrast, Pitt was perceived to represent British values of social order, tradition and Christianity.

Was King George III mad?

Revisionist historians McAlpine and Hunter (1969) proposed, based on contemporary descriptions of the king which included that his urine turned blue in colour, that the problem was a hereditary metabolic disorder called porphyria, which damages the nervous system and leads to mental instability. Garrard and Rentoumi (2013) have claimed that the blue-coloured urine was from medicine. They argue that George III's writings suggest a manic state indicating some form of mood disorder.

KEY TERM

Republican A political viewpoint in favour of a government without a monarch.

- In 1793, a failed radical attempt to form a National Convention in Edinburgh, and the government's unsuccessful 'Treason Trial' of the London Corresponding Society leaders (in 1794, see page 22) had convinced many Whigs that a real revolutionary threat existed.

Pitt exploited the Whig weakness and in 1792 approached individual Whigs to create a coalition. For example, he invited Portland to consult on the precise wording of legislation against seditious writings. Baron Loughborough was the first Whig to defect to Pitt in January 1793 in return for the title of lord chancellor. Soon afterwards, other Conservative Whigs, many with impressive aristocratic titles or connections, joined Pitt's government. Other Whigs refused to support Fox.

Pitt showed shrewd leadership by demoting several Tory supporters to allow more prominent Whigs, like Portland, to have key roles if they joined his coalition. Portland joined the coalition in May 1794 in return for the position of home secretary. Six of the thirteen cabinet positions went to Whigs who had opposed Pitt. However, he kept crucial long-time supporters in his cabinet.

In the short term, the significance of the Whig divisions in the 1790s was that the Tory government under Pitt was unchallenged in the early nineteenth century. As a direct result, following Pitt's death in 1806, the Tories remained dominant until 1830. More significantly in the long term, the formalising of the roles of government and opposition became the forebear of the more rigid party system which formed in the nineteenth century.

Rebellion and Union in Ireland

In 1798, the republican Wolf Tone led the **United Irishmen** in open rebellion. This was prompted by revolutionary ideas from America and France, combined with economic pressure. The rebellion was quickly crushed, due to divisions within it and the overwhelming power of the British army.

In 1801, Pitt's government passed the Act of Union. They overcame opposition from Irish republicans (who feared their loss of independence) and **Ulster Protestants** (who feared that parliament would be lenient on Catholics) by making good use of bribery and promising government offices and peerages.

The impact of the 1801 Act of Union was:

- To absorb Ireland into the British constitution, creating the United Kingdom.
- To abolish the Irish Parliament, and instead give seats to 100 Irish MPs and 28 Irish Peers in the British Parliament.
- To join the Church of Ireland with the Church of England, and guarantee in law the supremacy of the Church of England in Ireland.

Not everything changed. Ireland retained its own legal system, army establishment and system of landholding, and Irish affairs were still directed from Dublin on behalf of the British government.

Following the Act of Union, Pitt attempted to pass a Catholic emancipation bill, which would have given political rights to the 75 per cent of the Irish population

ONLINE EXTRAS OCR **WWW**

Develop your analysis of the impact of war on Pitt's government by completing Worksheet 3 at **www. hoddereducation.co.uk/ accesstohistory/extras**

ONLINE EXTRAS OCR **WWW**

Test your understanding of Whig opposition by completing Worksheet 4 at **www.hoddereducation. co.uk/accesstohistory/extras**

KEY TERMS

United Irishmen An Irish republican association which opposed British control of Ireland.

Ulster Protestants Protestants in the Ulster region of Ireland who supported British, Protestant control of Ireland.

ONLINE EXTRAS
Pearson Edexcel **WWW**

Develop your analysis
of disagreements over
parliamentary reform by
completing Worksheet 2 at
**www.hoddereducation.
co.uk/accesstohistory/extras**

who were Catholic. The king refused, and Pitt resigned on 16 February 1801 (though he continued to act as prime minister when another bout of 'madness' prevented the king appointing a new prime minister). Pitt was replaced by Addington, and Pitt joined the opposition. By 1804, Addington's government was unable to withstand opposition from Pitt and Fox, and Addington resigned. Pitt returned to office, although with a weaker government than before, as many of Addington's supporters chose to join the opposition.

Radical threats in the 1790s

In the 1790s, there was a growing radical demand for political reform. This was a challenge to Pitt's government for two reasons: the demands challenged the traditional power of the political elite, but also the government was very aware that in France, popular protest had led to a revolution which had overthrown the monarchy.

A sense of political dissatisfaction in Britain pre-dated the French Revolution. However, there was nothing resembling a popular protest movement before the 1790s. The closest thing to popular protest was the Society for Constitutional Information. This organisation was formed in 1780 by Major John Cartwright to oppose Lord North and support the American colonists. This middle-class organisation was strongest in Sheffield, although it was represented in many places. The principal idea was that reform would only be possible if information was shared, and so the society gave free leaflets to the public which called for reducing the time between elections and making political representation more equal. Although this shows evidence of some form of popular reformist thought, it was little more than a talking shop which lacked direction or clear goals. It foundered in 1783 due to a lack of purpose.

The French Revolution exposed radical ideas to the world, especially after 1791 when Thomas Paine wrote his influential *Rights of Man*. Paine not only defended the values of the revolution, but proposed the possibility of a society in which the government took responsibility for the welfare of the people. This invigorated an extra-parliamentary reform movement:

- The Society for Constitutional Information re-emerged. However, as a middle-class organisation the society was careful to avoid supporting excessively radical ideas such as changes to land ownership.

- The London Corresponding Society (LCS) was formed in 1792 by Thomas Hardy. It was primarily supported by artisans and small tradesmen and asked only a penny per week, twenty per cent of the cost of joining the Society for Constitutional Information. For most of the 1790s, the LCS probably had no more than 1000 members, but gained political attention through their campaigns of distributing printed handbills to the public.

- Similar organisations sprang up across the UK. Some abolished membership fees entirely. It is likely that by 1797 there were over 80 political societies nationally with about 10,000 members.

As well as parliamentary reform, many of these organisations also debated reforms of working conditions, the restoration of common land, lower taxes and shorter working hours – topics reflecting the lower-middle-class membership. Although they generally avoided Paine's most radical ideas, their ideals were radical in the context of the 1790s, for example, calling for **universal male suffrage**.

This meant that more working men were involved than in many other societies of the period. The Sheffield Corresponding Society, for example, was involved in many protests and strikes between 1791 and 1796, including a three-day protest in 1791 in which thousands of workers chanted 'no king', 'no taxes' and 'no corn bill'. This resulted in soldiers being permanently billeted in the town. These demands demonstrate the mixed political and social interests of reformist societies in the 1790s.

The Association of the Friends of the People, an aristocratic reformist organisation made up of Whig MPs, also formed in 1792. This movement was quite exclusive, and charged two and a half guineas per year, ten times the annual cost of the LCS. It aimed at limited reform, especially tempering the radical ideas of other political clubs across Britain.

These organisations put pressure on Pitt's government as they showed that the demand for reform was growing, and supported by members of different social classes. Although Pitt personally supported limited constitutional reform, the ideas of these organisations were two radical for the government to accept.

KEY TERM

Universal male suffrage
The right for all men to vote. (Suffrage is the right to vote, while universal suffrage is the right for men and women to vote.)

SUMMARY DIAGRAM

PRESSURES FACED BY PITT'S GOVERNMENT

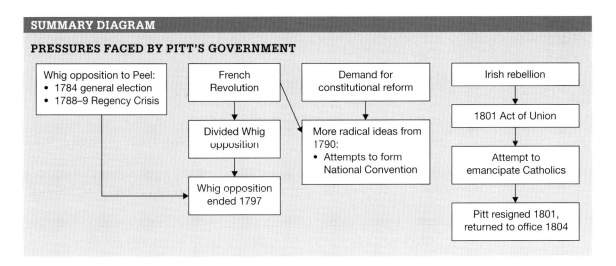

4 Opposition to reform

■ *Was government legislation the main reason that the radical movements failed?*

There was a growing reform movement but there was also significant opposition. Although some opposition came from Pitt's government, there was also opposition from the wider population in the form of a counter-reform movement.

The counter–reformist movement

While revolutionary ideals invigorated an extra-parliamentary reform movement in parts of the population, they prompted a conservative response in others. Property owners, especially landowners, feared stories of revolutionary excesses. Many **counter-reformist** associations formed. These tended to have financial backing and support from magistrates and clergy, which meant that their conservative message was clearly heard. Membership was confined to men of property, although they would call on the working classes when action was needed. The largest such association was the Reeves' Association for the Preservation of Liberty and Property against Republicans and Levellers. This was set up in 1792 by lawyer John Reeves. It grew to have almost 2000 branches nationally. This was genuinely an expression of popular opinion among members, since there was no government involvement in these organisations.

Staunchly Anglican 'Church and King' groups formed and used violence to attack suspected radicals. They were concerned about the challenge to both the propertied classes (by radical ideas) and the Church of England (by the heavily **Nonconformist** membership). Events in Birmingham, 1791, exemplify the dual concerns. Angered by a small local middle-class reformist group holding a meal to celebrate the **fall of the Bastille**, a three-day riot broke out, initiated by loyalists. One Baptist and two Unitarian meeting houses were sacked and burned, as were a number of shops and houses belonging to known reformists. In addition to spontaneous popular resentment of dissenters, there is evidence that the mobs were directed by local clergymen and magistrates, who also refused to prosecute offenders.

Pitt's repression of the radical movements

The extra-parliamentary reform movement was becoming organised and widespread, but it was fundamentally weak. Between 1793 and 1801, Pitt's government progressively cracked down on dissent in what has been referred to as his 'Reign of Terror'.

In 1793, when reformists tried to organise a National Convention to unify their associations, a number were arrested and tried in court. Fourteen were sentenced to **transportation**. In May 1794, based on the radical ideas in papers seized from the LCS, parliament suspended the **Act of Habeas Corpus**. This allowed the government to arrest radicals as political prisoners and hold them for an indefinite length of time. Thirty prominent LCS members, including the founder, Thomas Hardy, were tried for treason in October on the grounds that they had 'imagined the king's death'; under existing legislation, the jury had acquitted them all. Hardy's house was attacked by a mob and he retired from the movement.

In 1795, wheat prices increased due to a harvest failure to 170 per cent of 1792 prices. Mass protests were organised. In October, stones were thrown at the king's coach as he travelled to open a new session of parliament. Without any supporting evidence, the stone throwing was linked to a reformist meeting three days earlier. Pitt used this as an excuse to clamp down more, passing the so-called 'Two Acts':

- The Seditious Societies Act (1795) banned meetings of more than 50 people without a magistrate's consent.
- The Treasonable Practices Act (1795) extended existing treason laws to include speaking or writing against the constitution.

These Acts prevented public meetings – since magistrates would not grant a licence – and the ability to debate reform. In the House of Lords, only five peers voted against the bills, and the wealthy Bishop of Rochester declared that he could not see 'what the mass of people in any country had to do with the laws but to obey them'. Radical MP Fox (see page 6) voiced his concern when he claimed that these broad laws would even make discussing reform in parliament illegal.

Pitt's government passed further legislation to hinder radical groups from sharing their ideas, including:

- The stamp tax (1798): a tax on all printed media to inflate artificially the cost of newspapers.
- Newspaper Publications Acts (1798, 1799): required that all newspapers register with the government and publish the names of the author and publisher at the foot of the page. Journalists sharing reformist ideas could be brought before a specially selected jury by the attorney general, rather than a common jury.
- Seditious Meetings Act (1799): renewed and extended the Seditious Societies Act. This continued to ban groups of 50 or more from meeting without a licence but also required the licensing of properties used for debates or lectures.
- Combination Acts (1799, 1800): prevented specific groups of workers from combining to organise strikes to protest about pay or working conditions.
- Unlawful Societies Act (1799), also called the Corresponding Societies Act: prevented organisations that required a secret oath from forming branches.

KEY TERMS

Transportation Some criminals were punished by being sent abroad to serve their sentence. Australia was the main destination from 1787.

Act of Habeas Corpus An old English law which gave anyone arrested the right to face trial or be released.

ONLINE EXTRAS WWW
OCR

Develop your analysis of government responses to radical protest by completing Worksheet 5 at **www. hoddereducation.co.uk/ accesstohistory/extras**

ONLINE EXTRAS WWW
Pearson Edexcel

Develop your analysis of government responses to radical protests by completing Worksheet 3 at **www.hoddereducation. co.uk/accesstohistory/extras**

It can be easy to simply see Pitt's responses as heavy-handed, and a repression of free thought. However, Pitt's measures were intended to stave off what appeared to be a threat to the stability and social norms of the country. The chaos that had followed revolutionary action in France was a genuine worry.

The failure of the radical movements

By 1796, the protest movement had largely disappeared, partly due to Pitt's heavy-handed legislation. Table 2.3 shows other factors to consider. Some say that, although in the short term the movement failed, in the long term it created the legacy of organised socio-political discontent which resurged after the Napoleonic Wars, and eventually led to parliamentary reform, **Chartism**, the birth of modern trade unionism and the movement for women's rights.

KEY TERMS

Chartism A political movement which demanded political reform such as universal suffrage. Chartists were particularly strong in the north of England. Some of their main tactics were petitions and marches.

Agents provocateurs Government employees who would join radical organisations to identify the leaders and encourage radical behaviour so people could be arrested.

Table 2.3 Reasons for the failure of the reform movement

Factor	Detail
Government intimidation	• The government relied heavily on local magistrates, who were landed gentry and tended to oppose reform • Since magistrates were responsible for licensing pubs, they could threaten the loss of licences to landlords who allowed radical groups to meet on their premises • The government expanded the Home Office to have an Alien Section and a Secret Service Section, which directed spies and **agents provocateurs** who worked among radical groups. These reported back on meetings and identified ringleaders
Government propaganda	• The government promoted anti-reformist propaganda in publications like *The Oracle* and *True Briton* • Articles accused radicals of treachery and promoted the virtues of the British socio-legal system • They published cartoons, like those of James Gillray, showing terrifying imaginative scenes of the consequences of the French Revolution spreading to Britain
Counter-reformist attitudes	• There was patriotic support, such as the 'Church and King' clubs, for maintaining the *status quo* in Britain • Once radical clubs had collapsed or gone underground, many 'Church and King' members joined the government organisation the Volunteers, a paramilitary defence force with 450,000 members in 1804
Lack of co-ordination	• The effort in 1793–4 to create a national alliance failed. The associations were divided. For example, the LCS distanced themselves from more radical groups such as the SCS
Social division	• There was no unifying of working-class support with middle-class leadership • Societies with wealthier membership were more interested in reform more as academic debate than in achieving change • Working-class groups had little influential support

ONLINE EXTRAS [WWW]
Pearson Edexcel

Test your understanding of the weaknesses of the radical protest movement by completing Worksheet 4 at **www.hoddereducation.co.uk/accesstohistory/extras**

SOURCE A

Promis'd Horrors of the French INVASION, —or — Forcible Reasons for negociating a Regicide PEACE. Vide . The Authority of Edmund Burke.

A cartoon by James Gillray, entitled 'Promised Horrors of the French Invasion or Forcible Reasons for Negotiation of a Regicide Peace. Vide, The Authority of Edmund Burke. October 1796.' It was produced in response to a pamphlet by Edmund Burke on the dangers of making peace with France. In the image, French soldiers march down the road, while Fox beats Pitt the Younger.

SUMMARY DIAGRAM

OPPOSITION TO REFORM

Popular anti-reformist groups:
- Landowners and magistrates
- Reeves' Association
- Church and King groups

Government action:
- Suspension of *habeas corpus*
- The 'Two Acts'
- Seditious Meetings Act 1799
- Combination Acts

Other issues:
- Government intimidation
- Lack of co-ordination
- Social divisions
- Anti-reform propaganda

SOURCE QUESTION

What does Source A tell you about the cartoonist's opinion of the French at this time?

5 The abolition of the slave trade

■ *What were the reasons for abolishing the slave trade by 1807?*

Britain had been a leading contributor to international slavery, primarily with the so-called 'triangle trade' (see page 3) over the Atlantic Ocean. British ships, commissioned by British merchants and industrialists from ports such as Bristol and Liverpool, sailed to west Africa. There, African slaves were purchased from local tribal chiefs and professional slave catchers in exchange for coins, manufactured goods, woven cloth, alcohol and other commodities, especially guns. The most desirable slaves were healthy males of working age and female slaves aged 18–25, since they had the potential to give birth to more slaves. Children and nursing mothers were less popular as slaves due to the additional difficulties of transporting them.

Loaded down with slaves, the ships would sail westwards across the Atlantic. This journey, known as the **'middle passage'**, was one of horror. Hundreds, crammed into the ship, endured poor sanitation, diseases, infection, suffocation, and violence and sexual assault from the crew. Although in good weather the journey might last six to nine weeks, in less favourable conditions it could take as long as six months.

On arrival in the West Indies, slaves were unloaded, often into holding camps, before subsequently being sold into slavery, either individually or in batches. Most found themselves working the large plantations of the West Indies and North America, although many were purchased as domestic servants. With the wealth of the sale, captains would purchase commodities, commonly sugar, cotton and tobacco, before completing their journey by sailing back to Britain to share the profits with the merchants who had invested in the voyage.

At its height, between 1751 and 1807, an estimated 1.6 million African men, women and children were forcibly transported across the Atlantic. In Liverpool alone in the late 1780s, about 360 merchant firms were involved; Hugh Thomas (2015) estimates that this was an astounding 43 per cent of the total European trade. Britain was responsible for approximately 45 per cent of all slaves transported by European colonial powers.

The anti-slavery movement

Between the years c.1785 and 1807, a movement grew in Britain to oppose slavery. Historian Christopher Brown (2006) noted that it 'seemed to appear out of nowhere' in the 1780s and that before then 'public opposition to the abolitionists was negligible'. By the start of the nineteenth century, there had been several failed efforts to produce legislation which would standardise conditions on the slave ships. In 1806, parliament passed the Foreign Slave Trade

KEY TERM

Middle passage
The name for the stage of the slave-trading voyages in which slaves were transported across the Atlantic from Africa.

Act, which made illegal the transportation and sale of slaves to a non-British state or colony. Officially this was a war measure, but it was really designed to reduce the international trade in slaves.

In 1807, the British government passed the Abolition of the Slave Trade Act after a final ten-hour debate; it was passed in the Commons by 283 votes to 16. This law banned the trade of slaves between British colonies, which essentially ended the British involvement in the Atlantic slave trade, although slavery itself was not abolished in the British Empire until 1833. The bill was passed, despite strong opposition from the future King William IV of England, for which the port city of Liverpool, economically reliant on the slave trade, presented him with a golden casket. The bill was signed by George III on 25 March 1807. The law came into effect in January 1808, and the last British slave ship cleared Liverpool on 27 July 1807.

The work of the Abolition Committee

In 1783, an informal group of six Quakers formed to present a petition to parliament with 300 Quaker signatures. In 1787, the Society for the Abolition of the Slave Trade, commonly known as the Abolition Committee, was formalised. It consisted of nine Quaker members, with three Anglican members – since Quakers could not sit as MPs, the Anglicans were intended to bring greater respectability and influence. They were a prototype of the later political protest movements, led by a committee in London and reliant on a network of agents and supporters, largely Quaker, across the country. Crucially, this was not a local movement; there were representatives in every English county as well as in Scotland and Wales. The Abolition Committee was significant in raising national awareness of the issue and showing the strength of popular feeling.

The Committee produced books and pamphlets, and organised lectures. A key tactic was petition campaigns. Inspired by a Manchester abolitionist petition with 10,639 signatures, the Abolition Committee urged its own supporters to send petitions. During 1791 alone, 519 petitions reached parliament, the largest number ever submitted to the lower House on a single subject or in a single session. MP Sir Samuel Romilly wrote that 'it is impossible the trade should last many years longer'.

Humanitarian campaigning

The abolitionists focused on **humanitarian** arguments. This was calculated, as they would face more opposition with economic arguments:

- They widely publicised the case of the slave ship *Zong* (1783), in which the captain jettisoned into the sea 132 slaves with dysentery to protect the remaining slaves. The British public were shocked. Abolitionist Granville Sharp unsuccessfully attempted to have the whole crew charged with murder, which was reported nationally.

> **KEY TERM**
>
> **Humanitarian**
> Concerned with the well-being of human beings.

- In 1796, the *Tatham* v. *Hodgson* case was reported. Due to bad weather, a ship from Liverpool carrying slaves had taken six months to reach the West Indies. The captain had only taken enough food for nine weeks, and 128 slaves died. Even though there was no criminal charge for the deaths of slaves, the judge ordered that the insurance underwriter did not have to pay. This indicated the changing wave of popular opinion.

Newspaper reports included information about instances of rebellion on ships and began to support the idea of noble, repressed African warriors, fighting for their survival.

Fiction followed this trend, reaching its height in the years 1787–92:

- In 1787, Eliza Knipe published a narrative poem with the title *Atombaka and Omaza: An African Story*, which told of an African warrior chief and his lover, captured and forced to throw themselves overboard to avoid separation.
- William Cowper's poem *Pity the Poor Africans* (1788) was distributed in thousands by the Abolition Society with a superscription reading 'A Subject for Conversation at the Tea-Table'.
- In 1789, the 1688 novel *Oroonoko; or, The Royal Slave* was performed as a play with an anti-slavery prologue in Manchester and London. It was a tragic love story involving a noble African prince in slavery, ending in suicide. Poems about slavery, often reusing lines from *Oroonoko*, were published in newspapers.
- In 1789, Irish Quaker Thomas Wilkinson addressed his anti-slavery poem, *On Behalf of the Abused Africans*, to members of the clergy, colleges, the king, politicians and the British people in general.

Religious support for abolition

The essential characteristic of evangelical faith was the belief that good works were the chief means for obtaining God's grace and future salvation. Campaigning to end slavery made an ideal cause to support. From 1788, evangelicals were heavily involved in the abolitionist movement. Since many, including **William Wilberforce**, had political office, it brought respectability to the movement. That said, the ideas of evangelicals were not always respected. They did not yet have the broad support that evangelism would have in the nineteenth century, and they were seen by the more conservative members of the Anglican Church as being worryingly radical.

The Clapham Sect

A notable group of evangelicals was the Clapham Sect, which included Wilberforce. Several members, such as banker and economist Henry Thornton, were MPs. They sought to improve the moral quality of society from within the Church of England. As well as abolition, the Clapham Sect campaigned on other issues, including prison reform, preventing cruel sports, and encouraging good manners and religious learning among the poor. They were politically conservative and tended to be wealthy Anglicans, so they attracted support from

KEY FIGURE

William Wilberforce (1759–1833)

A British philanthropist and politician, and a leading member of the movement to abolish slavery. He served as an MP between 1780 and 1825. In 1791 he introduced a parliamentary bill to abolish slavery, and this bill was presented annually until it was successful in becoming the 1807 Abolition of the Slave Trade Act.

the rich, making the abolitionist campaign socially acceptable. They provided a network for encouraging discussion of abolition.

Quakers

A particularly influential group were Quakers, especially on the Abolition Committee, making up nine of the original twelve members. From the early eighteenth century, Quakers had been questioning the morality of the slave trade. They believed that every individual could experience salvation in their lives, regardless of race or gender. Without a belief in white supremacy, it was difficult to justify slavery. They denied original sin, the belief that imperfection was inherent to all human beings. They also denied the tradition that Africans were descended from Cain, a biblical character cursed by God, and that the inherent existence of sin justified slavery because of the curse.

Quakers were influential in industry and politics. Several American Quakers travelled thousands of miles through the American states between 1753 and 1756, observing the conditions of the slaves. They were highly critical of slave owners. Later, several of these made the trans-Atlantic journey to Britain where they shared their reports and experiences.

Women

Historian Clare Midgley (1992) has shown that women were a key support group to the abolitionists.

- Many abolitionist Quakers were women, such as American Rebecca Jones who travelled around Britain between 1784 and 1788 giving sermons and drumming up abolitionist support. Midgley notes that women had no decision-making roles within the Church.

- As supporters of abolitionist movements. For example, the 1788 list of the Abolition Society's members shows that women made up about ten per cent of supporters. Of these, only about 25 per cent had male abolitionist relatives, indicating an independent decision to support the movement.

- As signatories of petitions. The *Newcastle Courant* reported that 433 women had signed a local petition in 1792. Midgley notes that this was not universal, in London, the Abolition Committee opposed women signing petitions. A concerned Quaker activist reported that in Dundee 'by a mistaken zeal, some boys and three women have been allowed to sign' a petition.

- Women wrote, read and discussed literature on slavery, which helped to legitimise the topic for polite conversation.

- In boycotts. Women were targeted to boycott items such as sugar and rum, which were transported in the slave trade. Methodist Samuel Bradburn wrote an *Address to the People Called Methodists* (1792) calling on British women to boycott slave trade goods; an anonymous writer sent *An Address to Her Royal Highness the Duke of York* calling on her to ban these items from the royal household. The abolitionists claimed that 300,000 people supported the boycotts.

Efforts by freed black slaves

There was a small but growing number of free black people in Britain, mainly freed or runaway slaves, ex-sailors from slave ships, or liberated slaves from the American War of Independence. The likelihood is that several thousand black people lived in or near London in the 1780s, although no specific number is known.

Before the American War of Independence, there was no movement for abolition in Britain. Following the war, attention turned to the abolition of slavery as an institution. The British army during the war had granted freedom to many black slaves willing to turn against their former masters. Brigadier General Samuel Birch in New York City granted passports to some freed slaves to travel to Britain. In 1786, the British government established Sierra Leone as an experimental colony for freed black people. Further, in the late 1780s, a philanthropic movement had appeared in Britain specifically to help free black people, with organisations such as the Committee for the Relief of the Black Poor in 1786. Although largely led by white Quaker philanthropists, a number of black leaders, including Olaudah Equiano, emerged. These took the chance to publicise their experiences of the slave trade and were influential in promoting the ideas of the humanitarian and evangelical campaigns for abolition.

Efforts were not always positive for the abolition campaign. Most British anti-slavery writers took care to not criticise the popular institution of empire, but some writers were more radical in their criticism. Ottobah Cugoano, for example, in his *Thoughts and Sentiments on the Evil of Slavery* (1786), described the exploitation of the slaves as a symptom of the wider crimes of European imperialism.

Economic pressures

In the later 1780s, abolitionists began to incorporate economic arguments alongside moral reasoning. Thomas Clarkson's *Essay on the Impolicy of the African Slave Trade* (1788) entirely ignored moral reasons and focused on financial benefits. Economic arguments focused on three principal points:

- There were many important resources for British manufacturers in Africa, such as woods, spices, medicine, rice and tobacco, which could be purchased directly from Africa, shortening the trade journey.
- Shorter journeys with inanimate cargoes would result in fewer deaths of sailors.
- There were many successful plantations where the owners had not purchased slaves; anecdotal evidence claimed that free workers were more productive.

By the late eighteenth century, the slave trade was becoming less profitable:

- The Slave Trade Act 1799 limited the number of slaves that could be carried by a ship. It was harder to compete with other countries that did not follow the same regulations. In 1806, a British navy battleship captured a Dutch ship which had 413 slaves on board; had the ship been British it could have legally carried only 260.

- Wholesale slave shipment: local New World traders would buy the entire shipment for a low price and make a profit by selling the slaves individually around the colonies. British merchants were frustrated that their goods were being resold for such profits.

- Restricted ports: while the British allowed limited foreign trade into their ports under the Free Port Act, Spanish ports did not allow British merchants into theirs. In one instance in 1786, a Mr Leyland, being unable to obtain a licence to trade at the Spanish port of Cuba, sold his cargo to a Mr Blair at Dominica; Mr Blair then hired Mr Leyland's ship to transport the cargo to Cuba under his own licence, where he sold it for a large profit.

- Changes in Cuba: Havana had been a significant port for the sale of slaves, and many British merchants had instructed their captains to do business there for the best prices. In the 1790s, an oligarchy of merchants with Spanish loyalties became dominant. They either obtained slaves directly from Africa with their naval resources or purchased them from other Caribbean ports. Britain lost access to a major trading port.

Historian Eric Williams (1944) argued that the abolitionists' success was the result of the declining sale value of slaves and an economic need to move to a system of free labour which was less expensive and more productive. Free-trade supporters insisted that competition, market forces and free labour were essential for a strong international economy; slavery did not fit with this ideal.

Counter-argument

The economic argument has been closely argued. Robert Fogel and Stanley Engerman (1989) used an index of slave sale prices to argue that the real price of slaves between 1784 and 1794 remained at 89 per cent of the pre-1775 value. The 1790s also saw the largest increase in the number of slaves traded. This limits the impact of claims that the value of slaves was falling. James Walvin (1993) has pointed out that the economic impact was a concern to opponents of abolition, not abolitionists. As he pointed out, 'The British did not recruit millions of Africans simply for racial reasons.' More recent research has shown that the slave trade remained profitable and ports such as Bristol and Liverpool were highly dependent on the trade, as was the growing British industry in the north which needed cotton. The triangle trade itself from the 1770s was worth over £1.33 million, and the decreased profits per slave were being made up by the increased profits of selling cotton and sugar in Britain. This has been partly challenged by Stanley Engerman and David Eltis (2000), who argued that the slave trade made up a far smaller part of the British economy than generally assumed, only about three per cent of British shipping, and that the trade was never economically essential to Britain.

The role of individuals

Certain individuals played a key role in abolition.

Granville Sharp

Granville Sharp was a London clerk who took the first basic small-scale legal steps towards abolition. In 1766, he won a legal case to free an ex-slave who had been kidnapped back into slavery. He successfully used *habeas corpus* to free several slaves and in 1772, proved in court that it was not legal to enslave a person in Britain. In 1787, Sharp formed the Society for the Abolition of the Slave Trade with Thomas Clarkson. He was significant because:

- his actions set a precedent to challenge the legality of slavery
- as an Anglican, he broadened the appeal of the message to conservatively minded supporters
- he was instrumental in persuading William Wilberforce to take the lead with the Abolition Committee.

William Wilberforce

William Wilberforce was a friend of Pitt the Younger and Thomas Clarkson, and MP from 1780. He became spokesman of the Society for the Abolition of the Slave Trade in 1787, and a member of the Clapham Sect. Each year from 1791 until its passing in 1807, Wilberforce presented an abolition bill to parliament. Wilberforce also campaigned for other social issues, including tackling alcoholism, helping children to have better education in reading and religion, better hygiene and preventing cruelty to animals. He was significant because:

- He provided leadership to the movement.
- As a Cambridge-educated MP, he lent respectability to the movement, and he could present bills in parliament.
- He drew support from other philanthropists.
- Wilberforce was horrified by the French Revolution; his reputation helped to moderate fears that abolition was a revolutionary change.
- His decision in 1793 to postpone the use of petitions made the abolitionists look less radical during the height of French Revolutionary excesses.

Thomas Clarkson

Thomas Clarkson developed an interest in the legality and morality of slavery while at Cambridge University. In 1786, he published an essay on the legality of enslaving a person. In 1787, he formed the Society for the Abolition of the Slave Trade with Granville Sharp. He travelled widely to see slave ships and speak to eyewitnesses, including sailors and ex-slaves. His research was presented to parliament in support of petitions and debates, frequently with visual aids such as shackles and branding irons. He selected emotive examples, such as slaves dying from disease, or families being torn apart by the trade. He was significant because:

- Clarkson's evidence was detailed, thorough and hard to refute. He presented his arguments in an academic, persuasive style.

- His emotive reports affected audiences. In one report, he described a young female slave who knew that her father was on board the ship, but who was kept separated from him until the end of the journey. Supporters of slavery were unable to deny these claims. In a society which valued family, this further damaged the traders' reputations.

- As a practising Anglican, he broadened the appeal of the Abolition Committee.

- He was important in demonstrating the economic case for abolition to parliament.

Olaudah Equiano

Olaudah Equiano had been a slave-sailor on board various trade ships, including those carrying slaves, with the slave name Gustavus Vassa. He saved money to buy his own freedom. He had arrived in London in 1786, where he joined a group of free black abolitionists, known as the 'Sons of Africa'. He recorded his life in the autobiography *The Interesting Narrative of the Life of Olaudah Equiano, or Gustavus Vassa, the African, Written by Himself* (1789). It records his kidnap aged eleven from southern Nigeria, his experience of the middle passage, life as a sailor, the slave pens in the ports and the slave sales. Some parts of the account may be fictitious, yet overall it is considered accurate. He was significant because:

- Equiano's *Interesting Narrative* caught the attention of literate society in Britain. His detailed descriptions validated the poetry and novels of the humanitarian movement. People were shocked by his descriptions of conditions and also the feelings of hopelessness and psychological trauma experienced by slaves.

- His literate writing style and eloquent speeches during his national publicity tours humanised black people to his audiences. This was important in challenging the common abolitionist view of slaves as 'noble savages'.

The changing political climate

Despite public sympathy, the abolitionists had made little headway by 1791. They were associated with radicalism and could not overcome the evidence of supporters of slavery. For example:

- Ships' captains presented evidence that slaves were washed and fed well, and that the holds of ships were regularly cleaned.

- 'Specialists' blamed health problems on the naturally more diseased and inferior state of Africans compared to Europe and pointed out that slavery was an ancient institution in African countries.
- A series of respected admirals reported that not only were conditions in the West Indies good for slaves, they were better than in their own villages and were considered a paradise by slaves.
- Merchants claimed that any effort to abolish slavery would be economically disastrous.

Consequently, Wilberforce's abolition bill was dismissed by the House of Commons in 1791 by 163 to 88 votes. However, 1791 was a turning point:

- Reports reached Britain of a successful slave insurrection in Saint-Domingue, (modern-day Haiti). The majority population of 500,000 African slaves rose up against the 32,000 European colonists. There was continual fighting over the following decade. Reports of rebellions added to concerns about the economic viability of slavery and supported the humanitarian arguments for abolition.
- With the outbreak war with France in 1792, the issue of liberty seemed more relevant. Although the government was suspicious of reform, parliament listened to Wilberforce. From 1791 to 1807, the House of Commons heard Wilberforce's proposed bill. By the 1796 reading, the balance of opinion was shifting and Wilberforce lost by only four votes.

From about 1800, war, which had until that point distracted from the abolitionist campaign, now had a positive effect.

- In 1802, Napoleon reinstated slavery in France. Since slavery was now associated with Revolutionary France, it made the opposition to slavery a patriotic, anti-French stance.
- British armed forces in the Caribbean enjoyed consistent successes against French- and Dutch-held West Indian islands, which they captured one by one. British sugar plantation investors worried about competition from the plantations on these islands which could be supplied by British slave ships. They supported the abolitionists in passing the 1806 Foreign Slave Trade Act in order to limit the sale of slaves to foreign colonies and prevent them from weakening the British market hold on the sugar trade.
- The 1801 Act of Union had united Britain with Ireland, bringing Irish MPs to Westminster. These were sympathetic to anyone whom they perceived as being oppressed by the British Empire, and were willing to support Wilberforce's bill in parliament.
- By 1805, there was enough support in the Commons to pass the bill by 49 votes to 24, although the House of Lords blocked it from becoming law.
- In 1805, Henry Dundas, a strong opponent to abolition first in the House of Commons and later in the House of Lords, was impeached for mismanagement of funds.

6 Key debate

■ *Which factors were most important in the abolition of slavery?*

Although historians would accept the relevance of the factors considered in this chapter, different historians would emphasise different aspects. Extracts 1–4 below are examples of historians who have interpreted the role of factors such as economic concerns, religion and social ideals differently. Read them carefully to identify the different interpretation that each historian presents.

EXTRACT 1

Adapted from Christopher Brown, *Moral Capital: Foundations of British Abolitionism*, University of North Carolina Press, 2006, pp. 432–3.

The Quakers were central to the abolition movement. The Quaker propaganda campaign made a difference but informed opinion, alone, was not enough to make antislavery a vital political issue. The distinctive qualities that helped make Quakers pioneers in the antislavery movement – their separation from church and state, their marginal place in British society – handicapped their campaign. At the time the abolition movement began, polite society still looked down on religious enthusiasm. To introduce religious topics on social occasions showed poor taste and bad manners. The 'take-off' of Quaker abolitionism ultimately depended on the cooperation of allies outside the Society of Friends.

Thomas Clarkson had a decisive impact on the established Quaker campaign. He enlarged its ambitions and improved its prospects. His personality and personal experience helped Clarkson become an opponent of slavery, but the historical moment and his social position allowed him to become an abolitionist. He could build on the progress that others had made, using their knowledge, experience and networks. Others in Britain had cared and did care a great deal about the sins of slaving, but no other individuals gave their lives to the antislavery cause in the way Clarkson did.

EXTRACT 2

Adapted from James Walvin, *Black Ivory*, Wiley-Blackwell, 1993, p. 304.

The campaign which culminated in black freedom began in 1787 when a small group of Quakers launched a public campaign against the British slave trade. They were to be assisted by the effectiveness of their own campaign tactics. The campaign against slavery took place in years when more and more British people found their lives shaped by conditions in the towns. It was there that the nonconformist chapels took root and Baptist and Methodist congregations found a new social and political voice. Abolitionists were assisted by the social changes around them and the effectiveness of their own campaign tactics. At a time when British manufacturers, workers and economic theorists were promoting the virtues of free labour, the concept of owning a worker seemed to make no sense.

INTERPRETATION QUESTION

How do Extracts 1–4 differ in the reasons that they emphasise for the abolition of slavery in 1807? Which viewpoint do you most agree with?

ONLINE EXTRAS WWW
Pearson Edexcel

Practise your interpretation analysis skills by completing Worksheet 5 at **www. hoddereducation.co.uk/ accesstohistory/extras**

ONLINE EXTRAS WWW
Pearson Edexcel

Practise your interpretation analysis skills by completing Worksheet 6 at **www. hoddereducation.co.uk/ accesstohistory/extras**

ONLINE EXTRAS
Pearson Edexcel **WWW**

Practise your interpretation analysis skills by completing Worksheet 7 at **www. hoddereducation.co.uk/ accesstohistory/extras**

ONLINE EXTRAS
Pearson Edexcel **WWW**

Practise your interpretation analysis skills by completing Worksheet 8 at **www. hoddereducation.co.uk/ accesstohistory/extras**

EXTRACT 3

Adapted from Roger Anstey, 'The Pattern of British Abolitionism' in Christine Bolt *et al.*, editors, *Anti-Slavery, Religion and Reform*, Shoe String Press, 1980, p. 22.

When evangelicals did turn to political action, they were unsuccessful for nigh on twenty years. The decisive change came when a fortuitous combination of circumstances permitted the abolitionists to present the supply of enemy, other foreign, and captured territories with slaves by British slave ships as simple foolishness. In other words, the abolitionists, in 1806, had the wit to see that the abolition of about two-thirds of the British slave trade could be procured by disguising their own humanitarian motivation as elementary national interest in time of war. This made the 1807 measure of abolition successful, despite it serving no national interest. The manifest interest of Britain, by 1806–7, was to increase her own slave trade and deny slaves to her rivals.

EXTRACT 4

Adapted from Stanley L. Engerman and David Eltis, 'Economic Aspects of the Abolition Debate' in Christine Bolt *et al.*, editors, *Anti-Slavery, Religion and Reform*, Shoe String Press, 1980, pp. 281 and 283.

Anstey placed great stress on the abolitionists' ability to project the 1806 bill closing the trade to British 'enemies and competitors' as being in the national interest. [But] the parliamentary abolitionists frequently used various forms of the national interest argument before 1806, including bills which prohibited the slave trade to foreign colonies. Perhaps it is worth reiterating that much of the debate on abolition has always attempted to separate the economic from the humanitarian motive in a way that would have puzzled the abolitionists themselves. [Adam Smith's 1776] explanation of why planters used slaves when they were obviously the most expensive form of labour had profound moral and humanitarian as well as economic implications, however weak the initial premise.

SUMMARY DIAGRAM

THE ABOLITION OF THE SLAVE TRADE

The slave trade
- Britain → Africa → Americas → Britain
- Millions of Africans transported and sold
- British merchants traded for cotton, sugar and tobacco to sell in Britain

Abolition of the Slave Trade Act (1807)
- Banned trade of slaves between British colonies
- Did not ban slavery

7 Key debate

■ *How successful were Pitt's domestic policies 1783–1806?*

Pitt's economic and administrative reforms, and his management of radical groups, make up Pitt's main domestic policies. Historians have disagreed as to how far they can be considered a success.

Pitt was a principled, reforming leader, who made effective administrative and economic reforms

Early historians, between 1900 and 1950, tended to see Pitt as a principled leader who had a strong vision to reform Britain. His work was focused on a clear belief in the superiority of free trade and in the need to change the old, corrupt ways of governing. These historians focus on his proposals to reform the political system, which were radical for the time, as well as his removal of sinecures and other corruptions as a new economic approach to debt. This interpretation generally focuses on his achievements before the outbreak of war in 1793.

> **EXTRACT 5**
>
> Adapted from Thomas Macaulay, *William Pitt*, London, 1904, pp. 32–3.
>
> *No person could hear Pitt without perceiving him to be a man of high, intrepid and commanding spirit, proudly conscious of his own rectitude [goodness] and of his own intellectual superiority. His first administration lasted seventeen years. That long period is divided by a strongly marked line into two almost exactly equal parts in 1792. Throughout both parts Pitt displayed in the highest degree the talents of a parliamentary leader. During the first part he was a skilful administrator. With the difficulties which he had to encounter during the second part he was altogether incapable of contending.*

Historians also point out that there was little national opposition to Pitt's repressive policies, and that in fact loyalist organisations grew during this period. It is generally accepted that by 1796, the radical movement had been forced underground.

Pitt was a pragmatic leader, reacting to situations with reforms

An alternative viewpoint is that Pitt was an effective reformer, but that his role was more pragmatic, based on reacting to needs as they arose, rather than following a predetermined approach based on principles. Many of the ideas that Pitt introduced were not entirely new. For example, although he introduced new taxes, the idea of taxing luxuries was well established, and although he introduced the sinking fund, it was an idea that had been used previously in the 1730s on a limited scale, published in a pamphlet in 1772 by economist

INTERPRETATION QUESTION

How do Extracts 5–8 differ in their judgement of Pitt's leadership and the effectiveness of his policies?

ONLINE EXTRAS WWW
AQA

Practise your extract analysis skills by completing Worksheet 4 at **www. hoddereducation.co.uk/ accesstohistory/extras**

Richard Price and recommended by Lord North during his brief period as prime minister.

The idea that Pitt was reactive rather than proactive is also supported by the repressive governmental policies towards radical protest groups. That several policies were temporary would seem to support the idea that they were purely reactionary, not part of an overall plan.

EXTRACT 6

Adapted from Ian R. Christie, *Wars and Revolutions, Britain 1760–1815*, Edward Arnold, 1982, pp. 184–5 and 200.

In 1784, expenditure exceeded income, so that the debt, already viewed with alarm, was still increasing. Pitt did manage to improve the efficiency and value of taxes collected. But some of these taxes caused considerable difficulties for his victims as well as for himself, and the final impression left is one of a rather desperate and unsuccessful improvisation. Pitt put proposals for constitutional reform before the House of Commons. He himself still believed in the necessity, hoping for advantage both in Britain and in Ireland. Pitt's proposals were deliberately couched in moderate terms. Even these limited reforms were opposed by most of the cabinet ministers.

A good peacetime leader, not wartime leader

A common interpretation is that Pitt was a peacetime leader who became less effective once war broke out. Historians focus on:

- The failure of Pitt's government to appreciate that its strategic view was different from the view of its continental allies, or that the Revolutionary War would be a long, expensive affair. This meant that the British economy was not well prepared for the scale of war, which impacted on the domestic conditions.
- Pitt's economic policies, such as the sinking fund, were only effective during peacetime, without the costs of war. Apart from income tax, Pitt did not effectively adapt economic policies for a war.

Pitt's policies were less effective than they appear

A counter-argument suggests that Pitt's policies were less important in the improved economic position of Britain during the years 1784–93, even before the strain of warfare. The main evidence for this is that Britain's economic position was based largely upon the development of industry, which was not directed by the State, and international trade, which was established long before Pitt's time in office.

> **EXTRACT 7**
>
> Adapted from Eric Evans, *William Pitt the Younger*, Taylor & Francis, 1999, p. 23.
>
> *How much credit should Pitt claim for the so-called 'National Revival'? It is important to put the contribution of any individual into a wider context. There is much about a nation's economic performance which cannot be commanded by the policies of its governments. Britain's economic growth had only been temporarily checked by the American War. With the return of peace, trade boomed once more. The value of British imports almost doubled overall between the mid-1780s and mid-1790s. Concern about the state of the nation in 1783 rapidly came to be seen as alarmist. Also he inherited and adapted the ideas and policies of others. This still leaves substantial scope for recognising Pitt's own merits.*

Pitt's repressive policies failed to repress radical groups

Historian E.P. Thompson (1980) argued that protest did not end in 1796 but went underground. He cites as evidence:

- The United Irishmen's rebellion of the 1790s, including Wolf Tone's 1798 rebellion.
- The United Englishmen, an organisation which included members of the former LCS, operated between 1796 and 1802. Colonel Despard, a former United Englishmen member, and 35 others were arrested in London in 1802 on charges of treason for planning a *coup d'état* and executed.
- Naval mutinies in 1797.
- Food riots between 1799 and 1801.

There is some evidence of dubious origin, mainly from government spies, that secret northern societies were preparing weapons for a rebellion 1800 and 1802. This is referred to as the 'Black Lamp conspiracy'. Additionally, Thompson considers the Luddite sabotage of 1811 to 1813 (see page 47) to be part of this 'movement'.

Pitt's policies against the radical organisations were not justified

A further counter-argument suggests that the radical movement did not pose a credible threat to the government or Britain's ability to fight a war. There is little evidence of any widespread desire or ability among the protestors to exploit the economic strain the government faced. The few groups that did seem to understand the potential to use the economic situation to challenge the government, such as the so-called Black Lamp conspiracy, had little support and did not represent the wider working population. Therefore Pitt's repressive policies, far from being effective, were excessive, and his economic policies did not solve the economic conditions that caused the general discontent evidenced in such groups.

Pitt's repressive policies simply followed popular opinion

Historian Eric Evans (1991) has pointed out that in focusing on the repressive policies of Pitt's government, it is easy to overlook that this anti-reform attitude was a view supported by a huge proportion of the population, rather than Pitt's approach alone.

EXTRACT 8

Adapted from Eric Evans, *The Forging of the Modern State, Early Industrial Britain 1783–1870*, Pearson, 2014, pp. 88 and 92.

Radical propaganda laid down the gauntlet and the authorities were not slow to pick it up. However, the conservative reaction was not just a matter of sly counter-propaganda from Westminster. The counter-blast to radicalism in the 1790s was multi-faceted; it involved the press, the Church of England, local government and the militia among others. This counterblast was more effective than government repressive legislation in driving radicalism underground from 1795 onwards. Impressive demonstrations were redundantly staged against government legislation, but Pitt was unmoved and the ranks of the propertied remained unbroken.

CHAPTER SUMMARY

To King George III, Pitt was a good choice to restore stability, but he proved more than simply an obedient prime minister. His bold handling of the 1784 election strengthened his position, and he took decisive action to strengthen Britain through improved trade, increasing economic efficiency and removing some the corruption that was inherent to the political system. Many of Pitt's policies were effective by 1793, especially in reducing national debt.

However, Pitt's policies faced a challenge once Britain entered the Revolutionary War. Despite the end of formal Whig opposition to the government, the financial pressures of war limited Pitt's ability to continue his programme of reform. Revolutionary ideas also encouraged the growth of radical demands for parliamentary reform, and in turn, this created strong royalist, traditionalist opposition to reform. Pitt's 'Reign of Terror' made it increasingly difficult for radical groups to meet, let alone publish their ideas. By 1796, the radical movement was effectively underground and

ineffectual. The anti-slavery movement had also been growing, even though slavery had long been a staple of the expanding British economy. Britain, while not solely responsible in Europe, controlled a large proportion of the slave trade from Africa to the Americas.

Yet by the late eighteenth century, and especially after 1791, spearheaded by Nonconformist organisations and led by individuals such as William Wilberforce, Olaudah Equiano and Thomas Clarkson, concerns over the morality of slavery gained traction. By 1807, an effective anti-slavery movement had not only developed but also generated such pressure that the Abolition of the Slave Trade Act was passed by a large parliamentary majority. This was the result of a range of factors which had created the conditions under which parliament could accept such a reform. Although this Act did not end slavery in the British Empire, by banning the trade of slaves between British colonies, it effectively ended British involvement in intercontinental slave trading.

Refresher questions

Use these questions to remind yourself of the key material covered in this chapter.

1 What were the circumstances that led to Pitt the Younger becoming prime minister?

2 Why was the 1784 general election important for Pitt the Younger?

3 What policies did Pitt the Younger use to reduce national debt?

4 Give three examples of Pitt the Younger's administrative reforms.

5 Give three examples of corruption or unequal representation in the unreformed electoral system in 1783.

6 What was the Regency Crisis 1788–9?

7 Why did radical demands for political reform become more popular in the 1790s?

8 Give two examples of legislation used by Pitt the Younger's government to prevent radical reform.

9 Why was the 1807 Abolition of the Slave Trade Act a turning point in British history?

10 List four factors that contributed to the abolition of the slave trade in 1807.

Question practice: AQA

Essay questions

1 'Reducing the national debt was Pitt's greatest achievement in the years 1784–1812.' Explain why you agree or disagree with this view. [AS level]

EXAM HINT You need to analyse his financial achievements alongside other claims to success, and then reach a judgement.

2 'The radical reform movement was ineffective from 1783 to 1812 due to the counter-reform movement.' Explain why you agree or disagree with this view. [AS level]

EXAM HINT You need to look at the reasons for the failures of radical reform and assess where the causes lay, for example the strength of opposition to change or the weaknesses of the reform movement itself.

3 'In the period 1784–1806, Pitt proved to be an effective peacetime leader but ineffective during wartime.' Assess the validity of this view. [A level]

EXAM HINT There will be evidence for and against both parts of the quotation, and this needs to be reflected in your balanced analysis.

4 To what extent was the British government responsible for minimising the impact of radical protest between 1783 and 1812? [A level]

EXAM HINT You are being asked to analyse how the British government acted effectively and set this alongside other factors that minimised the impact of radical protest.

Interpretation questions

1 With reference to Extracts 5 (page 37) and 6 (page 38), and your understanding of the historical context, which of these two extracts provides the more convincing interpretation of Pitt's reforms? [AS level]

EXAM HINT Analyse the content of each of the two extracts in relation to your own knowledge. You must have a substantial section that compares the two in order to reach a well-argued judgement.

2 Using your understanding of the historical context, assess how convincing the arguments in Extracts 3 (page 37) , 4 (page 38) and 5 (page 39) are in relation to Pitt's reforms. [A level]

EXAM HINT Analyse the content of each extract in turn. Try to identify the main argument with subsidiary arguments that add substance, and then use your knowledge to analyse how convincing each one is. Do not include an overall conclusion about the three extracts.

Question practice: OCR A level

Essay questions

1 'Pitt's handling of the economy was effective.' How far do you agree?

EXAM HINT The opening might consider criteria against which effectiveness could be judged. Responses should then consider a number of ways in which Pitt handled the economy, explaining, through a balanced discussion of each, whether or not it was effective and reaching an interim judgement on the issue discussed. The interim judgements should then be used to reach an overall judgement on effectiveness.

2 'Radical reform 1783–1806 was a middle-class interest.' How far do you agree?

EXAM HINT In the opening, responses might explain what is meant by radical reform. For each of these elements responses could then analyse the extent to which it was a middle-class interest or an interest of another social group, reaching an interim judgement as to whether it was a middle-class interest before using the interim judgements to reach an overall judgement about the issue.

3 How important was Pitt's legislation in the failure of the radical reform programme?

EXAM HINT The opening should identify a range of reasons for the failure of the radical programme. It might raise issues such as Pitt's legislation, weakness of the radicals and events in France, and then offer a view as to which was the most important. In the following paragraph, the response should explain how the legislation did and did not help in the failure of the radical programme, allowing a judgement about its importance to be reached. The following paragraphs should discuss a range of other issues and explain how they did and did not contribute to the failure of the programme, with a judgement reached on each issue. The conclusion should bring together these interim judgements to reach an overall judgement as to the importance of the legislation in the failure.

4 'The Whigs offered little serious opposition to Pitt from 1783 to 1806.' How far do you agree?

EXAM HINT Responses should consider the opposition of the Whigs to Pitt in the period, and for each event or issue discussed analyse whether their opposition was serious, reaching an interim judgement on the issue discussed. The interim judgements should be used to reach an overall judgement as to whether they offered little serious opposition.

Question practice: Pearson Edexcel A level

Essay question

1 Was electoral corruption the main cause of demands for parliamentary reform 1785–1830?

EXAM HINT Examine the significance of electoral corruption and at least two other relevant factors before reaching a judgement on the question.

Interpretation questions

1 Study Sources B and C (page 35). Historians have different views about the reasons for the abolition of the slave trade. Analyse and evaluate the extracts and use your knowledge of the issues to explain your answer to the following question: How far do you agree with the view that the Quaker anti-slavery campaign was dependent on the work of individuals for success?

EXAM HINT Explain the role of Clarkson (Source B) and other prominent individuals such as George Fox and Olaudah Equiano. Source C refers to the role of Nonconformity in towns. Other points might include the role of women in the abolition movement, and the slave ship *Zong*.

2 Study Sources D and E (page 36). Historians have different views about the reasons for the abolition of the slave trade. Analyse and evaluate the extracts and use your knowledge of the issues to explain your answer to the following question: How far do you agree with the view that the abolition of slavery was due to the economic arguments used by abolitionists in 1806?

EXAM HINT Source D stresses the importance of the national interest in wartime, and Source E explains the arguments put forward by Adam Smith. Other points might include Clarkson's campaigning, and the growth of the petitioning movement.

CHAPTER 3

Government and a changing society 1812–32

Following Pitt's death in 1806, the Whig leader, William Grenville, held the office of prime minister for a little over a year. Tory prime ministers dominated the government for the next twenty years. Although Tories won the 1830 general election, following the death of King George IV, the resultant government was divided. This weakness allowed a Whig government under Earl Grey to take power. It was in these circumstances that the conditions needed for the 1832 Representation of the People Act, sometimes referred to as the Great Reform Act, were created. This chapter examines the Tory governments in office and the 1832 Reform Act through the following themes:

◆ The government of Lord Liverpool

◆ Tory governments under Canning, Goderich and Wellington

◆ The re-emergence of demands for popular reform

◆ The passing of the Reform Act

◆ The 'Great Reform Act'?

The key debate on page 64 of this chapter asks the question: What was the nature of Liverpool's government?

KEY DATES

1812		Lord Liverpool appointed as prime minister	**1830**	**Jan.**	First public meeting of the Birmingham Political Union (BPU)
1815		Corn Laws introduced after end of Napoleonic War		**Nov.**	Grey appointed as prime minister
1816		Spa Fields Riots			
1817	**Jan.**	Suspension of *habeas corpus*	**1831**	**March**	Reform bill passed in the Commons but rejected by the Lords
	March	March of the Blanketeers			
		Seditious Meetings Act		**Sept.–Oct.**	Reform bill passed in Commons but rejected by the Lords
	June	Pentridge Uprising			
1819	**Aug.**	Peterloo Massacre		**Nov.**	Rioting, and BPU declared a readiness to fight
	Dec.	Six Acts			
1820		Cato Street Conspiracy	**1832**	**March**	Reform bill passed in the Commons
1822		Corn Laws amended			
1824–5		Combination Acts repealed		**May**	Popular protest, including plans for a run on the banks
1827		Collapse of Liverpool's government			
1828		Corn Laws amended		**June**	Representation of the People Act allowed by the Lords and given royal assent
1829		Catholic Emancipation Act passed, contributing to fall of Wellington's government			

1 The government of Lord Liverpool

■ *Was Liverpool's government of 1812–27 reactionary or liberal?*

When Lord Liverpool took office in 1812 he faced many challenges, including the ongoing war, huge national debt and a Whig opposition, albeit weak and divided.

Liverpool was not the king's first choice for prime minister, yet he was a strong candidate. He had 22 years' experience in parliament. Among other more junior roles, he had held three senior cabinet positions: foreign secretary, home secretary and secretary for war and colonies. He had the favour of both the prince regent and parliament.

The first three years of Liverpool's government were focused on dealing with the war. As secretary for war and colonies, Liverpool had been a significant supporter of the military campaigns in Portugal and Spain. As prime minister, he supported Wellington's campaigns in Europe and the funding for continental coalitions, which ultimately proved decisive in defeating the French forces in 1814 and again in 1815.

In addition, Liverpool was concerned by:

■ Economic depression:

☐ There was a growing national debt (£861 million by 1815 with annual interest payments of £30 million).

☐ Income tax, introduced in 1799, was helping to cover the debt and producing 30 per cent of government income by 1815, but was unpopular.

☐ From 1806, a French blockade restricted British trade. The British economy, unable to trade openly, had become over-specialised in the production of war materials, causing inflation and rising prices.

☐ By 1815, European powers owed £57 million to Britain in war loans.

☐ There was a terrible winter at the end of 1811. By 1812, a bushel (eight gallons; approximately 36 litres) of grain averaged 126 shillings, whereas in 1793 it had been 49 shillings.

☐ Average wages of workers were falling. In Bolton, an extreme case, handloom weavers' weekly wages fell from 25 shillings to 15 shillings.

■ War with the USA 1812–15: This was caused by the British blockade of American ships trading with Europe under the 1807 'Orders in Council'. Peace was agreed in 1814 (fighting continued until 1815).

■ Unreformed parliamentary system: Liverpool was reliant on the fickle support of the prince regent. There was no formal party system yet; many politicians were independent and had to be persuaded to support a bill.

Luddism

Luddism was a working-class protest movement. Since 1811, Luddites had protested over the introduction of powered machinery in mills since they feared the loss of employment for skilled hand weavers. The protests included destroying machinery and writing letters to employers. The name came from the mythical leader of the movement, 'General Ned Ludd'. Yet they were not a unified group, simply a widespread demonstration of discontent. By 1812, when Liverpool was prime minister, Luddite protests had spread from Nottinghamshire into Yorkshire, Lancashire, Leicestershire and Derbyshire.

Measures introduced under Liverpool

By 1815, Liverpool was in a difficult position. Historian Norman Gash (1984) wrote that the impact of the war had been 'to create expectations while removing the means of satisfying them'. The war created more demand for change, while simultaneously limiting Liverpool's ability to act.

An example of this is the **Corn Law** in 1815. Like Pitt, Liverpool supported liberal economic ideals, including free trade, as a means of building economic strength. However, the economic depression had created a concern among the landed elite so that they demanded protectionist economic policies to maintain profits. Liverpool was forced to accept the Corn Laws, which banned the import of foreign grain until British prices were sufficiently high. The purpose was to keep food prices artificially high to prevent competition for landowners from cheaper imported grain. Liverpool had to accept a complete ban on importing grain until a quarter bushel (nine dry litres) had reached 80 shillings.

Similarly, Liverpool's government intended to renew income tax, since it contributed 30 per cent of national income. The bill introducing this was rejected in parliament in 1816. The government was forced to impose indirect taxation on basic goods such as tea, beer, candles, sugar and tobacco. Liverpool's government also passed the Game Laws (1816), making **poaching** an offence punishable by seven years in prison or transportation. This had an impact on rural communities, as hunting was a way of providing extra food for families.

Despite wanting liberal economics, it seemed that the poorest were being made to pay for the wealthiest. Liverpool was tied by facing a demand for reform while being unable to achieve it.

Liverpool's government by 1822

Between 1812 and 1822, Liverpool's government has been accused of reactionary Toryism: taking a right-wing, anti-reformist stance (Toryism) which was aggressively opposed to those demanding reform.

Luddism and other protests

The protests facing Liverpool's governments were larger than in the two previous decades:

ONLINE EXTRAS
Pearson Edexcel **WWW**

Get to grips with Lord Liverpool's policies by completing Worksheet 9 at **www.hoddereducation. co.uk/accesstohistory/extras**

KEY TERMS

Corn Laws Legislation introduced in 1815 which kept food prices high to protect landowners' profits. The Corn Laws were unpopular with working people.

Poaching Hunting animals on land owned by someone else.

ONLINE EXTRAS
OCR **WWW**

Learn how to plan an effective essay by completing Worksheet 7 at **www. hoddereducation.co.uk/ accesstohistory/extras**

- Luddite violence: riots, sabotage of machinery and protests continued through 1811 to 1816. A mass trial was held in York in 1813, with three men executed for murdering a mill owner, and, a week later, fourteen more executed for attacking a mill. Luddite rioting continued into 1816 but fizzled out due to improvements in the economy, government repression and a continuing lack of Luddite organisation.

- Spa Fields Riots, December 1816: a series of three open-air meetings was held at Spa Fields, London. Radical orator **Henry Hunt** criticised high prices and asked the audience to sign a **petition** which demanded universal male suffrage, annual elections and secret ballots. On the second day, a breakaway group robbed a gunsmith and made plans to burgle the Bank of England, before the meeting turned into an unplanned march to the Tower of London. It was broken up by soldiers. Four leaders were tried for treason, although acquitted.

- Attack on the prince regent, 1817: following Spa Fields, stones were thrown through the windows of prince regent's coach as he went to open parliament. Radical reformers were blamed for the violence.

- Reform petitions: petitions were a key method of the radical organisations. In 1817, parliament received almost 700 petitions as part of a national campaign.

- March of the Blanketeers, March 1817: a group of Lancashire weavers, each carrying a blanket, marched to London to present a petition to parliament. The government feared wider protest, so sent the army to break up the march and arrest the leaders.

The government was convinced that revolution was a real possibility. In early 1817, Liverpool's government rushed through a suspension of *habeas corpus* for four months. However, the March of the Blanketeers increased the fear of rebellion, leading to parliament passing legislation known together as the 'Gagging Acts':

- Seditious Meetings Act (1817): this banned meetings of more than 50 people without prior permission from local magistrates, stopped all meetings near Westminster Palace, and imposed the death penalty for mutiny in the armed forces. It was essentially a stronger version of the 1799 Seditious Meeting Act (see page 23).

- Suspension of Habeas Corpus: in place from January 1817 until March 1818, this allowed the government to arrest and detain people without trial.

From 1817, both protests and government reactions had become more extreme.

Pentridge Uprising, June 1817

The government assigned an *agent provocateur* to travel through the country and pretend to be a radical organising a revolution. Around 200–300 men from Pentridge, Derbyshire, marched on Nottingham with the intention of armed rebellion. They had been assured of support from men from other towns such as Birmingham. Instead, they were rounded up by the army; three were hanged and 30 were transported abroad.

Peterloo, August 1819

Henry Hunt called a large meeting at St Peter's Field, Manchester. His theme was parliamentary corruption. Between 50,000 and 200,000 people attended, including women and children. Local magistrates ordered the local yeomanry to arrest Hunt. Whether the outcome had been planned or was the result of panic among inexperienced yeomanry, violence broke out in which eleven protestors were killed and over 400 wounded. The event polarised opinion; supporters mocked the event with the name 'Peterloo' (in reference to the Battle of Waterloo in 1815), whereas opponents portrayed the protestors as a violent threat to peace in Britain.

The government responded to Peterloo by passing the Six Acts in December 1819. These are listed in Table 3.1 (see below).

Table 3.1 The Six Acts

Training Prevention Act	Prevented civilians learning to use weapons
Seizure of Arms Act	Allowed magistrates to seize weapons
Seditious Meetings Act	Renewed the 1817 Act and required magistrates to authorise large meetings
Blasphemous and Seditious Libels Act	Set penalties for libel at seventeen years' transportation
Misdemeanours Act	Speeded up the process of charging people and committing for trial
Newspapers and Stamp Duty Act	Raised the stamp duty to 4*d.* on all printed publications that appeared one or more times a month and cost less than 6*d.*

*The *d.* represents a penny. In the old currency system there were twelve pence to a shilling and twenty shillings to a pound.

Cato Street Conspiracy, February 1820

A small band of extreme radicals, led by Arthur Thistlewood, formulated a plan to murder the entire cabinet, behead them, and place their heads on display on Westminster Bridge. It was ridiculous but also an indication of the strength of radical feeling in some quarters. Unfortunately for the radicals, Thistlewood's second in command, George Edwards, was a spy for the police. The group was arrested; five were transported and five sentenced to death. The sentence was to be publicly hanged, and the dead bodies beheaded and cut into quarters. The government cancelled the quartering, fearing that it would cause outrage among the audience. Yet, the beheadings did not go well. The knife became damaged and a carving knife had to be found in the prison governor's dining room. Then an executioner dropped one of the heads, leading to shouts of 'butterfingers'. As a result, the government stopped publicly beheading executed criminals.

ONLINE EXTRAS **WWW**
Pearson Edexcel

Develop your analysis of Tory policies 1783–1820 by completing Worksheet 10 at **www.hoddereducation. co.uk/accesstohistory/extras**

ONLINE EXTRAS **WWW**
Pearson Edexcel

Test your understanding of the threat posed by radical groups by completing Worksheet 11 at **www. hoddereducation.co.uk/ accesstohistory/extras**

ONLINE EXTRAS
AQA WWW

Develop your analysis of the weaknesses of radical reformers to 1830 by completing Worksheet 7 at **www.hoddereducation. co.uk/accesstohistory/extras**

ONLINE EXTRAS
OCR WWW

Develop your analysis of Tory responses to the radical protest movement by completing Worksheet 8 at **www.hoddereducation. co.uk/accesstohistory/extras**

Spies and *agents provocateurs*

The use of spies and *agents provocateurs* was controversial. On the one hand, it was the only effective way that the government had to find out what was going on in the reform movements. On the other hand, it looked seedy and dishonest. For example, the Cato Conspirators (see page 49) claimed that Edwards had proposed the whole plan, and 'Oliver' had played some role in starting the Pentridge Uprising (see page 48). The morality of punishing radicals when a government employee was involved in inciting events was questioned.

Why had the radical reformers achieved so little under Pitt and Liverpool by 1820?

- Their aims seemed radical and dangerous to the landed elites.

- There was a lack of governmental support for reform.

- There was much state opposition, including legislation and direct action.

- Magistrates, who were from the landed elite, applied laws harshly.

- The movement was fragmented and radicals could be dealt with individually – there was no unified objective or organisation.

Liverpool's government after 1822

In 1941, historian W.R. Brock argued that Liverpool's apparent 'Reactionist Toryism' from 1812 changed to 'Liberal Toryism' after 1822. The following gives some evidence of this view.

A significant reshuffle of Liverpool's cabinet between 1819 and 1822

A cabinet reshuffle was caused by the Queen Caroline Affair (see the box, page 51), Whig general election successes in 1818 and the suicide of Foreign Secretary Castlereagh. Several ministers in new positions were associated with liberal actions between 1822 and 1827, such as Robert Peel, who became home secretary in 1822.

Peel reduced corruption and brutality in the legal system

Examples of Peel's reforms:

- The 1823 Gaols Act gave central government greater control over the prisons system. Local prisons would be inspected by magistrates with reports sent to the Home Office, and prison discipline, medical facilities and education should be standardised.

KEY TERM

Bloody Code A collection of laws for which the punishments were execution.

- Between 1825 and 1827, Peel abolished 180 capital offences in the **Bloody Code**, such as stealing five shillings from a shop. Additionally, 278 Acts were repealed and replaced with seven Acts. By 1830, 75 per cent of criminal offences were covered by laws passed since 1825.

- Peel abolished fees in some courts in 1828, instead paying officials a salary. This gave more access to the court system for the poor.

Economic reforms

Examples of the economic reforms included:

- Tariff duties on manufactured goods were reduced from 50 per cent to 20 per cent, and duties on other goods (like rum, silk, wool, glass and books) were reduced. This meant lower prices for consumers.

- In 1825, window duty was cancelled on small houses, which cut taxes for the poor.

- The Reciprocity of Duties Act 1823 agreed reciprocal, favourable duties with Prussia, Sweden, Denmark and some other European and South American states. It reduced tariffs and therefore costs.

- In 1823, the Navigation Acts, which had prevented non-British ships importing goods to Britain, were relaxed.

- In 1826, in response to riots over the introduction of power looms to mills, **William Huskisson** persuaded several employers to pay a fixed wage to loomworkers.

- In 1828, the fixed Corn Law tariff was replaced with a sliding scale, meaning that as British wheat became more expensive, duty on foreign wheat was reduced or removed. This limited how expensive food prices could become.

Repeal of the Combination Acts 1824

Reformers persuaded the government to repeal the 1799 and 1800 Combination Acts, which had effectively banned workers forming trade unions.

Changing attitude to the involvement of Catholics in politics

From 1822, Liverpool had two pro-Catholic ministers in his cabinet. Between 1821 and 1825, three bills, which would have improved the rights of Catholics, were passed in the Commons. Although they were rejected in the House of Lords, it suggested that a more liberal attitude was emerging.

The collapse of Liverpool's government 1827

Historians accepting the idea of Liberal Toryism see this as the result of division between **Liberal Tories** (Canning, Robinson, Huskisson and so on) and **Ultra Tories** (Wellington, Sidmouth and so on).

Queen Caroline Affair

The prince regent had separated from his wife, Caroline of Brunswick, in 1796. When Prince George succeeded to the throne in 1820, Caroline decided to claim her right as queen. Liverpool's government became dragged into dealing with the scandal, including proposing a bill of divorce, which failed. Although the government did not resign, the failure weakened the government and contributed to Liverpool's cabinet restructure.

KEY FIGURE

William Huskisson (1770–1830)

A Tory politician, and from 1823, president of the Board of Trade. He was influential in implementing free trade policies in the 1820s. He died as the first railway casualty during a demonstration of the Manchester to Liverpool line.

KEY TERMS

Liberal Tories Tory politicians in the 1820s who were more liberal.

Ultra Tories Tory politicians in the 1820s who were more conservative.

The counter-interpretation

Revisionist historians argue that there was no real change from a reactionary to liberal government by 1822:

■ Historians Norman Gash (1984) and John Plowright (1996) have argued that it is misleading to interpret the repression of the pre-1820 period as excessive. For example, *habeas corpus* was suspended in March 1817 for less than a year, and in that time only 44 people were arrested, of whom 37 were detained on suspicion of treason – hardly a police state reign of terror.

■ The lack of repressive action after 1822 against reformists is probably more due to the lack of reformist activity. The economy was improving; events such as Peterloo had discouraged further direct confrontation with the government; and middle-class support for the movement was still lacking.

■ Eric Evans (2001) has argued that Liverpool's government 1812–27 was not a reactionary development, but simply the continuation of Pitt's policies from the pre-war years (1784–93), in which free trade, mild reform and repression were used as necessary.

■ Many of the ministers in the reorganised cabinet had served in Liverpool's cabinet pre-1822. Canning was president of the Board of Control 1816–21, and Robinson had been president of the Board of Trade. The cabinet reshuffle was therefore not as significant as it might appear.

■ The idea of dividing politicians into 'Liberal' or 'Ultra' Tories did not exist at the time. A precise definition is very difficult; Liverpool, Peel and Canning, for example, could fall on either side. Canning's foreign policies were not as liberal as his opponents claimed.

■ Peel's legal reforms were intended to increase efficiency.

   □ Most of the capital punishments that Peel abolished were ones for which no one had been sentenced to death in years, or where pardons had become habitual.

   □ Under Peel, the number of death sentences awarded did not drop excessively (about 13.6 per cent of convictions in 1817–21 were death sentences, compared to 11.5 per cent in 1822–7).

   □ Peel's prison reforms were to standardise, not end, hardship – he favoured corporal punishments in prison like the whip or the treadmill, where prisoners walked for hours on end in a wooden cylinder.

   □ Many of the prison reforms were based on an 1819 parliamentary report completed before Peel was home secretary.

ONLINE EXTRAS OCR **WWW**

Test your understanding of Liverpool's government policies by completing Worksheet 9 at **www.hoddereducation.co.uk/accesstohistory/extras**

ONLINE EXTRAS OCR **WWW**

Develop your analysis of Liverpool's response to challenges by completing Worksheet 10 at **www.hoddereducation.co.uk/accesstohistory/extras**

- There is no evidence to support a newly liberal approach to economics in 1822–3.
  - ☐ The basis for the reforms was laid before Huskisson became president of the Board of Trade in 1823. Huskisson was supported in implementing the change by Robinson, chancellor the exchequer from 1823, who had himself been president of the Board of Trade before 1823.
  - ☐ The prime aim of reducing tariffs was increased profit for traders and landowners, as well as minimising the chance of revolution.
- Although the 1824 repeal of the Combination Acts allowed workers to form unions, these were not legally protected and could be taken to court if they interfered with trade. In response to new strikes, the Amending Act 1825 was passed, which allowed trade unions to be formed but banned any use of force. The prime concern was preventing agitation.
- Liverpool and key members of the cabinet, like Peel, remained completely opposed to any emancipation on the part of Catholic rights. Change for Catholics did not happen until 1829, after Liverpool's resignation.

Overall, it is more accurate to judge that the government was responding to a changing circumstance with a decline in radical protest and an improving economy, rather than changing its ideological viewpoint.

ONLINE EXTRAS **WWW**
AQA

Test your understanding of Pitt the Younger and Lord Liverpool by completing Worksheet 8 at **www. hoddereducation.co.uk/ accesstohistory/extras**

ONLINE EXTRAS **WWW**
Pearson Edexcel

Test your understanding of the impact of Liverpool's policies on the poor by completing Worksheet 12 at **www.hoddereducation. co.uk/accesstohistory/extras**

Figure 3.1 Convictions and use of the death penalty between 1817 and 1840.

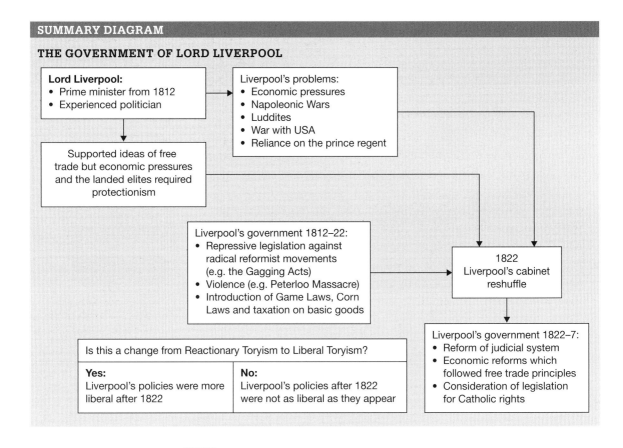

SUMMARY DIAGRAM

THE GOVERNMENT OF LORD LIVERPOOL

Lord Liverpool:
- Prime minister from 1812
- Experienced politician

Liverpool's problems:
- Economic pressures
- Napoleonic Wars
- Luddites
- War with USA
- Reliance on the prince regent

Supported ideas of free trade but economic pressures and the landed elites required protectionism

Liverpool's government 1812–22:
- Repressive legislation against radical reformist movements (e.g. the Gagging Acts)
- Violence (e.g. Peterloo Massacre)
- Introduction of Game Laws, Corn Laws and taxation on basic goods

1822 Liverpool's cabinet reshuffle

Is this a change from Reactionary Toryism to Liberal Toryism?

Yes:	**No:**
Liverpool's policies were more liberal after 1822	Liverpool's policies after 1822 were not as liberal as they appear

Liverpool's government 1822–7:
- Reform of judicial system
- Economic reforms which followed free trade principles
- Consideration of legislation for Catholic rights

2 Tory governments under Canning, Goderich and Wellington

■ *What were the main events of these Tory governments?*

In April 1827, Lord Liverpool resigned following a stroke, triggering a series of short-serving prime ministers.

Canning and Goderich

George Canning succeeded Liverpool, largely due to his assurances to King George IV that he would avoid the issue of Catholic emancipation. Canning's appointment split both Tories and Whigs as he pulled members from each into a coalition, while key senior Tories like Peel and Wellington and Whigs like **Charles Grey** refused to work with him. However, Canning died unexpectedly in August 1827, and Viscount Goderich (the former chancellor of the exchequer) succeeded him. He proved unable to hold a government together and resigned in January 1828.

Arthur Wellesley, Duke of Wellington

1769	Born in Ireland as Arthur Wesley, the third son of an aristocratic family
1787	Joined the British army
1796	Successfully commanded British troops in India
1805	Returned to UK, and was knighted for his military successes
1806	Began a political career as the member of parliament (MP) for Rye
1808	Began campaigning against France in Portugal
1814	Given the title Duke of Wellington in honour of his successes
1815	Defeated Napoleon at the Battle of Waterloo
1819	Began to serve in Lord Liverpool's government
1828	Appointed as prime minister by King George IV
1834	Short second term as prime minister
1846	Retired from politics when Peel resigned
1852	Died at Walmer Castle and given a state funeral in London

Background

Wellesley's father died when he was young and his mother neglected him. Despite an interest in music and a brief period at Eton College, he was academically weak and resorted to a career in the army.

Military career

He served in the failed Flanders campaign in 1794, before transferring to India, where his brother was governor general, and became a noted general. While there, the family changed its name from Wesley to Wellesley. He was knighted in 1805 for his achievements. He stood as MP for Rye in 1807, and became chief secretary for Ireland. However, he did little in these roles as he soon became involved in a British campaign in Denmark, followed by the Peninsular Campaigns in Portugal. His successes were rewarded with the title Duke of Wellington.

Political career

Wellington served in Liverpool's government before being appointed prime minister in 1828. This was short lived; his decision to pass the Catholic Emancipation Act, compounded by his opposition to parliamentary reform, split his support and contributed to his defeat in 1830 by Earl Grey. Other than a short spell as prime minister in 1834, most of the rest of his career was spent as a cabinet minister in Peel's government, until his resignation in 1846 following the repeal of the Corn Laws.

Wellington

George IV appointed the Tory Duke of Wellington as prime minister. In a sense, this was logical. Wellington was opposed to reform, including constitutional change and the extension of Catholic rights, which reassured the king. He was also indifferent to party politics, and in a rather high-minded, even arrogant, manner he thought that he could work above divisions and squabbling.

Metropolitan Police

One key reform of Wellington's government was the creation of the Metropolitan Police Force for London by the home secretary, Robert Peel, in 1829. This was a new approach to dealing with popular unrest. The police force, which numbered almost 1000 and grew to 3000 within a year, was a civilian solution to crime and protest in London, rather than using the army as had occurred with earlier popular protests. It became the model for other police forces, although the adoption of police forces elsewhere was slow. In 1835, the

Municipal Corporations Act empowered boroughs to form police forces, with counties receiving permission in 1839. However, it was not until 1856, when the County and Borough Police Act was passed, that all boroughs and counties were required to have a police force.

Wellington's decisions

Wellington was neither liberal enough to be a force for reform, nor Tory enough for the king's taste. Three decisions made by Wellington led to a split that would prove catastrophic for the Tories.

In March 1828, Wellington's government repealed the Test and Corporation Acts, which required government officials to take communion in a Church of England service. This effectively allowed Catholics and Nonconformists to take political office. In practical terms, it was insignificant since the Act had not been enforced in many years, yet in context it was seen by many, especially Ultra Tories, as a serious, fundamental attack on the establishment.

Additionally, following the 1826 election, Huskisson and his supporters pressured Wellington to remove the four parliamentary seats in the rotten boroughs of Penryn and East Retford and give them to Manchester and Birmingham. The Commons rejected the proposal for Penryn, and while East Retford lost its seats, they were redistributed to nearby Bassetlaw, which strengthened the political control of the Tory Duke of Newcastle. Huskisson and his supporters promptly abandoned Wellington's government, leaving it much weakened, since Huskisson's liberals included some of the best debaters in the Commons such as **Lord Palmerston**.

Finally, there was the Catholic Emancipation Act. The president of the Board of Trade, Charles Grant, was replaced by William Vesey Fitzgerald, who was the member of parliament (MP) for County Clare, Ireland. Under an archaic law, an MP offered ministerial office had to resign his seat and stand to be elected again. Fitzgerald stood against, and was defeated by, the Irish nationalist **Daniel O'Connell**, leader of the Catholic Association. Although O'Donnell, as a Catholic, could not sit as an MP, he was not barred from being elected. Wellington was left in an impossible position; to stand by the ban on Catholics serving as MPs he would trigger a wave of nationalist anger in Ireland, possibly even civil war. Yet if he emancipated Catholics, he would alienate his key support of Ultra Tories. In 1829, Wellington passed the Catholic Emancipation Act, legally allowing Catholics to serve as MPs. It was passed with Whig support, despite Tory opposition, and Wellington had to threaten to resign if the king refused to sign the bill. This completely alienated Ultra Tories and destroyed Wellington's reputation.

With the resulting division of the Tory party, Wellington had set the scene for constitutional reform on a scale that no one could have foreseen.

KEY FIGURES

Lord Palmerston (1784–1865)

A Tory politician who was one of the more Liberal Tories in Liverpool's government. With the fall of Liverpool's government, he drifted to the Whigs. He became foreign secretary in 1830 after Canning, a post he held for fifteen of the next 21 years. He became a Liberal politician, a party which better suited his political views. He served as prime minister 1855–8 and 1859–65.

Daniel O'Connell (1775–1847)

A Catholic, Irish lawyer who campaigned for Catholic emancipation from 1811. He refused to support revolutionary tactics, but instead formed a political group, the Catholic Association, to do this and seek political independence for Ireland. By the 1820s, it was the most significant Irish nationalist movement. He also used constitutional tactics to achieve Catholic emancipation in 1828.

ONLINE EXTRAS **WWW**
OCR

Get to grips with the reasons for the divisions within the Tory Party by completing Worksheet 11 at www.hoddereducation.co.uk/accesstohistory/extras

SUMMARY DIAGRAM

TORY GOVERNMENTS UNDER CANNING, GODERICH AND WELLINGTON

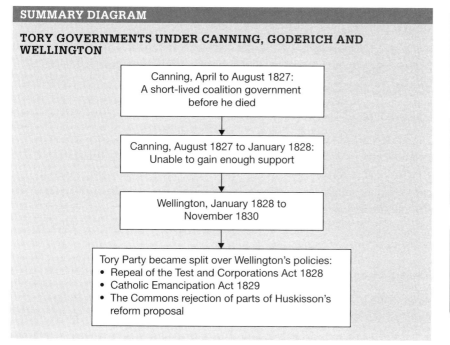

Canning, April to August 1827: A short-lived coalition government before he died

↓

Canning, August 1827 to January 1828: Unable to gain enough support

↓

Wellington, January 1828 to November 1830

↓

Tory Party became split over Wellington's policies:
• Repeal of the Test and Corporations Act 1828
• Catholic Emancipation Act 1829
• The Commons rejection of parts of Huskisson's reform proposal

3 The re-emergence of demands for popular reform

■ *Why did demands for reform re-emerge and what did Grey do about them?*

As was covered in Chapter 2, demand for parliamentary reform pre-dated the French Revolution, was subsequently shaped by the Revolutionary Wars, and, in the post-war period from 1815 to 1820, took on a new, more direct form. By 1820, the demand had been quietened. Although this was in part down to an upturn in the economy which alleviated some of the social discontent, it was also in a sense swept under the carpet by repressive government actions. So why did the demand re-emerge?

The Whigs

Led by Earl Grey, the Whigs supported the idea of parliamentary reform. They were back in power in 1830 for the first time since 1784. Grey introduced a reform bill proposing a reform to the franchise.

Continuing corruption

Somewhat ironically, Grey's government, while championing reform, demonstrated the character of aristocratic government. Grey had come to power not by popular election, but by political manoeuvrings in Westminster following Wellington's resignation. In 1831, Grey was appointed to the Order of the Garter, the most aristocratic order of chivalry in Britain. This inspired radical groups, long opposed to government corruption through nepotism, to react in the media through articles and cartoons.

O'Connell

The success of O'Connell's campaign (see page 56) inspired the formation of reformist groups such as the **Birmingham Political Union** (BPU) (see page 59) and National Union of the Working Classes (NUWC). Despite their general opposition to parliamentary reform, many Tories were concerned about the Catholic Emancipation Act. They hoped that a parliamentary reform might balance Irish Catholic voting by extending the franchise to non-Catholics in northern cities such as Manchester and Leeds.

The Swing Riots

From 1830 to 1832, a series of popular rural uprisings, known as the Swing Riots (as they were supposedly led by the mythical Captain Swing), broke out across the south and east of England. The primary aim was to remove threshing machines, which were reducing employment for labourers. Tactics included threatening letters, appeals to local leaders and destroying machinery. The Swing Riots generated public sympathy for reform. Despite the rioters being noted for their orderliness and not killing anyone, the government responded by sentencing 252 to death, 600 to imprisonment and 500 to transportation.

Grey's reform bill

Grey's bill was introduced to the Commons in March 1831. It proposed that some parliamentary seats should be taken from rotten boroughs and distributed to the unrepresented industrial districts. The bill also proposed introducing a uniform voting franchise to equalise national voting, whereby all men who owned property worth £10 a year would qualify.

It would be easy to interpret this as simply a liberal, reformist plan, but Grey's plan was inherently conservative. He did not envisage grand sweeping changes, and certainly not the extension of the franchise that would occur in subsequent decades. He was a landowner, interested in stabilising the existing system rather than redesigning it. The £10 voting qualification would open the door to middle-class voters but exclude the working classes, even in the industrial cities which would gain seats.

The first attempt passed in the Commons by one vote but was rejected in the Lords, which shows that the desire for reform was strong but not overwhelming within parliament. Grey persuaded the king to call a new election to gain support from the population; the gamble paid off and the Whig minority government became a Whig **majority government** by 130 seats. With this majority, Grey reintroduced the reform bill to the House of Commons.

KEY TERMS

Birmingham Political Union An influential political organisation led by Thomas Attwood which campaigned for parliamentary reform.

Majority government When a government has enough votes in the Commons to pass laws that they propose.

ONLINE EXTRAS
Pearson Edexcel **WWW**

Develop your analysis of factors leading to the 1832 Reform Act by completing Worksheet 14 at **www. hoddereducation.co.uk/ accesstohistory/extras**

> **SOURCE A**
>
> Grey speaking to the House of Lords, November 1832.
>
> *There is no one more decided against annual parliaments, universal suffrage, and vote by ballot, that I am. My object is not to favour, but to put an end to such hopes.*

SOURCE QUESTION

Study Source A. Why would Grey be keen to reassure parliament that he was opposed to further constitutional reform?

Extent of popular discontent

Although the reform bill was a parliamentary measure, the main support and pressure were extra-parliamentary, headed by industrialist **Thomas Attwood**. Attwood was inspired by O'Connell. He formed the BPU to unify wealthy leadership with popular working-class support, as the Catholic Association had done.

The majority of the membership, working-class men, supported universal suffrage for all men. In contrast, Attwood demanded representation only for middle-class industrialists such as himself. He argued that industrialists and their workers shared the same goal, since industrial success or failure would affect both. Despite his self-serving and conservative approach, Attwood and the BPU gained immense support. When he spoke at outdoor meetings, he drew crowds of 50,000–100,000.

Political unions and leagues were not new (see pages 20–1). What was different with unions from 1830 was how they allied popular support with wealthy political leadership. Previous efforts had never successfully married the two together. As historian Clive Behagg (2000) puts it, 'the lessons of 1815 -1820 had been learned, and the advantages of lining up behind men of wealth were recognized within the working community'. The strength of support for these unions was evidenced in 1832, when it appeared that the government would fail to pass the bill. Attwood and other leaders were able to whip popular support into a threat of civil disobedience and potential armed resistance.

It is hard to quantify how wide support was for reform and what people really thought. The conviction of members is evident from the fact that they were willing to threaten strong action in 1832. Yet, why would the working classes support Attwood's model, which offered only limited middle-class suffrage, when so many had been involved in earlier demands for universal suffrage? It seems likely that the majority saw this simply as a first step towards wider suffrage, rather than the single, final amendment that Grey was proposing.

Support for Attwood's model was not universal. Working-class radicals had not forgotten the demands of previous decades. The NUWC, for example, was founded in 1831. By means of an illegal political newspaper, the *Poor Man's Guardian*, and agitation by branches around the country, they campaigned for universal suffrage and proclaimed their distrust of the reform bill and the middle-class industrialists who were advocating it.

KEY FIGURE

Thomas Attwood (1783–1856)

A British banker, economist and political campaigner. He formed the influential Birmingham Political Union (BPU) to campaign for constitutional reform. He became a key voice in the campaign leading to the 1832 Great Reform Act.

SUMMARY DIAGRAM

THE RE-EMERGENCE OF DEMANDS FOR POPULAR REFORM

Demand for reform reappeared because:
- Outdated electoral system
- Grey's Whigs supported reform
- Grey's aristocratic government demonstrated corrupt behaviour
- O'Connell's Irish emancipation campaign inspired new tactics
- Some Tories saw reform as a defence against Catholic involvement in parliament
- Swing Riots raised awareness of discontent

Grey introduced a reform bill in 1831:
- Proposal appeared radical but was inherently conservative
- Proposed a uniform national voting qualification of owning property worth £10

- Political unions developed across the country, e.g. BPU
- Joined working-class support with middle-class leaders

---

4 The passing of the Reform Act

◼ *What did the 1832 Reform Act achieve?*

In 1832, an unprecedented constitutional reform was passed as legislation in the form of a Reform Act. This addressed key issues within the British political system. However, it was limited in scale and impact as it did not completely change the *status quo*.

The passing of the bill

The Commons passed Grey's reform bill in September 1831, although Robert Peel, Tory leader in the Commons, did not believe in wholesale reform – he denied that the existing system was exclusive, citing the example of his own father, an industrialist who entered parliament by purchasing a seat. However, he did accept that some corruption needed removing to restore public confidence.

Yet neither the aristocratic House of Lords nor King William IV was willing to support the bill. The Lords rejected the bill in October 1831. (Until the situation changed in 1911, the House of Lords had the power to reject Commons' bills completely.) This was out of a desire to protect the rights and influence of the aristocracy, whose power was held in rural areas, and a lack of awareness of the changing conditions in the industrial centres of the north of England.

The Reform Act

The full name of this Act is the 1832 Representation of the People Act; however, it is more commonly referred to as the 1832 Reform Act, or the Great Reform Act.

ONLINE EXTRAS
Pearson Edexcel **WWW**

Get to grips with the demand for reform 1830–2 by completing Worksheet 15 at www.hoddereducation. co.uk/accesstohistory/extras

---

The reaction to this rejection was extensive rioting in Nottingham, Derby and Bristol. The government had to use troops to suppress the disorder. The BPU declared that it was ready to start armed resistance in November. Although this was made illegal by a royal proclamation, and the BPU then abandoned the plan, their declaration demonstrated the scale of popular unrest.

Third time lucky?

Grey reintroduced the bill to the Commons for a third time with a more restricted franchise proposal. The Commons passed the bill again. Fearing another rejection, Grey demanded that the king appoint enough new Whig peers to the House of Lords to outvote their Tory opponents. The king refused, and Grey resigned in protest. The expectation was that Wellington was the only option to form a government and that he would crush the reform bill.

Leaders of the BPU and other political unions met in London to co-ordinate a response. They considered a **run on the banks**. They chanted the slogan 'To Defeat the Duke, Go for gold!' They also proposed non-payment of taxes, and the possibility of armed resistance. Attwood (see page 59) was at the forefront of this plan, and presented himself as the heroic figure in public speeches, ready to fight the government to the death for reform.

> **SOURCE B**
>
> **A speech by Attwood to an audience of about 200,000 at a BPU rally in Birmingham c.1831**
>
> *I would rather die than see the great Bill of reform rejected or mutilated … I see that you are all of one mind on the subject. Answer me then, had you not all rather die than live the slaves of the boroughmongers [those who buy or sell parliamentary seats]?*

The Tories were trapped. Wellington recognised that he could not form an effective government. He realised that he could not avoid passing some form of reform bill, but Peel and many Tories remained completely opposed. Any reform would split a Tory government more than the Catholic Emancipation Act had.

In desperation, the king agreed to the Whig demand for new Whig peers. Faced with the threat of losing control of the Lords, the Tories gave in. Over 100 Tory peers abstained from voting, which allowed the bill to pass with a majority of 84, but avoided the need for the king to appoint new Whig peers.

Therefore, the Reform Act was passed in 1932 due to a combination of:

- the Whig reform proposal
- popular pressure from organised radical groups
- fear of violence and riots by landowners
- Grey's tactics of resigning and demanding Whig peers
- the wider middle-class support for parliamentary reform.

ONLINE EXTRAS WWW
AQA

Develop your analysis of the reasons for the passing of the 1832 Reform Act by completing Worksheet 9 at **www.hoddereducation. co.uk/accesstohistory/extras**

KEY TERM

Run on the banks This was where protestors who had paper money would go to the London banks and demand the cash equivalent in gold, causing a cash crisis.

SOURCE QUESTION

Attwood was himself relatively moderate. He did not support more radical ideas, for example universal suffrage. Why would he present himself in such radical terms in the speech in Source B?

ONLINE EXTRAS WWW
OCR

Learn how to write effective introductions and conclusions by completing Worksheet 14 at **www.hoddereducation. co.uk/accesstohistory/extras**

ONLINE EXTRAS WWW
OCR

Learn how to develop an argument by completing Worksheet 15 at **www. hoddereducation.co.uk/ accesstohistory/extras**

ONLINE EXTRAS WWW
Pearson Edexcel

Test your understanding of the 1832 Reform Act by completing Worksheet 16 at **www.hoddereducation. co.uk/accesstohistory/extras**

ONLINE EXTRAS OCR **www**

Get to grips with support and opposition for reform in 1830–32 by completing Worksheet 16 at **www.hoddereducation.co.uk/accesstohistory/extras**

ONLINE EXTRAS OCR **www**

Get to grips with the reasons for the passing of the 1832 Reform Act by completing Worksheet 17 at **www.hoddereducation.co.uk/accesstohistory/extras**

ONLINE EXTRAS OCR **www**

Develop your analysis of the 1832 Reform Act by completing Worksheet 18 at **www.hoddereducation.co.uk/accesstohistory/extras**

The terms of the 1832 Reform Act

The terms included:

- Uniform voting rules were introduced in boroughs. Any man with property worth £10 or more per year could vote. In the counties, the existing 40-shilling qualification was retained.
- Fifty-six borough constituencies which were overrepresented lost MPs, including Old Sarum, with only seven voters, as well as other small constituencies such as Appleby and Whitchurch.
- Thirty overrepresented boroughs (for example, St Ives and Grimsby) lost one of their two MPs.
- Twenty-two constituencies were created, each with two MPs, in urban areas including Manchester, Stockport and Leeds, and twenty constituencies with one MP, including Rochdale, Kendal and Wakefield. Five seats were added for Ireland, eight for Scotland and four for Wales.

Divine retribution?

When the Houses of Parliament burned down in 1834, William IV's wife, Queen Adelaide, thought it was a punishment from God for passing the 1832 Reform Act.

SUMMARY DIAGRAM

THE PASSING OF THE REFORM ACT

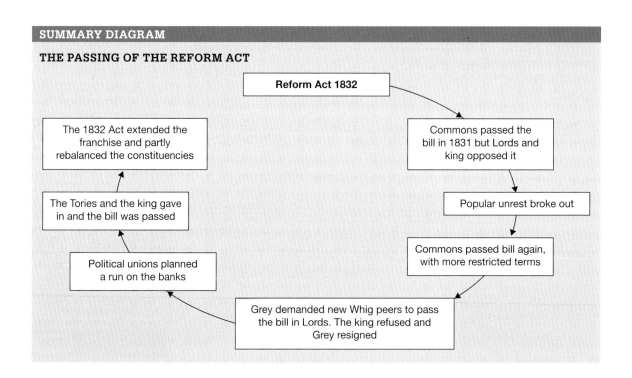

62

5 The 'Great Reform Act'?

■ *Is it accurate to call the 1832 Act the 'Great Reform Act'?*

The 1832 Reform Act is often referred to as the 'Great Reform Act' in comparison to the later Reform Acts of 1867 and 1884–5. Is it accurate to describe it as 'great'? Table 3.2 (see below) summarises the reasons for and against it being called 'great'.

Table 3.2 Was the 1832 Reform Act indeed 'great'?

Yes	No
• It represented a breakthrough in British political history as the first extension of voting rights	• Change to the electorate was limited; 90 per cent of adult males and all women could still not vote
• In 1831, only 11 per cent of adult males could vote; this rose to 18 per cent	• The make-up of parliament did not change; MPs continued to be wealthy men primarily from landed backgrounds. Despite becoming an MP, Attwood complained that there was no substantial improvement for men of industry. With no salaries for MPs, few middle-class men could consider standing as MPs
• New urban areas, critical to the economy, had political representation	
• Popular protest had impacted on government policy by forcing the king and Lords to accept reform	• Although in 1832 74 per cent of constituencies were contested, between 1832 and 1867 on average only 60 per cent of constituencies were contested
• The 1832 Act set a precedent for future reforms	• The limited extension to the franchise damaged the Whig reputation with working-class radicals
• Middle-class reformers had achieved their goal of political representation	• The enfranchisement of the middle-classes divided the alliance with working-class radicals which had been a strength of associations like the BPU
	• There was no change to how elections were carried out, so landowners could still pressure their tenants
	• The next reform bill would not be passed until 1867

Overall, the 1832 Reform Act may have been 'great' in terms of the precedent it set for future reform, but it was far more limited than the later reform acts considered in Chapters 6 and 7.

ONLINE EXTRAS
AQA `WWW`

Learn how to think analytically by completing Worksheet 10 at **www. hoddereducation.co.uk/ accesstohistory/extras**

6 Key debate

■ *What was the nature of Liverpool's government?*

Liverpool's government was reactionary until 1822, and liberal after

This view was first proposed by Brock in 1941 and developed by subsequent historians. It focuses on Liverpool's reconstruction of his cabinet in the years 1820–2, and compares policies before and after. Common comparisons focus on the significant events of anti-radical repression before 1820 and the imposition of the Corn Laws, whereas, in the 1820s, Liverpool's government addressed social issues (such as Peel's reforms to the judicial system), introduced new free trade measures and added a sliding scale to the Corn Laws.

> **INTERPRETATION QUESTION**
>
> After reading Extracts 1–4, do you think it is possible to label Liverpool's government as either reactionary or liberal? Is there enough evidence to support a change of policy in 1822?

EXTRACT 1

Adapted from W.R. Brock, *Lord Liverpool and Liberal Toryism 1820–27*, Cambridge University Press, 1941, pp. 170 and 191–2.

This reconstruction of the cabinet had been the work of Liverpool and no other. Every move might raise an alarm at the direction which the changes were taking. With the changes of 1821–23, Liverpool was able to gather around him a group of like-minded men ready to take whatever opportunities were offered for economic reform. The next two years were of the greatest importance in the history of economic policy. They saw the applications of free trade, and the launching of [liberal policies]. Liverpool did not initiate any of these policies; that was indeed the function of the departmental ministers concerned; but he did have to advise, to assent, and to co-ordinate.

There was no change to Liverpool's policies from reactionary to liberal in 1822

A generally accepted counter-argument is that there was no change in 1822. The main evidence is:

■ The policies after 1822 were not inherently liberal but rather were conservative in nature.

■ The idea of the cabinet shuffle is misleading; the change of offices hides the fact that most were active in the government before and after 1822.

EXTRACT 2

Adapted from Eric Evans, *The Forging of the Modern State, Early Industrial Britain 1783–1870*, Pearson, 2001, pp. 238–9.

Lord Liverpool's long administration has traditionally been divided into two unequal periods: a long 'reactionary' phase, 1812–22, and a shorter 'liberal' phase, 1822–27, associated with the policies and reforms of Liverpool's 'second-wave' ministers. In fact the division is misleading. Not only were the second-wave ministers serving lengthy and generally dutiful apprenticeships before 1822 but many of the reforms traditionally associated with them had been presaged by their supposedly reactionary predecessors. If turning points are sought, 1819 is a better candidate than 1822, but Liverpool's government never experienced anything so cathartic as an ideological conversion. The Prime Minister had always favoured free trade and stated his belief as early as 1812. However Liverpool and his ministers were no more in favour of a reform of the franchise in 1827 than they had been in 1819.

ONLINE EXTRAS AQA **WWW**

Practise your extract analysis skills by completing Worksheet 11 at **www. hoddereducation.co.uk/ accesstohistory/extras**

It is not accurate to see Liverpool pre–1820 as reactionary

Another interpretation is that pre-1820 policies were dependent on circumstances, not a reactionary outlook. For example, Liverpool was constrained by the post-war economic pressures, and faced large radical events like the March of the Blanketeers.

EXTRACT 3

Adapted from Derek Murphy *et al.*, *Britain 1815–1918*, Collins Educational, 1998, p. 45.

The period up to 1821 was not as reactionary and repressive as historians would have us believe. The government's response to a series of unprecedented circumstances between 1815 and 1821 represented a common-sense reaction on the part of a government that was at least trying to survive the difficulties of post-Napoleonic War Britain. The abolition of Income Tax in 1816 was opposed by Lord Liverpool but he was forced to accept it. There are other examples of so-called enlightened laws passed during the reactionary period. In addition, a number of important committees were set up to investigate known problems. Why didn't these policies come in sooner and assume the more official tone that they seemed to after 1821? The answer lies probably in the circumstances of the time that were not suitable for reform.

ONLINE EXTRAS AQA **WWW**

Practise your extract analysis skills by completing Worksheet 12 at **www. hoddereducation.co.uk/ accesstohistory/extras**

It has been suggested, for example, by Eric Evans (1989), that Pitt was simply continuing the policies of Pitt, in using economic reform and repressive policies as needed to deal with whatever political situation arose.

CHAPTER SUMMARY

From 1812 until 1822, Liverpool's government was focused on addressing economic pressures. His alternative solutions, such as indirect taxation on basic goods, led to an increase in popular protest and, consequently, forced him to take repressive action against radical groups. This has led to the first half of his time in office being interpreted as a reactionary period. From 1822, with the pressures of war fading, Liverpool enacted significant reforms to the legal system and the economy. In comparison to pre-1822, this has been interpreted as a liberal phase, although it is questionable how truly liberal these actions were. Liverpool's successful government contrasts with the short-lived ministries of Canning and Goderich, and Wellington, whose efforts to resolve issues over Catholic rights led to the split of the Tory Party.

Pressure for constitutional change was not new, but by 1830 the conditions were ripe for reform. There was a popular protest movement, unified with middle-class leadership such as Thomas Attwood, a Whig government with a prime minister (Grey) open to reform, and a public attitude which was more sympathetic than in the previous 30 years.

Even so, the 1832 Reform Act was only passed because of the fear of popular protest which groups like the BPU could command, the economic potential of a run on the banks, and the bold tactics of Grey. Ultimately, Tory peers and the king passed the bill mainly to avoid the loss of Tory dominance in the House of Lords through the creation of new Whig peers.

The 1832 Reform Act was a turning point in British politics. Although limited in terms of direct change, it established a precedent that the voting system and traditional constituencies could be challenged and changed. Equally importantly, it demonstrated the power of popular protest on government policy.

Refresher questions

Use these questions to remind yourself of the key material covered in this chapter.

1 What problems did Lord Liverpool face in 1812?

2 What was the Corn Law of 1815, and why did it have a significant economic impact?

3 Who were the Luddites?

4 How did the Gagging Acts (1817) and the Six Acts (1819) help the Tory government to restrict radical protest?

5 What happened at Peterloo?

6 Give two examples of Tory economic policies in the 1820s.

7 What changed with the 1824 and 1825 repeal of the Combination Acts, and what did not change?

8 Define 'Liberal' and 'Ultra' Tories.

9 What three decisions under Wellington's government split the Tory Party?

10 How was the Catholic Emancipation Act a turning point?

11 What events led up to the passing of the 1832 Reform Act?

12 What were the terms of the 1832 Reform Act?

Question practice: AQA

Essay questions

1 'The British government addressed the threat of radicalism with repressive legislation in the years 1812–32.' Explain why you agree or disagree with this view. [AS level]

EXAM HINT Analyse the evidence for and against the quotation, and then reach a judgement based on your own contextual knowledge.

2 'The main priority of Tory politicians in the years 1812–32 was to address economic concerns.' Assess the validity of this view. [A level]

EXAM HINT Analyse the importance of 'economic concerns' alongside other priorities in these decades. Reach a well-argued judgement on what you consider to be the main priority.

3 To what extent did the economic policies of Tory prime ministers from 1793 to 1830 remain fundamentally the same? [A level]

EXAM HINT You need to ensure that you cover the whole period and avoid a simple chronological narrative account. Think of aspects or themes across the period.

4 'The 1832 Reform Act fulfilled the expectations of extra-parliamentary protesters since 1812.' Explain why you agree or disagree with this view. [AS level]

EXAM HINT This is not straightforward because first you have to establish what the expectations were and then assess whether or not they were fulfilled by the Reform Act of 1832.

5 To what extent was the 1832 Reform Act passed because of the changing attitudes of politicians during the early nineteenth century? [A level]

EXAM HINT You need to assess the relative importance of changing attitudes by politicians against other factors. Reach a well-argued conclusion.

Interpretation questions

1 With reference to Extracts 1 (page 64) and 2 (page 65), and your understanding of the historical context, which of these two extracts provides the more convincing interpretation of Liverpool's government? [AS level]

EXAM HINT Analyse the content of each extract in relation to your contextual knowledge, and then argue in detail about which is more convincing. Ignore the provenance of each extract.

2 Using your understanding of the historical context, assess how convincing the arguments in Extracts 1 (page 64), 2 (page 65) and 3 (page 65) are in relation to Liverpool's government. [A level]

EXAM HINT Analyse the content of each extract in relation to your own knowledge to argue how convincing each one is. Try to find the main argument of each to aid your analysis.

3 With reference to Extracts 2 and 3 (page 65), and your understanding of the historical context, which of these two extracts provides the more convincing interpretation of the impact of the 1832 Reform Act? [AS level]

EXAM HINT Analyse the content of Extracts 2 and 3 in relation to your contextual knowledge to assess how convincing you find them. Reach a well-argued judgement as to which impresses you more.

4 Using your understanding of the historical context, assess how convincing the arguments in Extracts A, B and C below are in relation to the 1832 Reform Act. [A level]

EXAM HINT Analyse the content of each in turn in relation to your contextual knowledge, Try to identify the key argument and then any subsidiary ones. Reach a judgement on how convincing each one is in turn, as there is no requirement for an overall conclusion on the three.

EXTRACT A

From J.R.M. Butler, *The Passing of the Great Reform Bill*, Longmans, 1914, p. 426.

But it was the Reform Act of 1832 which showed that the fortress could be stormed and which marked out the line of assault. Though it in fact only enfranchised part of a single class, it established a precedent of permanent force for enfranchising all classes when they should reach the stage of political consciousness and power. It determined that those who have power outside Parliament must have power inside it, and sanctioned a readjustment of the Constitution for this purpose, even at the price of ancient forms and individual interests.

EXTRACT B

Adapted from Michael Brock, *The Great Reform Act*, HarperCollins, 1973, pp. 320–1.

After 1832, the middle classes not only remained as deferential as ever and as reluctant to engage in agitation. They also retained all their determination not to allow the workers a greater influence in politics. Although the Reform Act was regarded as a radical triumph, it was followed by a period of Conservative ascendency. This is no coincidence. Once the radicals seemed near power their partners became frightened. It was some years, however, before working-class people realised how little they could expect from the reformed House. By the 1850s, it was clear that the Act had not reduced electoral corruption.

EXTRACT C

Adapted from Robert Pearce and Roger Stearn, *Government and Reform: Britain 1815–1918*, Hodder Education, 1994, p. 50.

The legislation [in 1832] ended the crisis, re-stabilised politics and detached the middle classes from their political alliance with the working classes. Specifically, it brought about a redistribution of parliamentary seats and extended the franchise to include most middle-class males in the towns. The Reform Act ended the worst abuses of the old system; and yet, to modern eyes, it looks very much like a half-way house. The Act may have fulfilled its framers' intentions, but it disappointed many of its more radical supporters. A perfectly valid case can be made out for the Reform Act as a 'Great' measure, preventing revolution and reinvigorating the political system.

ONLINE EXTRAS AQA WWW
Practise your extract analysis skills by completing Worksheet 13 at **www. hoddereducation.co.uk/ accesstohistory/extras**

ONLINE EXTRAS AQA WWW
Practise your extract analysis skills by completing Worksheet 14 at **www. hoddereducation.co.uk/ accesstohistory/extras**

ONLINE EXTRAS AQA WWW
Practise your extract analysis skills by completing Worksheet 15 at **www. hoddereducation.co.uk/ accesstohistory/extras**

Question practice: OCR A level

Essay questions

1 'The government's willingness to use force was the main reason that radical protestors failed to achieve reforms by 1820.' How far do you agree?

EXAM HINT There should be a good paragraph analysing the use of force and a judgement reached on the importance of this factor. Responses should then consider other issues, such as divisions within the radical movement or economic issues, and analyse their importance and evaluate how important a role each played in the failure. These interim judgements would then form the basis of an overall judgement about the importance of the use of force.

2 How accurate is it to call Lord Liverpool's government 1812–27 'liberal'?

EXAM HINT The opening paragraph could explain what is meant by liberal and outline the issues to be discussed, such as economically or politically liberal. Responses should then analyse each of these areas, such as economic, judicial and political reforms, and reach a judgement as to how liberal the government was in the area under discussion before using the interim judgements to reach an overall judgement.

3 To what extent did the economy change between 1812 and 1828?

EXAM HINT The opening should identify the issues to be discussed, such as agriculture, industry and employment, and offer a view as to how far the economy did change. Paragraphs on each of the issues raised in the introduction could then consider the extent of the change in that area and reach a judgement before using the interim judgements on each issue to reach an overall judgement on the extent of change.

4 'The most significant reforms under Liverpool's government were to the judicial system'. How far do you agree?

EXAM HINT The opening could identify the scope of the reforms Liverpool's government brought in, including judicial, economic, social and political, as well as offering a view as to whether the judicial reforms were the most significant. Paragraphs should then be written on each area outline in the opening and a judgement reached about the significance of the reforms before going on to reach an overall judgement as to whether the judicial reforms were the most significant.

5 How far had Whig and Tory attitudes to constitutional reform changed between 1783 and 1832?

EXAM HINT The opening could identify some of the issues of constitutional reform and then offer a view as to how far Whig and Tory attitudes had changed. Each of the issues raised in the opening would then form the basis of paragraphs in which the extent to which Whig and Tory attitudes to the issue changed. Judgements should be reached on each issue, which would then form the basis of an overall judgement as to how far they had changed.

6 How significant were Whig actions in the passing of the 1832 Reform Act?

EXAM HINT The opening should outline the reasons for the passing of the 1832 Act and offer a view about the importance of Whig actions in its passing. The first paragraph should analyse the role of Whig actions and reach a conclusion as to their importance. Following paragraphs should analyse each of the other reasons and reach a judgement as to how important that reason was. The interim judgements should be used to form the basis of an overall judgement about the importance of Whig actions.

7 'The 1832 Reform Act failed to fix the problems in the political system.' How far do you agree?

EXAM HINT The opening paragraph should identify the problems in the political system, such as under-representation of some areas, rotten boroughs and corruption, and offer a view as to whether the Act did fail. Paragraphs should examine each of the issues and reach a judgement as to whether the problem was 'fixed', and these interim judgements should form the basis of an overall judgement as to whether the 1832 Act fixed the problems.

Question practice: Pearson Edexcel AS level

Essay questions

1 How far did parliamentary reform groups pose a challenge to the government in the years 1793–1820?

EXAM HINT Consider the impact of the war on domestic politics and the challenges to the government in the years 1815–20. Note the strength of the different reform groups.

2 To what extent was the demand for reform in the years 1793–1820 the result of economic distress?

EXAM HINT Examine the links between economic distress and the demands for reform, especially in the post-war years, and the lack of co-ordination of the reforming groups.

3 Was government repression the main reason for the lack of parliamentary reform between 1793 and 1830?

EXAM HINT Note the repressive measures used by Pitt and Liverpool, including the use of spies, and parliament's failure to consider any measures of reform.

4 Was popular pressure the main reason for the passing of the 1832 Reform Act?

EXAM HINT Examine the significance of popular pressure, and the growing unity between reform groups, especially between the Whigs and the radicals.

5 How far were parliamentary attitudes to reform in 1830–2 different from those in the years 1785–1819?

EXAM HINT Between 1785 and 1819, parties were concerned by the possibility of revolution and supported repressive measures. In 1830–2, reform was championed by the Whigs, and Catholic emancipation showed that a major reform was both possible and desirable.

CHAPTER 4

Foreign policy 1783–1830

The years 1783 to 1814 saw great upheaval for Britain. The American War of Independence (1775–83) had recently ended British influence in the Americas, and through the 1790s and early nineteenth century, Britain was engaged in the Revolutionary and Napoleonic Wars with France. British foreign policy had to adapt to meet the challenges. This chapter examines British foreign policy through the following themes:

◆ Pitt's pre-war foreign policy: ending isolation

◆ Foreign policy during war 1793–1814

◆ Foreign policy after war 1814–30

KEY DATES					
1783		American War of Independence ended	1814	May	Treaty of Paris ended hostilities in Europe
1793		France declared war on Britain		Sept.	Congress of Vienna began
1801		Armistice between Britain and France	1815	March	Napoleon returned to France
1803		War with France resumed		June	Congress of Vienna finished, with the signing of the Final Act
1808		British troops campaign in Portugal, beginning the Peninsular Campaigns		Nov.	Napoleon defeated at Waterloo
					Second Treaty of Paris signed
1814	April	Treaty of Fontainebleau; Napoleon abdicated and was exiled	1822		Canning replaced Castlereagh
			1830		Palmerston became foreign secretary

1 Pitt's pre-war foreign policy: ending isolation

■ What did Pitt's pre-war foreign policy achieve?

In 1783, Britain was an economic power largely dependent on international trade. Isolated from mainland Europe, Britain could maintain trade links across vast distances while remaining relatively disinterested in the dynastic struggles of its European neighbours. By the late eighteenth century, Britain was the dominant power in international trade. In particular, Britain was the leading power in the international slave trade (see page 26). However, Britain was not in an unassailable position. The loss of the thirteen American colonies in the War of Independence (1775–83) had affected British trade. Further, British isolation from Europe was starkly apparent when France and Spain offered to support the American colonists in 1778–9. Pitt's foreign policy aimed to end Britain's isolation (see Table 4.1, below).

Alliances

Initially, foreign policy under Pitt was not unified. Pitt's foreign secretary, the Marquis of Carmarthen, attempted to build an **anti-Bourbon** network to challenge France. Pitt did not support this and wished to maintain an isolationist stance to avoid Britain becoming entangled in military and diplomatic obligations.

Table 4.1 Pitt's foreign policy: some successes and failures

Successes	Failures
• In 1785, France challenged British trade in Europe by forming an alliance with Dutch opponents of the pro-British House of Orange in the Netherlands. Britain, Prussia and the United Provinces (Netherlands) signed a Triple Alliance in 1788 with the aim of protecting western Europe from French aggression • In 1790, when Spanish vessels raided a British trading base in western Canada and captured British ships, the British government was able to intimidate Spain into returning the ships. When Louis XVI attempted to mobilise the French navy to support Spain, the National Assembly refused to act against Britain	• British ambassadors, supported by Pitt, threatened Russia in 1791 over its control of the Black Sea port of Ochakov. Russia ignored the threats, internationally humiliating Britain. Pitt was criticised in parliament by his opponents, especially Fox, for his handling of the matter • British aggression towards Russia caused the Triple Alliance to collapse in 1791, leaving Britain again isolated

Economic relations

As a trading nation, Britain was heavily reliant on its commerce with areas outside its empire. Envoys were sent to negotiate with the governments of all the leading European powers, including Russia, Portugal and Spain. However, the negative response from almost all governments meant that there was very little to show by 1792.

The only real achievement was the Eden Treaty of 1786. This allowed for the French to export oil, vinegar, wines and spirits to Britain at a preferential rate. In return, Britain could export manufactured goods to France with a reduction of ten to fifteen per cent on tariffs. Although the deal appeared to favour France, the emerging industrial companies in northern England and the midlands were well placed to take advantage. By 1789, French traders were complaining that the treaty favoured their old enemies. By 1792, Britain's deficit of £2.5 million in trade to Europe had been improved to a surplus of almost £2 million. The treaty ended in 1792 with the French Revolution, but historian Eric Evans (2019) describes it as 'the first hint of that concealed monopoly which Britain was to enjoy as it became the world's first industrial nation'.

Pitt's government invested heavily in the navy. By 1792, the British merchant navy had 1.5 million tonnes of shipping, a 250 per cent increase from 1760. One-third of British naval vessels were constructed in America; America was not only a lost market but a new power with shipbuilding capabilities. In 1786, a Navigation Act was passed which required the registration of all ships over fifteen tonnes; only British ships could register, blocking American and French shipping. In 1787, a free port system was created which allowed a small number of American vessels to trade in certain West Indian ports. By 1785, Britain was back to exporting quantities to America equal to those in 1775.

The impact of the French Revolution

Pitt thought that the French Revolution was positive for Britain, imagining that it would reduce France's international influence:

- Officially, British foreign policy maintained a neutral stance to the revolution.

- As a safeguard in case Bourbon fortunes revived, Pitt reassured the younger brother of the French king (who was in London at the time) that Britain would not oppose any effort to restore the French royal family.

- Behind the scenes, Pitt and Carmarthen attempted to create a network of alliances which they hoped would allow Britain to become the power-broker of Europe. Carmarthen predicted that British diplomats would be 'strutting around Europe with an air of consideration unknown to us for some time'.

Ultimately, British efforts to build alliances failed. This was partly because Britain's aims were primarily to maintain the political *status quo*, not to seek territorial gains in Europe. By contrast, Prussia, Austria, Russia and Turkey were engaged in efforts to expand their power.

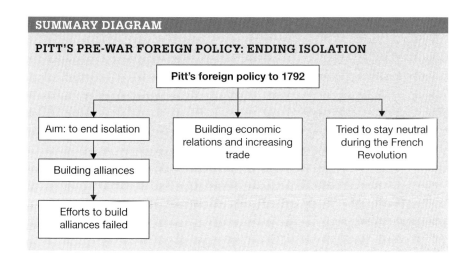

SUMMARY DIAGRAM

PITT'S PRE-WAR FOREIGN POLICY: ENDING ISOLATION

Pitt's foreign policy to 1792

- Aim: to end isolation
  - Building alliances
    - Efforts to build alliances failed
- Building economic relations and increasing trade
- Tried to stay neutral during the French Revolution

2 Foreign policy during war 1793–1814

■ *What were the main aims of Britain's wartime foreign policy?*

On 1 February 1793, the French National Convention declared war on Britain. This was a surprise to the British government, despite traditional anti-French feeling in Britain:

■ In 1792, Pitt had reduced defence spending to help balance government debts, stating that he considered war to be unlikely for at least fifteen years.

■ In November 1792, Whig member of parliament (MP) **William Grenville** declared that a French Republic might have a place among the governments of Europe.

■ In December 1792, Grenville informed the Russian ambassador that Britain would not interfere with French domestic politics.

However, from January 1793, Britain began to prepare for war. Self-defence was the main concern of other powers in Europe, but Britain's main concern was to prevent the threat of French domination of the lowlands of northern Europe, potentially challenging British security and trade.

Pitt's government was not interested in whether the French monarchy survived or was replaced. Rather, its foreign policy aims were to:

■ provide leadership for the countries opposing France

■ achieve minimal change to the *status quo* of Europe

■ contain French aggression

■ protect British trade in the lowlands.

On 5 February, Grenville sent a round of dispatches to European courts to create what became known as the First Coalition. Although France declared war on 1 February, the British government did not receive the declaration until 9 February, so the coalition was not simply a response to the French declaration of war.

With the outbreak of war in Europe, trade with America became more important. In 1794, the Jay Treaty agreed a ten-year suspension of trade restrictions with America. This benefited both countries; Britain gained more cotton for its northern mill towns and America gained a reliable market for its exports. By 1800, the USA was the destination for a full 25 per cent of British exports, with other parts of the Americas taking a further 25 per cent.

Pitt's wartime policies 1793–1802

Pitt's wartime policies can be divided into two main themes: blue water strategy and the use of coalitions.

Blue water strategy

Pitt focused much of his attention on the wider defence and extension of the British Empire. The phrase 'blue water' refers to naval strategy beyond local coastal defence. Between 1794 and 1796, Britain captured West Indian islands from the French and the Dutch. The cost was high: 40,000 British troops died fighting in the West Indies, with a similar number wounded; this was higher than the casualties of the entire **Peninsular Campaign**. In 1795, Guadeloupe and St Lucia were recaptured by the French.

Blue water strategy included Africa and Asia. When France overran the Netherlands and forced the Dutch to declare war on Britain, British troops could capture the Cape of Good Hope (South Africa) and Ceylon (modern-day Sri Lanka), which became vital trading posts. To support this strategy, the British government increased the size of the navy from 15,000 men in 1793 to 133,000 by 1801.

Naval supremacy protected Britain. In 1797, Britain defeated the Spanish navy, which was allied to France at the Battle of Cape St Vincent. This prevented Spain from supporting France at sea until 1803. The naval force supporting Napoleon's Egyptian campaign in 1798 was destroyed by Admiral Horatio Nelson at Aboukir Bay on the Nile, forcing Napoleon to abandon his Mediterranean plans and encouraging Austria and Russia to form the Second Coalition. In 1801, British supremacy was further consolidated when Nelson attacked and captured the Danish navy at Copenhagen in order to prevent its capture by Napoleon. As a consequence of British naval superiority, Napoleon abandoned all plans to invade Britain.

> **KEY TERM**
>
> **Peninsular Campaign**
> British campaigns against France in Portugal and Spain from 1808 to 1814.

Coalitions

The second string to British foreign policy was the construction of coalitions of nations to oppose France in Europe. By 1802, Britain had been involved in two coalitions:

- The First Coalition (1793) included Britain, Spain, Austria, Prussia, the Netherlands and the Italian state of Piedmont. It ended when France defeated Austria in Italy in 1797.

- The Second Coalition (1798) included Britain, Austria and Russia. This coalition was defeated quickly by Napoleon's ability to outmanoeuvre each nation.

- By 1802, Britain had spent £9.2 million in subsidies to coalition members to provide soldiers, weapons and an incentive to fight.

The main weakness of the early coalitions was the lack of co-ordination or combined strategy. Austria and Prussia, for example, had little trust in each other over their mutual claims of Polish territory. They also resented that Britain was paying for European nations to fight, with virtually no commitment of British troops.

A summary of Pitt's foreign policy up to 1802 is included in Table 4.2 (see below).

Table 4.2 Was Pitt's foreign policy working by 1802?

Yes	No
• The blue water strategy ensured that British economic interests were protected. By the 1800s over half of British exports went to the Americas • After 1802, the economic strength Pitt's policies had protected would allow Britain to continue the war with France until Napoleon's final defeat in 1815 • France was unable to defeat British naval power, making it impossible to invade Britain	• The policies were expensive. The cost of maintaining coalitions was a strain on the economy and caused high prices, contributing to discontent in Britain and rebellion in Ireland in 1798 • The coalitions were ineffective • Pitt avoided land campaigns on the Continent with British troops in France. Until this happened, Britain would be unable to do more than impose a naval blockade on France

From 1797, Grenville, at Pitt's direction, attempted to broker a peace deal to end the conflict with France. The defeat of the Second Coalition led to an armistice on 1 October 1801. Pitt resigned, and his brief successor, Addington (see page 20), negotiated the Peace of Amiens agreement on 25 March 1802. This deal was costly for Britain, which agreed to return recent gains, including West Indian conquests, land taken in Egypt, Ceylon, the Cape of Good Hope and Malta. The general feeling in Britain was that this was too high a price. The later prime minister, Canning, spoke at length about the 'gross faults and omissions' of the agreement, which he described as 'stupidity'. Yet Britain was a war-weary, overtaxed nation that was suffering from rising prices. Despite vocal criticism from some opponents, MPs in general ratified the treaty without even debating the terms in detail.

The second phase of the war: 1803–14

When war broke out again in 1803, Britain was better prepared than in 1793. During the short peace, Addington had revised the Militia Acts to draw a further 75,000 soldiers into a reserve army, and troops were left in the West Indies to reconquer the colonies that had been given back.

Britain initially continued the same strategies as pre-1802 (see Table 4.3, below).

Table 4.3 A summary of British foreign policy strategy after 1803

Blue water strategy remained important	Coalitions were funded to avoid British continental campaigning
• Strategic colonies in the West Indies were recaptured • Nelson's fleet decisively crushed the French fleet at Trafalgar (1805). There were only 1700 British casualties in contrast to 6000 French and Spanish, with a further 20,000 taken prisoner. This strategic victory meant that the French and Spanish navies took little part in the subsequent war with Britain	• Third Coalition (1805–6) of Britain, Russia and Austria was defeated in only four months • Fourth Coalition (1806–7) of Britain, Prussia and Saxony was defeated at the Battles of Pressburg and Jena

These tactics again led to stalemate. Each side tried to find an advantage:

- Napoleon challenged Britain's grip on naval trade.
  - ☐ From 1806 to 1812, Napoleon imposed the Continental System, laws which attempted to prevent any of the countries conquered by France or allied to them from trading with Britain.
  - ☐ France aimed to strangle British economic strength, to weaken the coalitions which relied on British funds to field armies.
- Britain responded with the British Orders in Council (1807).
  - ☐ These banned trade with France and allowed the searching of any vessels suspected of trading with France. This included stopping neutral ships.
  - ☐ Britain imposed blockades on any ports which followed the Continental System and refused to accept British goods.

Napoleon's Continental System failed because he did not have sufficient control of the policies of other European states. Spain and Portugal, for example, continued to trade with Britain. Likewise, the British Orders in Council was unpopular with neutral nations and had a negative impact on trade and the economy.

The Peninsular War

British foreign policy changed when Britain finally engaged in a land war in Europe. This change of strategy was the result of:

- The defeat of a French army in Spain in July 1808 at the Battle of Baylen. French General Dupont was forced to surrender, and his army disintegrated. The British public saw that Napoleon's troops could be defeated.
- Portugal, an ally of Britain which had been defeated by France, refused to accept the Continental System and called for British troops to help them to resist France.

A British army was landed in Portugal in 1808, led by Sir Arthur Wellesley (see page 55). As Britain realised the scale of the potential campaign, more troops were sent along with more two senior generals, Sir Harry Burrard and Sir Hew Dalrymple. The British troops quickly pushed the French out of Portugal for the following reasons:

- The quality of the British soldiers outclassed that of the French troops. France's long campaigns had drained their experienced manpower.
- The long supply chains that the French army relied on were vulnerable to attack by angry Portuguese civilians.
- The British army and its Portuguese allies were easily supplied by sea.
- Wellesley, a veteran of warfare in India, had experience of organising military campaigns over long distances.

Although the French were defeated, Dalrymple signed the Convention of Cintra. Instead of surrendering, the 25,000 French troops in Portugal were taken back to French territory by the Royal Navy, along with their weapons, cannon and any loot that they had taken. There was not even a clause preventing them from continuing to fight. Back in Britain, jubilation turned to bitterness. Wellesley, Burrard and Dalyrymple were recalled to Britain to face a court of inquiry. Wellesley alone was thanked for his role, as he had opposed the agreement; the others were pardoned but never given command again.

Sir John Moore took command and pushed into Spain. However, his initial successes were short lived and he was forced into a fighting retreat over 250 miles in mid-winter, during which he died. It was not an entire disaster, as France was unable fully to reconquer Portugal. Britain now had a foothold into Europe.

Wellington's campaign

In 1809, Wellesley, now the Duke of Wellington, returned to Portugal with a British army. French attention was focused on war with Austria, due to the creation of the Fifth Coalition (1809) of Britain and Austria. Although Austria was defeated, Wellington was able to liberate Portugal. Fighting from a 50-mile line of forts, Wellington defended against French attacks before pushing French troops from Portugal by 1811. In 1812, Wellington marched into Spain. After a temporary retreat, he again crossed into Spain in 1813. This time, the French military was in greater disarray, following a disastrous and costly campaign into Russia during 1812. Wellington's troops decisively defeated the French in June, and Wellington marched on France. By the end of March 1814, Paris had been captured. Napoleon's marshals forced him to **abdicate**, and he surrendered on 11 April 1814 in the Treaty of Fontainebleau.

ONLINE EXTRAS
OCR   WWW

Test your understanding of British strategy 1793–1815 by completing Worksheet 20 at www.hoddereducation. co.uk/accesstohistory/extras

KEY TERM

Abdicate When a monarch resigns from ruling.

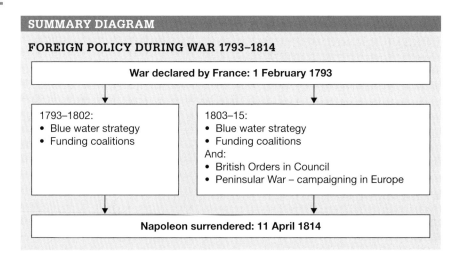

SUMMARY DIAGRAM

FOREIGN POLICY DURING WAR 1793–1814

War declared by France: 1 February 1793

1793–1802:
• Blue water strategy
• Funding coalitions

1803–15:
• Blue water strategy
• Funding coalitions
And:
• British Orders in Council
• Peninsular War – campaigning in Europe

Napoleon surrendered: 11 April 1814

3 Foreign policy after war 1814–30

■ *What did post-war foreign policy achieve?*

Castlereagh's foreign policy 1812–22

Viscount Castlereagh became foreign secretary from 1812 and was in office in the closing phases of the Napoleonic Wars. He supported Wellington's campaigning in Europe. By 1813, with the defeat of Napoleon becoming increasingly likely, parliament was concerned that any peace agreement had to benefit Britain. This would mean preventing any treaty between France and the other European powers which did not guarantee British interests in the Low Countries and the Peninsula. At the same time, Castlereagh was concerned that any peace should not further destabilise Europe and plant the seeds of further revolutionary struggles.

In early 1814, Castlereagh's negotiations led to the Treaty of Chaumont. This was signed in March by Britain and the eastern European powers. Castlereagh persuaded Austria, Prussia and Russia to guarantee to continue the war. Each country would commit to keep 150,000 men under arms for the duration of the war and subsequently prevent French aggression for twenty years.

Next, Castlereagh turned his attention to the French government. He did not favour forcing France to change its government, but with Napoleon's abdication and the return of the Bourbons supported by French royalists, he had to accept the new Bourbon government of Louis XVIII. Castlereagh preferred a generous policy towards France, since a brutal peace agreement would humiliate the new government and weaken it, leading to further instability and war.

The Peace of Paris was signed in May 1814 by France and the Allied nations:

- The borders of France returned to the 1792 lines. This included the complete surrender of the Netherlands, but meant that France kept some small areas of land captured early in the revolution.
- France received back colonies lost during the war, with the exception of the strategically important Tobago, St Lucia and Mauritius.
- Territory in northern Europe would be added to Holland in an enlarged Netherlands state.
- The countries involved would meet at the Congress of Vienna to agree the details of European borders.
- Despite Prussian demands, France would not be required to pay **reparations** to the victors.
- All Napoleon's captured artwork would remain in France.

KEY FIGURE

Viscount Castlereagh (1769–1822)

Born Robert Stewart, Castlereagh is best known as foreign secretary under Lord Liverpool. He was crucial in negotiating the balance of power following the Napoleonic Wars. However, his aristocratic background and aloof personality meant that he was disliked by many politicians.

KEY TERM

Reparations Money paid after a war by the losing side.

The Congress of Vienna

So many royals and statesmen from across Europe attended the Congress of Vienna, supported by entourages, that the population of the city increased by 30 per cent. As well as diplomatic meetings, there were balls, operas and concerts held all around Vienna to entertain the visiting nobility.

KEY TERM

Dutch East Indies
A Dutch colony in Southeast Asia which is now Indonesia.

The Vienna Settlement

Castlereagh's next challenge was keeping peace in Europe between the various continental powers. He wanted to create a system to avoid future conflict that might drag in Britain. He was involved in organising the Congress of Vienna. The Congress officially began in November 1814, although negotiations really began in September. The various nations involved used this as a forum to negotiate a series of agreements which would become part of a formalised system.

The aims of the Congress, Castlereagh insisted, should be restoration, legitimacy and compensation – in other words, the balancing out of power, guaranteeing the stability of governments and ensuring just treatment. It was not to be about making money for the victors. Various representatives who were present wrote letters in different languages, all using phrases synonymous with a balance of power.

Russia, Austria and Prussia all had long-standing intentions to control Poland, which made them rivals. This tension threatened to break the fragile alliance that Britain had formed and prevent stability in Europe. Castlereagh's big concern was Russian expansion. Ideally, he wanted to ally with both Austria and Prussia to prevent this, but they were competing over domination of the German states. No decision was reached in 1814.

Castlereagh's more successful plan, accepted by all powers, was that Austria should control Italy. This created a strong buffer against French aggression to the south. Britain also made a private agreement with the Netherlands in which Britain withdrew from the **Dutch East Indies** and paid £2 million to the Netherlands in return for keeping the strategic military and trade locations of Ceylon, the Cape of Good Hope and trading centres in Guiana – and a Dutch promise to strengthen the border with France.

It appeared that Castlereagh had constructed an overall policy to limit French aggression without weakening them and guarantee the stability of Europe. Two main problems threatened to end this hope (see Table 4.4, see page 81).

The agreement relating to the rearrangement of European borders, alliances and agreements was signed in June 1815 as the Treaty of Vienna, or the Vienna Settlement.

Fighting Napoleon a second time improved Britain's influence in Europe, whereas the lack of involvement of Russia or Austria in the second defeat of Napoleon gave them less voice in the treaty that followed, the Second Peace of Paris. Once again, Castlereagh insisted on a moderate policy, although less generous towards France this time. His aim remained preventing French aggression while maintaining political balance.

- Castlereagh and Wellington prevented plundering by Prussian and German forces.
- German states' demands for large areas of French land were denied.

Table 4.4 Castlereagh's policies to limit French aggression

Problem	Solution
The power struggle in eastern Europe threatened to end peace by November 1814: • Russia refused to accept any Prussian involvement in Poland • Prussia demanded the entire German state of Saxony as compensation • Austria opposed Prussian demands • This could potentially destroy the alliance that was designed to prevent future French aggression	Castlereagh made a controversial decision to join in a triple alliance with France and Austria: • With Britain and France behind Austria, Russia conceded a small area of northern Poland to Prussia • Austria agreed that Prussia could take a block of territory on the lower Rhine and in return Prussia agreed to govern only part of Saxony Although unpopular in Britain, the alliance reduced tensions and restored the balance in Europe, keeping Prussia as part of the system against France
Napoleon fled from exile on the island of Elba, and returned to France in March 1815 as a national hero in contrast to the unpopular Bourbon monarch: • Napoleon's return created new waves of popular support in France. Within two months he had 280,000 soldiers. British and Prussian troops in Belgium numbered 230,000 • Napoleon, if back in power, was unlikely to negotiate. Castlereagh's entire plan rested on negotiation	Wellington fought Napoleon at the Battle of Waterloo in June 1815 Napoleon's armies came close to winning, but ultimately Napoleon was defeated by Wellington's tactics as well as the arrival of the Prussian army late in the day Wellington returned to Britain as a victorious hero, whereas Napoleon went back into exile, this time on the more distant St Helena, where he died in 1821

■ France's borders were reduced from the 1792 frontier to the 1790 frontier, meaning a small loss of the Saar, Savoy and Landau.

■ France had to pay a heavy indemnity of 700 million francs.

■ France had to support an army of occupation numbering 150,000 for three to five years.

The second Peace of Paris established a sort of *status quo*, and Castlereagh's controversial willingness to enter an alliance with Austria and France supported this balance. Most importantly, Castlereagh had increased Britain's diplomatic importance far beyond its pre-war influence.

The Vienna Settlement was signed on 9 June 1815. It was an agreement that the eight nations involved (Austria, Britain, Prussia, Russia, Sweden, Spain, France and Portugal) would maintain the borders of European nations. This was achieved with very little change for the following 40 years. It also agreed on free trade between member states. Castlereagh also insisted on Clause Six of the Treaty of Vienna – that representatives of the involved nations meet regularly in conference to consult on European concerns and maintaining peace.

Congress diplomacy

The principle of using meetings and agreements to preserve peace became known as the **Congress System** or the Concert of Europe. Castlereagh backed this up by persuading Austria, Russia and Prussia to join Britain in the Quadruple Alliance, signed on the same day as the second Peace of Paris, 20 November 1815. The signatories agreed to guarantee that they would act together against French aggression at any point in the next twenty years.

ONLINE EXTRAS www
OCR

Get to grips with the events leading to peace 1814–15 by completing Worksheet 21 at **www.hoddereducation.co.uk/accesstohistory/extras**

KEY TERM

Congress System Also known as the Concert of Europe, this was the diplomatic network which protected the *status quo* in subsequent years. It is different from congress diplomacy, which is the principle of using meetings to maintain peace. Both of these are different from the Congress of Vienna (the meeting in Vienna 1814–15) and the Vienna Settlement (the 1815 agreement on borders and territories).

KEY TERM

Holy Alliance This agreement between Russia, Prussia and Austria was so-called because they agreed to base their relationship on Christian values.

However, pragmatic and moderate, Castlereagh refused to add the Russian demand that they guarantee to protect the Bourbon dynasty. As long as it was not Napoleonic or revolutionary, Castlereagh was happy to leave France to choose its own government. When, in September 1815, Russia, Prussia and Austria formed the **Holy Alliance**, agreeing to preserve the monarchies of Europe by resisting any demands for constitutional or democratic government, Castlereagh chose not to become involved.

Table 4.5 (see below) examines how successful Castlereagh was in his aims.

Table 4.5 Was Castlereagh successful?

Yes	No
• He prevented the collapse of France into further revolutionary and counter-revolutionary warfare	• Other countries tended to see the Congress system as a tool for strengthening their own spheres of influence
• The borders agreed at Vienna lasted for 40 years	• Russia saw it as a tool for preventing the development of liberal and democratic movements in Europe
• Castlereagh's objective, of maintaining the *status quo* of Europe, became a strand of British diplomacy until the 1870s	• From 1818, when Russia demanded action against democratic movements in Portugal and Spain, and Austria justified military action in Italy by saying that unrest there threatened their power, Britain stepped back from involvement in the Congress and disassociated itself from the Quadruple Alliance
• Britain avoided further warfare with France	• By 1820, Castlereagh was conducting diplomacy for Britain outside the Congress System. He was particularly concerned about the emergence of a Greek independence movement that appeared in 1821, which threatened to allow Russian expansion into the Balkans
• Castlereagh retained vital trade locations, such as the staging post at the Cape of Good Hope which enabled naval access to the growing empire in the east. Therefore, Britain in the nineteenth century was able to monopolise its hold on international trade	• Castlereagh's negotiations with aristocratic representatives of other nations, like Tsar Alexander of Russia and Prince Metternich of Austria, opened him up to accusations by his political opponents that he was dragging Britain into costly foreign affairs by his personal friendships. Castlereagh's disdain for explaining his actions did not help

KEY FIGURE

George Canning (1770–1827)

George Canning replaced Castlereagh as foreign secretary from 1822 until 1827. He also served as leader of the House of Commons during this period. In 1827, he briefly attempted to lead as prime minister, but his health failed and he died the same year.

Canning's foreign policy 1822–7

In 1822, frustrated by apparent failure to achieve a lasting system for peace and hounded by personal scandal, Castlereagh killed himself. His successor was **George Canning**. Canning and Castlereagh had been rivals for many years. In 1809, Canning had persuaded the prime minister, the Duke of Portland, to remove Castlereagh from his cabinet; when Castlereagh found out, he fought a duel against Canning. Canning missed Castlereagh, who shot Canning in the thigh. With such a long enmity between the two men, it is surprising that, in a political sense, Canning's foreign policy bore so many similarities to Castlereagh's. Canning believed in maintaining a peaceful *status quo* in Europe, intervening to prevent significant change in the balance of power.

Castlereagh's suicide

Castlereagh's death polarised opinion between those who respected him as a politician and gentleman, and those like Lord Byron, who wrote a poem encouraging travellers to 'stop and piss' on his grave. Yet his death contributed to a changing attitude to mental health. Previously, suicide victims would commonly be buried at a crossroads, not on Church grounds, but Castlereagh was buried in Westminster Abbey near William Pitt. A year later, a law was passed banning crossroad burials of people who died of suicide.

Speaking in Liverpool in 1822, Canning said that Britain's role lay in maintaining the balance between any nations which threatened the *status quo*, in which case 'England has only to maintain herself on the basis of her own solid and settled Constitution, firm, unshaken, not a partisan on either side, but, for the sake of both, a model, and ultimately perhaps an umpire.'

Three main themes summarise Canning's practical approach to foreign policy: deciding when to intervene, building trade overseas and imposing British ideas abroad.

Careful intervention

Selecting when to intervene was decided not on an ideological basis, but by estimating which events would be most likely to lead to a successful outcome by strengthening the British position in Europe (see Table 4.6, below).

Table 4.6 Canning's foreign policy approach

Issue	Canning's response	Reason
In 1822, the European Congress authorised French troops to enter Spain to stop a rebellion against the Spanish Bourbon monarchy	Even though Britain opposed the action, Canning did not send troops to intervene	There was little chance of improving British influence in the region
In 1826, a combined French and Spanish force threatened to invade Portugal	Canning sent 4000 British soldiers and a naval force to prevent invasion	Portugal was an old ally and trade partner, and gave Britain influence in south-west Europe. Intervention was likely to benefit Britain

Building British trade overseas

By 1815, five per cent of British exports were to Latin America. Canning chose to support a growing movement for independence among these countries in order to build British influence. In 1823, he persuaded the French ambassador to sign an acceptance of British dominance in the region. In 1824, Canning managed to persuade the British parliament to accept Buenos Aires, Columbia and Mexico as independent countries, and in 1825 helped to negotiate the independence of Brazil from Portugal. As a result, Britain gained influence in the region. Canning reportedly announced to an audience of merchants, 'Spanish America is free, and if we do not mismanage our affairs sadly [sic], she is English.' Between 1815 and 1825, British exports to Latin America had doubled.

Imposing British social ideas

Britain imposed social ideals in its imperial colonies, such as India, and regions where Britain had political influence, as in Latin America. They imposed governments with elites who shared British values and who would start to transform native societies into ones that more closely copied Britain by introducing the English language and British education. Religion was closely linked to this, and missionaries publicised Christian teachings in imperial colonies. The belief was that this would improve the quality of life and create greater stability.

The Greek question

The Greek question was a growing challenge that Canning inherited from Castlereagh, who was in office when the problem arose in 1821 – that of the emergence of a Greek independence movement, which enjoyed early successes against its Turkish political masters, since the **Ottoman Empire** was struggling to maintain control in the Balkans. Castlereagh and Canning were torn between the two sides; on the one hand, there was a deep-felt admiration for the Greek culture which had created democracy, and a love of classical Greek literature among the educated British elite, whereas the Ottoman Empire appeared to have a tyrannical and non-democratic government that was at odds with the British sense of democracy. On the other hand, Greek independence could allow Russia to extend its influence into the Balkans towards the Mediterranean, challenging British trade. Castlereagh had to maintain the balance of supporting the Greek ideal of independence while not allowing Russia to extend its influence.

Canning sent Wellington to negotiate with the Tsar of Russia, Nicholas I, in 1826. Shortly after Canning's death, in 1828, Russia agreed to accept Greek autonomy but also that Greece should remain under the nominal sovereignty of Turkey. This was a weak solution to a complex problem. It did not offer Greek independence, or satisfy the Turkish desire for Balkan power, or remove the Russian desire for expansion.

The Turks were defeated in the short Russo-Turkish war (1828–9). Britain and Russian continued to agree that they would support Greek independence, but now Russia had a military presence in south-east Europe. Britain and France's concern over Russian influence meant that in 1830 they insisted on fixed borders for Greece. These fixed borders prevented further Russian expansion, but at the cost of cutting off many Greeks who had fought for independence in territory still controlled by the Ottomans.

KEY TERM

Ottoman Empire
The empire of the country now known as Turkey.

ONLINE EXTRAS
OCR WWW

Learn how to write arguments rather than assertions by completing Worksheet 22 at **www. hoddereducation.co.uk/ accesstohistory/extras**

After Canning became prime minister, the Earls of Dudley and Aberdeen each briefly held office as foreign secretary, before Lord Palmerston held the office in 1830–4, 1835–41 and 1846–51. Palmerston continued to follow the core principles of Castlereagh and Canning's foreign policy, intervening only where necessary to maintain the balance of power in Europe.

ONLINE EXTRAS
OCR   **WWW**

Learn how to plan an effective essay by completing Worksheet 23 at **www. hoddereducation.co.uk/ accesstohistory/extras**

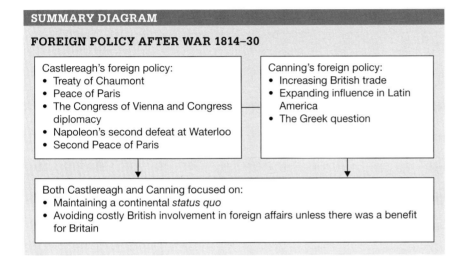

SUMMARY DIAGRAM

FOREIGN POLICY AFTER WAR 1814–30

Castlereagh's foreign policy:
• Treaty of Chaumont
• Peace of Paris
• The Congress of Vienna and Congress diplomacy
• Napoleon's second defeat at Waterloo
• Second Peace of Paris

Canning's foreign policy:
• Increasing British trade
• Expanding influence in Latin America
• The Greek question

Both Castlereagh and Canning focused on:
• Maintaining a continental *status quo*
• Avoiding costly British involvement in foreign affairs unless there was a benefit for Britain

CHAPTER SUMMARY

In 1783, Britain was at a crucial point internationally. Confidence had been shaken by the loss of the American War of Independence, and Pitt's government aimed to shore this up by building alliances and foreign trade deals, with limited success. This aim was disturbed by the outbreak of the French Revolution. Initially, Britain had little interest in what it saw a continental issue, but the declaration of war by France in 1793 dragged Britain into a long and costly war for which it was neither suited nor equipped.

British foreign policy focused on strengths throughout the war, using a blue water strategy to utilise naval power, and funding coalitions to use their economic strength. It was not until the successful campaigns of Wellington in Europe, however, that the deadlock was broken and Britain was victorious.

Following the war, the foreign secretaries Castlereagh and Canning followed a policy of protecting the *status quo* in Europe, ensuring British influence while avoiding costly entanglement in European conflict. This policy worked through the Congress System of diplomacy, and ushered in a period of relative peace in Europe.

Refresher questions

Use these questions to remind yourself of the key material covered in this chapter.

1 What was Britain's international position in 1783?

2 What did the Eden Treaty 1786 achieve for Britain?

3 What was Britain's foreign policy in response to the start of the French Revolution?

4 Define 'blue water strategy' and 'coalitions' in terms of British foreign policy during the Revolutionary Wars 1793–1802.

5 What were the 1807 British Orders in Council, and how did they affect the ongoing war with France?

6 What were Castlereagh's foreign policy priorities from 1815?

7 Define the Congress of Vienna and the Congress System.

8 How were Canning's foreign policies similar to Castlereagh's?

9 How did Canning build British trade overseas?

10 Why was the 'Greek question' a challenge for British politicians, and what was the solution by 1830?

Question practice: OCR A level

Essay questions

1 How important was Pitt's blue water strategy for victory against France?

EXAM HINT The opening paragraph should identify the factors that led to victory against France and offer a view as to how important the blue water strategy was. The first main paragraph should examine the blue water strategy and consider the arguments for and against its importance before reaching an interim judgement about its importance. The remaining paragraphs should examine other factors and reach a judgement about their importance. The conclusion will use these interim judgements to reach an overall judgement about the importance of the strategy.

2 'The Peace of Amiens was a failure for Britain.' How far do you agree?

EXAM HINT The opening paragraph should identify a number of the main issues of the peace and British aims and offer a view as to whether Amiens was a failure for Britain. Each paragraph should discuss an issue raised in the opening and reach a judgement, in light of British aims, as to whether it was a failure. The judgements on each issue should be used to reach an overall judgement in the conclusion.

3 'British foreign policy 1812–30 was consistently effective.' How far do you agree?

EXAM HINT The opening should identify the issues that would be needed for British foreign policy to be viewed as effective and should identify the issues to be discussed, such as balance of power, keeping France or Russia in check or naval dominance, and a view should be offered as to whether the policy was effective. Paragraphs should examine each of the issues and a judgement reached as to whether the policy was consistently effective in that area. The conclusion should use the interim judgements to reach an overall judgement as to whether policy was consistently effective.

4 How important was the Vienna Settlement to British foreign policy 1812–30?

EXAM HINT The aims of British foreign policy in the period could be outlined in the opening paragraph and a view offered as to how important Vienna was in relation to these aims. Paragraphs could be written on each issue and the relative importance of Vienna as against other events or developments considered before a judgement is reached. The interim judgements would then form the basis for an overall judgement about the importance of Vienna.

CHAPTER 5

The industrialisation of Britain 1783–1832

In the late eighteenth and early nineteenth centuries, Britain was leading the world in industrialisation. This process of great change brought in factories and mills, changing the face of the British economy. New areas of industry became important, and cities and transport networks were drastically transformed.

This chapter examines the industrialisation of Britain through the following themes:

◆ The Industrial Revolution

◆ The economic impact of the Industrial Revolution

◆ The make-up of society

◆ Changes to living conditions

KEY DATES

1776	Watt and Boulton manufactured a commercially available steam engine that could power a mill	**1802**	Health and Morals of Apprentices Act passed
1784	Technique for 'puddling' iron discovered	**1810**	Robert Owen invested in New Lanark
		1819	Factory Act passed
1789	Steam-powered cotton power looms became available	**1824–5**	Combination Acts repealed, permitting trade unions
1798	Thomas Malthus published an essay raising concerns over population growth, sparking a national debate	**1826**	County Bankers Act allowed joint-stock banks to be created
		1828	Repeal of the Corporation and Tests Act
1801	First census carried out	**1830**	Manchester to Liverpool line opened with first large-scale freight and public railway
	First public railway authorised by parliament		

A very British Industrial Revolution

If any period could be considered revolutionary, 1760–1830 would be the most appropriate. This is sometimes referred to as the first Industrial Revolution; the subsequent spread of industrialisation to other nations is referred to as the second.

1 The Industrial Revolution

■ *What were the main features of the Industrial Revolution?*

In the 1780s, Britain was industrialising rapidly. The term 'Industrial Revolution', coined in 1884 by historian Arnold Toynbee, has become a common name for the period to the mid-nineteenth century. Historians have debated what period should be considered to be the Industrial Revolution, and whether the word revolution can be applied to a process that lasted for decades. As Peter Mathias (2001) noted, 'the metaphor is over-dramatic and implies over-precision in dating. However, judged against the long perspective of history, the eighteenth century did see pivotal changes.'

From the 1780s onwards, the make-up of the economy changed. Older staples of the British economy such as woollen goods remained important, although newer trades and goods, such as steel smelting and cotton weaving, grew in significance. Cotton goods became central to the economy. Between 1780 and 1829, cotton goods increased from seven per cent to 62 per cent of British exports. The scale of the economy changed too: both imports and exports were increasingly rapidly, and by 1820 exports had overtaken imports, a sign of a thriving economy.

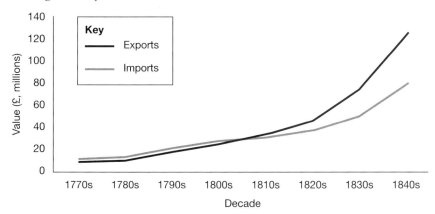

Figure 5.1 The value of British imports and exports. Adapted from data in C. Cook and J. Stevenson, *The Longman Handbook of Modern British History 1714–2001*, Longman, 2001.

Why was Britain industrialising?

There are several reasons that explain why Britain industrialised in this period:

- Industrialists had amassed wealth by profiting from the slave trade and the East India Company (see page 13). A flourishing banking system meant that affordable loans were easily available, essential for investment in industry.

- Britain had natural resources in large quantities. Industrialists could source iron, coal, tin, timber and stone, and Britain's navy and empire allowed the import of other resources.

- British terrain was perfect for industrialisation. Nowhere in Britain is out of reach of a coastal port, and there are many navigable rivers, like the Trent and Severn, for transporting goods more efficiently than roads. In the north of England were plenty of hills, for example the Pennines, with fast-flowing rivers to power water wheels.

- The climate, cold and damp, enabled efficient handling of cotton, since threads were less likely to snap than in warmer, drier climates.

- By the 1780s, Britain had a growing empire, meaning many markets in which to sell goods.

- The population was rapidly increasing, creating a large labour force (see page 90).

- Britain had a strong and growing middle class, the source of many industrialists.
- Britain had a stable political system. New scientific and economic ideas could be debated, and the population had more freedom to move than in other European states.
- New technological developments led to production methods which were faster and more cost effective.
- Agriculture had been improving through the eighteenth century and so was able to support industrialisation.
- The Revolutionary and Napoleonic Wars (1792–1815) created new demand for the iron, copper and lead industries for weapons production, which expanded the capacity of these industrial centres.

Individually these factors do not explain the change, since they all occurred in other countries too. Rather, it was the coexistence of these factors in Britain at this time that mattered. Crucially, the industrialisation process in Britain was managed not by the government but by individual entrepreneurs with a personal interest in success. The government did little to encourage innovation, or to mobilise capital for investment. With the exception of a few naval dockyards and military ordnance works, the government did not own or manage industrial sites. Until the 1840s, the government was not even willing to assume responsibility for the management of the social consequences of industrialisation, such as urbanisation, sanitation, health care and education.

Additionally, some of the reasons that explain industrialisation are also consequences of industrialisation. For example, population growth was both a result of, and cause of, industrialisation.

Population changes

By 1801, there was fierce debate over the question of whether the population was growing. Some, including minister and radical reformer Dr Richard Price, argued that Britain was a weak struggling country with a population that was decreasing. Others, such as **Thomas Malthus**, a professor of history and political economy, claimed that the population was increasing at such a pace that eventually it would overtake food production, leading to war, starvation and poor health. This was more than just a theoretical debate, as the contrasting views affected debates over political reform, social legislation and economic policy.

Prior to 1801, population figures were simply guesses based on evidence from parish registers of baptisms and deaths. A modern estimate is that the population of England and Wales was 7.5 million in 1781 and increasing at a rate of one per cent per year. In 1801, an official **census** was instituted, to be carried out every ten years, to resolve the debate. Even these figures were very unreliable until the introduction of recording names and ages from 1841 onwards. The census showed a continual growth across England and Wales, even allowing for the limited accuracy of the early methods (see Table 5.1, page 91). A similar pattern was emerging across Scotland and Ireland.

KEY FIGURE

Thomas Malthus (1766–1834)

A political economist and cleric who wrote *An Essay on the Principle of Population* (1798). He argued that the population would grow and outpace food production, causing war and starvation, which would, in turn, reduce the population.

KEY TERM

Census An official government collection of population data. In Britain, this has been completed every ten years since 1801.

Table 5.1 Population and growth of England and Wales 1801–21

Census year	Population	Annual increase
1801	8.9 million	1.10%
1811	10.2 million	1.43%
1821	12.0 million	1.81%

This growth was caused by the birth rate rising:

■ More jobs meant that young men became financially independent and able to marry sooner, and therefore were having children younger.

■ Urbanisation brought more men and women together to find partners than in smaller rural villages.

And, at the same time, the death rate was falling:

■ Agricultural improvements meant more access to more and better-quality food, often at lower prices during peacetime, which meant better health and fewer infant deaths.

■ Mass production of iron and steel tools began to improve the quality of medical equipment.

New methods of powering production

In 1776, James Watt and Matthew Boulton developed a steam engine that could power pumps in mines and ironworks and, by 1781, was capable of powering mill machinery. By 1800, at least 500 steam engines were in use, 40 per cent in cotton mills and most of the rest in mines and ironworks.

Water and steam power increased the output of mills and factories, which in turn required more workers and increased urbanisation. The increased availability of steam power also opened new possibilities in transport, such as steamships and railways. The iron and coal industries grew to meet the demand for materials.

As a consequence of the growing population, and the implementation of new sources of power, both industry and agriculture underwent significant changes, as explored in the next section.

ONLINE EXTRAS **WWW**
AQA

Develop your analysis of the reasons for economic growth in Britain 1783–1832 by completing Worksheet 16 at **www.hoddereducation. co.uk/accesstohistory/extras**

ONLINE EXTRAS **WWW**
Pearson Edexcel

Develop your analysis of the factors for industrialisation by completing Worksheet 17 at **www.hoddereducation. co.uk/accesstohistory/extras**

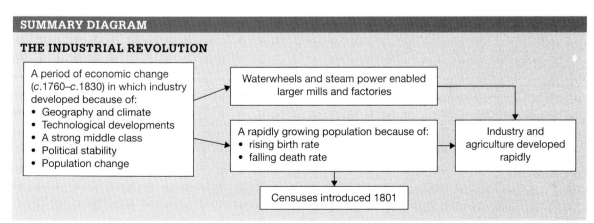

SUMMARY DIAGRAM

THE INDUSTRIAL REVOLUTION

A period of economic change (c.1760–c.1830) in which industry developed because of:
• Geography and climate
• Technological developments
• A strong middle class
• Political stability
• Population change

Waterwheels and steam power enabled larger mills and factories

A rapidly growing population because of:
• rising birth rate
• falling death rate

Industry and agriculture developed rapidly

Censuses introduced 1801

2 The economic impact of the Industrial Revolution

■ *How did the Industrial Revolution affect the economy?*

The Industrial Revolution had a large effect on the economy, significantly in the coal, iron, steel and cotton industries as well as the financial, agricultural and transport industries.

Coal

The demand for coal grew with the advent of steam power. Between 1750 and 1800, British annual coal production increased from 6 million to 10 million tonnes. Increased demand led to an expansion in the size and depth of mines, and an increased number of miners.

Working conditions in mines

In the efforts to extract more coal from deeper mine shafts and longer tunnels, mines became more dangerous. One major danger was flooding. This was partly solved with the Boulton–Watt steam engine that could continuously pump water from the mines. Another danger was gas, either carbon dioxide ('choke-damp') or explosive methane gas ('fire-damp'). The former was dealt with by the invention of an exhaust pump by John Buddle in 1790, which sucked in fresh air and could be steam powered; the latter was resolved in 1815, when Sir Humphrey Davy invented a safety lamp which protected the oil flame from the explosive gas. Steel cables, made possible by new factory processes, began to replace ropes from the 1800s to reduce accidents caused by strain on ropes in deeper pits.

Iron and steel

Large quantities of cast iron were essential for creating rails. In 1784, Henry Cort created a new production technique, called 'puddling', which created iron fifteen times more quickly than previous methods. Puddling required more complex ironworks and greater investment by owners. Whereas in 1786 Britain made less than 70,000 tonnes of pig iron per year, by 1806 250,000 tonnes a year were being produced. By 1850, it had grown to nearly 2.25 million tonnes per year. South Wales was particularly important, thanks to the coalfields and iron reserves, and by 1830 this region produced about one-third of British iron.

By the 1780s, steel production was growing. Though expensive, steel was stronger than iron and more flexible for machine parts such as springs. Sheffield became a steel centre: in 1770 there were only five steel manufacturers there; by 1856 there were 135.

Cotton

Wool, a long-time staple textile in Britain, was gradually replaced by cotton, which began as a luxury product and then became commonplace:

- Cotton was more comfortable, and had a wider international market, since wool is of little use in warm climates.
- The French Revolutionary War created a military demand for cotton cloth for uniforms.
- Cotton was more economical than raising sheep for wool. There was not enough land in Britain to raise the sheep needed for a quantity of wool equivalent to the cotton that was processed in British mills.
- The slave trade had established trade routes for importing cotton.
- New technologies, such as the **flying shuttle** (1733) and the **spinning mule** (1775), made cotton production faster and more economical.
- In 1789, Edmund Cartwright altered his power loom to use steam power, which doubled the speed of the weaving process.

Lancashire was the prominent cotton-producing region. Entire towns emerged around new mills across the breadth of Lancashire: Bolton, Accrington, Rochdale, Oldham, Preston, and others. This was because:

- There was an existing woollen industry with a workforce that was skilled in spinning and weaving.
- The port of Liverpool already imported cotton from Turkey and the Middle East, so was well placed for trans-Atlantic trade from North America.
- The Lancashire coalfields provided fuel for the mills with minimal transportation.
- The mid-eighteenth century had seen the construction of the Sankey Navigation Canal (1757), the Bridgewater Canal (1761–73) and the Trent and Mersey Canal (1777) and the start of the Leeds to Liverpool Canal (1770–1816), which made transporting goods, especially coal, easier.

> **KEY TERMS**
>
> **Flying shuttle**
> A powered mechanism which made cloth that was both wider and woven more quickly than was possible with earlier methods, and needed fewer weavers.
>
> **Spinning mule**
> A powered machine which span threads into yarn for weaving more quickly than older methods, with fewer workers.

Benjamin Gott

Benjamin Gott exemplifies the growth possible for textile entrepreneurs. He was a wool merchant who founded a textile works called Bean Ings Works in 1792. By 1820, he employed 1500 workers and owned more than £100,000 in capital (*c.£*9 million today).

The financial sector

Early industrial developments were funded by the private resources of industrialists and entrepreneurs. Investors purchased stocks in return for profits, if the business did well. This was especially apparent in the 1790s with a public demand to buy stocks in canal construction, and in the 1840s with the growth of railway networks.

Towards the end of the eighteenth century, banks took on a greater role. Industrialists and landowners required loans to pay workers and buy machinery, and a place to keep their profits. The Bank of England was dominant in London but did not play much of a role outside the city, where a range of smaller banks operated. Each bank printed its own banknotes. It was a symbiotic relationship: the small local banks deposited money in the London banks, and the London banks loaned money to industrialists via local banks.

By 1810, there were 721 private banks in England and Wales, including private merchants who made banking loans to customers or suppliers. Most were in Lancashire and Yorkshire. The rapid spread of banking made the Industrial Revolution possible. Without it, progress would have most probably stalled by the early nineteenth century. However, it was not a perfect system:

- Non-standardised printed money was easy to forge.
- The lack of regulation allowed fraudsters to steal money.
- There was no consumer protection, and if either the bank or customer went bankrupt, both were affected.
- There was no regulation on printing money, so banks often printed more than they could cover. There were several 'runs' on banks. For example, in 1825, 60 banks failed when customers lost confidence and tried to withdraw their money.
- The existing charter for the Bank of England prevented joint-stock banks, where more than six investors work together, which meant that independent banks were small.

In 1826, the government allowed joint-stock banks to form, as long as they were more than 65 miles from London. In return for losing its role as the only large bank, the Bank of England was permitted to have branches outside London. This move stabilised the financial sector, which benefited industry and began a series of further financial developments from the 1830s (see page 169).

The **invisible trade** sector grew alongside manufacturing. From 1816 to 1820, behind the annual deficit of £11 million in the trade of goods, was a surplus of £18 million in invisible trade. By 1830, this gap had extended, so that **visible trade** had an annual deficit of £15 million but invisible trades were profiting annually by £17 million. This shows the national importance of financial development.

Transport

By expanding the existing system that connected the ports of London, Liverpool, Hull and Bristol, the canal network grew in the 1790s. There were 50,000 'navigators', or labourers, many from Ireland. Between 1790 and 1796, 122 special Canal Acts were passed by parliament authorising new waterways. By 1830, Britain had 4000 miles of navigable inland waterways. The advantages and disadvantages of canals are considered in Table 5.2 (see page 95).

KEY TERMS

Invisible trade Financial transactions involving services, such as banking or insurance, not goods.

Visible trade Financial transactions involving goods and materials.

Table 5.2 The development of the canal system: advantages and disadvantages

Advantages	Disadvantages
• Canals were slow and steady; fragile goods such as pottery could be transported safely	• Canals were not standardised. The largest canals were three times wider than the narrowest. This meant unloading cargoes and repacking on different boats to continue the journey
• Canals were faster than roads and larger loads could be carried	• Canals were owned by a variety of companies, so merchants might pay several fees on one journey
• Canals gave growing industries access to raw supplies and markets that would have been too expensive by road	• Maintenance standards varied, and some areas had damaged locks, which allowed water levels to drop
• Thousands of workers were employed and capital was invested, stimulating other areas of the economy	• Many industrial areas are hilly, so long systems of locks were necessary. For example, near Birmingham, a series of 30 locks was created to climb 220 feet. This delayed journeys
	• While faster than roads, the average speed on canals was only 3 mph

Railways were superior to the canals:

■ Trains were faster and could pull heavier loads.

■ They handled hills better than canals.

■ Tracks could be mass produced and construction was less labour intensive than digging out canals.

The first public railway, the Surrey Iron Railway, was authorised by parliament in 1801. The first passenger line opened in Swansea in 1806, pulled by horses. By 1825, there were 30 passenger lines. The canals kept their dominance because the early public lines focused on passenger transport, not freight.

In 1826, parliament set a new precedent by authorising a large-scale freight line between Liverpool and Manchester. This opened in 1830 to great fanfare and national attention. Despite the accidental death of politician William Huskisson on the maiden journey, it was a great success. Trains carried 1200 passengers plus freight each day at 25 mph. It was a financial success. The money had been raised by shares bought for £100 each, and by 1835 investors were getting £10 profit per share, which was better than bank interest rates. Railways began gradually to replace canals after 1830. Many train operators bought out the nearby canals to monopolise transport in the area.

The significance of the expansion of transport, especially trains, was that industry could now spread. No longer did factories and mills need to be built near coalfields, as fuel could be cheaply transported around the country. This opened up new areas for industrial development.

Agricultural developments

Industrialisation did not mean that agriculture was pushed aside. The largest wealth still lay in the hands of landowners and bankers, with industrialists in second place. During the Industrial Revolution, agriculture became more productive:

- The development of mass production made equipment such as modern ploughs more cheaply available.
- By 1800, many farmers had built pits and tanks underground to store animal and human manure to use as fertiliser, and were experimenting with using soot from chimneys and marl, a clay with high lime content, to improve the quality of land.
- Between 1780 and 1855, in Norfolk, the treatment of farm land by fertiliser and marl increased rental values by 500 per cent.
- By 1800, breeders had become so successful at selectively breeding animals that top pedigree animals could sell at auction for £1000 each (equivalent to the combined annual earnings of 50 farm labourers).

Enclosure

To increase agricultural production, more land was required. Some farmers reclaimed wasteland by draining marshes, but others fenced off **common land**. This was called **enclosure**. In some areas, this was with the agreement of the community. Where there was no agreement, it could be done by law if 80 per cent of the property owners in the community agreed. Since, in many cases, the richest landowners owned 80 per cent of the property, this could be carried out even against the wishes of the entire village.

Enclosure required an Act of parliament to change the ownership of the land. This was not cheap, and the farmers who received land had to pay for new roads, walls, hedges and fences. Some small farmers were awarded land in the process of enclosure but could not meet the costs of enclosing the land. Many chose instead to sell their land to larger landowners. Others could not prove their right to the land they farmed before enclosure and lost their land. Landless farmers either became labourers for richer farmers or sought work in the growing cities:

- Before 1760, there had only been 130 enclosure Acts. Between 1760 and 1800, there were over 1000. By 1815, a further 800 had been passed. These Acts enclosed 7 million acres of communal land.
- The improvement in land quality increased rental and purchase values. This pushed poorer farmers to become labourers or move to cities.
- Village communities broke down. Although there had always been richer and poorer people in the villages, there was now a clear demarcation between those with land and those without. The landless now depended on employment from the wealthy.
- The larger farms created by enclosure benefited from the investment in technology and labour by wealthy landowners, and food production became more efficient.
- The changes intensified the social discontent, which was one reason behind the extra-parliamentary protest movement (see pages 20 and 57).

- In 1830, trouble erupted across southern England in which hay ricks and corn stacks were set on fire. These protests were known as the Swing Riots (see page 58).

Despite the increase in agricultural output, the population was growing at an average rate of 1.8 per cent in the early nineteenth century (France was growing at 0.7 per cent) and urbanising. Consequently, Britain's need for grain overtook its supply. Britain changed from being a nation which exported grain to one that was wholly reliant on imported grain:

- In the 1750s, Britain exported over 4000 tonnes of grain and flour annually.

- Imports overtook exports of food in the 1770s and 1780s.

- By the 1800s, Britain was importing almost 100,000 tonnes per year, an amount which continued to increase during the nineteenth century.

ONLINE EXTRAS
AQA **WWW**
Learn how to write effective introductions by completing Worksheet 17 at **www. hoddereducation.co.uk/ accesstohistory/extras**

SUMMARY DIAGRAM

THE ECONOMIC IMPACT OF THE INDUSTRIAL REVOLUTION

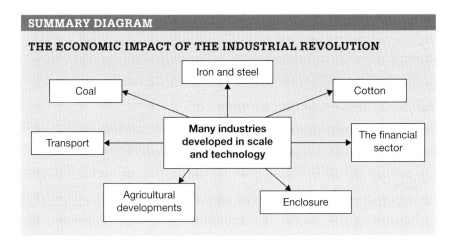

3 The make-up of society

- *How did society change from 1783 to 1832?*

The rapid changes to the economy created new pressures on society. British society was changed through urbanisation, which in turn led to social changes such as a developing middle class of industrial leaders and even religious changes.

Urbanisation

In 1750, approximately fifteen per cent of the British population lived in urban areas. This was higher than most European states, and by 1800, had grown to 25 per cent. Allowing for overall population growth, within 50 years the urban population had risen from just over 1 million to 2.2 million. This was just the start – by 1880, 80 per cent of the population, or 20.8 million people, were living in urban areas.

Table 5.3 Estimates of population growth in key British cities between 1701 and 1871

City	1701	1751	1801	1831	1871
London	500,000	750,000	1,100,000	1,900,000	3,900,000
Liverpool	5,000	35,000	82,000	202,000	493,000
Manchester	9,000	45,000	75,000	182,000	351,000
Norwich	25,000	35,000	36,000	61,000	80,000

Between 1783 and 1820, overcrowded, cheap housing provided by mill owners became more abundant. Clean water supplies and sanitation did not keep up with demand. Streets in poorer areas became filled with sewage and rubbish. The air was polluted by factories burning coal for power. From the 1820s, a further change occurred. Middle-class families began to move out of the centres of towns in search of larger houses with gardens, cleaner air and less overcrowding. Working-class urban dwellers, on the other hand, were more tied to the cheaper housing built near mills and factories. In London, due to its larger size, workers might live further from their place of work, but the lack of affordable public transport before the 1860s still required them to be within walking distance of their employment.

Why did urban populations increase?

No single factor can explain the change, but suggested factors include:

■ Improved quality of diet. Documentary evidence and the increasing height and weight of young people in the period suggests that, after 1780, working-class consumers were demanding more bread and meat. Potatoes and vegetables were eaten alongside the meat and bred, rather than as staples, to stave off starvation. This more nutritional diet protected babies, reduced miscarriages, reduced deaths of mothers in childbirth and increased life expectancy.

■ Migration from rural areas. However, evidence suggests that the movement was piecemeal rather than a mass exodus. Population numbers in rural areas also continued to rise through the early nineteenth century.

■ Improved medical care. Inoculation and vaccination (discovered in 1796) reduced the spread of smallpox as a killer disease. In the eighteenth century, charity hospitals became more prominent. Recent research has suggested that the lack of hygiene in these hospitals may mean that they had little impact on health, and, prior to 1852, the smallpox vaccination had little impact on the number of deaths.

■ Marriage in urban areas being more common. In urban Lancashire in 1800, 40 per cent of 17–30 year olds were married, compared to 19 per cent in rural Lancashire. In rural Britain, the average age of marriage was 27, in most industrial areas 24, and in mining areas about 20. The concentration of younger people in towns, and shorter apprenticeships in new trades, meant that men were independent sooner. More marriages at a younger age without effective contraception meant quicker population growth.

Religious change

A disproportionate number of leading industrialists were Nonconformists, especially Quakers and Unitarians:

- Nonconformist families benefited from financial and business support from their networks within congregations. For example, Quakers were more likely to support other Quakers with businesses and loans.

- There were concentrations of Nonconformists in industrial areas, so it was natural that they would make up a large proportion of industry leaders.

- Until the 1828 repeal of the Test and Corporation Acts (see page 56), Nonconformists and Catholics were excluded from public office. This meant that, unlike Anglicans, sons of these families had to focus on the financial sector rather than politics.

- Quakers and Unitarians drew their membership primarily from families with wealth, therefore they were more likely to become involved in finance and industry.

A new industrial elite

The existing social elites, essentially the landed gentry and nobility, maintained their important position as leaders of society. They were able to invest in new industry, make financial loans and profit from minerals on their land. However, a new industrial elite began to emerge in the late eighteenth century. The majority were merchants who became industrial entrepreneurs. By 1800, this new, largely urban middle-class of industrialists and professionals made up about 25 per cent of the population.

Josiah Wedgewood is a good example. He built on his family business in pottery. As well as improving the quality and look of his product, he sold to the British and Russian royal families in the 1760s and 1770s, after which he capitalised on his wealthy patrons by advertising himself as the 'Queen's Potter', an accolade which gained him customers from high society.

A small minority of the new industrial elite came from the workshop floor. These were men who were so successful that they were able to rise from apprenticeships and low social status to be industrial leaders. Examples include Joseph Bramah, a former engineering apprentice who invented the hydraulic press, and Robert Owen, a drapery apprentice who built a textiles empire (see page 104).

Employment and trade unions

The majority of urban workers were employed in mills and factories. This was a notable shift. Many would have been agricultural workers with their own plots of land or labouring on the land of wealthier men. Others would have been independent craftsmen working with their families at home or in small-scale workshops.

Instead of seasonal work, labour was now steady throughout the year. In place of working hours shifting with daylight and seasons, work was done on strict rotas, usually of twelve-hour shifts in factories which ran 24 hours a day, six days a week. The work was paid at an hourly rate, and many families lived hand-to-mouth, earning just enough to cover their costs for the week. They became completely dependent on industrialists for a living. Additionally, new jobs emerged within urban towns in the factories, such as machine operators. These began to replace the roles of traditional craftsmen since the industrialised processes could produce goods at a faster pace.

Up to twenty per cent of the workforce were children. Children were paid lower wages than adults and did lighter jobs which did not need an adult's strength. In some industries, children were essential; their smaller size made them useful in mines for moving materials in low tunnels, and in cotton mills for finding and fixing broken threads under machines.

Trade unions

Factory work created the potential for workers to have more power. They could unite, form a trade union, and put pressure on employers. These unions particularly represented skilled tradesmen, such as printers and mechanics. One example in 1793 was the London printers, who successfully used a petition to raise their wages. In this period, however, the unions were weak and ineffective due to:

- The lack of no central organisation, since there was no general council to direct efforts.

- Government legislation. In 1799 and 1800, Pitt's government passed the Combination Acts, which banned workers from combining into unions that would interfere with trade, and allowed such groups to be tried in court. Even though these were repealed in 1824, an amended law in 1825 meant that strikes were ineffective (see pages 51 and 53).

- '**Knobsticks**' (workers who continued to work despite strikes), which weakened the impact of the unions.

KEY TERM

Knobsticks
Strikebreakers; a derogatory term for workers who ignored strike action and continued to work.

ONLINE EXTRAS
Pearson Edexcel **WWW**

Learn how to use criteria by completing Worksheet 18 at **www.hoddereducation. co.uk/accesstohistory/extras**

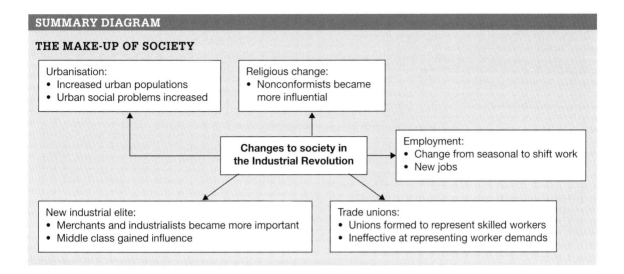

SUMMARY DIAGRAM

THE MAKE-UP OF SOCIETY

Urbanisation:
- Increased urban populations
- Urban social problems increased

Religious change:
- Nonconformists became more influential

Changes to society in the Industrial Revolution

Employment:
- Change from seasonal to shift work
- New jobs

New industrial elite:
- Merchants and industrialists became more important
- Middle class gained influence

Trade unions:
- Unions formed to represent skilled workers
- Ineffective at representing worker demands

4 Changes to living conditions

■ *What were the main changes to living conditions from 1783 to 1832?*

As society changed and became increasingly urbanised, living conditions also changed. While there were some changes to rural living, poor workers in urban areas faced increasingly dangerous conditions among the factories and mills.

Rural living conditions

Changes caused by enclosure, and migration towards urban areas, broke down the traditional bonds in rural communities that had existed for centuries, and changed the social balance. Unlike the industrial changes, these differences were small and gradual.

The power of the landowning elite was largely unchallenged. There was no growing middle class to share their economic control, unlike the industrial magnates of the cities. On the contrary, their monopoly on land for canals, trains and valuable resources increased their economic power.

Tenant farmers were reasonably wealthy, with some political influence. Many became wealthier by buying out smaller farmers, although there were fewer farmers overall. The poorest independent farmers, the yeomanry, now lost power and wealth. The costs of enclosure drove many to sell up and move to urban areas.

Despite the movement of labour to urban areas and changes to land management, it would be wrong to suggest that rural areas were becoming less important. As historian Peter Mathias (2001) has pointed out, in the first half of the century no English counties experienced rural depopulation, since the population of counties was rising more rapidly than the rate of migration to urban areas. By 1831, about 33 per cent of families were still working in

KEY TERM

Poor relief Financial support given to those in poverty under the Poor Law.

SOURCE QUESTION

How useful is Source A for showing the poor conditions faced by workers in factories and mills?

agriculture, although by 1841 this had fallen to 22 per cent. However, the majority of the rural population were now agricultural labourers who faced seasonal unemployment. This led to an increase in rural pauperism and reliance on **poor relief**.

The combination of the working poor leaving their land through enclosure or working as low-paid labourers for wealthier men caused discontent. This probably contributed to the growing demand for political change in rural areas through the nineteenth century.

Urban working conditions

For many workers, employment was in new factories and mills. These existed for profit, not comfort. Inside the cotton mills, it was dim, warm and humid. To prevent snapped cotton threads due to cold, dry conditions, windows were

SOURCE A

Cartoon showing abuse in the mills, published c.1810 by a newspaper which supported the campaign for factory reform.

kept shut, resulting in temperatures that could reach 30–40°C. Some overseers sprayed water to keep the air humid. This, combined with dust from cotton threads, led to several workers suffering from chest infections and breathing difficulties. It was also a fire risk. By the 1790s, mill fires were so common that insurers were paying out more in compensation than they were making from the premiums, so they had to amend the terms of what would be paid out in the event of fire.

The machinery was highly dangerous. Until 1844 there was no requirement to install safety guards. Accidents were common. Dr Ward, who investigated mill conditions in Manchester in 1819, claimed to have visited one school in which 47 of the 106 children working in mills had suffered injuries 'through the children's hands and arms having being caught in the machinery; in many instances the muscles, and the skin is stripped down to the bone, and in some instances a finger or two might be lost'.

Many mills had long shifts, commonly over twelve hours a day. Even for children, the working day was only limited to twelve hours in 1819. There were strict rules and workers could be fined. One list of rules from a mill in Tyldesley, Manchester, in 1823, listed a one-shilling fine for whistling, opening a window or being five minutes late, and six shillings for being off work ill without sending someone to cover the shift.

Reform movement

In response to the terrible working conditions, a small number of industrialists sought to reform their mills. Notable among these individuals is Robert Owen (see his profile on page 104), with his use of New Lanark as a model town of **philanthropic** principles. He introduced a standard eight-hour shift model and is credited with creating the slogan 'Eight hours labour, eight hours recreation, eight hours rest'.

Owen was not a lone voice. John Fielden, an industrialist and landowner from Todmorden, advocated a minimum wage and supported better wages and hours in his mills. He supported the right of working men to vote and he opposed the **workhouse** system (see page 189). One of the greatest philanthropists was Lord Ashley, who became the Earl of Shaftesbury in 1851. He used his position as member of parliament (MP) from 1826 to champion the reformist cause, especially in education and the mining industry.

A common link between reformers was that they were almost universally Nonconformist Christians:

- Owen was a religious free thinker who thought that religious organisations created prejudice and prevented reform. His utopian ideals were an early form of **socialist** thinking.
- Fielden was raised a Quaker and founded a Unitarian Nonconformist association.
- Lord Ashley was Anglican, but evangelical rather than conservative in his views.

ONLINE EXTRAS
AQA WWW

Learn how to write effective conclusions by completing Worksheet 18 at **www. hoddereducation.co.uk/ accesstohistory/extras**

KEY TERMS

Philanthropic The principle of promoting the welfare of others, often through charity to good causes.

Workhouse A place where people in poverty could go for financial support. After 1834, these became particularly horrible places that were feared by the poor.

Socialist A person who believes in socialism, the notion that the workers should own the factories in which they work and that society should function cooperatively, rather than the wealthy few controlling the economy.

Robert Owen

1771	Born in Newtown, Wales. His father was a saddler, ironmonger and local postmaster; his mother was from a farming family
1781	Apprenticed to a cloth wholesaler at the age of ten
1789	Borrowed £100 to establish his own cloth business
1792	Managed a mill with 500 employees
1793	Became a member of the Manchester Literary and Philosophical Society
1794	Established new mills in Manchester
1810	Purchased four textile mills in New Lanark for £60,000
1813–4	Published the essays *The Formation of Character* and *A New View of Society*
1816	Presented evidence on the state of the mills to parliament
1819	Factory Act passed, imposing a twelve-hour maximum working day for children
1858	Died and was buried in Newtown

Background

Robert Owen was born to an upper working-class family and apprenticed into the textile industry in Lincolnshire. He is an example of the small number of working-class men who became part of the new industrial elite. He gained broad experience working in textiles in London and Manchester, including part-owning a mill.

His connection to the Manchester Literacy and Philosophical Society brought him into contact with liberal thinkers and reformers who championed the value of social and political reform and education.

New Lanark

Owen purchased four mills in New Lanark, Scotland. In addition to profit, his aim was to create a community which demonstrated philanthropic principles. Owen believed fundamentally that people are good and simply shaped by their surroundings. Therefore, improving how they lived would improve them as people.

There were already 2000 people in New Lanark when Owen took over. He ordered the building of a school, purchased £500 worth of pictures to inspire the minds of younger children, and reduced the length of the working day for children. When his business partners objected, Owen bought their shares. He later sold shares to fellow reformers including Jeremy Bentham and several Quaker investors. The mills were kept clean, the town well ordered and well presented. A village store was also opened in 1813. The company bought goods in bulk and sold them at lower cost to the residents. In 1816, the Institute for the Formation of Character was opened, which doubled as a school and community centre offering lessons as well as evening classes, lectures and balls for adults.

The wider reform movement

Owen toured the country speaking about the value of responsible management of industry, spending £4000 in one two-month period. His essay *The Formation of Character* argued that society had an obligation to improve education. *A New View of Society* demanded a national system of education to reduce crime and poverty, laws to restrict the sale of gin and gambling, reforms to the prison system and the reduction of Anglican influence in society. Owen's campaigns were instrumental in the passing of the 1819 Factory Act. Karl Marx considered Owen to be the 'Father of Socialism'.

ONLINE EXTRAS
Pearson Edexcel **WWW**

Test your understanding of the significance of Robert Owen by completing Worksheet 19 at **www.hoddereducation.co.uk/accesstohistory/extras**

The role of education

One growing concern for reformers was the impact of work on children. Children from the mills as young as six years old were noted to be cursing and swearing like hardened workers. Consequently, a common reformist ideal was to improve education for children. Owen, for example, founded a school in New Lanark. He restricted work for children aged under ten and insisted that they attended school.

Between 1780 and 1783, a Sunday School movement emerged in Gloucester to provide a basic, Bible-based education for poor children. Similar schools were formed in other areas of Britain over the next twenty years. Around 1800, two reformers, Andrew Bell and Joseph Lancaster (working independently yet with similar ideas) created the idea of the Bell and Lancaster Monitorial System. This was a system to educate children without the cost of professional teachers. Bell and Lancaster taught their brightest students (the monitors) in the morning, then other children arrived and were grouped for the monitors who taught what they had learned that morning. The fees were a few pence each week, and for the poorest children, lessons were free. This model was copied by other charity organisations and individual reformers.

The moral focus of the reformers does not mean that they were interested in being 'soft'. They retained strict moral rules. For example, at New Lanark, parents who had illegitimate children were fined. Alcohol sales were strictly controlled. Coloured blocks were hung over the head of each worker, nicknamed 'silent monitors', and would be turned to show the rating of the quality of the work completed, including a black side to show an unacceptable quality of work.

What did the reformist movement achieve?

By 1830, the reformist movement had achieved some limited changes (see Table 5.4, below).

Table 5.4 Changes due to the reformist movement

Reform	Continuity
The reform movement created the first steps to the concept of responsibility by industrialists and investors …	… however, this was not widely accepted by many managers so had a limited practical effect
In 1802, the Health and Morals of Apprentices Act was passed. It limited apprentices to working only twelve hours per day and insisted on their receiving good accommodation and medical care …	… however, the Act did not apply to workers other than factory apprentices, and was not enforced
The 1819 Factory Act was passed, creating a twelve-hour working day limit in factories and a minimum working age of nine …	… but the law was not enforced, meaning that there were anecdotal reports of violations. It only applied to the cotton industry
The reformers represented the liberal sentiment among the growing Nonconformist religious groups which had campaigned for issues such as the abolition of slavery …	… however, Nonconformists were a minority, and their religious views divided them from people with conformist, Anglican views. For example, Owen's opposition to established religion divided him from influential reformers of the day such as William Wilberforce

The impact of evangelicalism

The growth of evangelicalism was important. It motivated reformist thinking by teaching that improvement was possible for all. At the same time, it encouraged people to help themselves. Therefore, reform campaigns focused on making changes that would allow people to help themselves.

ONLINE EXTRAS WWW
AQA

Learn how to plan effective essays by completing Worksheet 19 at **www. hoddereducation.co.uk/ accesstohistory/extras**

ONLINE EXTRAS WWW
Pearson Edexcel

Get to grips with the consequences of industrialisation by completing Worksheet 20 at **www.hoddereducation. co.uk/accesstohistory/extras**

ONLINE EXTRAS WWW
Pearson Edexcel

Learn how to write effective opening sentences by completing Worksheet 21 at **www.hoddereducation. co.uk/accesstohistory/extras**

ONLINE EXTRAS WWW
Pearson Edexcel

Get to grips with the social and economic consequences of the Industrial Revolution by completing Worksheet 22 at **www.hoddereducation. co.uk/accesstohistory/extras**

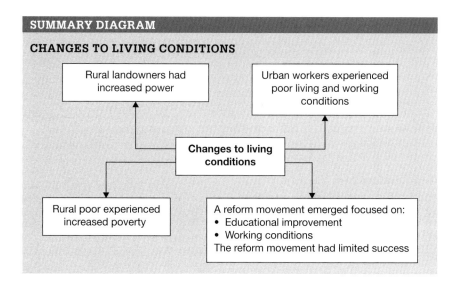

SUMMARY DIAGRAM

CHANGES TO LIVING CONDITIONS

Rural landowners had increased power

Urban workers experienced poor living and working conditions

Changes to living conditions

Rural poor experienced increased poverty

A reform movement emerged focused on:
- Educational improvement
- Working conditions

The reform movement had limited success

CHAPTER SUMMARY

The period 1783–1832 was one of great change for Britain, as it became the first industrialised nation in the world. It was, in 1832, on its way to becoming the 'workshop of the world'. The most important factor was the development of steam power. With the invention of commercial steam engines, industrialisation could spread beyond the confines of flowing rivers.

The changes caused developments across all industries, including coal, iron, steel and cotton, as well as agriculture, which became more efficient through enclosure and new methods. As production increased, so too did exports which brought in money that further generated economic developments. However, economic change caused wider impacts than purely industrial change. The population experienced rapid growth as well as urbanisation, and the make-up of society changed – the middle classes and Nonconformist religious groups became more influential, and new social problems emerged in the increasingly overcrowded towns. By the early nineteenth century, these social changes had given rise to the start of a movement for social reform, led by philanthropists such as Robert Owen, although significant reform would not be achieved until after 1832.

Refresher questions

Use these questions to remind yourself of the key material covered in this chapter.

1 What is meant by the term 'Industrial Revolution'?

2 What are five reasons for the Industrial Revolution in Britain?

3 Why did the development of steam engines affect the wider economy?

4 How did the financial sector change between 1783 and 1832?

5 Why did trains replace canals as a means of transport?

6 What was enclosure, and why did it affect communities?

7 Describe urbanisation in Britain in the years 1783–1832.

8 Give three examples of social changes caused by urbanisation and industrialisation.

9 Why were trade unions weak and ineffective in the period 1783–1832?

10 What social ideas did philanthropists like Robert Owen encourage in the years 1783–1832?

Question practice: AQA

Essay questions

1 'The positive benefits of industrialisation in the years 1783–1832 outweighed the negatives.' Explain why you agree or disagree with this view. [AS level]

EXAM HINT You need to analyse how industrialisation helped the working poor and set this alongside the negatives. Then reach a conclusion about which you think was the more significant.

2 'The economy fundamentally changed during the years 1783–1832.' Assess the validity of this view. [A level]

EXAM HINT You need to assess the extent of change. Analyse what changed and what remained relatively constant in the period. Make sure that the whole period is covered.

3 To what extent did society change during the years 1783–1832? [A level]

EXAM HINT You need to assess the extent of change. Analyse the aspects that changed and the aspects of society that fundamentally remained the same. One approach would be to look at different social groups in turn.

Question practice: Pearson Edexcel

Essay questions

1 How significant was urbanisation in causing social change in the years 1785–1832? [AS level]

EXAM HINT Consider the widespread social change brought by urbanisation, including living and working conditions, and the growth of trade unionism.

2 How far do you agree that the breakdown of rural communities was the main consequence of economic change in the years 1785–1832? [A level]

EXAM HINT Note the economic change and rural depopulation brought about by the agricultural revolution. Other aspects of the changing economy might include the growth of towns and cities, and the importance of industrialisation.

CHAPTER 6

Government and democracy 1832–68

From 1830 until 1841, Whig governments were in power, followed by Peel's Tories from 1841 to 1846. Between 1846 and 1859, the government changed between the two parties four times. From 1859, the two parties had become the Conservatives and the Liberals, and by 1868, both parties had spent time in office.

Governments from both parties struggled to adapt to the changed social and political situation in Britain. New pressures for change forced prime ministers to balance the demands of voters against those of their ministers and members of parliament. Additionally, with the 1832 Reform Act, the door was open for future change. Parliamentary reform had not exactly led to revolution and anarchy, which meant that proposals for future change could be considered. Chartism was an example of popular demand for further change. However, progress was not rapid, although the nature of the British political system did undergo substantial change during this period. This chapter examines the governments in office and the process of democratic change through the following themes:

◆ Whig and Tory politics in the 1830s

◆ Peel as prime minister from 1841

◆ Peel's fall from power

◆ Chartism

◆ Changes to party political structures by 1866

◆ The 1867 Reform Act

KEY DATES

1830–3		Tithe War in Ireland between tenants and landlords	
1832		Representation of the People Act, or Great Reform Act, passed	
1834	July	Melbourne replaced Grey as prime minister	
	Aug.	Poor Law Amendment Act (New Poor Law) passed	
	Dec.	Peel's Tamworth Manifesto	
1835	Feb.	Lichfield Compact between Whigs, radicals and Irish MPs	
	Sept.	Municipal Corporations Act	
1838		People's Charter published by the London Working Men's Association	
1839	June	First Chartist petition presented to parliament	
	Nov.	Newport Uprising	

1841	Peel became prime minister
1842	Second Chartist petition presented to parliament
1844	Banking Act and Companies Act passed, reforming the whole financial and business system
1845	The Maynooth Crisis and Peel's response damaged his government
1846	Corn Laws repealed and Peel resigned in response to Conservative opposition
1848	Third Chartist petition and Kensington Common March
1859	Agreement of the Liberal factions to form an alliance
1867	Second Representation of the People Act

1 Whig and Tory politics in the 1830s

■ *What were the main achievements of Whig and Tory governments during this period?*

In 1832, Grey's government had succeeded in passing the Representation of the People Act, or the Great Reform Act. Although this Act made moderate changes to the electorate and constituencies in Britain, its passing did not remove all demands for further reform. Over subsequent years, four main demands for reform were evident in political debates:

■ universal male suffrage (the vote for all men)

■ annual elections

■ secret ballots

■ further equalisation of the size of constituencies and political representation.

Grey's government after the Reform Act

Grey called for a new election in 1832 with the intention of capitalising on the goodwill of the newly enfranchised middle classes. The Whigs won a landslide 67 per cent of the seats in the Commons, which, with a smaller number of Irish and radical members of parliament (MPs), gave them control of 479 seats compared to the 179 of the Tories. This meant that the Whigs could introduce the following social reforms:

■ factory reform

■ abolition of slavery throughout the British Empire

■ Poor Law reform

■ reorganisation of the banking system.

Although they appeared to be in an unassailable position, the Whigs faced challenges which weakened their ability to quickly follow through on their intentions.

Initially, the fears that the 1832 Reform Act would lead to revolutionary change proved false. The immediate changes were fundamentally conservative and did little to alter the nature of democracy:

■ In 1832, only twenty per cent of adult men, approximately nine per cent of the adult population, could vote.

■ In the years from 1832 to 1867, an average of only 60 per cent of constituencies were contested. Therefore, many enfranchised people did not get to use their vote.

■ Although some of the middle classes had the vote, little changed in the social make-up of parliament. With no salary for MPs, it was limited to the minority of industrialists who could afford to leave their businesses to focus on politics. In 1841, for example, only 22 per cent of MPs were middle-class businessmen, 42 per cent were members of aristocratic families and 29 per cent were country gentry. Between 1832 and 1865, only one of the eight prime ministers (Robert Peel, see page 113) was not an aristocrat.

■ Without secret ballots, elections continued to be corrupt, with voters heavily influenced by their landlords.

However, in the longer term, the Reform Act proved to be a leak in the dam that would leave to a renewed demand for change, and, ultimately, further reforms to continue the process towards wider political representation in Britain.

Tensions between Whigs and radicals

Among the MPs elected in 1832 were about 60 radicals – neither Whig nor Tory, but men with reformist ideas that were radical at the time. These included Thomas Attwood (see page 59) and William Cobbett, a long-standing radical who believed in economic reform. Radicals tended to vote alongside Whigs but demanded even further reform to the franchise. They also quibbled over every detail of Whig reforms, and demanded further reforms with such enthusiasm that the more conservative Whigs were uncomfortable.

Tensions between Whigs and Irish nationalists

The Repeal Movement's demand for the removal of **Protestant Ascendency** and repeal of the Act of Union led to disturbances in rural areas of Ireland in the **Tithe War of 1830–3**. The Whig response was divided. Some Whigs, headed by **Lord Russell**, introduced minor reforms to Church and education in Ireland. Unsurprisingly, this did not satisfy wider demands or end the disturbances. The government, urged by **Lord Stanley** and his supporters, passed the 1833 Coercion Act, giving the authorities in Ireland stronger powers to suppress disturbances and impose curfews. Russellite Whigs responded by proposing 'appropriation', the use of Anglican Church money to fund education and social support for the uneducated, largely Catholic population. This created a political stalemate within the party. Lord Stanley resigned from Grey's cabinet in 1834 in protest at Russell's proposal for concessions, and a number of other senior Whig politicians followed suit. These Stanleyites later joined Peel's Conservative government.

The pressures leading to the Reform Act and the squabbling after over Ireland had weakened the government. Grey resigned as prime minister in August 1834, apparently in response to party disagreements over the terms of the coercion bill, although he had turned 70 and was doubtless more wearied by the continual political infighting.

What were the ideas of the Whigs?

The Whigs were the traditional opponents of the Tories. The name had originated as a term of abuse in the 1680s, and was a Scottish word for a horse thief. By the 1800s though, it had become a title of pride. What did they stand for?

KEY TERMS

Protestant Ascendency
The political, economic and social domination of Ireland by the minority group of landowners and Protestant clergy, all of whom belonged to the Anglican Church.

Tithe War 1830–3
The tithe was an obligatory payment by citizens in Ireland to pay for the upkeep of the Anglican Church. This was resented by Catholics, but after the 1829 Emancipation Act, more organised resistance to paying emerged. The government responded by seizing goods, and this led to outbreaks of violence.

KEY FIGURE

Lord Stanley (1799–1869)
Edward Stanley was a Whig MP from 1822. Under Lord Grey, he became the chief secretary for Ireland in 1831, and secretary of state for war and colonies in 1833. However, his views over Ireland led to his resignation from Grey's government in 1834. Having moved to the Conservative Party, he served in Peel's government and became the party leader from 1846 to 1868, the longest serving party leader to date. In 1851 he took the title Earl of Derby. He is also one of only four prime ministers to have had three or more separate periods in office (1852, 1858–9 and 1866–8) although paradoxically he spent only three years and 280 days in office.

- Whigs stood in opposition to the monarch and royal power.

- They wanted to retain a constitutional monarchy – they were not republicans – but they opposed government through royal favour.

- They supported the primacy of the House of Commons in the constitution as the main arena for governing the country.

- The Whigs were more likely to support the rights of Nonconformist and Catholic pressure groups than the Tories.

- They tended to favour social and political reform more than the Tories.

Having said that, they should not be seen as the 'reforming party' in an absolute sense in contrast to a traditionalist Tory faction. They were still very conservative in outlook:

- As with the Tories, most Whigs came from landed, aristocratic families. Whig lords sat in the House of Lords, and used their patronage to influence junior family members to gain seats in the Commons.

- They did not seek to weaken the landed interest in extending the vote. They saw giving the vote to the middle classes as a way of supporting the *status quo* against working-class unrest.

- In reforming the rotten boroughs in 1832 and equalising some constituencies, they sought primarily to weaken the Tory hold on these areas.

- They supported some measure of social reforms, and passed several key pieces of legislation between 1833 and 1835, but they saw this more as a way of preventing revolution than attempting to create an egalitarian society – they were not socialists.

Consequently, with the 1832 Reform Act and the small number of social and economic reforms passed in 1832–5, most Whigs felt that they had achieved fully their aims to reform Britain, stave off revolution and revitalise the political system. There were a number of more progressive Whigs who sought further reform but these were a minority.

How accurate is it to regard the Whigs as a group?

With the 1827 resignation of Lord Liverpool, party allegiances had become blurred. Examples that show this lack of party unity include:

- Peel's abandonment of the Ultra Tories in passing the Catholic Emancipation Act.

- The Whigs were entirely divided over the treatment of Ireland 1833–4.

- The 1833 Whig budget was opposed by Ultra Tories but also by radicals who supported Whig social reforms.

- Peel, a Tory, supported Whig government proposals in 1833 40 times out of 43.

Defined parties would begin to form slowly from 1835, with the Lichfield Compact (see page 115).

Robert Peel

1788	Born the son of a wealthy Lancashire mill owner and MP
1805	Studied Classics and Mathematics at Oxford University
1809	Entered politics as MP for Chashel
1822	Became home secretary in Liverpool's cabinet
1829	Created the Metropolitan Police Force
1834	Briefly served as prime minister
1841	Second term as prime minister
1846	Repealed the Corn Laws, which led to his resignation
1850	Died as a result of injuries from falling from his horse

Background

Unlike many Conservative MPs, Peel did not have a landed background, but was the son of a Lancashire mill owner and MP. He had an excellent education at Harrow and Oxford University.

Political career

Peel served as MP for several constituencies, starting with Cashel, Tipperary, and including Oxford University. He was noted for his conservative viewpoints, especially with regard to Ireland, where his Unionist beliefs led to the nickname 'Orange Peel'. From 1822 he served as home secretary under Liverpool and later Wellington; he introduced a number of key reforms including changes to the penal code, standardisation of the prison system and the introduction of a professional police force to London. However, he showed his willingness to change when he accepted the need for a new approach to Catholic emancipation, supporting Wellington's bill in 1828.

Prime minister

Peel served as prime minister 1834–5, and again 1841–6. His government passed several important laws, such as the Mines Act (1842) and the Factory Act (1844), which improved conditions for workers. However, his decision to repeal the Corn Laws split his party; after five months of debate, the repeal motion was passed but his opponents defeated him on another bill on the same day to show their displeasure, and he resigned as prime minister.

Melbourne as prime minister 1834

Following Grey's resignation, **William Lamb**, Lord Melbourne, became a Whig prime minister in August 1834. King William IV saw Melbourne as a good choice in the wake of Whig reform, since he was conservatively minded and had previously served in Canning's Tory cabinet (see page 54). The result was a Whig government which disappointed both liberal Whigs and the king. Melbourne refused to invite Peel and Wellington (see page 55) into his cabinet, to the king's frustration. He then attempted to appease the king by excluding radical Whigs, which isolated him from that side of the political spectrum. The king also became concerned when the Whigs investigated the system of appointments in the Church of England, discovering clear evidence of nepotism and pluralism. The king saw this as an attack on a key British institution.

Peel in opposition 1832–4

Peel's tactics as leader of the opposition in 1832 served to strengthen his party. Some historians have even suggested that his tactics formed the basis for the modern Conservative Party. Peel's tactics followed certain principles:

KEY FIGURE

William Lamb, Viscount Melbourne (1779–1848)

Melbourne was a Whig politician, but he had no strong political opinions either for reform or for reaction. The early part of his career had been overshadowed by scandal (his wife had an affair with the poet Lord Byron) and he was appointed as prime minister in 1834 as the 'least bad choice' for William IV. He benefited from a close friendship with Queen Victoria, but resigned in 1841 after a series of parliamentary defeats.

- Where possible, support the Whig government in its proposals instead of opposing them simply on partisan principle. This would prevent the formation of strong alliances between the Whigs, radical MPs and Irish MPs, by depriving them of a mutual opponent.
- Encourage divisions within the government where possible.
- Persuade more conservative Whigs to support the Tories by appearing more moderate than the radical or Irish MPs who had the sympathy of left-wing Whigs.
- Heal the division between the Tories and Ultra Tories that had occurred from 1828.
- Broaden electoral support by winning votes from the middle classes, while avoiding isolating the more traditional landed support.
- Work with the reformed political system instead of trying to reverse the 1832 reforms to show that Tories were relevant.

Why did Peel adopt these tactics in opposition?

In part, Peel's tactics were the result of clever political strategy. Peel wanted not only to weaken the Whig position for future elections but also to prevent the radicals using the Whig majority to push further reform. In a letter written in 1833, Peel said that justifying the Whigs working with the radicals would be 'tantamount to the adoption of the views and principles of the radicals and their practical enforcement through the Crown and government'.

Historian Norman Gash (1986) argued that Peel regarded his political party not as a mechanism to gain power, but as a means to an effective government. This explains Peel's lack of interest in opposition for its own sake. Peel also had a genuine fear of mob rule. He had been particularly worried by the threat of anarchy and popular protest during the passing of the 1832 Reform Act, and therefore may have wanted to ensure stable government, of whichever party, to prevent the breakdown of law and order.

Melbourne's dismissal: a constitutional watershed

When Melbourne appointed the radical Lord Russell as the chancellor of the exchequer, this was too much for the king, who dismissed Melbourne's government in November 1834. Although Melbourne's dismissal was a defeat for the Whigs, it paradoxically achieved one of their key aims – the weakening of royal power. The national negative response with which this was received, combined with the ineffectiveness of the subsequent minority governments, means that no monarch since 1834 has dismissed a governmental ministry simply on the basis of their personal opinion, or rejected a prime minister's request to dissolve parliament for a re-election.

Wellington was invited to form a caretaker government. He was reluctant to do so and recommended that Peel head the government. Peel formed a minority Tory government, although he was in Italy at the time. Since the new government was dependent on Whig goodwill in parliament, Peel asked for a new general election to gain parliamentary support. The king agreed and an election was held in January 1835.

Peel's first ministry

Peel held office for five months in 1834, a short-lived, but crucial, period in which he:

- Consolidated Tory unity. For example, he offered four cabinet positions to four Ultra Tories. This restored his reputation somewhat with that wing of the party.
- Went on to enjoy success in the January 1835 election with his minority government, winning about 80 seats. Most opposition came from the Whigs, rather than radicals.
- Began a process by which more modern political parties began to form.

Regarding the last point, the Tamworth Manifesto and the Lichfield Compact (see below) were important in this process.

The Tamworth Manifesto

In December 1834, Peel stood to be re-elected in Tamworth in the English midlands, and declared his political intentions to the voters. Unusually, however, his manifesto was agreed by his cabinet and printed in national newspapers. He stated that he considered the 1832 Reform Act to be final, that he would not seek to reverse it or make further reforms, and that he would stand to protect the Church of England as an institution. Peel's biographer, Norman Gash (1976), has interpreted this as Peel laying out party policies which would become the foundations for the modern Conservative Party. Other historians say the manifesto was simply a personal statement of his aims.

> **SOURCE A**
>
> Part of Peel's 1834 Tamworth Manifesto.
>
> *I never will admit that I have been, either before or after the Reform Bill, the defender of abuses, or the enemy of judicious reforms … With respect to the Reform Bill itself, I will repeat now the declaration I made when I entered the House of Commons as a Member of the Reformed Parliament – that I consider the Reform Bill a final and irrevocable settlement of a great Constitutional question.*

The Lichfield Compact

The Whigs were concerned after the January 1835 election, since the Tories had cut the Whig majority from 67 per cent to 58.5 per cent. In February, leaders of the Whigs, radicals and Irish MPs met at Lichfield House (the London home of a Whig politician) to discuss an alliance. This was a divisive decision; Melbourne, for example, was worried by the association with radicals and Irish nationalists. This agreement has been called the birth of the modern Liberal Party (see page 138).

SOURCE QUESTION

Study Source A. Why would Peel, a Tory, commit to considering the 1832 Reform Act to be 'a final and irrevocable settlement'?

ONLINE EXTRAS
OCR   **www**

Practise your source analysis skills by completing Worksheet 24 at **www. hoddereducation.co.uk/ accesstohistory/extras**

Melbourne as prime minister 1835–41

The Whigs, with their allies secured in the Lichfield Compact, were able to push Peel out in April 1835 to reinstate Melbourne in office. The name 'Liberals' began to be used to describe this alliance. By 1839, Russell, who had become the leader in the Commons, began to use the name to describe his faction. Melbourne's government had a much smaller majority than in the previous year, and now depended on the Liberal alliance of Whigs, Irish and radical MPs. Melbourne faced much criticism:

- Conservative Whigs thought that Melbourne had sold out to Irish MPs who were, according to one MP, controlled by the 'mob and priesthood'.
- The king met Grey (still active as a Whig) and expressed his concern that the Whigs were associating with 'dangerous men' such as O'Connell (see page 56).
- The Whig MP for Buckingham reported that his voters were concerned that the government was under the influence of O'Connell.

Peel's tactics in opposition were paying off. His moderate stance allowed the Whig weaknesses to cause division, and made the Tories appear as the patriotic English party.

What did the Whig governments achieve 1832–41?

Apart from Wellington's one-month caretaker government and Peel's five-month first ministry, and despite Peel's tactics to rebuild the Conservative Party, there was a Whig prime minister with a Whig Commons majority from 1832 until 1841. A summary of these governments' achievements is given in Table 6.1 (see page 117).

As Table 6.1 shows, despite their position, the Whigs achieved little notable reform in the 1830s. Most of their achievements were between 1832 and 1835. From 1835, their reforms fizzled out in quantity and significance, due to their inability to deal with their own internal problems and external pressures. But it also shows that, in passing the 1832 Reform Act, they were not striving to open a door to mass reform as their viewpoint had been rather more moderate in nature.

The key post-1835 reforms were aimed at reducing the power of the Anglican Church in society as a result of pressure from the Nonconformist (see page 3) supporters of the Whigs. These reforms did not do enough to truly satisfy Nonconformist demands, but they deeply concerned King William IV, a crucial factor in Melbourne's fall from power.

The decline of Melbourne's government

By 1837, when the death of King William IV caused another general election, the tide in parliament was turning in favour of Peel's Tories:

- The Whig majority fell to 51.7 per cent (344 seats), just 30 seats more than the Tories.

- About 40 MPs who had been reformers in 1832 switched sides to join Peel's faction.

- The unpopularity of passing the New Poor Law in 1834 had reduced Whig electoral support (see page 192).

The Tories were effective in their opposition as they had strength in both numbers and speakers. Key Tories, such as Peel but also Benjamin Disraeli and William Gladstone (see pages 150–1), as well as former Whig Stanley, were able to out-debate their Whig opponents in the House of Commons.

By 1839, Melbourne's government was in a critical position. Melbourne decided to resign and asked Queen Victoria (1837–1901) to invite Peel to form a government. Peel refused, unless the queen agreed to replace her **ladies of the bedchamber** with the wives of Tory ministers. The queen rebuffed the notion and Melbourne was forced to continue as prime minister. Peel's refusal was a surprising but wise tactic. Melbourne was left leading a divided government which barely controlled a majority vote, but he also appeared to have clung to power by relying on the queen's authority. This made him look weak, and was humiliating for a party which sought the reduce the monarch's influence in parliament. This event became known as the 'Bedchamber Crisis'.

> **KEY TERM**
>
> **Ladies of the bedchamber** Personal attendants to the queen. These were traditionally from noble families.

Table 6.1 Key achievements of the Whig governments in the 1830s

Year	Achievement	Notes
1833	The abolition of slavery	With the support of the Whig majority, abolitionists were able to extend the 1807 Act by passing a bill to ban slavery in the entire British Empire. However, the agreement to pay £20 million to former slave owners shows the continued influence of West Indian traders in parliament
	The Factory Act	The earlier Factory Acts of 1802 and 1819 were extended. The 1833 Act prohibited the employment of children under nine in textile factories, and limited working days to eight hours up to age thirteen, and twelve hours up to age eighteen
	Education Grant	A small grant of £20,000 was given for existing church societies that supported the building of schools in Britain
1834	Poor Law Amendment Act	The Poor Law 1601 was replaced by an amendment, becoming known as the New Poor Law. This abolished certain popular types of poor relief in favour of workhouses which were to be locally funded and managed
	Smallpox vaccinations	Vaccinations were provided free of charge through the Poor Law system
1835	Municipal Corporations Act	This law replaced old oligarchies of Tory, Anglican landed elites who ran towns. Instead, elected town councils with official powers were created
1836	Tithe Commutation Act	This law, which affected England and Wales, allowed people to pay their tithe to the Church in money, not goods. It mainly benefited farmers. It was extended to Ireland in 1837
	Marriage Act	Marriages could be held in Nonconformist churches, with a government registrar and two witnesses. To keep Anglicans happy, the licence needed was expensive and unnecessary in an Anglican marriage
1838	Pluralities Act	Clergymen were banned from holding more than one parish responsibility and salary without permission from the Archbishop of Canterbury

In 1841, a failed Whig budget and a vote of no confidence in Melbourne led to a premature general election and a comprehensive Whig defeat. Tories won 367 seats with 50.9 per cent of the vote; this increase, combined with the Whigs losing further seats to the new **Irish Repeal Party**, meant that Peel's government effectively had a majority of 76 over Liberal MPs.

The Conservative Party under Peel

How far had Peel reformed the Conservative Party by his policies in opposition?

Peel reformed the party in several ways:

- He unified it by bringing Ultras and more moderate Tories together.
- He presented the Conservatives as a moderate, patriotic party which would use reform to stabilise, not change British institutions.
- He encouraged the growth of a middle-class support base which broadened its support.

That Peel went on to repeal the Corn Laws in 1846 was evidence that the party had reformed into a more relevant, forward-looking party.

Historian Norman Gash (1986) sees Peel as a leader who formed a new party ideology and allowed the Conservative Party to be politically relevant. David Roberts (1999) argued that it was Peel's appeal to recently enfranchised industrialists, who represented the changing British economy and society, that made the basis for the reformed party.

The 1841 election showed the reformed strength of the Tories as the Conservative Party. It was the first time in British electoral history that a government was replaced by another purely on the results of an election; the electoral overthrow of a government would not happen again until 1874. However, the evidence of the 1841 election suggests that the victory was less the result of campaigning in newly enfranchised urban areas, but rather the winning back of traditional voters in rural areas. Ultimately, only a little more than three per cent of the population were able to vote and only 47 per cent of constituencies were contested. Of the 367 Conservative MPs elected, 212 (58 per cent) were unopposed. By contrast, only 42 per cent of Whig/Liberal-won seats were uncontested.

Additionally, much of the work of reforming the Conservative Party was organisational, done by Tory MPs restoring their powerbases, not by Peel. The Tory agent F.R. Bonham did much to create a national party structure, for example creating the Carlton Club, which acted as a headquarters for co-ordinating voter registration, candidate selection and canvassing for votes.

When did the Tories and Whigs become the Conservatives and Liberals?

There is no clear-cut point when the parties changed. The transformation can be seen as a process beginning with the Tamworth Manifesto (Conservatives) and Lichfield Compact (Liberals). From the 1841 election the Tories were operating as the Conservative Party. Newspapers were referring to members of the Whig and radical alliance as Liberals, but the Liberal Party as an organisation formed more slowly. Liberal Whigs and radicals of the 1830s bonded with Conservative supporters of Peel who split from the Conservative Party after the repeal of the Corn Laws in 1846. By 1859 they had become the Liberal Party.

ONLINE EXTRAS
AQA **WWW**

Learn how to construct arguments and counter-arguments by completing Worksheet 20 at **www. hoddereducation.co.uk/ accesstohistory/extras**

SUMMARY DIAGRAM

WHIG AND TORY POLITICS IN THE 1830S

Pressures on government:	Limits on the Whig reform programme:
• Irish nationalist demands • Anti-Poor Law League • Anti-Corn Law League • Chartism (from 1838)	• A shortage of strong party leaders • Melbourne as a conservative Whig PM • Peel's tactics

Conservative Party strengthened	Whig reforms limited in quantity and significance

---

2 Peel as prime minister from 1841

◼ *What were the achievements of Peel as prime minister?*

It has been argued that since becoming prime minister, Peel had taken on the role of national leader and betrayed his role as party leader. Reasons for this include:

▪ Peel's key reforms (the repeal of the Corn Laws, as well as other economic reforms and the treatment of Ireland) divided the Conservative Party and were not the protectionist policies that many Tory MPs had used to win their seats.

▪ In 1841, Peel wrote that he saw the role of prime minister as based on his 'sincere conception of public duty' and that he must be 'the instrument of maintaining opinions and feeling which I myself am disposed to repudiate'. Some historians have interpreted this to mean that he thought that the interests of the political party should be subordinate to national interest.

Additionally, historian Terry Jenkins (1999) argued that Peel saw himself as the queen's minister first and foremost, and a Conservative second, and therefore would follow national interest before his own party. Yet, it could be argued that Peel was continuing his 1830s' policy, and, rather than betraying his party, he was striving to use moderate, controlled reform to keep his party relevant. Norman Gash (1976) has taken this a step further by claiming that Peel's national leadership was more effective than his party leadership, and that, for Peel, there was no conflict between the two roles.

Peel's leadership

One hallmark of Peel's leadership was that he was almost dictatorial. The young William Gladstone, in the cabinet from 1843, noted that business was conducted by Peel individually with each department head, rather than as a whole cabinet, particularly foreign policy. He would often scrutinise and even amend dispatches written by the foreign secretary, Lord Aberdeen, before they were sent to British ambassadors. He felt that Aberdeen was too pacifist, especially where France was involved.

Financial reform under Peel's Conservative government 1841–6

Like Pitt (see pages 10–14), Peel was particularly focused on addressing administration and the economy. This is understandable; he had come to power amid the economic crisis that contributed to the growth of Chartism (see page 127). He believed that lowering tariffs and stimulating trade was crucial to reduce the £7.5 million budget deficit and avoid social discontent. Peel's financial policies (see pages 174–7) spanned three main areas:

- *Budgets.* In 1842 and 1845, Peel introduced budgets which reduced tariffs, particularly on corn. By the late 1840s, many tariffs were either substantially lower (such as on sugar) or had been completely abolished.

- *Income tax.* Peel reintroduced income tax temporarily to compensate for the reduction of tariff income.

- *Legislation.* As well as legislation which affected tariffs, Peel introduced measures aimed at stabilising the financial system. He passed the Bank Charter Act (1844), which among other duties gave the Bank of England an administrative role over other banks, and the Companies Act (1844) to regulate businesses. These contributed to a stronger economy.

Administrative reform under Peel

Peel also drove administrative reform, although much of this work was due to William Gladstone (the Board of Trade) and Sir James Graham (the Home Office), who were known for careful attention to detail. The management of government business became more professional and efficient:

- **Royal Commissions** were assigned to research social and economic issues. Findings were used as evidence for shaping social and economic policy. Examples include investigating:
  - ☐ ways of improving the quality of the London metropolis and communications within it (1843–51)
  - ☐ large cities, with a focus on diseases and public health (1843–8)
  - ☐ railway gauges (1845–6).
- Economic reforms, such as the aforementioned Bank Charter Act (1844) and the Companies Act (1844).
- District bankruptcy courts were established which addressed local cases of **insolvency**. This ended prison as a punishment for being in debt.
- District county courts were organised into a uniform system.

Peel's handling of Ireland

When Peel came to power in 1841, the Irish Repeal movement (see page 118) was re-emerging. Peel saw the need to act against O'Connell's radical ideas, but he equally recognised that there was an underlying social discontent to be resolved. His policies concerning Ireland were therefore to undermine and prevent the radical Repeal movement, while encouraging the Irish middle class to appreciate the benefits of developing strong links with Britain. This meant treating Catholics as equals and making the emancipation laid out in the 1828 law (see page 56) a greater reality in practice.

Peel refused to accept any of O'Connell's demands for political concessions, and opposed the Repeal movement's political activities. The movement's tactic was the so-called 'Monster Meetings' (coined in the British newspaper *The Times*, in mockery). These were an attempt to show political strength to the government through a series of public meetings at key Irish historical sites. O'Connell was the main speaker, addressing an enthusiastic crowd about reinstating the Irish Parliament. At one meeting in August 1843, the crowd reportedly reached 800,000. Peel sent troops to Ireland to prevent mass protest. In October, Peel's government banned a Monster Meeting of the Repeal movement at Clontarf. O'Connell backed down and cancelled the meeting, but was arrested and imprisoned a week later on charges of seditious conspiracy. This effectively ended the threat of the Repeal movement at that time.

To alleviate the fundamental problem behind this movement, Peel took action to improve the situation of the Irish middle classes:

- In 1844, he appointed Lord Heytesbury as lord-lieutenant of Ireland, who was willing to recruit Catholic magistrates and civil servants.
- In 1844, Peel established a commission on the question of **land tenure**, rural poverty and landlord–tenant relations in Ireland.
- The Charitable Bequests Act 1844 made it easier for Catholics to leave money or land to the Catholic Church in their will.

KEY TERMS

Royal Commission A committee formed by the monarch to investigate a specific issue for the government, with the aim of informing future legislation.

Insolvency When a person or business does not have the money to cover their bills.

Land tenure The issue of who owns the land and what their rights are.

- In 1845, he tripled the budget of the Catholic seminary at Maynooth to £26,000 and made it a permanent responsibility of the British government. Additionally, he made a one-off payment of £30,000 to improve the quality of the institution. It had a reputation for low academic standards, which meant that only sons from lower social orders were sent there. Peel thought that this was contributing to the link between the Catholic Church and the nationalist movement. By raising standards, more moderate families would send their sons, which would in turn moderate attitudes within the Church.

- Peel established three new secular colleges, in Belfast, Galway and Cork, for middle-class Catholics to train for careers in law or the civil service. Catholics and Protestants alike criticised these 'godless colleges'.

The Maynooth Crisis

Peel's decision to fund the training of Catholic priests was opposed by many hard-line Anglicans. The Duke of Wellington wrote in his diary that it was a 'popish plot'; Gladstone resigned from the cabinet for similar reasons. *Punch* magazine described Peel as 'turning and twisting like an eel'. For many, this was the renewal of the Catholic emancipation debate (see page 56). Peel's calculation was that the decision was necessary to alleviate the growing pressure in Ireland, despite the damage to his reputation.

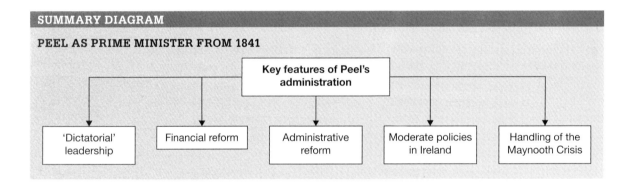

SUMMARY DIAGRAM

PEEL AS PRIME MINISTER FROM 1841

Key features of Peel's administration

- 'Dictatorial' leadership
- Financial reform
- Administrative reform
- Moderate policies in Ireland
- Handling of the Maynooth Crisis

3 Peel's fall from power

- *Why did Peel have to resign in 1846?*

The dual strands of Peel's focus on economic policy and Irish discontent combined in his policy on the Corn Laws.

Peel and the Corn Laws

The Corn Laws had been in place since 1815 (see page 47). Maintaining the Corn Laws was seen as a betrayal of the working population of Britain, as well as industrialist Tories who were concerned that their workers were facing high food prices solely for the benefit of rural landowners. The strongest opposition came from the **Anti-Corn Law League** (ACLL). Yet, if Peel repealed the Corn Laws, he ran the risk of betraying the party, many of whom had won seats in 1841 on a campaign of protectionism; at the time, the *Buckinghamshire Herald* grandly declared 'the great struggle of the general election will arise from the question of [the Corn Laws]'.

Peel's decision to repeal the Corn Laws

In 1845, Peel announced his intention to repeal the Corn Laws and, a year later, introduced the budget to make this law. There are various interpretations of this decision:

- The decision was a response to the Great Famine. In October 1845, famine broke out in Ireland following the failure of the potato crop, a staple food. Peel opened British ports to imported food without tariffs. Peel insisted that the British public would not accept the reimposition of tariffs. He announced his intention to repeal the Corn Laws in December 1845, shortly after the outbreak of the famine. He had not made an explicit statement of intention prior to the famine.

- It was always Peel's long-term goal. Historian Boyd Hilton (1979) argued that Peel used the circumstances of 1846 with famine in Ireland and the ACLL to act, but that he would have acted by the early 1850s anyway. Peel had been in government when Huskisson amended the Corn Laws in 1828 with a sliding tariff scale, so was aware that it was an issue. In the 1842 and 1845 budgets, he showed an intention to reduce tariffs on trade goods.

- Peel adapted his policy in response to his 1842 budget. Peel did not see the repeal of the Corn Laws as a realistic possibility until after he has seen the success of his 1842 budget and subsequent tariff reductions in the face of Conservative backbench opposition. Historians A.A.W. Ramsay (1971) and David Eastwood (1996) consider the changing point to be between 1842 and 1845. There is no evidence that prior to 1844 Peel intended to repeal the Corn Laws, and the earlier 1842 budget was an experiment in tariff reform but it was not directly a challenge to the Corn Law.

- Peel was under pressure from the ACLL. The ACLL created a pressure for Peel to act. Historian G.M. Trevelyan (1945) saw them as a powerful political force in key industrial constituencies. Stephen Lee (1994) revised this view to argue that the role of the ACLL was more in publicising the debate, persuading the Whig opposition to support repeal and give speeches, and in pressuring the House of Lords to pass the Commons bill through fear of popular unrest. The ACLL had a strong middle-class support; Peel wanted to win over this part of the electorate. A number of politicians in 1841 and subsequent by-elections, such as **Richard Cobden** and **John Bright**, won seats on manifestos that supported free trade. Peel may have been affected by the many speeches given in the Commons by supporters of repeal.

KEY TERM

Anti-Corn Law League
A political movement, formed initially in 1836 and which became a national movement in 1838. It focused on persuading the government to abolish the Corn Laws.

· ·

KEY FIGURES

Richard Cobden (1804–65)

An English industrialist who was heavily involved in the movement for free trade and also a founder of the Anti-Corn Law League. He gained a reputation as an MP for being vocal in demanding reform in these areas.

John Bright (1811–89)

A Quaker politician, and political partner of Cobden in leading the Anti-Corn Law League. He was renowned as a public speaker, and regularly gave speeches on free trade, the Corn Laws and religious freedom. He was known as a defender of the middle classes against the privileged position of the landed elite. When he joined Gladstone's first cabinet in 1868, he became the first Nonconformist politician to sit in a government cabinet.

· ·

- The reform was a strategic retreat. J.D. Chambers and G.E. Mingay (1966) argued was that Peel was protecting the Conservative Party and traditional elites with the same tactics he had followed as an opposition leader. He was protecting trade and the landed interests, despite their fears, and using moderate reform to prevent radical reform. He wanted to keep the Conservative Party relevant in a changing age. The Tamworth Manifesto of 1834 had shown his view of using limited reform to protect. Peel had previously shown willingness to act in what he saw as national and party interests regardless of party responses. Peel was aware of the broader danger from Irish nationalism and Chartism if food prices stayed high.

How Peel fell from power

Despite the transformation of the Conservative Party, it was still not a cohesive force. Peel's fall from power in 1846 was either the result of his poor management of the party, which divided into factions, or because he was overwhelmed by the backbench opposition from Conservatives who did not agree with his policies.

The events of the fall

The backlash to Peel's intention to repeal the Corn Laws in 1845 was instantaneous. The inflexible Lord Stanley resigned from Peel's cabinet rather than accept a policy that contradicted his protectionist viewpoint. Peel, recognising that he would struggle to pass the bill, offered to resign in favour of a Whig government under Lord Russell which could cooperate with free-trade Tories to repeal the Corn Laws. Russell considered that such a government would lack a sufficient majority to govern effectively, and rejected the idea. Peel accepted the invitation of Victoria to remain in office in order to pass what he saw as a measure of compelling national importance.

Many Tories felt doubly betrayed by Peel's decision to repeal the Corn Laws and then to continue in office. In parliamentary debate, Tory MPs Lord Bentinck and Benjamin Disraeli took the lead in ferociously opposing repeal. Disraeli was outspoken and fierce. His eloquent speeches were motived by genuine opinion and the knowledge that the removal of Peel would move him up in the seniority rankings of the party. He called Peel a betrayer, inefficient and short sighted.

The repeal bill passed a second reading in the Commons by 339 votes to 242, but of the 339, only 112 were Conservatives. Over two-thirds of the party had voted against Peel, and only Whig support pushed the bill through. The greatest opposition was from rural constituencies, from which 86 per cent of Tory MPs opposed the law. In urban areas, 50 per cent opposed the bill. The Corn Laws were thus abolished in 1846.

Peel had offended the protectionist Tory MPs who formed the core of the party, and they wanted revenge. Shortly afterwards, Peel's government proposed a new coercion bill to enforce law and order in Ireland.

Despite this being a fairly standard Tory approach to Ireland at the time, protectionist Tories were prepared to support the Whigs in defeating the bill. Bentinck and 70 Tories voted against the bill, while a further 80 abstained from voting. Peel resigned as prime minister four days later.

The legacy of Peel's fall from power

Peel's fall caused an irreparable split in the Conservative Party. The party majority turned to the leadership of the Earl of Derby (see Lord Stanley, page 111) and Disraeli. Disraeli gave speeches in which he clearly insisted that the loyalty of party leaders was to the party, whether they were national leaders or not. Peel's supporters remained loyal to him on the backbenches, forming a large faction known as 'Peelite Conservatives', but they could not gather enough support to form a majority government. Neither could Derby's Conservative supporters construct a unified Conservative majority.

Peel died as a result of a riding accident in 1850, but the division within the Conservative Party continued. It did not resolve itself until 1859 when the Peelites formed the Liberal Party with the Whigs, and the core Conservative Party did not form a strong majority Conservative government until 1874, when Disraeli became prime minister.

SOURCE B

'The Fallen Minister', published in the satirical journal *Punch* shortly after the repeal of the Corn Laws in January 1846. It shows Peel, surrounded by Conservative politicians, including Disraeli and Bentinck, who are jeering him.

SOURCE QUESTION

Look at how the artist has portrayed Peel and the Conservatives in Source B. What message was he presenting?

Table 6.2 (see below) considers whether it was solely Peel's own fault that he fell from power.

Table 6.2 Was it solely Peel's fault that he fell from power?

Yes: Peel was responsible	No: there were other reasons
• Peel failed to appreciate the strength of the backlash from the Conservative backbenchers, despite their opposition to previous tariff reductions and policies like the Maynooth grant bill • Peel's style of leadership and confidence in his own opinions did not take into account the viewpoints of other politicians, which created resentment • Peel acted as a national leader even without the support of the majority of his party, which would inevitably shorten his period in power • Peel betrayed what many of his MPs had campaigned for in the 1841 election when he abandoned protectionism and introduced reform in Ireland	• Peel's economic policies were not new – he was continuing an approach followed by Pitt before the Revolutionary Wars and Robinson and Huskisson in the 1820s • The idea that Peel was the leader of a party in the modern sense is anachronistic, despite Disraeli's insistence that the party was supreme. Party political organisation was still developing, meaning that there were no mechanisms to enforce party discipline • Peel faced circumstances, such as the Irish famine, Irish nationalism and Chartism, which required action, whether or not Tory MPs were willing to accept this • The 1850s was a time of great economic change; Peel could be seen as simply adapting to changing socio-economic circumstances

ONLINE EXTRAS
AQA **WWW**

Develop your analysis of Peel's significance by completing Worksheet 21 at **www.hoddereducation. co.uk/accesstohistory/extras**

ONLINE EXTRAS
AQA **WWW**

Learn how to link key points by completing Worksheet 22 at **www.hoddereducation. co.uk/accesstohistory/extras**

SUMMARY DIAGRAM

PEEL'S FALL FROM POWER

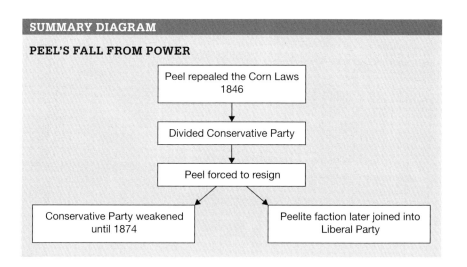

4 Chartism

- *What were the aims and methods of the Chartists?*
- *What was the impact of the Chartists?*

The Chartist movement was a large political protest group. It emerged in the 1830s, frustrated at the limited political rights and poor economic conditions of the working classes in Britain. It saw political reform as the solution. The movement formally emerged in 1838, while Melbourne's Whig government was in office. It continued through Peel's Conservative ministry and fizzled out after 1848, during Russell's Whig government.

The 1832 Reform Act bought renewed demands for the extension of democracy. Radical thinkers from working-class backgrounds felt cheated by the limitations of the Act, especially since many in the political unions had been instrumental in the popular unrest that had influenced the king and House of Lords to accept the bill.

This feeling of betrayal was made worse by the fact that the Whig Factory Act 1833 did not enforce the ten-hour working day that many workers had wanted, nor did it regulate the working hours of those over eighteen years old. Soon afterwards, the Poor Law Amendment Act abolished **outdoor relief**, which had been popular with many poor labourers, in favour of unpleasant workhouses with poor conditions (see page 189). Many labourers found themselves excluded from support or forced to accept terrible circumstances. This was especially problematic when the Act was applied in the north of England, where the scheme designed with rural areas in mind did not suit the conditions of a largely urban workforce. The negative feeling about Whig 'reformers' was exacerbated when a depression hit in 1837 and caused high bread prices and increased unemployment.

> **KEY TERM**
>
> **Outdoor relief** Money, food and clothing that was given to people in poverty. It was 'outdoor' in the sense that they received the help without having to enter a workhouse.

Not only was there a strong anti-government popular sentiment in the 1830s, but there was also a pre-existing radical tradition for extra-parliamentary protest. This had developed in the late eighteenth and early nineteenth centuries, and became revitalised with organisations such as the Birmingham Political Union (see page 59) during the late 1820s. In London and industrial centres such as Manchester and Leeds, there were core groups of politically aware, working-class men who continued to demand the same political rights that radicals had insisted on for the previous 40 years. Even the charter that they agreed on was based on proposals that radicals had been discussing since the 1780s.

Who were the Chartists?

The Chartists were initially formed from a core of the London Working Men's Association (LWMA), led by the radicals William Lovett and Francis Place. They were joined by six radical MPs and several reformist groups, and wrote and signed a People's Charter in 1838, from which they took the name Chartists. The charter contained six principles:

- Universal suffrage for all men aged over 21 who were of sound mind and were not criminals. Some individuals wanted universal suffrage to include women, and Lovett claimed to have included female suffrage in the first draft of the charter, but then removed it to seem more moderate.
- Secret ballots in elections, to free voters from control by landlords and reduce corruption.
- Abolition of the property qualifications for MPs (£600 in rural constituencies, £300 in urban constituencies).
- Introduction of salaries for MPs, to open parliament to candidates without a private salary.
- A redrawing of constituency boundaries to equalise the size of the electorate.
- Annual parliamentary elections to make MPs more accountable to the electorate.

Some historians have seen the Chartists as 'hunger politics', political demand driven by political crises. It is true that the greatest support was in 1838–9, 1842 and 1848, years of economic depression. Yet the political aim of the movement should not be forgotten; the anger at political decisions in the 1830s was just as important in motivating protest. If the Chartists were purely an economic protest, one would expect that the reforms of Peel's government, such as reducing tariffs, should have reduced the need for Chartist protest. Yet the resurgence of Chartist activity in 1842 coincided with some of Peel's key reforms – which improved economic conditions. Chartism was not simply a response, therefore, to economic circumstances. The demands of the movement were about giving a voice to those who had been underrepresented.

ONLINE EXTRAS
Pearson Edexcel **WWW**

Develop your analysis of the factors behind the emergence of Chartism by completing Worksheet 23 at **www.hoddereducation.co.uk/accesstohistory/extras**

Chartist leadership

Rather than one leader, there were several individuals who led the Chartists. The two most significant were William Lovett and Feargus O'Connor (see Table 6.3, page 129).

What were the methods of the Chartists?

The prime tactics of the Chartists were conventions, petitions and rallies. Behind this, there was a simmering threat of violence.

The organised Chartist campaign began in 1839 with a meeting known as the National Convention to discuss making a petition to Parliament. The National Convention consisted of 53 members, 25 of whom were from London, twenty from northern England and eight from Birmingham. Initially, they met in London but soon disagreements broke out over the use of force, the role of local organisations in a national movement and what to do if the petition failed. The National Convention moved to Birmingham and planned a so-called 'sacred month', or general strike, and a run on the banks.

Table 6.3 Chartist leadership

William Lovett	Feargus O'Connor
• Founding member of the Chartists and secretary to the LWMA	• An Irish lawyer and MP, until he was disqualified for not meeting the property qualification
• He was involved in writing the People's Charter	• He owned the Chartist newspaper, the *Northern Star*, which was a main method of spreading the Chartist message – it sold 36,000 copies weekly
• Secretary for the National Convention	
• Insisted on non-violent protest	• In 1847 he was again an MP, which gave the Chartists a voice in parliament
• Spent a year in prison for protesting against the police use of violence against Chartists	• He was deeply divisive
	• His political ideas were unfocused and often impractical
• Focused on uniting working- and middle-class support, and worked closely with the middle-class Birmingham-based Universal Suffrage Association	• His Land Plan, an investment scheme for workers to buy plots of land, turned into a humiliating failure
	• He wrote articles criticising almost every other Chartist leader, and used the *Northern Star* to publish them
• Also gave his time and attention to other issues, including educational reform and anti-slavery campaigns	• He spoke of using violence as a tactic, which worried moderates, but never became personally involved in such tactics, which led to accusations of cowardice from some Chartists

Chartist petitions

The first Chartist petition was presented to parliament in June 1839 with 1.2 million signatures. This was rejected by parliament by an overwhelming majority of 235 votes to 46, a result which caused chaos among the Chartists: radicals were ready to turn to rebellion while moderates wanted to continue with constitutional methods. The proposed general strike was rejected. Riots broke out in Birmingham and violence occurred between Chartists and the police.

In November 1839, an uprising broke out in Newport, south Wales. Five thousand miners, many of who were armed, marched to protest about imprisoned Chartists and demanded their release. Violence broke out between the marchers and soldiers sent to stop them, leading to the deaths of 24 Chartists and the arrest of 125. Twenty-five of these 125 were charged with treason. Between June 1839 and June 1840, over 500 Chartists were arrested. By late 1840, the Chartist movement was leaderless and all but disintegrated.

The National Charter Association

The National Charter Association (NCA) was formed in 1840 in Manchester to continue the struggle. Initially, this grew slowly; the financial subscriptions were unaffordable for many potential members, and the 1799 Corresponding Societies Act (see page 23) banned organisations which had local branches. This put many off joining. The radical Feargus O'Connor was also heavily involved, which discouraged more moderate Chartist leaders. Once a way around the 1799 law was found – local leaders were assigned instead of being chosen, which avoided the definition of 'local branches' – numbers rose, until in late 1842 there were 70,000 registered members.

In 1842, the movement re-emerged when a second National Convention was organised. A new petition was written and contained 3.3 million signatures. On top of the main six Chartist aims (see page 128), this petition also attacked the 'unconstitutional police force', the 1834 Poor Law, factory conditions, Church taxes on Nonconformists and the high income of Queen Victoria in comparison to the national working majority. This was rejected again, by 287 votes to 49. A series of mass strikes broke out in response, first by miners in Staffordshire and then by Lancashire textile workers. Mobs of strikers toured the north and midlands of England, enforcing strikes by removing the plugs from boilers to prevent work; this led to the nickname 'Plug Plot' for the strikes. Between July and September 1842, fifteen English and Welsh counties and eight Scottish counties were affected. Yet, without a strong central leadership or system of unions, the strikes fizzled out and the convention dissolved again. The NCA also lost many members, although they remained the central national organisation through the 1840s.

? SOURCE QUESTION

What can you learn from Sources C and D about the Chartist movement?

SOURCE C

Part of a song published in the *Northern Star*, the Chartist newspaper, in February 1841.

Loud roar'd the people's thunder,
And tyrants heard the storm,
They trembled, and knocked under,
And gave us mock reform.

At length the People's Charter
Shoots forth its beacon rays!
She deepens now her water,
The tide around her plays.

Our pilot, brave O'Connor
We soon will get on board
More sail we'll crowd upon her,
And get her richly stored.

SOURCE D

Extract of a fictional story, called *The Confessions of a King* by Ernest Jones. Jones was a Chartist who helped O'Connor to publish a sister journal for the *Northern Star*, called *The Labourer*. In this passage, Jones imagines an unnamed king about to die who has realised the folly of his aristocratic ways.

I'm a bad man – I confess it, I'm a humbug – for I tried to blind the world and blinded only myself… I owed my elevation to the throne, to a blunder made by a silly old fellow who thought to crush the people… and the people then, having it in their power to establish a republic, were fools enough to make me king instead. I though, as they were so stupid, I should be able to do what I liked with them, but I have since found, it was not the people but the middle class that did it, and the day of the former was yet to come.

ONLINE EXTRAS OCR **WWW**

Practise your source analysis skills by completing Worksheet 25 at **www. hoddereducation.co.uk/ accesstohistory/extras**

Physical force versus moral force

There was a division in ideology over the best tactics to be used. Some Chartists, headed by William Lovett, believed that the petitions and marches needed to be rooted in peace and avoid violence. They were concerned that outbreaks of violence villainised the Chartists and weakened their moral argument. On the other hand, there were some groups, such as the strikers involved in the 'Plug Plot' strikes, who believed that physical action was needed. The memories of the protests that had contributed to the 1832 Reform Act justified more direct action. This was exacerbated by the speeches and articles of O'Connor, who encouraged violence as a tactic, although he never took such action himself.

1848: A desperate fiasco

In 1848, a revolutionary fervour was spreading across Europe, and at the same time an economic depression led to riots across Birmingham and Glasgow. A third National Convention was organised. The Chartist leaders, primarily Feargus O'Connor, attempted to use this to further their own importance within the movement. A third petition was presented to parliament by the Chartist leaders, with O'Connor declaring that it held 6 million signatures.

O'Connor organised a meeting on Kennington Common in London followed by a march on Westminster to present the petition. The government, fearing violence in the capital, summoned soldiers and recruited special constables to control the event. The government banned the march, although not the peaceful meeting. The threat of government force and an untimely downpour meant that few turned out for the march – the Chartists claimed that 150,000 attended but the government insisted only 12,000–15,000 attended. Three days later, the Commons Committee for Public Petitions claimed to have counted the signatures and found only 2 million. They further claimed that fraudulent signatures (such as Her Majesty, Duke of Wellington and Sir Robert Peel) and joke signatures (such as 'Flat Nose' and 'No Cheese') were on the petition. O'Connor claimed that this governmental review was a lie, but the petition was discredited. In the end, only fifteen MPs voted to accept it.

Support for Chartism

There were several forms of support for Chartism.

Massed national support

Although Chartism was fundamentally comprised of local organisations, it was simultaneously a national movement. O'Connor's NCA offered a national structure, as did touring national leaders and lecturers. Each petition had between 2 and 3 million signatures (assuming the parliamentary commission was correct about the third petition), which is impressive considering the national population in 1841 was about 10 million. O'Connor's radical newspaper the *Northern Star* had peak sales of 50,000 per issue, which historian John

SOURCE QUESTION

What can we learn from Source E about the 1848 rally? Does this photograph change or confirm your view of the Chartist movement?

SOURCE E

This image, the only surviving photograph of the Chartist movement, is of the 1848 rally on Kennington Common. It was taken by William Kilburn.

Charlton (1997) suggests may mean a readership of 200,000, given that newspapers were regularly passed around.

Traditional trades

The names on the three petitions show a predominance of handcraft workers: weavers, framework knitters and wool-combers from the textiles industry, shoemakers and tailors. Of the 716 delegates to the general council of the NCA in 1841, these five jobs made up 47 per cent. These were jobs that were being threatened by the increase in industrialised processes in the 1830s and 1840s. This supports the claim that the Chartists were primarily motivated by economic concerns. However, there were a variety of other trades involved, including school teaching, engineering, printing and hairdressing, which were not trades that were disappearing.

Regional support

The initial Chartist movement was predominantly based in southern England. The LWMA (see page 127) and half of the first National Convention were from London. Southern Chartists tended to be more moderate. The movement was also supported in Birmingham, where there was a core radical support existing in the Birmingham Political Union (see page 59).

Increasingly, the north of Britain became more important in the Chartist movement. It was the attempts in 1836–7 to apply the Poor Law to the north that gave impetus to the movement, when the new system of workhouses impacted heavily in industrial areas, to a far greater degree than in southern, more rural counties. The areas with the worst economic conditions, such as Manchester, Leeds, Stockport, Newcastle and Glasgow, were those most politically underrepresented. For example, Manchester was given only two MPs in the 1832 Reform Act for a population of over 144,000, the majority of whom did not qualify to vote. This inspired the demand for political representation as a step towards dealing with economic discontent. Evidence of northern influence can be seen in the first national petition, in which 19,000 signatures came from London but 100,000 from the West Riding of Yorkshire (an area in the north of England).

Northern Chartists had the tendency to be more radical. During the years of the petitions, particularly 1838–9, they collected weapons and formed local militias. As northern support grew, the more moderate southern support waned, which skewed the movement to the north of England even more.

Class support

The Chartist movement was predominantly working class, motivated by concerns over the lack of political representation, economic hardship and the imposition of the Poor Law.

However, there was also middle-class, and, to a limited degree, landed gentry (see page 2) support for the Chartist movement. This included industrialists who sympathised with the rights of their workers. Initially, middle-class support was important. Several attendees of the first National Convention were middle class. With the Birmingham riots and Newport Uprising in 1839, middle-class support nationally decreased. One exception was Birmingham, where a group called the Complete Suffrage Union united working- and middle-class supporters in demanding universal suffrage and the repeal of the Corn Laws.

Support from women

The People's Charter demanded universal suffrage for men aged over 21 and the movement itself was predominantly male, yet had large support from women. In the 1840s there were over 100 female radical organisations in Britain. In Hyde, near Manchester, for example, the local organisation had 300 male members and 200 female members. Chartist women did not take the lead in giving speeches, but they did sew banners, join marches and give gifts to visiting speakers. Women may have made up to twenty per cent of audiences at public Chartist events.

A good number of Chartist women were charged with public order offences. When a Chartist speaker was pelted with stones in Cirencester in 1839, those responsible were reportedly 'given a thrashing' by a group of female Chartists.

Some women formed female-only Chartist organisations, such as the East London Female Patriotic Association. These groups usually campaigned to

ONLINE EXTRAS
Pearson Edexcel WWW

Test your understanding
of the strengths and
weaknesses of the Chartist
movement by completing
Worksheet 24 at www.
hoddereducation.co.uk/
accesstohistory/extras

Hustings

The election day was
known as the hustings.
In simple terms, voters
had to make their way
to a wooden platform
and declare who they
were voting for. These
were drunken, violent
affairs. It was common for
supporters of candidates
to try to prevent opposing
voters from reaching
the platform, while the
candidates themselves
often provided free beer
to people coming to vote
for them. Candidates
would give speeches
while the supporters of
the opposing candidates
tried to drown them out
by shouting. It was not
uncommon for rioting
to break out following
the announcement of
the winner in contested
elections.

extend the idea of universal suffrage to include female suffrage. This was met with a mixed response from male Chartists; many opposed the possibility of women holding political office. This was especially the case with Feargus O'Connor's Physical Force Chartists, who believed that women did not have the physical capability for political roles. This was for two reasons. First, it was not considered safe for a woman to attend election days, or hustings, because they were usually violent (voters were provided with alcohol and thugs were paid to disrupt the elections). Second, it was claimed at the time that women did not have the mental or physical capability to cope with discussing political topics.

The impact of Chartism

The Chartist movement had very little impact in a direct sense. Chartists failed to achieve any of their objectives during the time that they were active. The main impact of Chartism could be said to be that it gave valuable political experience to thousands of men and women. Many of these people would later become involved in more successful movements, such as the movement for women's suffrage, the trade unions and socialist organisations. Many of the members of the Chartists went on to be involved in these organisations, and they took their ideas and tactics with them. For this reason, later political protest organisations were heavily influenced in using marches, petitions and speeches.

The Chartists also demonstrated the existence of a political consciousness among the working classes which was not just a mob but a group demanding specific political aims. This awareness contributed to the increased involvement of grass-roots organisations within political parties between 1840 and 1885 (see pages 137 and 142). Many former Chartists became involved in these organisations.

Although the Chartists cannot claim any direct impact, their ideas did not die out. By 1918, five of the six demands of the Chartists had become law. However, it is crucial to note that the circumstances for each of the five changes were not a direct consequence of the actions of Chartists (see Table 6.4, below).

With the failure of the 1848 petition, the Chartist movement disappeared. Different factors and interpretations explain this.

Table 6.4 Chartist demands and their later outcomes

Chartist policy	Later Act that introduced the change
Universal suffrage	1918 Representation of the People Act
Secret ballots	1872 Ballot Act
Abolition of the property qualifications for MPs	1858 Property Qualification for Members of Parliament Act
Introduction of salaries for MPs	1911 Parliament Act
Equally distributed constituencies	1885 Redistribution Act
Annual parliamentary elections	Not achieved

Economic issues

- The simplest explanation is that the movement was motivated by the distressing economic conditions which deteriorated in 1836–7, exacerbated by the Poor Law. Consequently, when the economy improved by the late 1840s, the appeal of, and support for, Chartism, declined.

- This partly explains the collapse. However, studies have shown that the improvement in the economy was not as sustained as sometimes assumed. For example, historian Hugh Cunningham (1994) showed that in eight of the fourteen years between 1851 and 1864, real wage values were below pre-1850 levels.

- The growth of the railways meant that by the 1850s, the iron, steel and coal industries were stronger, and economic growth was greater than in the 1830s. This benefited more workers in the north.

- Legislation which introduced New Model Unions (see page 218) meant that the wealthiest ten to fifteen per cent of the working classes, previously potential leaders of local working-class discontent, had a role working with managers. They were more likely to work with middle-class managers than against them, and to seek gradual change rather than wholesale revolutionary reform.

Inherent weaknesses

- The Chartists were a national movement, but they lacked a unifying structure. The leaders did not offer a clear vision or direction.

- Individual local organisations had different aims, including different views on female suffrage.

- The division in ideology between physical force and moral force created not only internal division but also regional division.

- There was division between the leaders. Lovett, for example, was moderate and objected to the aggressive tactics of O'Connor. O'Connor, in turn, used his newspaper and speeches to attack moderate Chartist leaders as well as the government.

- The movement suffered when the leaders were distracted. Lovett was heavily involved in other campaigns over slavery and education. O'Connor was sidetracked by theories on land ownership. His complicated **Land Plan**, an investment scheme to buy plots of land, collapsed in legal and economic problems and discredited the Chartists.

- The Chartists could not agree on whether ending the Corn Laws was an important aim or only useful if accompanied by laws controlling wages. This alienated a middle-class pressure movement which could have been a strong support.

- The Chartists demanded too much, too quickly. In contrast, the Anti-Corn Law League, which focused on repealing one single, simple piece of legislation, was successful (see page 123).

> **KEY TERM**
>
> **Land Plan** Chartist leader Feargus O'Connor organised an investment scheme to buy land, with the idea that shareholders would get enough land to gain the vote. The scheme was badly planned, and it could not provide all shareholders with land. The government investigated it and found that it did not meet the requirements for legal registration. It was shut down in 1851. The whole scheme discredited the Chartist leadership.

State opposition

- The government used repression to prevent Chartist protests. When the Kensington Common meeting (1848) took place, Chartists faced 7000 soldiers, 4000 regular police and thousands of temporary special constables. This was an overwhelming force.

- Ministers supported the use of force. In 1842, when protestors in Preston were shot, the home secretary sent his personal congratulations to the mayor of Preston on having the courage to take action.

- The 1835 Municipal Corporations Act empowered local authorities to have professional police forces. This enabled local justices of the peace to manage local strikes or protests with ease.

- Sir **Charles Napier**, assigned to command the troops in the north of England, was an effective leader. He disciplined his troops and avoided bloodshed where possible. This prevented Chartist deaths which could have inspired further protest.

KEY FIGURE

Charles Napier (1782–1853)

A soldier with a distinguished military record. He was assigned to command British army units in the north of England. He sympathised with those who suffered as a result of poor economic conditions and so restrained any military action by his officers, instead allowing limited Chartist protests.

ONLINE EXTRAS WWW
AQA

Develop your analysis of the failure of political protest movements 1830–50 by completing Worksheet 23 at **www.hoddereducation. co.uk/accesstohistory/extras**

ONLINE EXTRAS WWW
Pearson Edexcel

Learn how to write balanced arguments by completing Worksheet 25 at **www. hoddereducation.co.uk/ accesstohistory/extras**

ONLINE EXTRAS WWW
Pearson Edexcel

Learn how to address the concept of significance by completing Worksheet 26 at **www.hoddereducation. co.uk/accesstohistory/extras**

SUMMARY DIAGRAM

CHARTISM

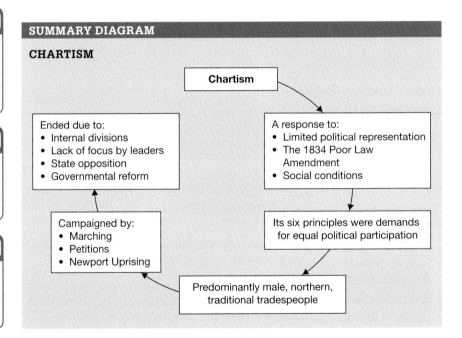

5 Changes to party political structures by 1866

■ *How did the changing political system lead to changing party organisation?*

Throughout the period from 1780 to 1866 the structures of the political parties began to change. They moved from the loose factions of the late eighteenth century to the start of the modern party political system, where politicians are organised into identifiable groups, with clear party manifestos.

Factors contributing to the changing structures

- The gradual reduction in royal power, beginning with the economic reforms of the 1780s (see page 10) and the rise of Pitt's cabinet governments (see page 13), carried on through the 1800s. This was clearly demonstrated in 1834 when King William IV removed Melbourne as prime minister, only to fail in his appointment of Peel which resulted in Melbourne being reappointed (see page 116). Party politics became more important than royal support for building effective governments.

- The 1832 Reform Act accelerated this process by requiring that voters were registered. This immediately forced factions to be more organised about registering supporters, which was initially carried out by local solicitors acting as voluntary agents. However, the parties soon established centralised organisations to register voters in the form of the Conservative Carlton Club (1832) and the Whig Reform Club (1836). Although their links to local areas were still forming, it was a step towards the idea of a formal party. In addition, increasingly, politicians needed to win voters over, not just return seats that they controlled, as the number of contested elections increased after 1832.

- The 1834 Tamworth Manifesto (see page 115) was printed nationally and has been considered an early prototype of a national manifesto with a whole-party policy (although many Tory MPs campaigned in the following elections on policies that contradicted the manifesto).

- The 1835 Lichfield Compact brought Whig, Irish and radical MPs into an alliance that held for several years and became known as, collectively, Liberals. The practice of agreeing areas of common interest contributed to the formation of a party mindset in a more modern sense.

- In the 1840s, Peel's policies split the Conservatives, leading to his eventual resignation following the repeal of the Corn Laws (see page 124). In this can be seen clearer ideologies forming along more defined party policies. The majority stayed loyal to Bentinck and Disraeli, but about 100 followed Peel. While nominally Conservatives, they acted as a separate faction. This showed that clear identities were forming among the groups of politicians.

Over the twenty years following the 1832 Reform Act, the Conservatives and Liberals struggled with their identities. The Conservatives struggled to accommodate the concept of abandoning trade protection. Instead, they focused on their traditional support of landed interest and rural voters. Party leader Earl of Derby was unable to provide clear leadership, and Disraeli was unable to gain enough party support for his policies of abandoning protectionism. As a result, the Conservatives failed to win a single general election between 1841 and 1874. Between 1846 and 1868, every government was either Whig or Whig–Liberal, with the exception of three short-lived minority Conservative governments.

It is therefore surprising that the Whigs and Liberals did not achieve more in this period. But they were also struggling to form a unified party. The Whigs still saw radical MPs as a dangerous ally, and radicals still saw the Whigs as aristocrats who relied on family connections and were not reforming quickly enough. Four times in the 1850s, Whig–Liberal governments were brought down after losing votes on amendments that had been initiated by radical MPs.

The Peelites did not fit into either side in this period. They were unable to resolve their differences with the core Conservative Party, but unwilling to form a new, smaller political party, and viewed the Whigs as inferior administrators. They also disagreed with the Whigs in key areas, such as expenditure on the military as part of foreign policy.

The 'Who? Who? Ministry'

One of the three short-lived minority Conservative governments between 1846 and 1868 was the Earl of Derby's 1852 ministry, which lasted from February until December. It received the mocking nickname, the 'Who? Who? Ministry' after the now very elderly and deaf Duke of Wellington shouted out 'Who? Who?' as the list of inexperienced cabinet ministers was read out.

The formation of the Liberal Party

Although they were divided on some matters, the Liberal factions of Whigs, radicals and Peelites shared two main areas of agreement:

- broad agreement that free trade was a good thing for an economy
- support for liberal and nationalist movements in Europe.

When, in 1859–60, **Italian unification** became a real possibility, it sparked a debate in Britain about political unification. This led to a meeting in 1859, where the Liberal factions agreed that they would cooperate politically over their shared support of Italian unification.

This closer alliance led to the formation of the Liberal Party, out of Whig, radical and Peelite MPs in the years 1859–68. The first leader of the Liberal Party was Lord Palmerston (see page 56). He gives a good idea of the middle ground that the party had formed from. He was an aristocrat, had started his career as a Tory MP, become a Whig from 1830, and now led a party which was formed of both. Following Palmerston's death in 1865, Lord Russell, the former Whig prime minister (1846–52), who had supported reformist policies for his career, replaced Russell as party leader (see page 110).

The party was not in itself new, nor did its social make-up differ from earlier parties. In the 1860s, only about one third of Liberal MPs came from middle-class backgrounds. Their leader was an aristocrat, as were many of the leaders of the party, and a number of their seats were still in the hands of landowning families.

KEY TERM

Italian unification
The process of the Italian states overthrowing their Austrian masters and forming a country. In 1859, Sardinia and France succeeded in forcing Austria out of most of Italy, making unification a possibility.

However, the support base for the party was new. The core strength of the party outside London lay in the growing industrial areas of Lancashire, Yorkshire and the midlands. The majority of Liberal voters were from middle-class, Nonconformist backgrounds, who became politicised by their involvement in local council affairs after the 1835 Municipal Corporations Act (see page 117), and through articles in newspapers such as the *Manchester Guardian*, *Leeds Mercury* and *Sheffield Independent*.

The Liberal Party was, therefore, closely connected to reformist and Nonconformist ideas:

- The National Reform Union, a middle-class organisation with mainly former ACLL members, campaigned for the franchise to be extended to all male ratepayers.

- The Reform League, a working-class equivalent to the National Reform Union (which had many old Chartists in its ranks), was more radical and demanded universal male suffrage. Both the Reform League and the National Reform Union were connected to the Liberal Party.

- The Liberation Society, a Nonconformist organisation for the abolition of Church of England tithes and rates, was active within the ranks of Liberal supporters.

- The United Kingdom Alliance (for restrictions on the alcoholic drinks trade) and the National Education League (for reform to provide free education) were supported by Nonconformists and strongly connected to the Liberal Party.

ONLINE EXTRAS **WWW**
AQA
Learn how to link key points by completing Worksheet 24 at **www.hoddereducation. co.uk/accesstohistory/extras**

SUMMARY DIAGRAM

CHANGES TO PARTY POLITICAL STRUCTURES BY 1866

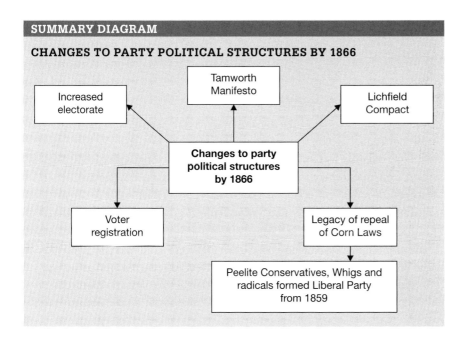

6 The 1867 Reform Act

■ *How did the 1867 Reform Act change the British political system and affect political parties?*

Although the 1832 Act had been judged by many Whig and Conservative politicians to be a complete reform, it had instead created a precedent for reform which led to greater demand. In 1867, a further Reform Act was passed. But whereas 1832 had been a contested struggle between those who supported and those who opposed the Act, in 1867 it was a case of the Liberals and Conservatives competing to pass a Reform Act that favoured their political views.

Gladstone's bill 1866

In 1866, Gladstone, the Commons leader of the Liberal Party in Russell's Liberal government (see page 110), proposed a reform to the parliamentary election system that would extend the terms of the 1832 Reform Act. This was partly the result of Liberal tendencies to reform and a desire to remove corruption from the system, but it was also the result of pressure from the National Reform Union and Reform League (see page 139). The proposal was not radical – Gladstone was a moderate reformer. He proposed that the £10 rental qualification in boroughs be reduced to £7, and a flat rent value of £14 in the counties be applied. The impact of this would add about 200,000 voters, but, more importantly, for the first time this would enfranchise the better-paid artisans among the working classes, while still excluding the uneducated poorest of society. This proved too radical for right-wing Liberals. Robert Lowe, their leader, argued that extending the vote to the working classes would causes a dramatic decline in the character of parliament, due to the influence of people whose only objective was self-interest. The bill was defeated.

The Conservative response

The Tory leaders at the time, Derby and Disraeli (see page 151), realised quickly that if they capitalised on the division among the Liberals, they could create an 'unholy alliance' by working with Liberal MPs who opposed the bill. They proposed an amendment to Gladstone's bill which was passed, forcing the Liberals to resign. Derby formed a Conservative government.

In March 1867, Derby and Disraeli proposed their own version of a reform bill. The intention was to direct the terms of the reform proposed by the Liberals, and to gain credit for it. Disraeli proposed giving the vote to all male householders in the boroughs, but restricting this by a two-year residence qualification and the requirement that householders must pay their own rents. In other words, although all male householders could qualify, the poorest – who often paid their rates in their rent (so-called 'compounders') or who moved house frequently when they were between work – would not qualify. The measures would allow about 400,000 new voters to qualify. Over a series of debates, however, the Conservatives accepted a series of amendments which made the bill more radical. The bill was passed by the Commons and the Lords in 1867.

What were the terms of the 1867 Representation of the People Act?

Like the 1832 Representation of the People Act, the 1867 Act brought parliamentary reform by redistributing seats and amending the voting qualifications. However, the terms of the 1867 Act were far stronger than those of the 1832 Act.

- Redistribution of seats:
  - 53 boroughs which were overrepresented lost their seats; these were redistributed
  - nine new boroughs were created with one seat each
  - two single-seat London constituencies were given a second seat
  - Birmingham, Leeds, Liverpool, Manchester and Salford were given an extra seat each
  - five Scottish boroughs and three Scottish counties were given an extra seat
  - 25 seats went to counties
  - one seat went to Wales
- New voting qualifications:
  - In boroughs, all male householders who paid local rates could vote, and all lodgers who paid £10 a year in rent. The only limit on both was a one-year residency requirement.
  - In the counties, the £50 property qualification was reduced to £12.

In practical terms, the Act added about 700,000 new voters, mainly working class, although still excluded the poorest working classes.

Derby, Disraeli and the Conservatives

It might seem strange that Disraeli would want to extend the franchise with this reform, especially in a more radical form than Gladstone's bill, but there are several explanations which show why it was a logical choice:

- Disraeli knew that the majority Liberals would probably be back in office, so he needed to control the reform and take credit for it before the Liberals could pass it.
- The majority of new voters from 1832 were in the boroughs where the Liberals dominated. Disraeli's redistribution of seats did not give the Liberals much additional advantage, but it strengthened Conservative control in rural areas by separating them from Liberal borough voters.
- There was strong campaigning by the National Reform Union and the Reform League over the winter of 1866–7, in which harsh weather conditions, an economic slump and a **cholera** epidemic increased discontent.

ONLINE EXTRAS AQA WWW

Learn how to write effective introductions by completing Worksheet 25 at **www. hoddereducation.co.uk/ accesstohistory/extras**

ONLINE EXTRAS Pearson Edexcel WWW

Get to grips with the 1867 Reform Act by completing Worksheet 27 at **www. hoddereducation.co.uk/ accesstohistory/extras**

KEY TERM

Cholera A water-borne disease which causes severe dehydration and death.

A protest meeting in Hyde Park in London in May 1867 saw a crowd of 100,000. Despite the government sending at least 10,000 police and soldiers, the government abandoned any attempt to disperse the crowd as it was simply too large. This humiliation for the government showed the potential threat of popular pressure and the working-class solidarity which could not be ignored.

The impact of the 1867 Reform Act

The impact of the 1867 Reform Act is summarised in Table 6.5 (see below).

Table 6.5 The impact of the 1867 Reform Act

Electoral change	• The number of adult males who qualified to vote rose from 20 to 30 per cent • The number of voters in boroughs increased significantly: Manchester from 21,542 in 1866 to 48,256 in 1867; Leeds from 7217 in 1866 to 35,510 in 1867; Birmingham from 15,500 in 1866 to 42,000 in 1867 • There was still an imbalance. For example, south-west England had 76,612 borough voters and 45 MPs, whereas the north-east had 232,431 voters but only 32 MPs • There were still 140 constituencies with electorates under 2000
Constitutional change	• After 1867, general elections became the common way of changing government. Before 1867, most governments had fallen following failed parliamentary bills • General elections were increasingly seen as the way of measuring the opinion of the population on key issues
Party politics	• The two-party system became more important. While not as fixed as in modern politics, MPs relied more on party support and discipline to win seats
A changed view of the vote	• Before 1867, the vote was seen as a privilege. After 1867, the vote was seen more as a fundamental democratic right. This contributed to the rise of the women's suffrage movement in the following decades
A changing role of political parties	• Parties had a far greater role in registering people to vote. They worked to help people carry out the registration process and persuade them to vote • The larger electorate necessitated an increased use of the media and clearer party messages in order to persuade *en masse*. Gladstone, for example, in the 1879–80 election campaign, toured the country by rail, stopping to give speeches which were then printed in newspapers • Parties took a closer interest in selecting local candidates and organising election campaigns
A growth in political activism	• From 1867, Liberal and Conservative organisations spread in towns across the country. Far more people became members • Party organisations began to offer leisure activities with the dual purpose of keeping voters loyal and improving the working-class voters through exposure to middle-class values
Party structure	• The Conservative Party formed a national party structure, through the appointment of a national party agent from 1870 and the spread of Conservative local organisations under the umbrella of the National Union of Conservative and Constitutional Associations • The Liberals developed more slowly. The Reform League functioned as an agency. By 1877, the National Liberal Federation was acting as a central party organisation by overseeing local groups

ONLINE EXTRAS www
Pearson Edexcel

Develop your analysis of
the significance of the 1867
Reform Act by completing
Worksheet 28 at **www.
hoddereducation.co.uk/
accesstohistory/extras**

ONLINE EXTRAS www
Pearson Edexcel

Learn how to plan an
effective essay by completing
Worksheet 29 at **www.
hoddereducation.co.uk/
accesstohistory/extras**

SUMMARY DIAGRAM

THE 1867 REFORM ACT

Gladstone's Liberal bill defeated → Conservatives proposed bill → Reform Act 1867 passed:
- Seats redistributed
- New voting qualification
→
- Working-class voters
- Changed party role and structure
- Increased political activism
- Vote seen as a right and not a privilege

CHAPTER SUMMARY

In 1832, many people expected a programme of reform to follow the Reform Act and landslide Whig victory of 1832. However, further reforms were limited in both impact and range. This was due to less enthusiasm for reform among Whig leaders like Grey and the pressures that the government was under. Radical MPs and the Irish Repeal movement continued to divide both Tories and Whigs. Yet the 1832 Act did create a precedent for future reforms. A key example of this demand was the Chartists. Although they failed to achieve their goal of wider political representation, they showed that the demand for further reform could not be ignored.

The 1830s saw the rise of Peel and Tory MPs beginning to form a modern Conservative Party. By the time Peel became prime minister in 1841, he had clear policies for dealing with the economy, government administration and Ireland. However, despite Peel's clear aims, the concept of parties with a unified ideology had not fully

formed. Ultimately, Peel's policies, especially the repeal of the Corn Laws, divided the Conservative Party. This division ended the Conservative domination, but also created factions that would later form the Liberal Party.

Further, the changes to the electorate had made party organisations necessary. It was no longer enough to rely on loose alliances of like-minded MPs; parties now needed to be united organisations with clear political aims that reached out to the electorate. The Conservative Party was the quickest to adapt, but the Liberal Party soon emerged with a party structure.

No longer was the issue of reform one of supporting or opposing bills; the reality of reform meant that parties had to try to control and direct, not prevent, reform. Consequently, the Reform Act of 1867, a further extension to the electorate, became a political conflict over which party could pass a bill that would benefit them the most.

Refresher questions

Use these questions to remind yourself of the key material covered in this chapter.

1 What were some of the challenges faced by the Whig majority government after 1832?

2 Why were the Tamworth Manifesto and Lichfield Compact turning points in British political history?

3 Give three examples of achievements of the Whig governments of the 1830s.

4 Why have some historians seen Peel as a key figure in the formation of the modern Conservative Party?

5 What financial reforms did Peel introduce as prime minister?

6 What was the Maynooth Crisis, what was Peel's response, and why did it lead to criticism of Peel?

7 What factors contributed to Peel repealing the Corn Laws?

8 What happened to the Conservative Party after Peel's resignation in 1846?

9 What were the aims of the Chartists?

10 What were some of the main Chartist strategies?

11 What were some of the key political ideas of the Liberal Party?

12 How did the 1867 Reform Act affect the political system?

Question practice: AQA A level

Essay questions

1 'The most important political change in the years 1832–68 was the development of party political structures.' Assess the validity of this view.

EXAM HINT Analyse the importance of the development of party political structures as against other political developments in the period, such as parliamentary reform. Reach a clear judgement on the validity of the quotation in the question.

2 To what extent was the purpose of the 1867 Reform Act to address problems that had existed since the 1832 Reform Act?

EXAM HINT You will need to consider the problems that existed since 1832 and set these alongside the purposes of the 1867 Reform Act. Do they match? Or were there other factors in play which led to the passing of the 1867 Act?

3 To what extent were governments from 1832 to 1868 following programmes of political reform?

EXAM HINT You will need to assess the motivations of governments in this period to determine how far they were concerned with political reform. Make sure that you cover the whole period adequately.

4 To what extent had the Conservative Party of the 1820s changed by 1846?

EXAM HINT You will need to assess the extent of change. Avoid a narrative descriptive approach. Think of aspects of change and aspects of continuity.

5 'Chartism was the greatest political challenge to governments between 1832 and 1885.' Assess the validity of this view.

EXAM HINT The question is asking you to analyse how Chartism posed a political challenge and then set this alongside other political challenges. Avoid describing events. Instead reach an argued conclusion.

Question practice: OCR A level

Source questions

1 Using Sources 1–4 below in their historical context, assess how far they support the view that the aims and tactics of the Chartists were radical.

EXAM HINT Group the sources according to whether or not they support the view in the question. Each source should be explained in relation to the question, its provenance evaluated and contextual knowledge used to test the view of the source. A judgement about each source in relation to the question should be reached, allowing an overall judgement about whether the sources support the view that the aims and tactics were radical.

2 Using Sources 5–8 below in their historical context, assess how far they support the view that Peel was responsible for his own downfall.

EXAM HINT Group the sources according to whether or not they support the view in the question. Each source should be explained in relation to the question, its provenance evaluated and contextual knowledge used to test the view of the source. A judgement about each source in relation to the question should be reached, allowing an overall judgement about whether the sources support the view that Peel was responsible for his own downfall.

SOURCE 1

From an article in the *Ipswich Journal*, 9 November 1839, on the Newport Uprising.

Newport, Monday, 11 o'clock a.m. The Chartists have almost entire possession of the town. 7,000 or 8,000 have marched in from the hills, and attached the Westgate Inn, where magistrates are sitting. I have heard 30 or 40 shots fired, and learn that several of the Chartists, as well as soldiers, are killed …

Newport, 1 o'clock p.m. I was mistaken in saying that any soldiers are killed. There is one (sergeant Daly) wounded with some slugs in the forehead but not dangerously … Of the Chartists 9 lie dead in the yard of the Westgate Inn, besides several others … whose wounds will prove fatal.

SOURCE 2

From an article in the *Caledonian Mercury*, 24 October 1842, on a meeting of female Chartists.

A meeting of female Chartists was held on Monday evening, in the National Charter Association Hall, Old Bailey, for the purpose of forming a 'Female Chartist Association' to cooperate with the male association … Mr Cohen expressed the high degree of satisfaction which he had received from [the proposal] but could not help saying that women would be more in her proper character and station at home, where she was the pride and ornament of the 'domestic hearth' than in the political arena. (Sensation among the ladies.) … He was for maintaining the 'social rights' of women. 'Political rights,' such as he understood that meeting to aspire to, [they] could never, in his opinion, attain.

SOURCE 3

An extract of the *People's Charter*, published in 1838 by the London Working Men's Association.

We are induced to believe that the enlightenment of all will sooner emanate from the exercise of political power by all the people, than by their continuing to trust to the selfish government of the few. A strong conviction of these truths, coupled, as that conviction is, with the belief that most of our political and social evils can be traced to corrupt and exclusive legislation – and that the remedy will be found in extending to the people at large, the exercise of these rights, now monopolised by a few, has induced us to make some exertions towards embodying our principles in the following Charter.

SOURCE 4

A letter to the Commissioner of the Metropolitan Police by a group of householders in a wealthy, middle-class area of London following the large Chartist demonstration on Kennington Common, London, in 1848.

To the Honourable the Commissioner of the Metropolitan Police

We the undersigned cannot allow this time to pass without expressing our entire approbation [appreciation] of the good conduct of the Police in our District, in keeping order and protecting us from these repeated attempts to disturb the Public peace in this and the adjoining neighbourhood by a class of misguided persons calling themselves Chartists.

SOURCE 5

From a memorandum which Peel wrote and had read to his cabinet in 1845. He wrote it to lay out his reasons for his decision to support repeal of the Corn Laws.

There is the prospect of a lamentable deficiency of the ordinary food of the people in many parts of Ireland, and in some parts of this country, and of Scotland. The evil may be much greater than present reports lead us to anticipate. Inaction and indifference might involve the country in serious danger … I greatly fear that partial and limited interference with the <u>Corn Law</u> … will be no solution of our difficulties. We must make our choice between determined maintenance, modification, and suspension of the existing Corn Law. I am fully aware of the gravity of the considerations connected with this part of the question.

SOURCE 6

From a report from 1843 into the economic conditions in Ireland, written by Captain Kennedy, secretary to the Royal Commission. It was published in 1847 as part of a collection of evidence about land ownership in Ireland.

It has been stated almost universally throughout the evidence, that the lands in nearly every district of Ireland require drainage. That the most valuable crops and the most profitable rotations cannot be adopted on wet lands, etc. Some attribute the apathy that exists … to the fact of the occupiers not having any certainty of receiving compensation, if removed immediately after having effected valuable improvements. A close analysis of this subject would probably lead to the conclusion, that the potato … as compared with other food stuffs grown in this climate, supplied the largest amount of human food on the smallest surface. Its peculiar cultivation enabled the occupier of land to plant it in the wettest soils.

SOURCE 7

A letter written by J.W. Croker, a leading Ultra Tory MP, to his friend, Sir Henry Harding, the governor-general of India, in April 1846.

For all my affection to [Peel], I cannot excuse this latest u-turn and, above all, the deception of endeavouring to attribute it all to the potato famine in Ireland … What the real cause of the change of opinion was I cannot possibly assert … There was, perhaps, some original inclination to idealise free trade and the advancement of the manufacturing interest, and some latent hatred of the 'proud aristocracy'. But the main and immediate cause was terror, cowardice – terror of the League.

SOURCE 8

From the 5 April 1845 diary entry of the Duke of Newcastle, a Tory who opposed Peel's policies for Catholics in Ireland.

Sir R. Peel has brought forward his popish scheme as regards Maynooth. An endowment of £27000 a year, settled an enlargement of their power of tenure of lands to £3000, a year … and an additional grant for the year of £30000. This will do, I presume and show our prime minister in his true colours – but will the Nation endure it? I think not – Their feelings are too strongly excited to permit a relapse & at present they are quite up in arms.

ONLINE EXTRAS
OCR **WWW**

Practise your source analysis skills by completing Worksheet 26 at **www. hoddereducation.co.uk/ accesstohistory/extras**

ONLINE EXTRAS
OCR **WWW**

Practise your source analysis skills by completing Worksheet 27 at **www. hoddereducation.co.uk/ accesstohistory/extras**

ONLINE EXTRAS
OCR **WWW**

Practise your source analysis skills by completing Worksheet 28 at **www. hoddereducation.co.uk/ accesstohistory/extras**

ONLINE EXTRAS
OCR **WWW**

Practise your source analysis skills by completing Worksheet 29 at **www. hoddereducation.co.uk/ accesstohistory/extras**

ONLINE EXTRAS
OCR **WWW**

Practise your source analysis skills by completing Worksheet 30 at **www. hoddereducation.co.uk/ accesstohistory/extras**

Question practice: Pearson Edexcel A level

Essay questions

1 How accurate is it to say that popular pressure led to political change in the years 1830–68?

EXAM HINT Examine instances where popular pressure led to change, but also the limitations of popular pressure such as the failure of the Chartist movement.

2 How significant was the Chartist movement in developing tactics for demanding reform?

EXAM HINT Examine the methods used by Chartism, such as the NCA, the Chartist Convention, and petitions, and the extent of their success. Also note the movement's divided leadership.

3 Was government policy the main reason for the passing of parliamentary reform in the years 1830–67?

EXAM HINT Compare the significance of government policy (by Grey and the Whigs in the 1830s, and Derby and Disraeli in 1866–7), with extra-parliamentary protests during both periods.

4 How successful was the Reform Act of 1832 in meeting the demands for parliamentary reform?

EXAM HINT Compare the often radical demands for reform in the country with the terms of the 1832 Act, and the extent to which those demands had been met.

CHAPTER 7

Gladstone and Disraeli's rival ministries 1868–85

From 1868, two statesmen came to personify the Conservative and Liberal parties: Benjamin Disraeli and William Gladstone, respectively. Their personal rivalry represented the competition between the two parties. However, in turn as prime minister, each leader contributed to legislation which left a lasting social and political impact on Britain. This chapter examines the governments of Disraeli and Gladstone through the following themes:

◆ Rival statesmen

◆ The competing ministries of Gladstone and Disraeli

◆ Changes to the democratic process

KEY DATES				
1868	**Feb.**	Disraeli's first ministry	**1883**	Corrupt and Illegal Practices Act passed
	Dec.	Gladstone's first ministry	**1884**	Reform Act passed, extending the franchise
1872		Ballot Act passed		
1874		Disraeli's second ministry	**1885**	Redistribution Act passed, redefining constituencies
1880		Gladstone's second ministry		

1 Rival statesmen

■ *How were the political ideas of Gladstone and Disraeli different?*

Gladstone and Disraeli (see their profiles on pages 150 and 151, respectively), both Conservative members of parliament (MPs) in the 1840s, became great rivals to the degree that their relationship as opposing politicians has become representative of British politics in the 1870s and 1880s. Both men are two of only three nineteenth-century prime ministers (the third was Peel) who were from non-aristocratic families.

Rivalry between the two emerging leaders

The two men were in many ways very different. Gladstone's reputation was as an honourable, hard-working English gentleman. In contrast, Benjamin Disraeli was considered an outsider due to his foreign background and past scandals. There was also animosity between the two over Disraeli's leading role in the political attacks against Peel, whom Gladstone considered a mentor.

The rivalry became more direct when each became leader of his political party:

■ Disraeli became the Conservative Party leader in 1848. The Conservative prime minister, Derby, could not be party leader in the Commons as he was an aristocrat.

- Gladstone became Liberal Party leader following the death of Palmerston in 1865 and Russell's retirement in 1867.

The two developed a rivalry based on their personal as well as political differences:

- Disraeli was a dandy and a creative author; Gladstone was very serious and unimaginative.
- Disraeli led the attack on Peel, Gladstone's mentor, over the Corn Laws which forced his resignation, whereas Gladstone attacked Disraeli's 1852 budget, causing Derby's government to fall.
- When Disraeli presented his first budget as chancellor of the exchequer, he made rude personal comments about several opposing MPs, including Gladstone. Gladstone lectured him in parliament on his manners.
- Many Liberals called Gladstone GOM: 'Grand Old Man'. Disraeli said it stood for 'God's only mistake'. Gladstone referred to Disraeli as 'Dizzy' and accused him of being unprincipled.

The rivalry was intense and has been interpreted as hatred. Perhaps it is more accurate to say that they failed to understand each other's politics and personalities.

Gladstone and Disraeli's political ideas in 1868

Free trade and protectionism

Gladstone believed fundamentally in free trade, without high tariffs or State controls. Disraeli had been involved in persuading the Conservatives to abandon protectionism by 1852.

The State

Both Disraeli and Gladstone believed that the government should take a *laissez-faire* role and avoid unnecessary interference in the lives of citizens. Disraeli defended the traditional institutions of the monarchy and the Church of England. Gladstone used the Whig motto of 'peace, retrenchment and reform' to mean opposing unnecessary warfare (peace), keeping government spending low, which would also lower taxes (retrenchment), and improving corrupt and inefficient government (reform).

Government

Gladstone believed that governments should be run by individuals with a history of service to the State and too much wealth to be tempted by bribes – in other words, an aristocracy and monarchy. Disraeli saw the country as two nations – a majority working population and a small, mainly Whig group of aristocratic families who were in power. He sought to unify the two 'nations' behind the Conservatives. Disraeli was keen to unite groups who had not previously supported Conservatives, such as trade unionists in urban areas.

William Gladstone

1809	Born in Liverpool; his father was a wealthy merchant and MP
1828	Studied Classics and Mathematics at Oxford University
1832	Elected as Tory MP for Newark
1840	Began a personal crusade to help London's prostitutes
1845	Resigned from the government over Peel's Maynooth policy
1867	Became leader of the Liberal Party
1868	First term as prime minister
1880	Second term as prime minister
1886	Third term as prime minister
1892	Fourth term as prime minister
1898	Died and was buried in Westminster Abbey

Background

William Gladstone was born to a merchant family with landed interests, including a plantation in the West Indies. He studied Classics and Mathematics, gaining a double first. He was deeply religious and contemplated a career as a priest before turning to politics. He was driven by his moral religious values. Gladstone was a committed defender of the Anglican Church and the rights of the West Indian slave owners, including his father. Later in life, he also made a personal campaign of trying to help women escape from prostitution and find alterative work.

Political career

Gladstone entered parliament in 1832, helped by his family connections. He quickly became known for his strong political views and was appointed to a junior ministerial role in Peel's Conservative government in 1834. Gladstone had a moral approach to politics. For example, he resigned on principle when Peel did in 1835. Later, Gladstone again resigned in response to Peel's grant of money to Maynooth Seminary because he had published a book criticising the idea.

By the 1850s, he had become a Liberal, committed to free trade and reform. After his first term as prime minister ended, he resigned as Liberal leader, but his anti-Conservative feeling made him return to campaign against Conservative imperialist politics in 1879.

Gladstone focused on policies that were important to him, such as Ireland. He tended to divide opinion; his supporters called him GOM ('Grand Old Man') whereas his opponents saw his as preachy and inflexible.

Gladstone served four terms as prime minister, finally resigning in 1894.

Foreign policy

Gladstone made Irish reform, particularly the disestablishment of the Church of Ireland (the official Anglican Church), a priority of his time in power. This was both a serious political issue and a way to unite his Liberal Party. Gladstone also wanted to reduce troop numbers by withdrawing from self-governing colonies, while Disraeli and the Conservatives wanted to defend the outposts of empire and saw Gladstone's foreign policy as a desire to dismember the empire.

Social policy

Having been elected by a Nonconformist Liberal electorate, Gladstone was under pressure to introduce social reforms. Disraeli saw social reform as a necessary process to stabilise and win votes from a broader section of the electorate. It was also a tool to outplay the Liberals. Disraeli's earlier Young England ideas meant that he saw social reform as key to national stability.

ONLINE EXTRAS AQA WWW

Test your understanding of Gladstone and Disraeli by completing Worksheet 26 at **www.hoddereducation.co.uk/accesstohistory/extras**

ONLINE EXTRAS Pearson Edexcel WWW

Develop your analysis of Gladstone by completing Worksheet 30 at **www.hoddereducation.co.uk/accesstohistory/extras**

Benjamin Disraeli

1804	Born in London to a Jewish middle-class family
1817	Converted to Christianity
1821	Became a trainee solicitor
1837	Began a political career as MP for Maidstone
1841	Was rejected for a role in Peel's cabinet
1846	Opposed Peel over the repeal of the Corn Laws
1852	Became leader of the Commons and chancellor of the exchequer
1868	First term as prime minister
1874	Second term as prime minister
1879	Given the title Earl of Beaconsfield by Queen Victoria
1881	Died and was buried in the churchyard near his home

Background

Benjamin Disraeli was the son of a Jewish-Italian writer, although he became Anglican at the age of twelve when his father formally converted to the Church of England for political reasons. This was significant, since Jewish people were not allowed to stand as MPs until 1858, so this change opened up a political career. He was known throughout his life for his indulgent lifestyle. He also faced significant debts arising from failed business ventures as a young man. Scandal followed his political career, when he took a married woman, Henrietta Sykes, as his mistress, and persuaded an older heiress to marry him, mainly for her money.

He led a group of young aristocratic gentleman, although not himself aristocratic, who discussed ideas of Social Toryism, the idea of a nation with a strong monarch and established Church which created social reform to deal with the problems faced by the population. Disraeli shared these ideas in a trilogy of novels, including *Sybil, or a Tale of Two Nations* (1845).

Political career

Disraeli entered the Commons in 1837 as MP for Maidstone on his fourth attempt to be elected. He was mocked during his maiden speech in parliament. In 1841, Peel failed to offer him a cabinet position and Disraeli became bitter. Once Peel decided to repeal the Corn Laws, Disraeli attacked him in parliament and helped to bring down his government. Although this built a reputation for Disraeli as a talented politician, he would not gain political office until 1852, in Derby's government. Later, he would go on to be prime minister twice and achieve a range of important legislation. Central to this was Disraeli's coining of the idea of 'one-nation Conservatism', the idea of using social reform to unite all classes behind a Conservative government. Disraeli built a strong friendship with Queen Victoria, based on his charm and imperialistic policies.

SUMMARY DIAGRAM

RIVAL STATESMEN

Gladstone:
- Liberal
- Committed Anglican
- Believed in Christian moral principles
- Supported free trade, aristocratic government, Irish reforms and social reform

Disraeli:
- Conservative
- Anglican with a Jewish-Italian background
- Was associated with scandal
- Supported the abolition of protectionism, one-nation Conservatism and limited social reform

A strong rivalry based on political and personal differences

2 The competing ministries of Gladstone and Disraeli

■ *What were Gladstone and Disraeli's main ideas and policies during their ministries?*

Disraeli's first ministry, February to December 1868

Disraeli finally became the Conservative prime minister in February 1868. Derby resigned due to ill health. Neither Liberals nor Conservatives wanted to hold a general election immediately, as the new lists of registered voters from the 1867 Reform Act had not yet been compiled. Therefore, Disraeli took office on Derby's recommendation, knowing that it was reasonably likely that he would only be there for a short while until a new general election would bring back a Liberal majority. As it happened, the new election led to a Liberal government in December 1868.

One major issue of 1868 was a debate over the Irish Church. Tensions had reached a high between the Anglican Church of Ireland and the majority Catholic population who had to fund the Church. Disraeli entered negotiations with the Church, but Gladstone introduced the 1869 Irish Church Act which gave the Church of Ireland independence. This unified the Liberals and prepared them to win the general election as a united party, gaining a strong majority government of 382 seats to 276 Conservative ones. This was in part the benefit that the Liberals gained from the increase in working-class Nonconformist voters, but this should not be overstated – there was a wider trend towards Liberal majorities in every election between 1857 and 1874.

Gladstone's first ministry 1868–74

Gladstone's first ministry was formed in 1868 as he became Liberal prime minister in December that year. The cabinet was composed of Whigs, Liberals, Radicals and Peelites. All belonged to the Church of England, except for John Bright, a Quaker MP and the first Nonconformist in a British cabinet (see page 123).

What did Gladstone's first ministry achieve?

Gladstone's government targeted reforms in a number of key areas.

Reform in Ireland

■ 1869 Irish Church Act: this broke the connection between the Anglican Church of Ireland and the State, removing its financial support. The Church became a voluntary organisation and was given £10 million in compensation for losses. The Act also allowed farmers on Church land to buy the land and reduced grants to the Presbyterian Church and Catholic Maynooth College (see page 122) to equalise the situation for each Church.

■ 1870 Irish Land Act: this protected the rights of tenant farmers by allowing evictions only if they failed to pay the rent. It also forced landlords to compensate tenants for improvements they made to the property when they left. The Bright Amendment (proposed by John Bright) also allowed tenant farmers to purchase land by borrowing two-thirds of the cost from the State.

■ 1870 Peace Preservation Act and 1871 Westmeath Act: these extended police powers in Ireland in response to civil unrest in rural areas. To balance these Acts, Gladstone freed Irish nationalist prisoners in 1870.

Social reform

■ 1870 Education Act (or the Forster Act): this set up school boards in areas where religious organisations did not provide education. The boards could make local education compulsory if need be. Local ratepayers were responsible for appointing school boards, and education had to include non-denominational Bible teaching. The Act also empowered existing religious schools to continue independently, and increased the value of State grants.

■ 1872 Public Health Act: this established local urban and rural authorities to be responsible for managing public health, and required local medical officers to be appointed.

■ 1872 Licensing Act: this gave magistrates the power to control the licensing of pubs and check the quality of alcoholic drinks on sale, in particular to seek evidence of the addition of salt to make drinkers thirstier. It gave local authorities the power to set closing times for pubs.

Trade union reform

■ 1871 Trade Union Act: this established the legal right of **trade unions** to exist. Any previous laws which criminalised trade union activities were repealed.

■ 1871 Criminal Law Amendment Act: this stated that 'intimidation' was still illegal in strikes. This weakened the power of unions. The government intended the law to prevent violence, but justices of the peace often applied the word 'intimidation' quite widely to include things such as peacefully picketing.

Administrative reform

■ 1870 Civil service examinations: this introduced examinations to enter the civil service in almost all departments. Appointments were no longer wholly by patronage or family connection but by ability.

■ 1871 University Tests Act: Nonconformists were allowed to teach and hold posts at Oxford and Cambridge Universities; previously only Anglicans had been allowed.

KEY TERM

Trade unions
Organisations of workers formed to protect their rights against their employers. One tactic is to organise strikes to demand better conditions or pay.

- 1868–74 Cardwell reforms: a series of measures proposed by Edward Cardwell, minister of war, including:
  - ☐ abolition of the purchase of commissions
  - ☐ abolition of flogging as a punishment in peacetime
  - ☐ shortened terms of service from twelve years to six years of active service and six years in reserve
  - ☐ reorganisation of the structure of regiments
  - ☐ purchase of more modern weaponry such as breech-loading rifles
  - ☐ reorganisation of the War Office into distinct departments.
- 1872 Ballot Act: introduced secret ballots instead of open voting at elections.
- 1873 Supreme Court of Judicature Act: the Liberals established a streamlined high court system with the aim of making the court system more effective.

Why did Gladstone's government fall by 1874?

Although Gladstone's Liberals had passed a raft of reforms, in doing so they had alienated support on all sides (see Table 7.1, page 155).

In 1873, Gladstone proposed an Irish universities bill. This would have created a non-denominational University of Dublin by combining the Anglican Trinity College with smaller Catholic colleges. Gladstone underestimated the backlash from both Catholics and Anglicans, and so, when the bill was defeated, he offered to resign in favour of Disraeli. He was hoping to follow the same pattern as the previous two decades: a Liberal government was weakened, a short-lived Conservative government came to power, the Liberals reunited and swept back in with a new majority government. However, Disraeli tactically refused the offer to break the cycle. Gladstone was forced to attempt to keep his ministry together. After eleven months, he gave up and called a new general election in 1874. When he lost the election, Gladstone reportedly blamed the Licensing Act, stating 'We have been swept away in a torrent of gin and beer.' He resigned as leader of the Liberal Party in 1874, although he remained as an MP.

Disraeli's second ministry 1874–80

Disraeli took power in the 1874 election, winning 350 seats for the Conservative Party. The Liberals won 242 seats, and an alliance of Irish nationalists, the **Home Rule** Party, won 60 seats for the first time.

Disraeli did not have a distinct plan for his time in office in 1874. One cabinet minister recorded his disappointment that Disraeli did not have any clear suggestions of policies, and that he relied on suggestions from his cabinet ministers. This does not necessarily mean that he was not ready to be prime minister. It possibly reflects Disraeli realising that Gladstone had been partly responsible for his own defeat through his wide raft of reforms which alienated many supporters. Consequently, Disraeli was far more likely to focus on managing smaller reforms to stabilise his government.

KEY TERM

Home Rule Irish nationalists campaigned in parliament for the right for independent political rule in Ireland.

Table 7.1 Liberal reforms and their lack of support

Alienated group	How this measure lacked support
Nonconformists	• The Education Act (1870) had extended education, a Nonconformist demand, but had not weakened the Anglican control. Anglican schools still outnumbered other religious groups by three to one and they secured a larger share of the funding • The Licensing Act (1872) did not go far enough for the majority of Nonconformists in simply providing powers to control pubs; they had wanted a reduction in the number of pubs
Anglicans	• The disestablishment of the Church of Ireland, the support for non-Anglican School Boards and the opening of university posts at Oxford and Cambridge to Nonconformists offended more traditional Anglicans
Irish people	• The Irish land changes alienated Irish landowners, but did not actually make enough of a difference to tenants – many were still evicted despite the law, and few could afford the one-third of the cost of purchasing their own land they needed to benefit from the Bright Amendment • The new Coercion Acts extending police powers generated resentment among the Irish masses
Working classes	• The Licensing Act (1872) imposed fixed closing time and annoyed those in the drinks trade and drinkers. Many working-class men, recently enfranchised in 1867, were alienated • The Criminal Law Amendment (1871), mainly due to the anti-union way that it was interpreted by justices of the peace, alienated many working voters
Aristocratics	• The Cardwell reforms removed the ability to purchase commissions as officers, and the civil service exams prevented appointment by family connection. These had been two key ways that landed families had found careers for sons and relatives. The reforms were opposed by many landed politicians, to the point that the abolition of commissions had to be proposed as a royal warrant, not a bill in parliament • The Ballot Act weakened the influence of landowners over the voting of their tenants, since they could no longer know who their tenants had voted for • Many aristocratic families were Anglican, and so were also alienated by the 1869 Irish Church Act, 1870 Education Act and 1871 University Tests Act

What did Disraeli's ministry achieve?

The key reforms of Disraeli's ministry were all passed in the first few years, 1874–6, and focused on addressing social problems.

Reforms to living conditions

■ 1874 Licensing Act: an alteration to Gladstone's unpopular 1872 Act. Although it theoretically offered longer opening hours, in many cases local authorities used it to shorten hours further, so it was less successful than Disraeli hoped.

■ 1875 Artisans Dwelling Act: this enabled councils to buy land occupied by poor slum housing and redevelop it. This had little effect, as opposition from within the Conservative Party led to it being a law that permitted, rather than required, councils to take action. Many Conservatives saw it as an attack on the rights of private property owners. Records suggest that, due to the high cost of redevelopment, only ten towns in England and Wales had taken action by 1881.

- 1875 Public Health Act: this crucial piece of legislation combined previous public health legislation into one law. More importantly, it obligated local councils to take responsibility for clean water and sewage, provide street lighting, deal with dangers to health and report outbreaks of infectious disease.

- 1875 Sale of Food and Drugs Act: set standards for food and drugs on sale to avoid contamination or **adulteration**. It had limited effects as it was not enforced, but its passing into law showed a changing attitude to State involvement.

- 1875 Rivers Pollution Act: intended to reduce pollution in rivers, but it was not enforced.

Reforms to working conditions

- 1874 Factory Act: this law built on previous Factory Acts (see pages 211–15), setting a ten-hour working day for children and women and raising the age limit for child workers from eight to ten. It did not impose a limit on working days for men, but the need to adapt shift times for women and children led to shorter days and a reduction in weekend working for everyone.

- 1875 Conspiracy and Protection of Property Act: reversed Gladstone's 1871 Criminal Law Amendment Act and protected the rights of strikers to peacefully picket.

- 1875 Employers and Workmen Act: previously, it was a criminal offence for a worker to break the terms of a contract, but a civil offence for an employer (a less serious offence). This legislation equalised both groups by making it a civil offence for everyone.

- 1875 Friendly Societies Act: this Act, originally a Liberal proposal, created a register for so-called 'Friendly Societies', which were similar to trade unions, in the sense that they were clubs for workers. They essentially acted as an insurance scheme that offered sickness benefits. The register was designed to protect members from losing money they had paid.

- 1876 Merchant Shipping Act: proposed by a Liberal MP and was intended to prevent the overloading of ships, which posed a danger to sailors. The government accepted a proposal that ships would have a 'Plimsoll line' painted on the side to show the maximum loading point, but they refused to enforce this, which meant that ship owners could decide where to paint the line.

- 1876 Trade Union Amendment Act: extended the Liberals' 1871 Trade Union Act by enhancing existing rights for trade unions to have protected funds.

- 1878 Factory and Workshops Act: ensured that both factories and workshops were subject to government inspections: a simple way to improve conditions for many workers.

Reforms to education and religion

- 1876 Public Worship Regulations Act: designed to support traditional Anglican groups, this banned the adoption of Catholic rituals into Anglican worship, what is known as 'High Anglicanism'. This nearly split the Conservative Party and led to a decade of attempts to repress Anglican priests who refused to accept the ban, before the law was abandoned.

- 1876 Education Act: created school attendance committees in areas without a school board (where there were voluntary Anglican schools). The committees encouraged children under ten to go to school, and could pay fees for poor children if needed. This essentially meant that schools were now available everywhere for under-tens.

Land reforms

- 1875 Agricultural Holdings Act: based on Gladstone's Irish Land Act (see page 153) but applied to Britain. It protected tenants from eviction and required landlords to pay compensation for any improvements carried out by tenants. However, it was not enforced so many landlords ignored it.

- 1876 Enclosures Act: made the enclosure of public land (see page 96) more difficult, and protected existing common land for public use.

Gladstone's second ministry 1880–5

Although Gladstone had resigned as party leader in 1874, he soon stepped back into the political spotlight. He was angered by reports of Turkish brutality against Christians in Bulgaria during the **April Uprising**, and especially by Disraeli's claims that the reports were exaggerated. He became the *de facto* leader of opposition to Disraeli's foreign policy, which was to work with the Turkish Ottoman Empire as a balance against Russian imperialism. Gladstone's campaign became known as 'Agitation', and he published a pamphlet called *The Bulgarian Horrors and the Question of the East* which attacked the Turks for their crimes and Disraeli for his complicity. The Agitation had no significant effect, as the Liberal leaders were not prepared to challenge Disraeli, but it rebuilt the Nonconformist, grass-roots support that Gladstone had lost in 1874. It also showed Gladstone that if he was to take on Disraeli, something he felt morally compelled to do, it would have to be as party leader.

In 1879, Gladstone agreed to stand as candidate for Midlothian in Scotland. Using the railways and the media to great skill, he gave speeches in town after town which were then published in national newspapers. Some speeches were accompanied by bonfires and firework displays. He repeatedly attacked '**Beaconsfieldism**', as he referred to Disraeli's imperialist policies. He focused on the public dissatisfaction with Conservative imperialism. For example, Disraeli's government had sent troops to fight in the **Anglo-Zulu War** and **Second Anglo-Afghan War**, which, while victorious, had been expensive, while in Britain there had been poor harvests, several bank failures and a rise in unemployment.

KEY TERMS

April Uprising A rebellion in 1876 by Bulgarian nationalists led to reprisals by the Turkish government. Turkish military units, who were Muslim, massacred many Bulgarians, who were primarily Christian. Reports reached Britain of brutal violence and piles of rotting bodies and skulls. Official British estimates suggested 15,000 dead.

Beaconsfieldism This was the term Gladstone used for the Conservative imperialist foreign policies, which included the Zulu and Afghan Wars. The name was a reference to Disraeli's title of Earl of Beaconsfield.

Anglo-Zulu War A six-month invasion in 1879 of Zululand in order to create a South African colonial federation. Although victorious, there were many British losses, such as when 800 British soldiers were killed when Zulu troops destroyed a British column at Isandlwana.

Second Anglo-Afghan War A British invasion of Afghanistan between 1878 and 1880 to prevent Russian involvement which would have left British India vulnerable to future invasion. Although victorious, it involved 50,000 British troops.

Gladstone spoke of the government's 'mischievous and ruinous misdeeds' which endangered the 'most fundamental interests of Christian society'. By 1880, his speeches had broadened to attack all parts of the establishment, including landed elites and clergy who supported Disraeli.

Even though economic depression and party organisation were probably more important in the following landslide election in 1880 (352 Liberal seats to 237 Conservative) than Gladstone's campaigning, he had made it impossible for Hartington, Liberal leader in the Commons, or Earl Granville, Liberal leader in the Lords, to form a government without him. The queen offered Hartington the office of prime minister; Gladstone refused to serve under him, and so she was forced to offer him the chance to form a government.

A new focus on moral-issue politics

One unintended impact on politics from this period was a more moral angle to campaigning. This became a greater feature of political campaigning in the later nineteenth century. This was a result of:

- The developing party political organisations that were trying to engage popular support made greater use of moral messages than before.
- Gladstone's campaign messages against 'Beaconsfieldism' were designed to inspire moral outrage in the population at large.

? SOURCE QUESTION

What judgement of Gladstone's government was the artist portraying? What details show this?

SOURCE A

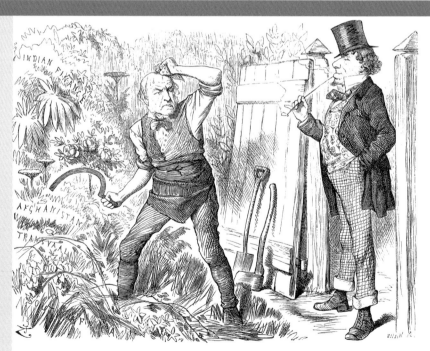

LABOUR AND REST.

Ex-Head Gardener (*retired from business*). "WELL, WILLIAM, YER DON'T SEEM TO BE MAKIN' MUCH PROGRESS—DO YER!"
New Head Gardener. "WHY NO, BENJAMIN; YOU LEFT THE PLACE IN SUCH A PRECIOUS MESS!!"

A political cartoon published in *Punch* magazine, 19 June 1880. Set shortly after Gladstone's successful election, it shows Benjamin Disraeli (right) as the ex-head gardener of an overgrown garden looking in on William Gladstone (left) as the new head gardener.

The divisions in Gladstone's ministry

Despite the overwhelming majority, Gladstone's second ministry was less effective than the first because of Liberal divisions:

- The split between radical and conservative Liberals was growing. With Gladstone's victory, the radicals expected their agenda to be addressed, but Gladstone formed a conservative Liberal cabinet.

- Apart from attacking Beaconsfieldism (see page 157), Gladstone had neither a coherent programme nor the interest in building one. He seemed to want to deal with the threat of Conservative foreign policy and then retire.

- The Bradlaugh case strained Liberal ideology (see the box, below). Liberals stood for Nonconformist religious freedoms against an official State Church, but the idea of atheism and removing religion from parliament entirely was a challenge.

- Four Conservative MPs formed a so-called 'Fourth Party', disrupting proposals and holding up government business. Their taunts and comments goaded Gladstone, causing him to lose his temper in parliament and appear out of control.

- The 'Irish Question', which Gladstone had hoped to have solved with legislation in his first ministry, kept rolling on, to the embarrassment of the government.

The Bradlaugh case

An atheist republican, Charles Bradlaugh was elected in 1880. He refused to take the religious parliamentary oath and requested a secular oath instead. Although he eventually took the religious oath, his contempt led to objections to his taking his seat in parliament. He was elected and was rejected twice more. Finally, he was re-elected and allowed to take a non-religious oath of allegiance. The government attempted to pass legislation in 1883 to allow this, but was outvoted.

The impact of Irish nationalism on Gladstone's second ministry

The ongoing pressure of Irish nationalism became a focus of Gladstone's ministry and a continual problem for British government:

- In the 1840s, Irish nationalist groups called Young Ireland sought independent rule as well as a revival of Irish culture.

- By the 1860s, a number of secret Irish nationalist societies had formed under the umbrella title of the Irish Republican Brotherhood, often referred to as **Fenians**.

- By the late 1870s, falling grain prices in Ireland meant that many tenants were unable to pay their rent and faced eviction. Large sections of the population were reliant on charity to survive.

KEY TERM

Fenian A member of the Irish Republican Brotherhood, a revolutionary nationalist Irish organisation which sought Irish independence.

- The National Land League emerged to address this issue. Between 1879 and 1882, the League fought for tenants' rights against landowners by picking examples of landlords who charged excessive rents and focusing public attention on them. This became known as the 'Land War'.

- The Land League tied together the nationalists in the Fenian organisations with the mass support of those affected by financial problems. They were led by MP Charles Stuart Parnell, which gave them a voice in the British parliament.

- When a bill for compensation to evicted Irish tenants was rejected in the House of Lords in 1880 and a new coercion bill was passed to keep the peace, Irish nationalist MPs started to use a tactic of **obstructionism** as a policy to disrupt government business. Although this was soon addressed with a law that prevented the tactic, it showed that Irish nationalism could not be ignored.

KEY TERM

Obstructionism
A political tactic of using long speeches to disrupt government business in parliament.

A change to Irish nationalism in parliament

In 1881, Gladstone passed the second Irish Land Act. This law extended the terms of Gladstone's earlier 1870 Irish Land Act (page 153). It introduced the 'three Fs':

- Fixity of tenure (tenants in Ireland could not be evicted if they paid the rent on time).

- Free sale (the right for compensation to tenants who had improved the property if the property was sold).

- Fair rents (rents at reasonable prices).

The Act included legislation to allow tenants to borrow 75 per cent of the money from the State to buy the property from the landlord, and the right of tenants to appeal to the land court if their rent was unreasonably high – most cases taken to the land court resulted in a fifteen to twenty per cent reduction. Although the Act gave some protection to tenants, it did not help the many in Ireland who were already in rent arrears and could be evicted.

The Act divided Irish nationalism, between those who accepted the 'three Fs' and those who demanded Irish independence. Parnell was arrested for speeches which appeared to attack the Land Act, and the Land League dissolved.

While Parnell was in Kilmainham gaol, Dublin, Gladstone's government entered secret negotiations with him, which became known as the Kilmainham Treaty. The deal was that Parnell would use his influence in Ireland to call off agitation, and in return, Parnell and his supporters would be freed, the coercion bills repealed and legislation created to protect tenants in rent arrears from eviction.

On Parnell's release, the chief secretary for Ireland resigned in protest. The new chief secretary, Lord Cavendish, and his under-secretary, Thomas Burke, were murdered in May 1882 by an extreme nationalist group known as The Invincibles while strolling in Phoenix Park in Dublin. Parnell was shocked and considered resigning from politics; Gladstone was forced to introduce a new coercion bill.

The Kilmainham Treaty and the Phoenix Park murders led to a change in the role of Irish nationalist MPs in British politics. Parnell became convinced that more constitutional methods were needed, and he formed his MPs into an organised political party, the Irish Parliamentary Party (IPP, also known as the Irish Nationalist Party). By offering or withholding their support, the IPP could negotiate with subsequent governments. Parnell's party policy was to support whichever major political party looked more likely to support Irish Home Rule. Initially, this was the Liberals but when Liberal Joseph Chamberlain introduced a proposal to establish an Irish council with very limited powers, they switched their support to the Conservatives and helped them to defeat the Liberal government in 1885.

What did Gladstone's second ministry achieve?

Gladstone's second period in office was marked by limited success in terms of legislation. That said, there were three main areas of significant reform.

Domestic reform

- Burial Act 1880: allowed Nonconformists to bury their dead in parish churchyards.
- Ground Game Act, 1880: allowed tenants to kill vermin on their land; this changed the previous law which gave the landowner the sole right to all hunting.
- Education Act, 1880: basic schooling became compulsory for all children up to the age of ten. Government spending on education increased from £1.25 million in 1870 to £4 million; by the 1890s, 82 per cent of children were receiving compulsory education to 10 years of age.
- Army Act 1881: consolidated parts of a law already passed in 1879; among other amendments to army discipline, it abolished flogging as a punishment in the army and navy.
- Employers' Liability Act 1881: introduced the concept of employer responsibility for injuries in the workplace, although there were many loopholes.
- Married Women's Property Act 1882: extended an earlier law from 1870 in giving married women more rights to own property.

Constitutional reform

- Third Reform Act 1884: extended the size of the electorate by including many working-class men.
- Corrupt and Illegal Practices Act 1883: introduced fairer political practice for elections.

In 1885, Gladstone's second ministry came to an end when his budget was defeated by the Conservatives, supported by Parnell's IPP. Although Gladstone would be back in office twice more in 1886 and 1892, for six and eighteen months, respectively, the period of his political dominance was ended.

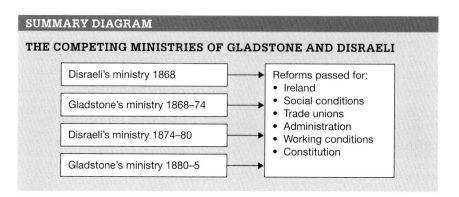

SUMMARY DIAGRAM

THE COMPETING MINISTRIES OF GLADSTONE AND DISRAELI

Disraeli's ministry 1868	→	Reforms passed for:
Gladstone's ministry 1868–74	→	• Ireland • Social conditions • Trade unions
Disraeli's ministry 1874–80	→	• Administration • Working conditions • Constitution
Gladstone's ministry 1880–5	→	

3 Changes to the democratic process

◼ *How were the twin problems of corruption and representation in the political system addressed?*

Between 1868 and 1885, under Gladstone and Disraeli, several key pieces of legislation were passed which continued the process of democratic change. Although there would be crucial legislation in later generations, for example in reforming the House of Lords and introducing a universal franchise that included women, the reforms in this period went a long way towards creating the basis for the modern political system by continuing what had been achieved by 1867.

The problem of corruption

Many MPs recognised that there was too much scope for corruption within the existing political system. Committees formed in 1835 and 1868 had shown that corruption had become a greater problem since the reforms. Two laws were passed to resolve this.

The 1872 Ballot Act

This replaced public voting with secret voting, in which voters marked a printed slip with an 'X' and placed it into a sealed ballot box. Consequently, voters could vote anonymously – landlords could no longer direct their voting. The hustings became less social, drunken affairs, with less intimidation and violence. Anecdotal evidence suggests that bribery may have increased, since voters could accept bribes from both sides.

The 1883 Corrupt and Illegal Practices Act

This defined acceptable election practices, and banned campaign tactics such as bribery, paying to transport voters to the poll and employing more than two party workers per 500 voters. It imposed spending limits which were linked to the size of the constituency, and set harsh punishments for breaking these terms. Consequently, elections became less violent (see page 134) and spending was reduced, although some MPs found a way round the limits by spending more money in constituencies before election campaigning began. There were fewer complaints that election results were invalid. Some poorer voters lost the chance to vote as they had relied on the free transport. Parties became more organised as they relied on teams of local volunteers.

The problem of representation

By 1884, both Conservatives and Liberals agreed not only that further constitutional reform was needed, but also that it was inevitable. Therefore, whereas the 1832 Reform Act had been a hard-fought Whig victory, and the 1867 Act a Conservative hijacking to outmanoeuvre the Liberals, the 1884 and 1885 Reform Acts were agreed between the two parties as a political necessity.

The existing 1867 reforms had left the electoral constituencies unbalanced. Two-thirds of MPs were still elected by one-quarter of the electorate, and industrial workers who would qualify to vote but lived outside the official borough boundaries could find that they did not qualify under county qualifications.

The Liberals were under pressure from their radical members, including cabinet members such as Joseph Chamberlain and Charles Dilke, to reform the political system. Gladstone supported electoral reform; this was a combination of genuine personal opinion and the desire to find an issue to unite his weakening Liberal Party.

The Conservatives, led by Salisbury after Disraeli's death in 1881, initially opposed a Reform Act on party principles. However, they soon saw reform as a chance to win seats. By dividing up the towns into smaller, single-seat constituencies, they would be able to win seats from newly created middle-class suburban constituencies.

Gladstone and Salisbury met at Salisbury's house in Arlington Street, London, along with their deputies; the deal that they reached became known as the Arlington Compact. They agreed that Salisbury would order the Conservatives to allow the reform bill through the Commons and Lords, and in return, Gladstone would follow it with a redistribution bill.

The 1884 Reform Act

This resulted in a uniform franchise across all counties and boroughs. Those enfranchised under the 1832 and 1867 Acts retained the vote. Additionally, the vote was given to all male householders who paid rates, lodgers in properties worth £10 a year, if they had lived there for at least a year, and anyone who owned property worth £10 a year. Plural voting was not abolished. Consequently, the number of eligible voters rose from 3 million to 6 million – almost twenty per cent of the adult population – including many working-class men.

The 1885 Redistribution Act

This resulted in:

- removals of boroughs with populations under 15,000
- boroughs with populations between 15,000 and 50,000 losing one of their two MPs
- 138 seats being redistributed to generate new constituencies
- 647 out of 670 constituencies now having a single MP.

Consequently, constituencies were now of approximately equal population, and the north–south imbalance was removed. Cornwall, for example, went from 44 MPs to seven, while more populous Lancashire went from fourteen to 58.

Overall, in the short term, the reforms of 1872–85 benefited the Conservatives more than the Liberals, and partly explain the Conservative dominance from 1885 until 1902:

- The twelve-month residence qualification meant that at any one time, over 1 million men may not have qualified to vote due to changing residence. These are more likely to have voted Liberal.
- The new constituencies favoured the Conservatives. In the rural areas, the Conservatives kept their lead while winning seats in newly formed suburban constituencies where the middle-class voters were more influential through being divided off from more working-class constituencies.
- The Conservatives had been ahead of the Liberals on party development, and party structures, like the Primrose League, now had a new importance with the new regulations over election campaigning.
- The retention of the first-past-the-post voting system through the reforms meant that only a small shift in voting balance could result in a major swing in the election results. In the 1886 general election, the Conservatives and a breakaway group of Liberals won 402 seats with 50.3 per cent of the vote, while the Liberals only won 183 seats despite winning 45 per cent of the vote.

What was the political situation in Britain in 1885?

Between 1832 and 1885, a slow but unstoppable process of democratisation occurred. From an unrepresentative, corrupt electoral system, a far more balanced system had developed. By 1885:

- Twenty per cent of the adult male population could vote, including some working-class voters.
- Constituencies were approximately equal in size, meaning that representation was even across the country.
- Corruption in the form of campaign tactics and landlords controlling the votes of their tenants had been removed.
- Two organised, structured political parties, the Conservatives and Liberals, had emerged from the general coalitions of politicians, and had organisations aimed at actively building support from the electorate.

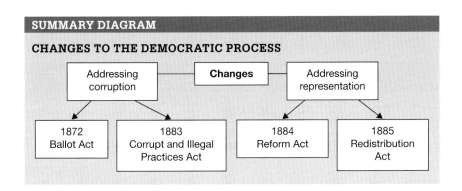

SUMMARY DIAGRAM

CHANGES TO THE DEMOCRATIC PROCESS

Addressing corruption — Changes — Addressing representation

1872 Ballot Act

1883 Corrupt and Illegal Practices Act

1884 Reform Act

1885 Redistribution Act

CHAPTER SUMMARY

Despite their shared Conservative past, the personal rivalry of Gladstone and Disraeli has come to represent their political differences, although politically they were more similar in terms of how their periods in office have become associated with reform. For Gladstone, reforms took place due to a moralistic, liberal outlook and pressure from the Nonconformist organisations which supported his party; for Disraeli, reforms took place as a means to a political end, through his policy of one-nation Conservatism.

Consequently, the period 1868–85 saw a raft of legislation which affected social issues that were not previously addressed by governments, such as housing, public health and education. More importantly, there was a change from reforms which were permissive, to later Acts such as the 1875 Public Health Act, in which the government claimed the right to enforce the law. This was a change to role of the State in public life. Further, this period saw the extension of the franchise to working-class men in 1884, but also a fundamental change to politics through legislation which removed much of the corruption that was inherent to the political system.

Refresher questions

Use these questions to remind yourself of the key material covered in this chapter.

1 What were Gladstone and Disraeli's backgrounds?

2 How did Gladstone and Disraeli's political ideas differ?

3 Give five achievements of Gladstone's first ministry.

4 What was the 1873 Irish universities bill, and why was it significant for both Gladstone and Disraeli?

5 Give five achievements of Gladstone's second ministry.

6 What was Beaconsfieldism, and why was it important to Gladstone's 1879 electoral campaigning.

7 Why was Gladstone's second ministry less effective than his first?

8 What did the 1870 and 1881 Irish Land Acts achieve?

9 Give five achievements of Gladstone's second ministry.

10 What problems in the political system were resolved between 1868 and 1885?

Question practice: AQA A level

Essay questions

1 'Gladstone achieved more political reform than other prime ministers in the period 1841 to 1885.' Assess the validity of this view.

> **EXAM HINT** Analyse Gladstone's political achievements alongside the achievements of other prime ministers. You will need to plan effectively so that you do not write a descriptive account about each prime minister in turn.

2 To what extent had the problems of the 'old corrupt' political system before the 1832 Reform Act been resolved by 1885?

> **EXAM HINT** You will need to consider each so-called cause of corruption in politics and assess show far it had been dealt with through legislation by 1885. Avoid a narrative-style approach.

Interpretation question

1 Using your understanding of the historical context, assess how convincing the arguments in Extracts A, B and C below are in relation to political reform 1867–85.

> **EXAM HINT** Study each extract in turn. Assess the validity of its main argument and any subsidiary ones in the light of your own contextual knowledge. There is no need to reach an overall judgement on the three extracts – just a reasoned judgement on each one in turn.

EXTRACT A

Adapted from H.C.G. Matthew, 'The Liberal Age (1851–1914)' in Kenneth O. Morgan, editor, *The Oxford Illustrated History of Britain*, Oxford University Press, 1984, pp. 497 and 499.

By increasing the electorate, the Reform Acts of 1867 and 1884 presented parties with a much larger, though by no means universal, body of voters. Accustomed to losing, the Conservatives began to win. Their target was the boroughs: to obtain political power they had to enlarge their base from the counties to the expanding towns and suburbs. This they did with considerable success in the 1870s and 1880s, by linking an aristocratic and Anglican party with the aspirations of the expanding middle and lower middle classes in the great cities. Disraeli advocated a policy of social reform, supposedly of particular appeal to such members of the working classes as had recently become voters. The early years of the Conservative government of 1874–80 were marked by a burst of social reforms. They affected middle-class perhaps more than working-class interests and because the social measures were permissive rather than compulsory their effect was more limited than might have been expected.

EXTRACT B

Adapted from Annette Mayer, *The Growth of Democracy in Britain*, Hodder Education, 1999, pp. 59, 66 and 69.

After 1868, both the Liberals and the Conservatives engaged in a review of party policies. This analysis of ideas was clearly driven by motives of pragmatism and self-interest. Both parties realised the enormous potential of support created by the process of democratic reform. The second major impact of political reform was the need to restructure party organisations. As patronage declined, so voting behaviour became less predictable. The most obvious method of attracting votes and increasing support was to build up local associations which would encourage grass-root involvement in politics.

[continued overleaf]

Through these associations, politics came to the people, men and women, subtly disguised in the form of popular entertainment: tea dances, excursions, summer fetes, cricket matches and garden parties. Political education would be a feature of the entertainment, but it was never permitted to detract from social enjoyment.

EXTRACT C

Adapted from Clive Behagg, *Labour and Reform: Working-class Movements 1815–1914*, Hodder Education, 2000, pp. 95–6.

Gladstone's biographer argues that: 'the third Reform Bill moved the country almost all the way towards political democracy'. This is not a very accurate appreciation of a political system that, despite the changes, represented only a small proportion of society and which remained heavily distorted against the interests of labour. Women were still not enfranchised and parliamentary motions to give them the vote were rejected in every parliamentary session between 1870 and 1885. Under the 1884 Act plural voting continued, and, needless to say, plural voters were not generally working-class voters. There were a variety of restrictions that disenfranchised many working-class men. Nor, we should remember, was this an unfortunate by-product of badly devised legislation. It had been accepted in 1867 and 1884 that residential qualifications and voter registration were useful devices to restrict working-class participation. The political system appeared democratic yet, in practice, it was heavily distorted against the working community.

ONLINE EXTRAS AQA **WWW**	**ONLINE EXTRAS** AQA **WWW**	**ONLINE EXTRAS** AQA **WWW**	**ONLINE EXTRAS** AQA **WWW**
Practise your extract analysis skills by completing Worksheet 28 at **www. hoddereducation.co.uk/ accesstohistory/extras**	Practise your extract analysis skills by completing Worksheet 29 at **www. hoddereducation.co.uk/ accesstohistory/extras**	Practise your extract analysis skills by completing Worksheet 30 at **www. hoddereducation.co.uk/ accesstohistory/extras**	Practise your extract analysis skills by completing Worksheet 31 at **www. hoddereducation.co.uk/ accesstohistory/extras**

Question practice: Pearson Edexcel A level

Essay questions

1 How far were Liberal governments responsible for legislation to improve the lives of the urban poor between 1850 and 1870?

EXAM HINT Examine the government's measures to improve conditions in towns and cities. Compare their achievements with those of individuals and organisations such as trade unions and different religious denominations.

2 How far was the political system of 1870 different from the political system of 1785?

EXAM HINT Examine the nature of change concerning, for example, the size of the electorate, the growth of parties and the declining power of the monarchy. Reach a conclusion on the extent of change overall.

CHAPTER 8

Industrialisation and the economy 1832–85

From 1832, the processes of industrialisation and change that had altered the economy of the early nineteenth century continued. As well as improvements in industry, transport flourished with railway mania and the expansion of shipping, creating more British potential for trade, alongside social impacts which particularly changed the lives of the poor. By the 1850s, Britain was in a mid-Victorian boom, but this soon gave way to the so-called 'Great Depression of Agriculture'. This chapter examines the economic changes through the following themes:

◆ Economic developments of the 1830s and 1840s

◆ Economic legislation in the 1840s

◆ Mid-Victorian boom to 1873; Great Depression from 1873

KEY DATES

1834	Poor Law Amendment Act (New Poor Law) passed	**1846**	Corn Laws repealed
1844	Banking, Railways and Companies Acts reformed the financial, transport and business sectors	**1851**	Great Exhibition held in London, which was a great success
		1863	London Underground train network opened
1845 Aug.	A new Enclosure Act created a commission to oversee future land enclosure	**1873**	Great Depression (agriculture and industry) began
Sept.	Potato famine started in Ireland	**1885**	Royal Commission formed to investigate the causes of the economic depression

1 Economic developments of the 1830s and 1840s

◼ What were the key features of the growing economy?

Employment in the 1830s and 1840s

Earlier developments in mining, factory production and transport had laid the basis for the ongoing Industrial Revolution (see pages 92–7). However, in 1832, Britain was not an industrialised society in the sense of having moved entirely away from older production methods. By 1851, the two largest employment groups identified in the census were still agricultural labourers (1.8 million) and domestic service (1 million), not factory workers. For example, there were only 811,000 workers in the cotton and wool industry, and about one-third of these were in small workshops rather than mills and factories. Trade and agriculture still dominated the economy. The process of industrialisation and migration to towns was underway, but not complete.

British agriculture and transport had changed greatly by 1830, but in the 1830s and 1840s there was a real increase in technological developments in these areas. Transport was particularly important, as it not only aided economic development but also had a direct influence on the lives of the population.

Agricultural developments

A range of factors contributed to a growth in agricultural strength in the 1830s and 1840s:

- The 1834 Poor Law cut costs to landowners for poor relief by almost half; this money was often invested in farming.

- The process of enclosure (see page 96), largely completed by the end of the 1840s, had made farming more profitable.

- Improved steam-powered technology was in common use by the 1840s. This included stationary steam engines to power threshing machines, and, from the later 1840s onwards, steam traction engines which acted as early tractors.

- Steam-powered drainage machines improved the quality of soil by making waterlogged ground suitable for farming. One machine could drain 6000 acres.

- Traditional farming tools were improved with industrial iron-working techniques. Lighter ploughs and tools were created, which needed fewer men and horses to use.

- Despite steam machinery, many tasks were still performed by hand, though even simple techniques improved. Traditional farming methods had used sickles for harvesting, but research showed that scythes were more cost-effective, leading to a change of tools.

- Improvements were made in fertilisers. In 1843, Sir John Bennet Lawes and Sir Joseph Henry Gilbert formed the Rothamstead Agricultural Laboratory. Their tests into soil quality and plant nutrition led to improvements in fertiliser quality. By 1858, it was claimed that their new fertilisers had improved wheat yields by 25 per cent.

- Agricultural societies formed, such as the Royal Agricultural Society (1842). These offered lectures and produced journals which shared new developments.

Shipping developments

Trade by shipping was essential to the British economy. In 1800, almost all British shipping was carried in wooden sailing ships. However, the British supplies of oak suitable for shipbuilding were dwindling, whereas the American shipping industry had unlimited supplies. By the 1840s, when the 1842 **Treaty of Nanjing** opened up trade with China, British companies invested in American-built clippers, faster sailing ships, that increased trade.

KEY TERM

Treaty of Nanjing At the end of a war between Britain and China (the Opium War) in 1842, China ceded the rights for British merchants to trade freely at five Chinese ports.

From 1822, shipbuilders began to make ships out of iron. Although iron deteriorated in water and needed to be treated regularly, it was easier to build larger ships in iron and therefore carry more goods.

Steam became a more common method of power through the nineteenth century. Steam-powered ships were not inherently faster than sailing ships, but since they could travel in a direct line (sail ships have to tack across the wind), they could make journeys more quickly and more regularly. However, there were many disadvantages to steam-powered ships: the paddlewheels were ineffective in high seas, they could not be manoeuvred in small spaces, and they needed huge quantities of coal.

A crucial development was **Isambard Kingdom Brunel**'s steam-powered screw propeller in 1836, which was used on the SS *Great Britain* in 1843, and was far more effective than paddles. In 1854, the compound steam engine was invented, halving the amount of coal needed to power a steamship. These ships still had sails, for use in good conditions, but steam engines allowed good speed in the worst conditions. For example, while a sailing ship would take 32 days to travel from Liverpool to New York (one reported journey in 1837, in very bad conditions, took 100 days), a steamship called *Columbia* made the same journey in just ten days in 1843.

By 1857, Brunel had built a steamship of record dimensions, the SS *Great Eastern*. It was 200 metres long, could carry 4000 passengers or 10,000 soldiers, had sails, paddle wheels and a giant screw propeller 8 metres across, and even contained a farmyard for fresh meat on the journey.

Improved sea travel in the mid-nineteenth century had several impacts on the British economy:

- Guano (bird and bat droppings) was imported from South America to fertilise British farmland.
- The cost of imported wheat from America fell from £2 per tonne to 6 shillings (30p) per tonne by the end of the nineteenth century.
- Industrialists could more easily access foreign markets to export industrial goods.

Railway mania

Investing in railways became highly popular. Trains were new and exciting, and a way to make money. By 1836, northern English towns such as Leeds and Sheffield were developing links to connect to the existing Manchester to Liverpool line. In 1837, the Grand Junction Railway linked the line to Birmingham and the English midlands under its chief engineer, Brunel. In 1838, a new line linked London to Birmingham, and in 1841, the Great Western Railway, also directed by Brunel, linked London to Bristol.

The growth of railways during the 1840s was known as 'railway mania'. The name reflects the chaotic speed with which the railways grew:

KEY FIGURE

Isambard Kingdom Brunel (1806–59)

A British engineer noted for inventions which revolutionised industrial processes. Among his achievements were the construction of the Great Western Railway, steam-driven, propeller-powered ships, the first tunnel under a navigable river, dockyards, improved bridges and army hospital structures.

- In 1844, there were 49 Railway Acts submitted to parliament but by 1846, this had increased to 219 Acts.
- In 1832 there had been only 100 miles of track, but by 1846, there were 4000 miles.

The name also reflects a lack of regulation. In many areas, there were two or more lines doing the same job, with competitors building lines where another company was already providing a service, or lines were built where there was insufficient demand. There was no standardisation of track. Many train operators followed George Stephenson's 1.4 metre gauge track, while Brunel preferred a 2.1 metre gauge. This meant that different trains could not always use other tracks.

After the initial creative surge, many companies merged under the control of key industrialists. Whereas in 1843 there had been about 200 smaller companies, by 1850 there were 22 larger companies and a few smaller ones. George Hudson, a member of parliament (MP) who controlled 1000 miles of track in the north of England, became known as the 'Railway King'. He merged a number of companies to create the Midland Railway, and did much to encourage the expansion of the rail networks (until he was accused of fraud in 1849). Another industrialist, Thomas Brassey, built about one-third of Britain's railways.

The impact of the railways

The impact of the railways was enormous. They began to replace obsolete forms of transport. Stage and mail coaches vanished quickly – in 1829, there were 29 stagecoaches a day between Manchester and Liverpool, but by 1832 this had fallen to just two. **Coaching inns** went bankrupt, and **turnpike roads** went unused. William Chaplin, a London businessman who owned 500 horses for carrying the post, sold most of them and changed his business to carrying messages on behalf of the London and Birmingham Railway. Canals were slower to decline, in part because they were often subsidised by rail companies, or owned by the same businessmen.

In addition:

- The railways created huge demand for iron, coal, steel, machined parts, timber, bricks and other manufactured goods – massively stimulating the economy.
- Many more jobs were created – not only makers and drivers of the trains, but also station masters, porters, cleaners and other related roles – than were destroyed by old methods of transport becoming obsolete.
- Dock towns flourished. Trains brought more goods to transport, as well as opening up markets for imported goods. Seaside resorts flourished, with recreational businesses like shops, hotels and promenades.
- Industrial sites could be built away from coalfields as coal could be transported, so factories spread to new areas of Britain.

KEY TERMS

Coaching inns
Businesses which provided food, drink and accommodation to people travelling by coach.

Turnpike roads Private roads, set up by private investors, which charged a toll, or fee, for people travelling on them.

- Manufacturers began to work on the branding of their goods as they could sell to a wider national market more easily. Advertising became more common.

- Farmers could buy coal to power steam machinery and therefore send their produce to further markets to sell.

Socially, the impact was more mixed, as is considered in Table 8.1 (see below).

Table 8.1 Social impacts of railway development in the 1830s and 1840s

Positive impacts of the railways	Negative impacts of the railways
• National newspapers flourished, giving people access to national information • Passengers visited the sea, and seaside resorts such as Blackpool and Scarborough emerged • People could have holidays and days out. In 1830, for example, it cost £1.20 to travel to Brighton from London and took five hours by stagecoach; by train in 1840 it cost 40p and took less than three hours. In 1851, 6 million people attended the **Great Exhibition**, many on cheap-day excursions • Middle-class suburbs developed, where commuters could travel by train to their business while avoiding the more industrial centres of cities • Town centres grew bigger, as it was easier for customers to travel in to shop. Department stores were built in cities such as Manchester • Public schools thrived as children could travel to them, and school inspectors could travel more easily to distant schools	• There was public hysteria when the trains were created. Many believed that the speed and movement of the train would cause brain injury, leading to manic behaviour. The newspaper *Illustrated Police News* regularly produced cartoons claiming to report instances where passengers had gone mad and attacked people, before returning to normal when the train stopped, and *Punch* magazine produced a series of satirical cartoons criticising the railways • Landowners complained about the impact on their land, although they often made a profit selling the land and later using the trains to sell goods • Shareholders in other transport companies, such as the canals, as well as owners of inns and people involved with maintaining turnpikes, risked financial disaster • Country people complained about the trains scaring their livestock or starting fires from sparks • Huntsmen complained that their traditional hunting grounds were disrupted as they could not chase foxes across train tracks and embankments

SOURCE A

A satirical description of railway mania in the 1830s, in the novel *Hard Cash*, by Charles Reade, and published originally in 1863 as a serial in Charles Dickens' journal.

When this sober state of things had endured some time, there came a year that money was loose, and a speculative fever due in the whirligig of time. Then railways bubbled. New ones were advertised, fifty a month, and all went to a premium. High and low scrambled for the shares, even when the projected line was to run from the town of Nought to the village of Nothing across a goose common. The flame spread, fanned by prospectus and advertisement, … princes sat in railway tenders … our stiffest Peers relaxed into Boards [of Directors]; Bishops warned their clergy against avarice.

SOURCE QUESTION

Study Source A. What is the writer's view of railway expansion?

KEY TERM

Great Exhibition
A public event at Crystal Palace, London, in 1851 which showcased British industrial and imperial strength.

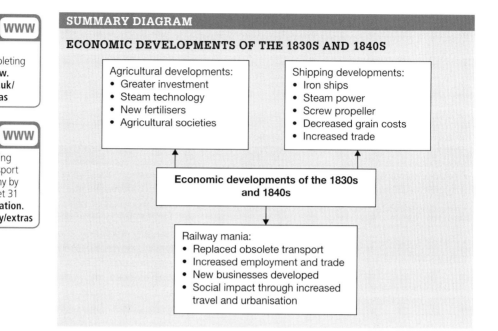

SUMMARY DIAGRAM

ECONOMIC DEVELOPMENTS OF THE 1830S AND 1840S

Agricultural developments:
• Greater investment
• Steam technology
• New fertilisers
• Agricultural societies

Shipping developments:
• Iron ships
• Steam power
• Screw propeller
• Decreased grain costs
• Increased trade

Economic developments of the 1830s and 1840s

Railway mania:
• Replaced obsolete transport
• Increased employment and trade
• New businesses developed
• Social impact through increased travel and urbanisation

2 Economic legislation in the 1840s

■ *How did the government control the economy in the 1840s?*

Despite their powerful position following the 1832 Reform Act victory (see page 110), the Whig governments of 1832–41 were not particularly forceful with reform. Although they did pass the 1833 Factory Act and 1834 Poor Law Amendment Acts, these had a social impact more than an economic impact on Britain.

Economic change came instead from the Conservative governments of the 1840s under Peel. Peel was particularly focused on addressing administration and the economy, similar to Pitt's earlier approach. This is understandable; Peel had come to power amid the economic crisis that had contributed to the growth of Chartism. Between 1837 and 1842, the government deficit had grown to £7.5 million.

Peel's legislation to reduce tariffs

Peel was concerned on financial grounds, but he was also worried about the social discontent that economic problems cause. He believed that lowering tariffs and stimulating trade was crucial to improvement. In 1842, he introduced a budget which lowered duties on imported corn significantly, as well as reducing many other tariffs. To offset the cost, income tax was reintroduced for three years for those earning over £150 annually. Peel had also wanted to lower sugar duties, but this was held back by fierce Tory backbench opposition.

Between 1842 and the next budget in 1845, Peel introduced three pieces of legislation to reduce tariffs (see Table 8.2, below).

Table 8.2 Peel's legislation to reduce tariffs

Year	Action	How did Conservative backbenchers react?
1842	The import duty on cattle was lowered	Opposed by 85 Conservative backbenchers but passed
1843	The Canada corn bill allowed the import of corn from Canada at a very low tariff	Opposed by 60 Conservative backbenchers but passed
1844	An amendment to the sugar bill reduced duties on sugar imported from foreign, non-colonial countries	Opposed by 62 Conservative backbenchers. The government was defeated. Peel threatened to resign and the amendment was passed in a second vote

In 1845, Peel extended his 1842 policies with a new budget. Export duties on British goods were abolished, as were import duties on most raw materials, such as cotton. Sugar duties were further reduced, and Peel announced that the new income tax would be extended for a further three years. This allowed him to reduce indirect taxes, which he felt had a greater impact on people's lives.

By 1845–6, the deficit had turned to a surplus of £1.2 million.

During his second ministry (1841–6, see pages 119–24), Peel passed legislation which reformed three other areas of the economy: banks, the organisation of companies and railways.

SOURCE B

Lord Hatherton, a Whig peer in the House of Lords who was heavily involved with Whig reform campaigns in the 1830s, writing in his diary upon Peel's death in 1850.

Peel always seemed to me the most faultless of Ministers. The steadiness of his application and his facility of research, acquired from habit and good memory, were quite wonderful; he always appeared to me to do everything with great ease. Naturally he did not appear to me good-tempered, but his temperament was not hasty, and his feelings were held under wonderful control. He frequently carried the House away with him, but it was by his greater knowledge of his subject, and his superior power in handling facts, and by the moral character of his sentiments.

SOURCE QUESTION

How reliable might Source B be in considering Hatherton's view of Peel?

ONLINE EXTRAS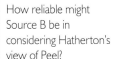
OCR

Practise your source analysis skills by completing Worksheet 32 at **www. hoddereducation.co.uk/ accesstohistory/extras**

Banking reform

Peel's Bank Charter Act 1844 regulated the banking system (see page 120). It ensured that the Bank of England was the only institution that could issue banknotes. Other existing banks could issue only a limited number of banknotes, restricted to the average that they had issued in the three months prior to the Act. New banks, or banks that amalgamated (joined together to make larger banks), were not allowed to issue banknotes. Some banks in Scotland, such as the Bank of Scotland, retained the right to print notes. The Bank of England itself was limited to issuing £14 million of banknotes, after which any additional notes had to be covered by the bank's **gold bullion** reserves.

There were two main aims of this legislation:

- The Act made the currency more reliable. The Bank of England came to dominate the supply of notes, and since it had to guarantee the value with its gold reserves, investors could rely on the value. This stimulated trade and investment. It also created enough confidence in banks for a cheque system to develop, whereby businessmen could pay with a cheque, with the recipient trusting the validity and value of the currency.

- In the process of change, smaller banks amalgamated to form larger banks. This was necessary to allow businesses to take out the larger loans that they needed to maintain financial growth. The continued large-scale operation of smaller banks would have stifled the economy.

This Act stabilised the banking sector. It established the Bank of England as the main administrative bank in Britain and supported trade in a growing empire. This essential piece of legislation was crucial to British economic success until the early twentieth century.

> **KEY TERM**
>
> **Gold bullion** Bars of gold kept by a bank to guarantee the value of its printed money.

> **SOURCE QUESTION**
>
> What danger was Peel referring to in Source C?

SOURCE C

Part of the official parliamentary record of a speech given by Peel over the 1844 Bank Charter Act.

When I call to mind the danger to which the Bank of England has been exposed, … then indeed I rejoice on public grounds in the hope, that the wisdom of Parliament will at length devise measures which shall inspire just confidence in the medium of exchange … .

[Footnote by civil servant: Peel explained that Parliament had the power … to reconsider the charter of the Bank of England, provided it did so within a few months. The state of the nation demanded, in his opinion, that Her Majesty's Government should accept this opportunity. He therefore asked members of the House to give consideration to the subject no matter what pressure should be applied to them by country bankers who feared curtailment of their existing privileges.]

Reform to the organisation of companies

Prior to 1844, there was a genuine concern about how easy it was for disreputable businessmen to defraud customers by setting up fake businesses to steal investments, or for company directors to make unwise financial decisions and lose investors' money. In 1844, a Select Committee investigating this found that there was no system of accounting in place or control measures to prevent poor management.

The Joint Stock Companies Act 1844 introduced the post of Registrar of Companies. All companies with more than 25 members and transferable company shares had to be registered, issue a prospectus covering their business, and publish audited accounts annually. This did not prevent all fraud, neither did the Act cover all businesses. Smaller companies, for example, were exempt, as were businesses formed by Act of parliament, such as the railway companies. But it did reduce corruption in larger businesses.

The Act gave investors confidence in businesses. They were safer from fraud or mis-advertising, and this stimulated greater investment in British businesses.

Railway reform

By the 1840s, 'railway mania' was well underway. Peel introduced key legislation which regulated and standardised the system:

- 1842 Railway Clearing House: as train companies began to share lines, it became complicated to organise the division of ticket fares. For example, a passenger could get on a train owned by one company, travel along sections of track owned by another company, and get off at a station owned by yet another company. The clearing house was an organisation that divided the money for each company.

- 1844 Railway Act: this law required companies owning tracks to provide at least one train service per day in each direction on the track. They could charge a maximum of 1p per mile and travel at a minimum speed of 12 mph. This became known as the 'parliamentary train'. Although it tended to be a slow travel option, it opened up cheap transport every day to the working classes.

- 1846 Broad Gauge Act: there had been a division between tracks made to Stephenson's 1.4-metre gauge design, and those on Brunel's 2.1-metre gauge; this was known as the 'gauge wars'. This Act set 1.4 metres as the standard for all tracks, although the Great Western Railway did not complete the conversion of its tracks until 1892. The law also required train companies to share their lines with other companies.

The repeal of the Corn Laws

A significant change to the British economy was Peel's decision to repeal the Corn Laws. Although the consequences were political as well as economic, it was essentially an economic decision (see pages 122–6). The main economic impact was to establish free trade as a principle for the British economy. The actual financial impact of the repeal on the economy was slow. There was no collapse of food prices, as opponents had predicted. However, it did prevent food prices from rising, which benefited the poor. Ireland did not see a notable improvement until the 1850s, at which point it benefited from the same upturn in the economy that the rest of British enjoyed. Combined with the agricultural developments of the 1840s mentioned earlier in this chapter, the resulting free trade led to a stable prosperity in agriculture in the 1850s.

ONLINE EXTRAS **WWW**
AQA

Learn how to write counter-arguments by completing Worksheet 32 at **www.hoddereducation.co.uk/accesstohistory/extras**

ONLINE EXTRAS **WWW**
Pearson Edexcel

Learn how to address the concept of significance by completing Worksheet 32 at **www.hoddereducation.co.uk/accesstohistory/extras**

SOURCE QUESTION

How are the views of Prince Albert expressed in Source D of use to a historian?

SOURCE D

Part of a memorandum about Peel's economic policies written by Prince Albert (Queen Victoria's husband) on 25 December 1845.

Sir Robert has an immense scheme in view; he thinks that he shall be able to remove the contest entirely from the dangerous ground upon which it has got – that of a war between the manufacturers, the hungry and the poor against the landed proprietors, the aristocracy, which can only end in the ruin of the latter … He will adopt the principle of the [Anti-Corn Law] League, that of removing all protection and abolishing all monopoly, but not in favour of one class and as a triumph over another, but to the benefit of the nation. Farmers as well as manufacturers … The experiments he had made in 1842 and 1845 with boldness but with caution had borne out the correctness of the principle.

SOURCE QUESTION

To whom is Disraeli referring in Source E and what is his opinion of him?

SOURCE E

Part of Disraeli's speech to parliament in response to the third and final reading of the bill to repeal the Corn Laws, 15 May 1846.

But was it not strange that, after so much agitation, after all these schemes, after all these Machiavellian [scheming] manoeuvres, when the Minister at last met the House and his party, he acted as if we had deserted him, instead of his having left us? … Yet even then the right hon. Gentleman had no cause to complain of his party. Why, what a compliment to a Minister – not only to vote for him, but to vote for him against your opinions, and in favour of opinions which he had always drilled you to distrust … When I examine the career of this Minister, which has now filled a great space in the Parliamentary history of this country, I find that for between thirty and forty years … that right hon. Gentleman has traded on the ideas and intelligence of others. His life has been one great appropriation clause. He is a burglar of others' intellect.

ONLINE EXTRAS
OCR   WWW

Practise your source analysis skills by completing Worksheet 33 at **www.hoddereducation.co.uk/accesstohistory/extras**

ONLINE EXTRAS
OCR   WWW

Practise your source analysis skills by completing Worksheet 34 at **www.hoddereducation.co.uk/accesstohistory/extras**

SUMMARY DIAGRAM

ECONOMIC LEGISLATION IN THE 1840S

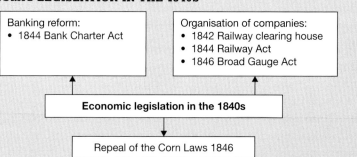

Banking reform:
- 1844 Bank Charter Act

Organisation of companies:
- 1842 Railway clearing house
- 1844 Railway Act
- 1846 Broad Gauge Act

Economic legislation in the 1840s

Repeal of the Corn Laws 1846

3 Mid-Victorian boom to 1873; Great Depression from 1873

■ *Why was Britain's economic success so strong until 1873?*

■ *Why could the scale of economic success not be maintained after 1873?*

From the late 1840s until the early 1870s, the British economy was at the height of its economic and industrial power. With free trade established following the repeal of the Corn Laws, the last bastions of protectionism crumbled. The Navigation Acts, which had acted for decades to prevent foreign competition in naval trade, were repealed in 1849 (for foreign trade) and 1854 (for coastal trade). Tariffs on sugar were phased out. Successive governments strengthened free trade. For example, Gladstone (as chancellor of the exchequer under Lord Aberdeen and then Lord Palmerston) removed duties on soap in 1853 and paper in 1861. *The Times* newspaper in 1859 stated: 'Free trade is henceforth, like parliamentary representation or ministerial responsibility, not so much a prevalent opinion as an article of national faith.' By the mid-nineteenth century, British trade and industry was so strong that 40 per cent of manufactured goods traded in the world were produced in Britain, and about 25 per cent of world trade passed through British ports. Britain was the 'workshop of the world'. The British Empire provided both a source of raw materials and an extensive market to which to sell.

The British economy benefited from socio-political stability. Taxes were low and food prices were steady. The agricultural and transport developments of the 1840s meant that there was a variety of food available in urban areas. The middle classes, with the right to vote, and influential in local government (see the 1835 Municipal Corporations Act, page 117), were a stabilising factor on the country. As well as industrialists and landowners, professionals and shopkeepers were represented on town councils. The working classes also had trade unions to represent their demands. There were none of the radical threats that had threatened the peace in the 1830s and 1840s. Living conditions for the majority, although not for those in deepest poverty, were improving.

On top of the world

Nowhere was this combination of economic strength, imperial power and socio-political stability as evident as at the 1851 Great Exhibition of the Works of Industry of All Nations. This was a huge display of British and imperial power, creativity and patriotism in a purpose-built glass building in London, one-third of a mile long, known as the Crystal Palace. Six million visitors turned up during the five-month exhibition, many using cheap train tickets. Of the 14,000 exhibitors, more than half were British or colonial. This major event took place only two miles from Kennington Common, where only three years earlier

Feargus O'Connor had organised a march on parliament which had caused such panic that thousands of soldiers and police were brought in to keep the peace (see page 131). Yet at the Great Exhibition, the police dealt with nothing worse than pickpocketing.

The golden age of agriculture

Excluding a brief dip in 1850–2, which caused some mild panic when farm rents had to be reduced, by 1853 British farmers were harvesting successively high yields. The developments of the 1840s in steam technology, lighter iron tools, better drainage and fertiliser had created a boom in agricultural produce.

Many farmers adopted a practice called 'high farming': moving from traditional methods, referred to as 'low farming', to styles of farming aimed at maximising production. There were three key strands to high farming:

- Adopting mixed farming. Instead of focusing on a limited range of produce, many farmers chose to diversify their work, producing grains and root crops as well as livestock. This protected farmers from fluctuations in the prices of products from year to year, compared to farmers who specialised in one product.

- Investing in new methods. Farmers invested in steam machinery to drain their land and improve the quality, as well as threshing machines and other new mechanisms. They purchased high-quality fertilisers, either imported guano or industrially produced fertiliser.

- Developments in animal husbandry. Some farmers raised specific breeds of livestock, such as cattle which provided superior beef, to improve the quantity and quality of meat and dairy products.

High farming led to high profits. Successful farmers built large farmhouses and enjoyed a luxurious lifestyle. In the cities, British farmers made meat and dairy products available at prices that the majority could afford, which increased quality of life. But not all farmers benefited from high farming. Those without the money or land to diversify and invest were forced to continue in low farming techniques, particularly farmers in the north and west of Scotland.

Industrial and transport developments

One major reason for the economic golden age was developments in industry and transport.

An increased labour force

The population increased from 27.3 million in 1851 to 31.4 million in 1881, a fifteen per cent increase. The increase was particularly high in industrial areas – between 1851 and 1871, the population of the north-west of England increased by 34 per cent, while London increased by 39 per cent. The larger workforce allowed the development of larger industrial projects. The growing population kept agricultural prices from falling due to increasing demand.

An increase in coal mining

The market for coal had increased as it was required for transport, such as railways and steamships, as well as the manufacture of materials such as iron and steel. Wire ropes and steam-powered winding gear made the removal of coal from mines faster. In 1850, annual coal production was 49.4 million tonnes, of which 6.8 per cent was exported. By 1875, 131.9 million tonnes were being produced and 13.5 per cent was exported. Larger quantities of coal allowed other industries to flourish. For example, by 1870 the iron industry was using one-third of the coal mined in Britain.

An increase in iron and steel production

In 1827, John Neilson developed the 'hot blast' technique of preheating air before it was blown into the blast furnace, improving the efficiency of iron and steel production. In 1844, James Nasmyth designed the steam hammer, which produced large iron and steel goods more quickly. And, in 1856, Henry Bessemer, an industrialist in Sheffield, designed a method for mass-producing high-quality steel. Production increased annually; by 1880, Britain was producing 1.3 million tonnes annually. Iron and steel were required in the production of ships, railways, industrial and agricultural machinery. Iron ore production increased from 9 million tonnes in 1855 to 15 million by 1875.

Improvements to railways

Railway lines were extended into rural areas of Wales and Scotland. Many of the new lines were aimed at passenger transport and linked large towns together or to seaside resorts. Developments in precision engineering enabled improvements in engines and rolling stock. In 1863, the London Underground opened its first line, the Metropolitan Line. It carried over 21 million passengers in the first two years alone. By 1871, British trains were carrying 322 million passengers annually, 166 million tonnes of freight, and taking £41.3 million in receipts. The railways continued to stimulate coal, iron and steel production and helped to create and maintain jobs in other industries, for example, seaside resorts benefited from an influx of holidaymakers and day-trippers.

Improvements to shipping

The production of coal, iron and steel allowed Britain to stay ahead of competing nations in iron ship production, aided by earlier improvements in steam power. British steamship production increased from 11,800 tonnes in the 1840s (nine per cent of shipping production) to 107,000 tonnes in the 1860s (34 per cent of shipping production). British steamships allowed Britain to outcompete with other nations, like the USA, by reaching further markets – for example, they used the Suez Canal to dominate trade with India, China and Australia. Shipbuilding stimulated other industries, like coal and iron, and industrial docking areas such as the Clyde region.

The impact of increased trade

The impact of the increased trade for Britain was varied:

■ Trade allowed Britain to build up its staple industries of raw materials. These played a crucial role in British exports. By the 1860s and 1870s, for example, iron and steel made up about sixteen per cent of British exports, while machinery and coal each made up another four per cent.

■ The capital raised through trade allowed continual investment into these key industries.

■ The British economy's reliance on international trade contributed to the development of an isolationist international policy. Britain stayed out of the wars of the mid-nineteenth century after the Crimean War (1853–6), avoiding wars like the American Civil War (1863–6) and the Franco-Prussian War (1870–1). This kept military costs down, while also capitalising on the disruption these wars caused to economic competitors such as the USA.

■ The booming trade allowed Gladstone's Liberal governments to keep taxes down, which especially benefited entrepreneurs and industrialists, who built personal fortunes.

■ Employment was high due to trade; wage earners created a demand in the economy by their desire to buy consumer goods and travel on the railways.

ONLINE EXTRAS **WWW**
AQA

Develop your analysis of the strength and stability of the British economy, 1832–70, by completing Worksheet 33 at **www.hoddereducation. co.uk/accesstohistory/extras**

The Great Depression (agriculture and industry) 1873

Historians have questioned the extent to which the Great Depression of agriculture in 1873 was a true depression – there was certainly stagnation in parts of the economy, but it did not collapse.

The agriculture in the 1850s and 1860s had benefited enormously from the British dominance in shipping. By the 1870s, other nations such as the USA were starting to challenge that dominance.

Depression in agriculture

■ Grain imported from the USA was sold at lower prices, causing economic difficulties for British farmers.

■ From 1873, a series of wet summers and poor harvests damaged the farming industry. The high yields of the previous twenty years were over.

■ Disraeli, previously a hard-line protectionist, was prime minister from 1874 to 1880. He had become a firm believer in free trade and decided not to reintroduce protectionist policies such as new Corn Laws (see pages 47 and 123).

■ The landed elite, who wanted the reintroduction of tariffs, no longer had the political dominance of previous decades.

■ Falling agricultural prices contributed to the increase in Irish nationalism, including the emergence of the Land League in 1879 (see page 160).

Depression in industry

- Part of Britain's earlier success had been due to being ahead of the world in its Industrial Revolution. By the 1870s, other countries such as Germany were offering greater competition.

- British industrialists, despite continued innovation, failed to keep up with changing scientific trends. The family nature of many businesses and a confidence that older, traditional industries such as cotton would remain a staple of the economy contrasted starkly with countries such as the USA and Germany. Germany, for example, was investing heavily in scientific apparatus and chemical industries.

- The home markets in other modernising countries were stronger than the British home market because of their relative size. For example, in 1880 the USA had a population of over 50 million, compared to less than 35 million in the UK.

- Industry continued to expand but at a far lower rate than in the previous twenty years.

- Overproduction was beginning to have an impact, as supply had outpaced demand both in the UK and abroad. This led to falling prices and, consequently, falling profits.

- British education was not modernising, despite Liberal improvements. Most youngsters left school by twelve with a basic, traditional education. In Germany, by contrast, youngsters were given an education more focused on industrial training.

The depression continued for the remainder of the nineteenth century. Historians Neil Tonge and Michael Quincey (1980) refer to this as a 'paradox of depression amidst prosperity', as the volume of trade and industrial production was still increasing, but the value of economic growth was falling as other nations drew closer to overtaking them. Britain would not be fully overtaken economically until the First World War.

It is clear that the government recognised this as a period of depression. In 1885, a Royal Commission was formed to investigate the causes of the depression, and it reported back in 1886; one of the conclusions was that Britain was disadvantaged by having industrialised first and now needing to adapt to the changing requirements of international competition.

ONLINE EXTRAS
AQA WWW
Get to grips with the reasons for the Great Depression by completing Worksheet 34 at **www.hoddereducation. co.uk/accesstohistory/extras**

What was the economic condition of Britain in 1885?

Britain had undergone a rapid process of industrialisation which had left the country urbanised and created a strong economy with a huge share of international trade. By 1885:

- Britain had an extensive rail network which transported goods but was also used by passengers for the purposes of migration and leisure.

- Britain had an enormous trade empire, supplied by steam-powered iron and steel ships.

- Agriculture had become modernised, with scientifically developed methods of animal husbandry and technological developments that made crop growth more efficient.
- Britain had a thriving heavy industry base which was producing huge quantities of iron, steel and coal.
- Despite the growth, in 1885 Britain was experiencing the effects of the depression which had set in during the 1870s. This was in part due to other nations such as Germany and the USA catching up with Britain's industrial advantage.

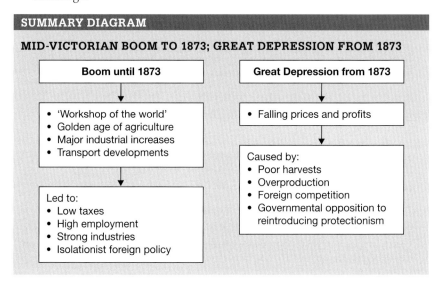

SUMMARY DIAGRAM

MID-VICTORIAN BOOM TO 1873; GREAT DEPRESSION FROM 1873

Boom until 1873	Great Depression from 1873
• 'Workshop of the world' • Golden age of agriculture • Major industrial increases • Transport developments	• Falling prices and profits
Led to: • Low taxes • High employment • Strong industries • Isolationist foreign policy	Caused by: • Poor harvests • Overproduction • Foreign competition • Governmental opposition to reintroducing protectionism

CHAPTER SUMMARY

By the mid-nineteenth century, the position of Britain as the 'workshop of the world' was secure. The Industrial Revolution had established the basis for the economy, but after 1832, the expansion of faster, steam-driven shipping expanded international trade and, along with developments in agriculture, ushered in the mid-Victorian boom. A major development was the expansion of the railways with 'railway mania'. As well as expanding the economy and creating new jobs, it had an enormous social impact as the population became more mobile. Tourism became a reality and the expectations of working-class life in Britain developed.

Crucial to the stability of this growth was the decision, largely under Peel, for the government to introduce economic legislation and become directly involved in the economy. This stabilised the economic growth in Britain.

Despite these successes, there was a downturn from 1873, in the form of the Great Depression. While the name is an overstatement, in that it was a slowing down rather than a collapse, it showed that the British economy, while strong, was soon to face strong international competition from Germany and the USA.

Refresher questions

Use these questions to remind yourself of the key material covered in this chapter.

1 What key developments in shipping happened during the nineteenth century?

2 What was 'railway mania'?

3 Give one positive and one negative social consequence of the development of railways after 1832.

4 What was the economic importance of the 1844 Bank Charter Act?

5 Why did Peel's reforms to the railways benefit the economy?

6 Why was the 1851 Great Exhibition a key moment for British imperial and economic power?

7 What was 'high farming' and how did it impact on agriculture?

8 Describe the British economic position between *c.*1850 and *c.*1870.

9 Why did increased trade affect the British economy?

10 How did the Great Depression from 1873 affect industry and agriculture?

Question practice: AQA A level

Essay questions

1 To what extent were social consequences the most significant results of developments to transport between 1832 and 1885?

EXAM HINT Make sure that you cover the whole period and the different branches of transport. Were social consequences for the British people more important than economic opportunities?

2 'The "golden age of agriculture" was the main reason for the economic strength of Victorian Britain in the period 1850–73.' Assess the validity of this view.

EXAM HINT You are being asked to assess the reasons for Britain's economic strength. How far was it due to agriculture? How much to other factors such as industry, empire and finance?

3 'The positive economic benefits of industrialisation in the period 1832–85 outweighed the negative economic effects.' Assess the validity of this view.

EXAM HINT You are being asked to assess whether the positive or negative effects were more prominent. Avoid describing. Analyse effects and reach a judgement.

Question practice: OCR A level

Source question

1 Using Sources B (page 175), C (page 176), D (page 178) and E (page 178) in their historical context, assess how far they support the view that Peel had a programme of effective economic legislation in the 1840s.

EXAM HINT Group the sources according to whether or not they support the view in the question. Each source should be explained in relation to the question, its provenance evaluated and contextual knowledge used to test the view of the source. A judgement about each source in relation to the question should be reached, allowing an overall judgement about whether the sources support the view that Peel had a programme of effective economic legislation in the 1840s.

Question practice: Pearson Edexcel A level

Essay questions

1 Was the development of transport the main consequence of the increase of industrialisation, 1832–70? Explain your answer.

EXAM HINT Explain the growth of employment in the stated period. Note also the impact of the railways on matters such as trade, the coal industry and leisure activities.

2 How significant were government attitudes towards industrial development in the growth of the British economy between 1832 and 1870?

EXAM HINT Compare legislation in the stated period with other factors, including the growth of the navy and the impact of the empire on trade and the economy.

CHAPTER 9

Dealing with the poor: social developments 1832–85

By the 1830s, social problems were an increasing concern for the government, particularly the growing issue of poverty. The governments of 1832–85 increasingly recognised the need to legislate to relieve the most serious issues. This chapter examines the social reform that occurred through the following themes:

◆ The problem of poverty

◆ Social reform 1832–53

◆ Social reform 1853–85

◆ Cooperative organisations and self-help

KEY DATES

1832	Feb.	Royal Commission formed to investigate poverty and the operation of the Poor Law	1854		Dr John Snow demonstrated the link between dirty water and cholera
	June	Representation of the People Act passed	1865		Louis Pasteur published evidence on the link between bacteria and disease
1834		Poor Law Amendment Act (New Poor Law) passed; applied in the south of England	1867		Representation of the People Act passed
1837		Poor Law applied in the north of England	1870		Forster's Education Act passed
			1871		Vaccination Act passed, with powers for the State to enforce the law
1842		Chadwick published a report on poor sanitation			
1843		Royal Commission initiated into the causes of death in areas of poverty	1875		Public Health Act passed, with powers for the State to enforce the law
1844		Equitable Pioneers of Rochdale opened the first cooperative store	1880		Education Act extended to make education compulsory until ten years of age
1845		Andover scandal			
1848		Public Health Act passed			

1 The problem of poverty

■ *How did the government attempt to deal with poverty?*

Despite the passing of the 1832 Reform Act (see pages 62–3), Britain was still very much a divided society. Most of the population were working class, and many lived on low wages. There was a significant difference between the poorest, who relied on poor relief to live, and the wealthiest. This did not change substantially through the nineteenth century. An analysis published in 1876 estimated that just 4000 families owned more than 50 per cent of the land in Britain, whereas 95 per cent of the population owned no land at all.

It was not only land ownership that demonstrated the divide. In the 1850s, the average labouring family might earn on average £41 per year, while the wealthiest would annually earn thousands. The 1851 census showed that there were about a million outdoor agricultural labourers, and half a million indoor farm servants. Most of these were labourers. Their employment was dependent on good harvests and sufficient work. Since many lived in cottages tied to the work, losing their work could mean losing their home as well.

Generally, no matter how successful a society, there will always be those with less than the majority. In the nineteenth century, poverty was more severe in rural areas, due to 'congregation', or the development of areas with populations that lived closely together in cramped conditions. This was a result of a combination of factors, including:

- urbanisation (the movement of people from rural areas to towns)
- the factory system (which provided low-income work)
- poor-quality housing (which led to many people living in close proximity in poor conditions)
- a *laissez-faire* attitude to social reform.
- rapid population growth.

KEY TERMS

Laissez-faire
Government policy of leaving an issue alone and not interfering.

Lodging houses Cheap hostels where a person could pay for a bed.

Overcrowded urban areas

In the nineteenth century, houses in the poorest urban areas were overcrowded, with several families sharing one building with one room each. Some houses might have up to 60 people. In Liverpool in the 1840s, 40,000 people were living in cellars, with an average of six people per cellar. The worst areas were **lodging houses**, where beds were crammed in so that 30 or more people could live in one building. The nineteenth-century statistician William Farr estimated that the 1860s' population of Liverpool was 66,000 per square mile, which meant that there were 39 square metres per person (modern Liverpool has 124 square metres per person).

Disease

A consequence of the overcrowding was a growing problem with sanitation and disease. This was partly due to people living in close proximity, since diseases could spread with great speed. For example, a typhus epidemic occurred in 1837, 1839 and 1847 which killed 10,000 in the north-west of England in 1847 alone. A smallpox outbreak also spread in the years 1837–40, killing at least 10,000 people. Children were particularly vulnerable; in the mid-nineteenth century, one-quarter of children died by their first birthday.

Poor health was also due to a lack of basic sanitation. The State did not provide sufficient facilities for the sheer growth in population. In some areas, a lack of maintenance for water supplies led to polluted water, which caused the cholera outbreaks of 1831 and 1849. In 1849, there were 53,293 reports of cholera.

Those in poverty were unable to avoid these unsanitary conditions, and were forced into dangerous situations. For example, there were reports of families having to keep the dead body of a relative inside for up to two weeks until they could afford the basic funeral costs.

Crime

The emergence of large, overcrowded towns caused a rise in crime. This was the result of the combination of poverty, the anonymity of large populations and crowded areas where it was easy to disappear, and the breakdown of community spirit due to the fluctuating population. However, violent crimes were still relatively rare; most crime was petty theft.

The Poor Law

Poor relief was provided under the Poor Law, established in 1601. The principle of the law was that the poor were to be looked after by local parishes. The impotent poor (those who could not care for themselves due to sickness, age or disability) were to be looked after in poorhouses, while the able-bodied poor (those healthy enough to work) were to be given the opportunity to work in a workhouse. From the 1720s, many parishes deliberately made their workhouses unpleasant places, and made entering the workhouse a condition of receiving aid – the so-called 'workhouse test'. The idea was that only a person genuinely in need would be willing to live in the workhouse, where people were treated harshly and made to do tiring, difficult work (see page 190).

Many parishes chose to use outdoor relief as it was simpler than providing sufficient workhouse spaces for the poor. This meant giving financial aid to **paupers** without them having to move into a workhouse. This was particularly used for seasonal labourers, since they might have work at some points of the year.

> ### KEY TERM
>
> **Pauper** A person in poverty who needed financial assistance. While some people spent their whole lives as paupers, others who lived close to the poverty line could drift in and out of being a pauper.

The provision of aid was inefficient and varied greatly. As local ratepayers had an eye on the cost of providing aid, different areas tried different systems. Some of the most important were:

- Speenhamland system: created by magistrates at Speenhamland, Berkshire, this system was introduced in 1795 and copied by many other parishes. It worked by calculating the amount of money a family needed based on the cost of a loaf of bread and the size of the family, and subsidising the wages of labourers until they could meet that cost. Some parishes varied this system by offering goods, such as flour, in place of money. This system was common in the south and east of England, but rarely used in the north.

- The labour rate: about twenty per cent of parishes, particularly in the north, operated a system whereby ratepayer could either hire labourers for a fixed daily wage, or pay a parish rate to support local paupers. If they paid less in wages than the parish rate would cost them, they had to pay the difference.

- Roundman system: local paupers were hired by local ratepayers, who paid part of their wages, and the local parish paid the rest.

The workhouse regime

Although some local unions attempted to create a more humane workhouse experience, most workhouses forced the poor to live in terrible conditions:

- On entering a workhouse, families were split up.

- Children were required to attend the workhouse school, and when they turned nine or ten could be apprenticed, often to a local cotton mill, without the consent of their parents. This could include being apprenticed to tradesmen who would take them a long way away.

- Inmates were dressed in uniforms which may or may not have fitted.

- They bathed once a week. Men were allowed to shave once a week. All this was watched by the workhouse staff to prevent attempts at drowning or self-mutilation, which added to the feeling of humiliation.

- No personal possessions were allowed.

- The day was designed to be long, hard and boring. People worked from 8a.m. to 6p.m. and were expected to be in bed by 8p.m.

- People would be put to work in laundries and kitchens, or as cleaners. Other work included picking old ropes to pieces to make fibres for new ropes, chopping wood, smashing rocks or breaking down bones for fertiliser. This was similar to the work convicts did in prison.

- Meals were designed to have enough nutrition for survival, but to give no pleasure. They included oatmeal and bread, with low-quality cheese or meat. Until 1842, meals were to be eaten in silence. Many workhouses refused cutlery and some deliberately served the food cold.

- Workhouses were often rowdy, violent places. There is evidence of bullying and even sexual abuse. Although there were standard punishments, such as reducing rations, and a ban on women being beaten, some workhouse masters introduced their own punishments, such as forcing disobedient paupers to sleep in the mortuary.

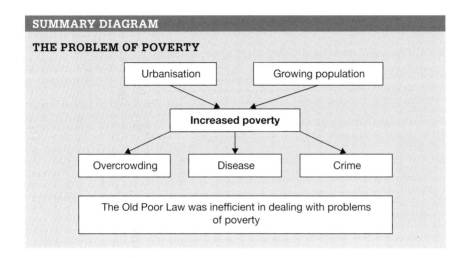

SUMMARY DIAGRAM

THE PROBLEM OF POVERTY

- Urbanisation
- Growing population

→ **Increased poverty** →

- Overcrowding
- Disease
- Crime

The Old Poor Law was inefficient in dealing with problems of poverty

2 Social reform 1832–53

◼ *How did the government reform the Poor Law system, and with what effect?*

By 1832, there was substantial pressure for change in social conditions.

The pressure for change: long-term concerns

- The Poor Law system was almost breaking under the cost of poor relief (see pages 189–90).
- There was a growing belief that the administration of the Poor Law was corrupt. Contracts for workhouse supplies or maintenance were frequently awarded to local merchants, often on the same committee who administered the Poor Law.
- There was some worry that the Poor Law was counterproductive. Critics thought that outdoor relief did not make life difficult enough for the poor to avoid supporting those who were simply lazy. Others worried that the Speenhamland system encouraged the poor to have large families, or that the labour rate and Roundman systems encouraged the poor to expect the parish to take care of them.
- The Napoleonic War years caused economic strain which continued in the post-war period. There was high unemployment caused by fluctuating food costs. The Corn Laws (see page 47) simply maintained high prices for the poor and created national resentment.

The pressure for change: short-term concerns

- The **Swing Riots** of the 1830s showed the level of discontent among the working classes. That this was mainly in the south, where the Speenhamland system was in wider use, was taken as evidence that the Poor Law system was increasing poverty. It encouraged employers to keep wages down (as they would be topped up by the local parish) and labourers to have larger families (to receive a larger allowance).

- There was a fear of revolution, since France was again caught up in revolution in 1830, and it seemed like this could spread to Britain.

- The reform crisis which led to the 1832 Reform Act had shown the potential for popular protest to cause change.

The Whig government which came to power during the reform crisis believed that action was necessary to stabilise the country.

The Poor Law Commission 1832

In 1832, Earl Grey's Whig government formed a Royal Commission to investigate the operation of the Poor Law. It consisted of 29 assistant commissioners tasked with investigating the Poor Law in the 15,000 parishes, and reporting back. The Commission was dominated by the ideas of **Utilitarianism**, mainly by the influence of the commissioners Nassau Senior and **Edwin Chadwick**. Utilitarian ideas had been developed by Jeremy Bentham, Chadwick's mentor, who proposed that a successful society would be one where the happiness of the greatest number of people was achieved. Therefore, supporters of Utilitarianism opposed the Poor Law on two grounds:

- It forced the greater number to support a minority in poverty.

- By supporting those in poverty, it prevented them from working to achieve their own happiness.

Some utilitarian thinkers believed in a completely *laissez-faire* approach, allowing people to be entirely independent. And so, the Commission started with a fixed conclusion: the Poor Law needed to be replaced. Senior and Chadwick even wrote large parts of their conclusions before the evidence was collected. Assistant commissioners used three petitions, asking questions designed to gain answers to support these conclusions, and only ten per cent of parishes replied.

The Poor Law Amendment Act

The Commission produced an 8000-page report in 1834, based on the thirteen volumes of evidence collected. The evidence showed that poor relief in 1832 was costing nearly £7 million; to this, Chadwick added £5 million in unsatisfactory health measures and £2 million in dealing with crime, claiming that the true total cost of poverty was £14 million.

The report was immediately accepted by the Whig government (there were never more than 50 votes against it in the Commons or Lords) and by August

1834 it had passed the Poor Law Amendment Act. Those who spoke against the Act – for example, Tories who saw it as an attack on *laissez-faire* policy, or old radicals like William Cobbett (see page 111) who saw relief as a human right – were a minority who could be easily ignored.

The Act broadly followed the proposals in the report:

- A central authority should be set up to administer the Poor Law.
- Parishes should form Poor Law unions to organise efficient relief.
- Each Poor Law union was required to have a workhouse.
- The conditions in the workhouse were to be worse than the conditions of an independent labourer.
- Outdoor relief was discouraged, but not abolished.

The Act did not stipulate how the Poor Law should be carried out beyond these terms. This was left in the control of the three Poor Law commissioners, who had contracts for five years. Chadwick was only appointed as secretary to the Commission; he had expected to be a commissioner and bitterly clashed with the Commission many times over the next fourteen years. The Commission was independent of parliament, which was an advantage in that it was free to apply the reforms how it wanted without bothering with public opinion. However, this meant that it had no voice in parliament, and lacked direct power to force parishes to follow its instructions.

Instead, from 1834 to 1837, the Commission imposed the Poor Law by pressuring parishes in the south of England to form Poor Law unions. The aim was to create one workhouse per 10,000 people. While some areas followed the recommendations, many ignored the order, especially in areas which had already formed unions under the Old Poor Law.

The government also passed:

- the 1842 Outdoor Labour Test Order, which commanded parishes not yet following the reforms to require paupers to work in a labour yard before receiving outdoor relief
- the 1844 General Outdoor Relief Prohibitory Order, which completely banned outdoor relief.

By 1837, the New Poor Law was working to some degree in the south of England. Many farmers and landlords, benefiting from several good harvests, accepted it without too much opposition. Rural protest was limited, partly due to the recent **Tolpuddle Martyrs**, which made labourers fear protesting.

The Anti-Poor Law League

The Commission turned its attention to the north of England. By this time, however, the economy had taken a downturn. Added to that, the system which suited the south reasonably well was not at all adapted for the northern mill towns, where unemployment was cyclical, and workers might find themselves in need only of short-term relief during a temporary downturn in the local mills.

KEY TERM

Tolpuddle Martyrs
A legal case in 1834, in which six agricultural labourers from the village of Tolpuddle in Dorset were convicted of swearing an oath as members of a labour union, and sentenced to transportation.

Working-class radicals and Tory paternalists such as John Fielden and Richard Oastler fought together against the New Poor Law, forming the Anti-Poor Law League. Unlike earlier discontent movements, this was well organised, with petitions and meetings. However, it was not a sophisticated or moderate movement – many of the pamphlets and speeches were emotional outbursts threatening violence and showing the Poor Law commissioners as inhuman tyrants. Some relied on anecdotes of cruelty that were not true. There were also violent protests and riots that were put down by militia. These factors meant that the League was not taken very seriously by wealthy supporters of the New Poor Law. Ultimately, the Anti-Poor Law movement was short lived, and faded by 1839.

How 'new' was the New Poor Law?

Table 9.1 (see below) summarises the changes to the Poor Law brought about by the Poor Law Amendment Act of 1834.

Table 9.1 A comparison of the New and Old Poor Laws

Change	Continuity
• There was a central Commission overseeing what had been a local parish responsibility • The State was taking a direct role, albeit with little hands-on control from the government • The expenditure on poor relief fell by 27 per cent in the years 1834–7 and a further three per cent by 1843 (see Figure 9.1, page 195) • There were local Poor Law guardians with responsibility for the administration of the local workhouse, rather than the local 'select vestry'	• Many areas continued to operate unions under older legislation • Settlement Laws, originally passed in 1662 and 1697 to stop paupers moving to an area and claiming relief, had to be enforced to prevent rural paupers swamping urban areas in search of relief • Despite the 1842 and 1844 efforts to end outdoor relief, most parishes continued it in some form; it being cheaper and easier. Until 1870, up to 70 per cent of paupers may have continued to receive outdoor relief; even in 1871, less than twenty per cent of parishes had fully abolished outdoor relief • Many of the guardians were the previous workhouse administrators

The impact of the Poor Law Amendment Act

ONLINE EXTRAS
Pearson Edexcel WWW
Learn how to use criteria to support your arguments by completing Worksheet 33 at www.hoddereducation. co.uk/accesstohistory/extras

■ *Discontent among those receiving poor relief.* Many paupers, especially in the north of England, found themselves facing a situation worse than the one that they were already in. It created a fear of the workhouse for generations to come. This discontent was shown through armed riots in such as Oldham, Todmorden and Bradford, and attacks on representatives of the Commission and the workhouses. Many protestors used aggressive rhetoric which concerned the government (see Source A, page 195).

■ *Criticism from ratepayers.* While ratepayers in southern England were generally less critical, northern ratepayers were particularly concerned. They objected to building workhouses for use during temporary economic downturns, only for the workhouse to be nearly empty in better times.

Across the country, ratepayers and influential citizens used their positions to circumvent the Commission.

■ *Chartism.* When opposition fell apart, those who still opposed the Poor Law supported the Chartist movement (see pages 127–36). For many Chartists, universal suffrage would mean protection from legislation like the Poor Law.

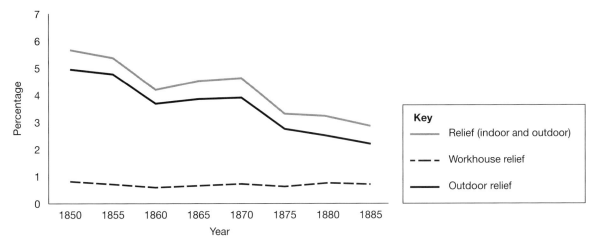

Figure 9.1 The percentage of the UK population receiving relief by year.

SOURCE A

From a speech about the 1834 Poor Law, delivered 1 January 1838 in Newcastle upon Tyne by Joseph Rayner Stephens, a Chartist leader and Methodist minister who was an associate of O'Connor.

And if this damnable law, which violated all the laws of God, was continued, and all means of peaceably putting an end to it have been made in vain, then, in the words of their banner, 'For children and wife we'll war to the knife.' If the people who produce all wealth could not be allowed, according to God's Word, to have the kindly fruits of the earth which they had, in obedience to God's Word, raised by the sweat of their brow, then war to the knife with their enemies, who were the enemies of God If the musket and the pistol, the sword, and the pike were of no avail, let the women take the scissors, the child the pin or needle. If all failed, then the firebrand—aye, the firebrand—the firebrand, I repeat. The palace shall be in flames.

SOURCE QUESTION

What limitations does Source A have for an investigation into the views of opponents of the Poor Law?

ONLINE EXTRAS | **www**
OCR

Practise your source analysis skills by completing Worksheet 35 at **www. hoddereducation.co.uk/ accesstohistory/extras**

Education reforms

The concerns over poverty fed into a concern over education. The idea of individuals being responsible for themselves raised a crucial issue over education, since on the one hand education was necessary for self-improvement, yet on the other the government had a *laissez-faire* attitude.

The solution was the 1833 Education Grant. Each year, the government issued a grant to educational institutions, which was to be split between the Church of England's National Society and the Nonconformist British and Foreign School

Society. The idea was to improve education by allowing the institutions to construct schools, without the government directing the reform. In 1839, a Privy Council on Education was formed to oversee the grants, the first government department overseeing education, although not providing education itself. This council discussed matters relating to improving education, such as the qualifications to work as a teacher or regulating the use of pupils as teachers for the class.

Between 1841 and 1852, the government also passed five School Sites Acts to purchase land for new schools. By 1843, the State also offered grants to help in equipping schoolrooms. Although education would not become compulsory until 1870, these steps began to improve the quality of education.

Public health reform

In 1842, Chadwick led an investigation into public health, concluding that:

- there was a link between the environment and poor health
- a solution was needed for urban sewage by the construction of sewerage systems
- centralised State control was needed for drainage, paving, water supply and street cleaning.

While a professional, such as a doctor or solicitor, in Derby might live to 49 or in Rutland to 52, a labourer in Liverpool had an average life expectancy at birth of just fifteen years, or in Bethnal Green, London, just sixteen. Chadwick's reports led to the creation of a new pressure group, the Health of Towns Association, which campaigned for legislation to reform public health in towns. The reports also led to a Royal Commission into sanitary conditions in towns in 1844, since the home secretary, Sir James Graham, wanted research that was more official than Chadwick's personal crusade.

Since the Poor Law was the only large-scale national administration of a social issue, it made sense to use that administration for public health reforms. For example, education for working-class children and the Vaccination Act 1840 were administered using the Poor Law.

Even after a Royal Commission in 1843 followed up on Chadwick's research and concluded that his link between poor sanitation and water supplies and high death rates was correct, the government was slow to act. The first response was a range of minor legislation between 1846 and 1848:

- A Liverpool Sanitary Act (1846) established a health official in Liverpool and gave the council authority to carry out improvements to sewerage, water supply and drainage systems.
- A series of Nuisance Removal Acts from 1846 enabled local authorities to remove unwholesome houses, foul drains and cesspits.

- The 1846 Baths and Washhouses Act enabled local authorities to use public money to build baths and washhouses.
- The 1847 Towns Improvements Clauses Act defined the rights of towns to lay water supplies, improve drainage schemes and control nuisances.

The Public Health Act 1848

These laws all enabled local authorities to make changes but did not force them to take action. The Public Health Act followed this trend when finally proposed in 1847. It was first rejected by parliament, before a cholera outbreak led to its passing in 1848. The Act:

- established the General Board of Health in London for advising on policy with a five-year contract
- enabled local ratepayers to set up a local board of health if ten per cent of ratepayers petitioned for it
- empowered the board to encourage local health boards to reform public health.

Most larger towns ignored the Act and continued to use private Acts of Parliament to make reforms. By 1854, only 182 local boards had been set up and only thirteen had established water and sewage schemes. Even where boards were formed, the General Board had little authority to insist on reform. Where changes were carried out, they were done with limited awareness of sanitary engineering, which led to instances of new sewer systems flushing into the nearest river – which was also a source of drinking water. Eventually, the General Board was abolished in 1854 due to a combination of lack of public support and the abrasive nature of Chadwick, whose dogmatic manner enabled his opponents to portray the General Board as bullying the nation into cleanliness.

The Andover Workhouse Scandal 1845

At this workhouse, paupers were being deliberately underfed, to the point that they were fighting to eat marrow from the bones that they were forced to smash up for work. This led to an investigation which unearthed other abuses, including attempts to seduce female paupers by both the master and his seventeen-year-old son, and stories of babies not being baptised to save money. This directly led to a change in the New Poor Law, as the Poor Law Commission was replaced with a Poor Law Board which had more authority and included a member of the cabinet. It also contributed to forcing the government to look at the issues of poverty in Britain.

ONLINE EXTRAS WWW
AQA

Develop your analysis of changes in the treatment of the poor by completing Worksheet 35 at **www. hoddereducation.co.uk/ accesstohistory/extras**

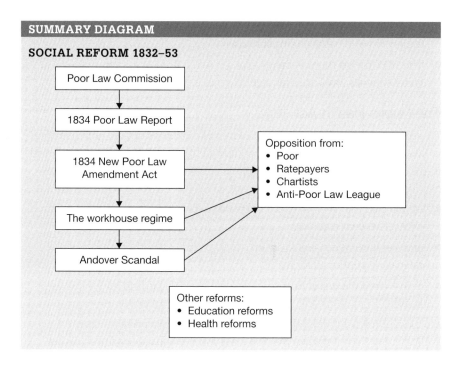

SUMMARY DIAGRAM

SOCIAL REFORM 1832–53

Poor Law Commission
↓
1834 Poor Law Report
↓
1834 New Poor Law Amendment Act
↓
The workhouse regime
↓
Andover Scandal

Opposition from:
• Poor
• Ratepayers
• Chartists
• Anti-Poor Law League

Other reforms:
• Education reforms
• Health reforms

3 Social reform 1853–85

■ *How did the State take more responsibility for social reform after 1853?*

Progressively, from the 1840s to the 1860s, a new public view of poverty had developed. Whereas previously people had had a tendency to see poverty as the fault of the individual, either due to decisions made or a poor work ethic, people began to see poverty as also stemming from circumstances beyond the control of the pauper. An influential development was the cotton famine in Lancashire in the 1860s; many mill workers found themselves out of work because the American Civil War had disrupted the supply of cotton. This coincided with another cholera outbreak in 1866.

The attitude of **individualism** continued to be widely accepted; in 1859, Samuel Smiles published a bestseller, *Self-Help*, which gave advice on how individuals could help themselves out of difficult situations. It contained many anecdotes of individuals in challenging circumstances who improved their position through hard work. The idea of **self-help** became popular. However, the increased sense that poverty was not always down the actions or attitude of the pauper led to the start of a move away from individualism, the belief that the individual was the best judge of his own affairs, to **collectivism**, which assumes that the State is the better judge of the individual's affairs and that each citizen has a claim on society for the State to provide a good quality of life.

Reasons for change

As well as a better sense of collectivism, another change in attitude was the 1867 Reform Act, since it gave the vote to a larger part of the population. Although many working-class men, and especially paupers, did not qualify to vote, the Act extended the idea that individuals had rights within society and that governments represented the population. There was also a practical concern: as the votes opened up to larger parts of the population, the parties had to consider not only policies from their own political outlook but also policies which would win votes. With the extension of the vote in 1884 to a far larger number of men, this became even more important.

The influence of writers

The social concerns of the day were reflected in the writings of a number of notable authors:

- **Charles Dickens** wrote books such as *David Copperfield* (1849), *Great Expectations* (1859) and *A Tale of Two Cities* (1860), which publicised a grim vision of social conditions for the working poor. It is no coincidence that Dickens, who lived near a workhouse at two points in his life, was so critical of workhouses. Most famously, *Oliver Twist* (1837–9) describes the terrible abuses of power by the master of the workhouse, and was published at the height of public opposition to the Poor Law. *Hard Times* (1855) was highly critical of the misery caused by Chadwick and others who had applied Utilitarianism (see page 192) in the Poor Law Amendment Act.

- Elizabeth Gaskell wrote, among other novels, *Mary Barton: A Tale of Manchester Life* (1848), which addressed the social conditions in the industrial north of England.

- Charles Kingsley wrote the children's book *The Water-Babies* (1863), a fairy story with an underlying message exposing child labour.

These authors described social conditions to the parts of literate society who had no experience of them, with characters who could often garner sympathy.

New ideas about health

Through the nineteenth century, some doctors were analysing the link between poverty and poor health. Various ideas were considered, including the traditional view that good health was linked to faith, prayer and living a moral life. There is evidence of a widespread belief that death and illness were linked to poor morals such as drunkenness and prostitution. This was in line with the thinking which had supported the creation of the New Poor Law. As late as 1871, when the Prince of Wales recovered from typhoid, many people believed that it was the result of national prayers.

But new explanations started to emerge. In 1842, Chadwick had produced a report on public health which linked disease to poor sanitary conditions. This was not widely accepted until 1854, when John Snow, a London doctor, carried

KEY FIGURE

Charles Dickens (1812–70)

A British philanthropist and author. Dickens had first-hand experience of the conditions of poverty, both in London and elsewhere, and he portrayed this in his fiction. Most of his stories were first published as serials in weekly or monthly journals, which made them affordable and widely read.

out an experiment in which he showed that cholera was a water-borne disease. During the Crimean War, Florence Nightingale became a national hero when she improved the cleanliness of Scutari Hospital and drastically reduced the mortality rate of patients. At the same time, Charles Darwin was developing his theory of evolution, published in *On the Origin of Species* (1859); while not universally accepted at the time, it did alter thinking about health and survival to a more biologically, rather than morally, based explanation.

By 1865, medical knowledge had extended further. The French scientist Louis Pasteur had conclusively proven the link between bacteria and disease, leading the chief medical officer of health to the Privy Council, John Simon, to finally accept Snow's research into polluted water as a cause of disease by 1870.

How significant was cholera?

Cholera outbreaks were important in pushing legislation; for example, outbreaks influenced the passing of the 1848 Public Health Act and 1866 Sanitary Act. Cholera was not the most serious killer: the 1865–6 outbreak killed 20,000 but annually 50,000 people were dying from common diseases. Yet the horrible manner of death combined with the fear that cholera epidemics generated helped to stimulate reform. Without the outbreaks of smallpox, it is unlikely that legislation for vaccination would have progressed.

ONLINE EXTRAS
AQA   **WWW**

Get to grips with reasons for social reforms, 1853–85, by completing Worksheet 36 at **www.hoddereducation. co.uk/accesstohistory/extras**

Reforms to public health

Public health also followed the trend of greater government responsibility and centralised control. Political parties became more open to this after the 1867 Reform Act created a greater urban electorate:

- 1858 Local Government Act and 1858 Public Health Act: taken together, these two laws replaced the General Board of Health (which had not been renewed after 1854) with a Local Government Act Office. A medical department of the Privy Council was formed and local health boards were given greater powers. In the following ten years, 568 towns set up health boards and began to implement health reforms.

- Joseph Bazalgette, an engineer, oversaw the construction of a sewerage system for London which included underground tunnels and pumping stations. It was opened in 1865, although not completed for another ten years.

- 1866 Sanitary Act: this breakthrough Act put more pressure on local authorities to take action. They were given more authority to deal with sanitation issues, and the definition of 'nuisances' was extended to include domestic properties and overcrowding. The big change was that if local authorities did not take action, central government could step in and charge the local authority for the work.

A photograph from the second half of the nineteenth century showing Joseph Bazalgette (top right) overseeing the construction of Outfall Sewer, the largest sewer in London.

SOURCE QUESTION

What can be inferred from the posed nature of the photo in Source B about the creation of sewers? Hint: how often in modern times do the builders of sewers pose for photos like this?

- 1872 Public Health Act: ensured that the whole country was covered by sanitary authorities, whether town councils or local guardians, and that each had a local medical officer of health.

- 1875 Public Health Act: tied together about 30 previous laws into one legislative package. It confirmed that local authorities not only had the authority to make sanitary reform, but now had an obligation to do so.

The trend of social reform in the nineteenth century

Public health reform therefore followed a clear pattern:

- recognition of a problem and allowing people to take individual action
- passing permissive legislation to allow local authorities to take action
- passing legislation to pressure local authorities to take action
- passing legislation which enforced action.

This same process is repeated in various aspects of social reform in the period.

Reforms to medical care

Vaccines

- From 1834, smallpox vaccinations were available free of charge through the Poor Law system.

- In 1840, following a smallpox outbreak in 1837–9, the 1840 Vaccination Act was passed, which permitted anyone to receive a free vaccination administered through the Poor Law system. It was still voluntary.

- The 1853 Vaccination Act responded to the low take-up of free vaccinations by requiring parents to have their children vaccinated in the first three months of life, but without enforcement.

- The 1871 Vaccination Act, following an outbreak in 1870–3 which killed 44,000 people, required local health boards to enforce vaccinations by appointing vaccination officers and fining or imprisoning parents who refused vaccination.

General medical care

- 1841: poor people could receive medical care from a Poor Law medical officer.

- 1850s: Poor Law unions set up public dispensaries for the public as well as paupers.

- 1852: a poor person who could not afford medical treatments automatically qualified for outdoor relief (which was a contradiction of the efforts to abolish outdoor relief).

- 1860s: medical care for the poor could be provided at home, not only in the workhouse.

From the 1860s, public opinion turned against pauper hospitals in workhouses. Complaint letters were published in *The Lancet*, a medical journal, and *The Times* published articles criticising workhouse hospitals. The Poor Law Board changed its policy, allowing paupers to be cared for in hospitals away from the workhouse. For the first time, there was official recognition that those in poverty deserved a basic standard of health care from the State. By the 1880s, Poor Law unions were providing a growing network of general, specialist, isolation and mental hospitals, with 30 institutions in London alone by 1882. This was the beginning of a national care system for paupers which would be in place by 1900.

Reforms to the Poor Laws

The cost of providing poor relief had risen after the initial reduction in the 1830s. The cost was not evenly spread, since the financial burden within each Poor Law union was placed on the individual parish from which the paupers came. Since generally these were also the parishes least able to afford to pay, this was not an affordable system. The following changes took place:

- The 1865 Union Chargeability Act standardised the system by dividing the cost across parishes – a step towards greater recognition of a wider societal responsibility to care for the poor.

- The 1869 Poor Law Loans Act allowed local guardians to extend loans from the public works' fund to 30 years, meaning that they could take out larger loans to improve Poor Law facilities without substantially increasing local poor rates.

- Despite passing laws banning outdoor relief in 1844 and 1852, outdoor relief continued to make up about 80 per cent of all poor relief nationally. This was because outdoor relief remained:
  - □ more cost-effective (in 1862 London, outdoor relief cost 2*s*. 3*d*. per pauper each week, whereas workhouse relief cost 4*s*. 8*d*.)
  - □ easier to administer, since it did not require building facilities
  - □ better suited to cyclical unemployment in the north of England.
- In recognition of the failure to end outdoor relief, the government introduced the 1863 Public Works Act. This allowed local authorities to borrow public works' money to employ paupers in work schemes. Essentially, the government had ended their efforts to abolish outdoor relief.

In 1871, the Local Government Board took control of the Poor Law to try to reduce pauperism by:

- Issuing a circular condemning the use of poor relief. It claimed that this discouraged the poor from saving for bad times.
- Supporting local authorities that continued to enforce harsh conditions in workhouses.
- Enabling local guardians to set up emigration schemes, where certain categories of paupers, even whole families, were sponsored to emigrate abroad.

Additionally, Joseph Chamberlain, president of the Local Government Board, issued a circular in 1886 which encouraged local guardians to provide work schemes such as street sweeping to avoid sending them to workhouses or their needing outdoor relief.

These policies did reduce the numbers claiming poor relief, since in 1860, 4.6 per cent of the population had been receiving poor relief and only 2.9 per cent were still claiming it in 1885, but outdoor relief continued to make up over 75 per cent of poor relief.

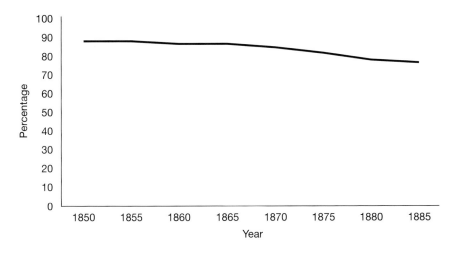

Figure 9.2 Graph showing the percentage of all poor relief that was provided as outdoor relief, between 1850 and 1885. How far does the graph support the idea that the Poor Law had failed to end outdoor relief?

Reforms to education

Children aged under sixteen comprised about one-third of the Poor Law population. From the beginning, the Poor Law commissioners could see that children mixing with adult paupers was undesirable, which was one reason so many were apprenticed out of the workhouse. As the concept of State responsibility to help individuals changed through the nineteenth century, the expectations of help, particularly education, for pauper children became more evident:

- 1834: schools were established in workhouses. In some cases, this meant that workhouse children received more education than most children of working labourers.
- 1844 Poor Law unions could combine to provide a district school. Some, as in Manchester and Leeds, provided progressive industrial schools where children learned valuable trade skills.
- 1846: a government grant was made available for Poor Law guardians to pay salaries for workhouse schoolteachers.
- 1850s: some Poor Law unions abandoned district schools and returned to educating children in the workhouse, mainly trade skills for boys and domestic skills for girls.
- 1860s: some guardians began to send pauper children to board with working-class families to get them out of the workhouse.
- The 1870 Forster's Education Act set up boarding schools, with Poor Law guardians encouraged to send pauper children to attend with working-class children.

Reforms to housing

ONLINE EXTRAS **www**
Pearson Edexcel

Get to grips with developments in living conditions by completing Worksheet 34 at **www. hoddereducation.co.uk/ accesstohistory/extras**

- Local reports in 1842 flagged up the link between poor housing, poor sanitation and high death rates.
- Some local towns (for example, Liverpool in 1842, Manchester in 1844, Nottingham in 1845 and Newcastle in 1846) passed by-laws which allowed them to have some control of new buildings and cellar dwellings. However, these were rarely enforced, even by the same councils that had introduced them.
- The 1851 and 1853 Common Lodging Houses Acts required all lodging houses to be registered and receive police inspections. This was rarely enforced.
- The 1855 Nuisances Removal Act empowered local authorities to deal with overcrowding.
- The Local Government Act 1858 allowed governments to pass local building regulations, although these were rarely enforced.
- The 1866 Sanitary Act created limits on the use of cellars for occupation, and empowered central government to take action if local authorities did not.

- The 1868 and 1875 Artisans' Dwelling Acts established the right of local councils to force landlords to repair insanitary houses, or to buy the house and demolish it. Councils could clear entire slum districts under this law. This extended State involvement more directly, although it did not provide housing for those left homeless, who often simply moved to create new slums elsewhere.

ONLINE EXTRAS **WWW**
AQA
Learn how to write effective conclusions by completing Worksheet 37 at **www. hoddereducation.co.uk/ accesstohistory/extras**

ONLINE EXTRAS **WWW**
Pearson Edexcel
Learn how to plan an effective essay by completing Worksheet 35 at **www. hoddereducation.co.uk/ accesstohistory/extras**

SUMMARY DIAGRAM

SOCIAL REFORM 1853–85

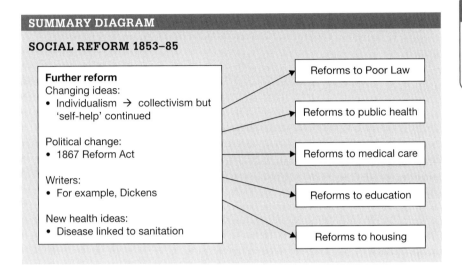

Further reform
Changing ideas:
- Individualism → collectivism but 'self-help' continued

Political change:
- 1867 Reform Act

Writers:
- For example, Dickens

New health ideas:
- Disease linked to sanitation

Reforms to Poor Law

Reforms to public health

Reforms to medical care

Reforms to education

Reforms to housing

4 Cooperative organisations and self-help

■ *How did cooperative associations impact on the lives of some workers?*

Another source of social support for the working class, which came from the idea of self-help (see page 198), was the rise of cooperative organisations. The idea was that, instead of buying food and supplies in small quantities as individuals from a merchant who was making a high profit, communities should join to buy goods in larger quantities wholesale at better prices:

- Robert Owen, industrialist and philanthropist, is seen as the founder of the cooperative movement in the sense that he developed New Lanark as a model town with a cooperative shop where workers enjoyed social benefits for their hard work. He preached his theories in speeches and pamphlets nationally.

- By 1827, Owen had taken his ideas to the USA, but in Britain, William King, a doctor, adopted the principles. He published a journal, *The Co-operator*, which encouraged people to found cooperative organisations. Although he published the journal for only two years, it further established Owen's ideas.

- A congress of supporters of cooperative thinking was held in Manchester in 1831, and several short-lived cooperative organisations were founded.

The first modern cooperative society was in Rochdale, a mill town near Manchester. Twenty-eight weavers founded the Equitable Pioneers of Rochdale. By investing £1 each, they leased a property in 1844 and began to sell butter, sugar, flour, oatmeal and candles. The profits were reinvested into the business and new branches were opened. It operated on the basis that anyone could join and invest, making profits as the shop profited. The effect was to allow local workers to buy goods at lower prices and make a profit from the community shops.

Other similar cooperative associations copied the Rochdale model, and the government recognised them in law in 1852. To give the organisations the ability to control prices, they joined into the North of England Wholesale Society in 1863 (renamed the Cooperative Wholesale Society in 1872), since they could buy larger quantities as a network than working separately. Over the next two decades, this organisation branched out to provide a wider range of services, including producing its own clothes and shoes, insurance and founding the Cooperative Bank.

As well as offering lower prices, cooperative shops became part of the growing community identity of the working class, which contributed to the rise in trade union activity.

CHAPTER SUMMARY

By the 1830s, poverty was a significant social concern. The common perception was that something had to be done to address poverty, but that the existing Poor Law was ineffective. This problem was addressed in 1834 by the Poor Law Amendment Act. This Act, created on the basis of utilitarian principles and with the aim of reducing the cost to ratepayers, legislated that poor relief should only be given through the workhouse, in conditions so terrible that only those in the most dire need would ever seek help.

Rather than solving the problem, this generated opposition from many quarters. It also showed the conditions of the poor, especially with scandals should as Andover House. As a consequence, attitudes began to change in the mid-nineteenth century, so that ideas of collectivism began to be considered alongside individualist philosophies. By 1885, a number of social reforms had been passed which reformed public health, medical care, education and housing.

Refresher questions

Use these questions to remind yourself of the key material covered in this chapter.

1 Why was poverty a big concern in the early nineteenth century?

2 What was the workhouse system and how was it intended to discourage poverty?

3 What was 'new' about the 1834 Poor Law Amendment Act?

4 Why was the 1847 Public Health Act significant, and what limitations did it have?

5 What was the Andover Workhouse Scandal, 1845, and how did it affect the Poor Law system?

6 How did writers such as Charles Dickens affect social reform?

7 What was important about the 1875 Public Health Act?

8 What was the repeated pattern in the introduction of various types of social reform through the period 1832–85?

9 What was the importance of the 1870 Forster's Education Act?

10 Explain what the cooperative society model was.

Question practice: AQA A level

Essay questions

1 To what extent did legislation lead to substantial improvements in the lives of people in poverty between 1832 and 1885?

EXAM HINT Think of the consequences of legislation in this period. How far did working people benefit? How much were their lives still dominated by poverty?

2 'The main cause of social reform in the years 1832–85 was changing public attitudes.' Assess the validity of this view.

EXAM HINT How much social reform was due to changing public attitudes? And how much because of other factors? Did these other factors in themselves influence public attitudes?

Question practice: OCR A level

Source question

1 Using the four Sources 1–4 below in their historical context, assess how far they support the view that the Poor Law Amendment Act 1834 was effective in dealing with the problem of poverty.

EXAM HINT Group the sources according to whether or not they support the view in the question. Each source should be explained in relation to the question, its provenance evaluated and contextual knowledge used to test the view of each source. A judgement about each source in relation to the question should be reached, allowing an overall judgement about whether the sources support the view that the New Poor Law was effective in dealing with the problem of poverty.

SOURCE 1

From an official report from the Poor Law Board overseeing the Market Harborough Union, written in 1836. Market Harborough was a new union, established following the amendment.

People who never could be made to work have become good labourers, and do not express any dissatisfaction with the measure. In most parishes the moral character of the poor is improving: there is a readiness to be more orderly and well-behaved … The great body of labouring poor throughout the Union have become reconciled to it; the workhouse is held in great dread; cases of bastardy are on the decline.

SOURCE 2

From the Third Annual Report of the Poor Law Commissioners, published in 1837.

The administration of relief by the Nottingham Board of Guardians had hardly begun before the mass interruption in the American [cotton] trade led to massive unemployment. It became evident that a need would soon arise for relieving more persons than could be provided for within the walls of the union workhouses. We felt it to be our duty to authorise the Guardians that the rule which prohibited them from giving relief to able-bodied male persons except in the workhouse should be suspended whenever they found it necessary to do so.

SOURCE 3

From an official record of comments made by the MP Sir John Easthope, an opponent of the Poor Law Amendment Act, during a parliamentary debate in 1839.

While he fully approved of the leading principle of the Poor-law Amendment Act, he could not conceal from the House that he felt considerable misgivings … It appeared that a few individuals connected with some paupers in the [Worcester] workhouse had been in the habit of furnishing them with snuff, tea, and sugar … This they had done with the knowledge … of the local guardians, and also with the knowledge of one of the assistant commissioners visiting the establishment … But a new assistant commissioner having come to the place, he insisted that the practice must be at once discontinued as an infringement on the rules of the commissioners, and that the furnishing of the articles must be immediately stopped.

SOURCE 4

From a passage in Charles Dickens' *Household Words*, a weekly journal of short stories and social journalism, published in 1850. Dickens is describing a visit to a workhouse.

We have come to this absurd, this dangerous, this monstrous pass, that the dishonest felon is, in respect of cleanliness, order, diet, and accommodation, better provided for, and taken care of, than the honest pauper … The men and women paupers gratify their aspirations after better board and lodging, by smashing as many workhouse windows as possible, and being promoted to prison … 'Most of them are crippled, in some form or other,' said the wardsman, 'and not fit for anything.' They slunk about, like dispirited wolves or hyænas; and made a pounce at their food when it was served out, much as those animals do.

Question practice: Pearson Edexcel A level

Essay questions

1 How significant were the Swing Riots as a cause of concern over the effectiveness of the Old Poor Law?

EXAM HINT Examine the different reasons for the riots, including the injustices of the Old Poor Law, reductions in wages and the introduction of agricultural machinery. Link these to the introduction of the Poor Law Amendment Act in 1834.

2 How far was the operation of the New Poor Law in the years 1847–70 different from its operation in the years 1834–46?

EXAM HINT Note the change in organisation from the Poor Law Commission to the Poor Law Board, and the latter's achievements (such as pauper schools and regulation of outdoor relief). Examine the extent and significance of organisational change.

3 How significant were leading individuals as a factor driving social reform in the years 1832–70?

EXAM HINT Consider the role of prominent individuals in the making of social reforms. Also note the role of organisations, such as the Liberal Party, trade unions and various religious groups.

CHAPTER 10

Changes to the workplace 1832–85

As the workplace changed, so did the demand for reform. Once trade unions became legalised after the repeal of the Combination Acts (see page 51), the modern concept of a trade union began to form, leading to the creation of 'New Model Unions', trades councils and the Trades Union Congress. This chapter examines the development of trade unions through the following themes:

◆ Changes to working conditions after 1832

◆ The development of trade unions

◆ Trade union activity 1866–85

The key debate on page 225 of this chapter asks the question: Had living conditions improved between 1793 and 1885?

KEY DATES

1819		Factory Act passed	**1851**		Amalgamated Society of Engineers became first 'New Model Union'
1824–5		Repeal of the Combination Acts			
1833		Factory Act passed	**1868**		Formation of the Trades Union Congress
1834	**Feb.**	Grand National Consolidated Trades Union formed by Robert Owen	**1869**		Royal Commission into trade unions published major and minor report
	March	Trial of the Tolpuddle Martyrs	**1871**		Trade Union Act passed, giving legal protection to trade unions
1842		Mines Act passed			
1844		Graham's Act passed	**1878**		Consolidation Act passed
1847		Ten Hour Act passed			
1850		Compromise Act passed			

1 Changes to working conditions after 1832

■ *How did government legislation affect the workplace?*

By 1832, Britain was comprehensively industrialising, and while the majority of the population still worked in agriculture, the majority of the urban population were finding employment in mills, factories and workshops of varying sizes. These were, generally speaking, dark and dangerous places, described famously by poet William Blake as the 'satanic mills' in 1808. It was especially dangerous for children, who were often required to crawl around machinery to retrieve broken cotton threads. The only efforts to legislate had been for cotton mills, with the 1802 Health and Morals of Apprentices Act (1802) and the Factory Act (1819), which together had limited the working day for children to twelve hours, and prohibited children working before the age of nine years of age. However, as with many other social reforms of the early nineteenth century, these were not enforced and so had little impact. Neither did they affect the many workers, adult or child, employed in other industries (including mines and foundries), who regularly worked more than twelve-hour shifts, for low wages, with little protection from injury.

The Ten Hour Movement

In 1830, concerned by the working conditions in the mills, Richard Oastler and John Fielden formed the Ten Hour Movement. Initially, the movement sought a ten-hour limit on the working day for all workers, but Oastler soon realised that this was an unlikely goal. Instead, the movement focused on reducing the working day for women and children. Rather like earlier radical movements, they campaigned through pamphlets, speeches, petitions and demonstrations.

Some opposition was to be expected from employers concerned about the loss of profits. There was also opposition from some politicians, including a worry about foreign competition and increased unemployment, as well as a ridiculous theory by economist Nassau Senior that most profits were made in the last hour of the working day. There was also some opposition from workers themselves, since this would impact on their families' wages.

Workplace legislation

The 1833 Factory Act

In 1831, the Tory member of parliament (MP) Michael Sadler introduced a ten-hour bill to parliament. Although this was outvoted, the evidence included with Sadler's bill about factory conditions drew attention. Tory MP Lord Ashley reintroduced the bill in 1833, when it led to a Royal Commission. The commissioners supported the need for legislation to protect children in factories. Ashley withdrew his bill, and it was replaced with a governmental bill prepared by Lord Althorp, passed as the 1833 Factory Act.

Terms of the Act:

- Children under age nine could not work in factories; children aged nine to thirteen could only work nine hours per day and 48 hours per week, and children aged thirteen to eighteen could only work ten hours per day and 69 hours per week.

- Workers under eighteen could not work at night.

- Employers had to keep a register of all children they employed and check certificates verifying the age of children.

- Children aged nine to thirteen were to receive two hours' education a day.

- All workers were entitled to an hour and a half break each day.

- The building had to be whitewashed at least once a year.

- Four full-time inspectors were employed by the government to inspect factories to enforce the law.

- Local authorities could fine mill owners who broke the rules.

Table 10.1 Outcomes of the 1833 Factory Act

Positive consequences	Negative consequences
• The law established the government's right to enforce working conditions in factories • Fines did, in some cases, reduce abuses in factories. Factory inspector Leonard Horner claimed in 1840 that the 'chief evils have been remedied to a great extent'	• The inspectors complained that many local councils, whose members were often mill owners, did not apply the fines • Some workers, wanting to protect their family income, supported employers who evaded the rules • The inspectors complained that some doctors wrote false age certificates, either through believing parents who lied or through deliberate fraud • The legislation only applied to cotton mills, not the majority of other employment locations

The 1842 Mines Act

After the 1833 Act, Ashley tried to pass new factory bills with ten-hour clauses in 1838, 1839 and 1840, all unsuccessfully. In 1840, Ashley chaired a commission which investigated how the 1833 Act was working, and concluded that government intervention was the best policy. This was almost immediately halted by Peel, who, as prime minister from 1841, declared that the government was opposed to a ten-hour bill.

The movement to reform working places was revived in 1842, by a Royal Commission report into working conditions for children. There were descriptions of brutality and dangerous conditions, and vivid illustrations were included. Public opinion was horrified, and the government response was swift. Through the following decade, legislation was passed which primarily affected children and women in employment. However, no real progress was made on the aim of achieving a ten-hour working day.

Terms of the Act:

- All women, as well as boys under ten, were banned from working underground in mines.

- New safety regulations were instated.

- No one under the age of fifteen could operate machinery.

- A mines inspector was employed to enforce the law.

Table 10.2 Outcomes of the 1842 Mines Act

Positive consequences	Negative consequences
• The law protected women as well as children • It affected an area beyond the mills, showing that employment legislation was becoming broader • It copied the 1833 Factory Act in having an inspector to make sure it was followed	• The law received a lot of opposition, including from the influential Anti-Corn Law League, as they saw it as an attack on *laissez-faire* • It only applied to a specific area of industry, the mines

The 1844 Factory Act

In 1843, Sir James Graham, the home secretary, attempted to pass a factory bill with strong clauses to introduce compulsory education by funding factory schools. This met strong opposition, including the claim that if a government could impose compulsory education, they could impose compulsory religion. Graham withdrew the bill and proposed it again in 1844, without educational clauses.

Terms of the Act:

■ Children could start working younger, at eight, but until age thirteen could only work half-time and no more than six and a half hours daily.

■ Children aged thirteen to eighteen and women were limited to a twelve-hour day, and nine hours on a Saturday.

■ Night work for women and children was forbidden.

■ More inspectors were appointed to check on factories.

■ Dangerous machines had to be screened off to protect workers, and women and children could not clean moving machinery.

Table 10.3 Outcomes of the 1844 Factory Act

Positive consequences	Negative consequences
• The law continued the Mines Act in protecting women and children • The requirement to shield machinery protected all workers • More inspectors meant more visits, which encouraged compliance	• There was still no legal limit on working hours for adult males • There were still many factory owners who failed to comply with the terms

The 1847 Factory Act

In 1846, Lord Ashley resigned his seat to support Peel over the Corn Laws, and John Fielden took his role as the leading politician in workplace reform. He passed the 1847 Factory Act.

Terms of the Act:

■ All women, as well as boys under eighteen, were limited to a ten-hour working day, with a maximum of 58 hours per week.

■ Men were not included in the law, but reformers thought that the reduction for women and children would naturally lead to a reduction for men as factories could not continue working once half the workforce finished their shift.

Table 10.4 Outcomes of the 1847 Factory Act

Positive consequences	Negative consequences
• Many factories naturally shifted to a ten-hour system for all workers, including men	• Some factory owners, determined to keep twelve-hour shifts, set up systems of relays and lunch breaks which in practice meant that all workers were still working twelve-hour days • When inspector Horner took a test case to court, the court ruled that this was legal

The 1850 Factory Act

Terms of the Act:

■ Women and children from age thirteen had to work their entire shift between either 6a.m. and 6p.m. or 7a.m. and 7p.m. This effectively ended relays for women and children which lengthened the working day.

■ Children from eight to thirteen had to complete their shorter working day within the same time frames.

■ As a compromise, the Act extended the working day to ten and a half hours.

Table 10.5 Outcomes of the 1850 Factory Act

Positive consequences	Negative consequences
• The shorter work pattern was protected for women and children • A more accurate version of the law, with more thorough wording, was passed as the 1853 Factory Act. It removed some of the loopholes • In practical terms, since the effective working day was now limited to ten and a half hours plus lunch break, most factories in practice also reduced the adult males' working day to match	• The legislation was rushed in response to Horner's 1850 test case, and there were many loopholes until 1853

Subsequent Factory Acts

From 1862 to 1866, another Royal Commission investigated the conditions of children working in industry, resulting in further Acts that are summarised in Table 10.6 (see page 215).

Table 10.6 Outcomes of further Factory Acts

Act	Positive consequences	Negative consequences
The 1864 Factory Act, which extended the existing factory legislation to six dangerous industries which had previously not been covered, including the production of gunpowder and matches	Workers in dangerous industries were more protected, and the limited working day of cotton mills now applied to some other industries	The legislation still only covered a proportion of the working population
The 1867 Factories Extension Act and Workshop Regulation Act: • the previous Factory Acts now applied to all factories with more than 50 employees • the Workshop Regulation Act applied similar terms to workplaces with fewer than 50 employees	The majority of workers were now covered by the protection of the Factory Acts	Smaller workplaces were not inspected as much as the larger factories
The 1874 Factory Act (the 'Health of Women and Children Act'): • maximum 10-hour shifts for women and children • minimum working age raised to ten	Created a new standard for women and children in textile factories. Many men also benefited as often employers found it easier to change shifts for everyone	Only impacted workers in the textile industry
The 1878 Factory Act (the 'Consolidation Act'): • All previous terms were consolidated into one law • In addition, a minimum employment age of ten years was set across industries • The importance of compulsory education was confirmed	All the achievements of legislation to this point were consolidated and applied across industry	Trade unions complained that there were not enough inspections

How did workplace legislation affect the lives of workers?

Adult workers

Although most of the legislation affected children, adults benefited as well, directly and indirectly. Machines became safer due to the installation of safety guards, and there were more safety regulations in dangerous industries. The eventual reduction in working hours benefited all workers in terms of reducing shifts.

It is possible that there were negative economic consequences for some families, particularly those without a father, since the working hours of women and children, then adult men, were reduced. It is also possible that the greater educational prospects of children may have helped families as they became adults.

ONLINE EXTRAS
Pearson Edexcel **WWW**

Develop your analysis of progress in working conditions by completing Worksheet 36 at **www.hoddereducation.co.uk/accesstohistory/extras**

ONLINE EXTRAS
Pearson Edexcel **WWW**

Learn how to write effective opening sentences by completing Worksheet 37 at **www.hoddereducation.co.uk/accesstohistory/extras**

Another impact was that the changes for women working somewhat reinforced Victorian stereotypes of women as the weaker sex, which the late Victorian female suffrage movement would struggle against. Again, this impact was probably minimal as the roots of this stereotype were far wider than female employment.

Child workers

Children gained the most from the legislation. They did earn less, but since most wages for children were passed to their families, this would be less of a direct impact in the sense of affecting the overall family unit. However, children benefited from the introduction of shorter days, safer conditions in factories and compulsory education which, although basic, helped them to gain work as adults.

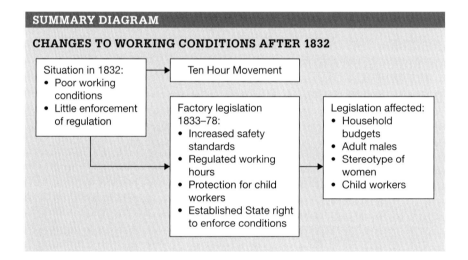

SUMMARY DIAGRAM

CHANGES TO WORKING CONDITIONS AFTER 1832

Situation in 1832:
- Poor working conditions
- Little enforcement of regulation

Ten Hour Movement

Factory legislation 1833–78:
- Increased safety standards
- Regulated working hours
- Protection for child workers
- Established State right to enforce conditions

Legislation affected:
- Household budgets
- Adult males
- Stereotype of women
- Child workers

2 The development of trade unions

■ *How did trade unions become legally recognised organisations?*

Trade unions by the 1830s

Trade unions were a cause of great fear to the middle and upper classes. They not only represented a means by which workers could demand more pay and better conditions, but also represented a means of uniting the working masses as a force – a truly revolutionary concept, in the context of the eighteenth and early nineteenth centuries.

Consequently, Combination Acts had been passed in 1799 and 1800, banning workers from uniting to form a strike action. Simply put, these outlawed any union type of action against employers. In 1823, they were enhanced by the Master and Servant Act. If a worker did something which left work incomplete, this was now immediately a breach of contract and was charged as a criminal offence. Employer actions were only charged as civil offences, with lesser consequences.

In 1824, the Combination Acts were repealed. Theoretically, this meant that workers were free to form unions, such as the Association of Colliers in the Rivers Tyne and Wear. This union formed in 1825 with 4000 members and was holding meetings with up to 20,000 people by 1831.

However, in practical terms, the workers were still limited. The 1824 Repeal Act was replaced in 1825 with a tougher Act, since the government was concerned that the 1824 Act was too lenient. It banned any form of violence or intimidation on threat of up to three months in prison. Magistrates and justices of the peace applied this very strictly. Chants, glaring looks and shouts all counted as violence or intimidation.

Friendly Societies

An alternative to trade unions was Friendly Societies. These were informal organisations where members would pay money into a fund as an investment, and would receive a payment in the case of certain specified events. These included burial costs as well as fires, illness, the death of a cow or other causes of hardship. They were popular as they gave a measure of financial protection to members which might mean avoiding the workhouse, although there was no legal protection of funds until 1855. They also fitted into the nineteenth-century idea of 'self-help' (see page 198), by working hard and making investments that would allow individuals to protect themselves. Some lasted for a year before collapsing, while others became strong organisations. From 1846, Friendly Societies could register with a government registrar for legal recognition.

Friendly Societies were not trade unions and did not have a role in industry, but they did serve as a model for the benefits that some unions tried to offer, especially from the 1850s, and became tied into the legal recognition of the unions in the 1860s and 1870s.

Trade unions in the 1830s

Despite legal limits, the Association of Colliers did have some success in 1831 when they went on strike for seven weeks and achieved a 30 per cent pay increase. But when they tried to repeat their success in 1832, mine owners evicted them from homes and replaced them with 'blackleg miners', or strike-breakers, from Wales. This demonstrated the inherent weakness of the early regional unions which lacked national support.

The problem was that it was not possible to create a national union with sufficient strength. In 1830, a Lancashire cotton spinner, John Doherty, tried to form a national union called the National Association for the Protection of Labour by uniting workers from his regional union, the Grand General Union of Operative Cotton Spinners (GUOCS), with unions from different industries. It collapsed after less than a year when Doherty's GUOCS was defeated in a series of cotton strikes.

The Grand National Consolidated Trades Union

The first nearly successful attempt at a national union was by the philanthropist mill owner, Robert Owen (see page 104). He formed the **Grand National Consolidated Trades Union (GNCTU)** in February 1834 to give workers a unified basis from which to demand better conditions of work.

However, the GNCTU immediately hit problems. Just one month after its formation, the Tolpuddle Martyrs stood trial after forming a union, and were sentenced to transportation. Shortly afterwards, 1500 factory workers were locked out in Derby for joining a union, and two Oldham union leaders were murdered. By August, panicked by recent events, support for the GNCTU dissolved and it disbanded. There was a lack of national co-ordination between unions, too much fear of poverty to take risks, and too many workers willing to act as strike-breakers and take jobs.

The Tolpuddle Martyrs

In 1833, six Dorset agricultural workers were arrested. Although the issue was that they had formed a union, which was not illegal after the repeal of the Combination Acts, they were tried under outdated laws intended for dealing with naval mutinies and charged with swearing illegal oaths. They were sentenced to seven years' transportation. Although public opinion led to their sentences being repealed, they did not all return home until 1838. This damaged worker confidence in unions.

The 'New Model Unions'

Although the large general unions failed to stand up to early challenges, this was not an end of all unions. Through the 1830s and 1840s, a number of loosely knit groups of workers formed. While these did not have the size and organisation of groups like the GNCTU, they were more able to survive, in part because they were far less ambitious.

A number of amalgamations of smaller unions meant that by the start of the 1850s, there were several unions that had larger size, with some having up to 2000 members and 80 branches. As they grew, they also became more formalised, employing full-time national officers by the 1840s.

Therefore, the emergence of the **Amalgamated Society of Engineers (ASE)** in 1851, labelled a '**New Model Union**', was really the end of a process of amalgamation since 1834. This union was created by the fusion of several smaller, local unions for skilled engineers, combined with the larger Society

---

KEY TERMS

Grand National Consolidated Trades Union (GNCTU) Robert Owen's attempt to form a national trade union in 1834.

Amalgamated Society of Engineers (ASE) A New Model Union of skilled engineers formed in 1851.

New Model Unions Organisations of smaller unions working together. They developed formalised structures and management.

of Journeymen Steam Engine Makers, which provided 75 per cent of the membership of the ASE.

The ASE grew quickly, from 5000 members in 1851 to 54,000 in 1888. Other unions grew in the same period, including the United Society of Boilermakers and Iron and Steel Shipbuilders, and the Society of Operative Stonemasons. These New Model Unions shared certain common traits:

- They were organised by a central executive committee which provided paid, full-time leadership. These were usually based in London, for example the ASE. They were national unions, not regional, which had been made possible by the train as well as the introduction of the penny post in 1840.
- The membership was exclusively skilled workers, such as engineers. Unskilled members were not allowed to join, and generally could not have afforded to. The higher wages of skilled workers allowed them to pay high membership costs, which could be as high as five per cent of their income.
- The unions offered welfare benefits to members, including sickness and unemployment benefits and provision for old age. This was only possible due to the high fees.
- They cultivated a middle-class, moderate image. They preferred to negotiate with employers around a table than engage in industrial action.
- They organised industrial action, where necessary, nationally. Only strikes approved by the committee would be financed, since they managed the funds centrally.

Not only did the unions work for their workers, but there was also a measure of unofficial cooperation between them because the secretaries of five unions, including the ASE, met on an unofficial committee nicknamed 'the **Junta**'. They worked together within the **Conference of Amalgamated Trades**, which represented a number of unions. They, like the unions they represented, cultivated a respectable, middle-class reputation, and helped to bring a level of organisation that made the new unions more efficient.

How important were the New Model Unions?

The traditional view

The traditional view, put forward by Beatrice and Sidney Webb in 1894, was that the GNCTU had been an important union, followed by a lull in union activity. Then the New Model Unions had emerged, offering a clearly structured style of union. These became centrally important to the overall trade union movement and represented a leap forward. In particular, the Webbs saw the Junta as a forward-thinking group which was directing the trade union movement. Keith Laybourn (1992) agreed that the Junta shaped the trade union movement into a pressure group to extend worker rights. W. Hamish Fraser (1999) also agreed that the unions were an important step forward, focusing on the key difference being in the size and range of benefits offered to workers, beyond what local unions could offer.

KEY TERMS

Junta An unofficial committee of the secretaries of five influential unions which co-ordinated with each other.

Conference of Amalgamated Trades An organisation that formed to represent a number of unions from different industries. It acted as a forum to unite labour organisations.

Counter-interpretations

- There was no lull before the 1850s: A.E. Musson (1972) argued that the GNCTU had far less significance than previously imagined, and there was no real lull in the 1830s and 1840s. Therefore, the 1850s' unions are better seen as a simple development rather than a leap forward.

- The New Model Unions were not 'new': Clive Behagg (1991) argued that many features of the ASE and other new unions were adopted from previous unions. For example, the stonemasons had had professional officials since 1834. Henry Pelling (1987) pointed out that many organisational principles of the ASE were simply adopted from the largest member union, the Journeymen Steam Engine Makers, which had been founded in 1826. Further, when these unions did engage in industrial action, such as in 1859–60 when they spent £3000 supporting strike actions for builders, they were not so different from other unions except for being nationally organised.

- A 'labour aristocracy': the socialist interpretation, presented by Eric Hobsbawm (1968), is that the union actually represented the dominance of an elite group of workers, those with skills and higher wages, who only made up ten per cent of the working population, and, therefore, these unions did not represent the more militant local unions.

- Most workers were not represented by the New Model Unions: most workers, including unskilled workers, were represented by older, local unions. In particular, the cotton and mining industries were mainly represented by local unions. The local unions often opposed the New Model Unions on two key issues: they disliked that they took members from local unions, and they saw their moderate negotiation tactics as a betrayal of the working classes.

- The Junta was not very influential: it did not become involved with the Trades Union Congress (TUC), which represented the provincial and local unions across the UK, until 1871, three years after it began. When it did become involved, it faced strong opposition from leaders of older, more traditional unions. A major opponent was George Potter, secretary of the Committee of the London Building Trades' Workers. He challenged the Junta at London Trades Council meetings and in *Beehive*, the working-class newspaper he owned and published.

- The Junta was not a unified force through the period: Fraser (1999), while seeing the new unions as a move forward, argued that it is incorrect to see the Junta as a unified, forward-thinking force. Instead, he argues that they only provided a form of national leadership during the 1867 crisis.

Trades councils

From the 1850s, **trades councils** gained in importance as a trade union tool. Simply put, they were meetings of delegates from unions with the purpose of allying together. They aimed to unite their efforts to support workers during

KEY TERM

Trades council
A meeting of representatives from different unions with the aim of uniting their demands.

industrial disputes, for example using workers in one area to raise funds to allow striking workers in another area to continue the strike, and to improve the image of trade unions with the general public by providing respectable representatives to speak on behalf of workers. Between 1855 and 1864, at least 24 trades councils had formed, and many became permanent town organisations.

An important example was the London Trades Council, formed on the suggestion of William Allen, secretary of the ASE and member of the Junta. It brought together many London-based societies. This was formed in response to a failed strike by builders in London in 1858, when workers were locked out for demanding a reduction in the working day from ten to nine hours; employers said the lockout would only end when workers signed an agreement not to join a union. The best the unions managed to do was negotiate to allow workers to be in a union; they failed any improvements to the working day. Allen realised that more strength was needed in future industrial actions.

The trades councils did lead to an improved government response as the reputation of trade unions improved.

■ 1855 Friendly Societies Act: this law protected the funds of Friendly Societies, mutual organisations for sharing funds to create pensions and benefits. Unions assumed that they benefited from this law.

■ 1859 Molestation of Workmen Act: this law allowed peaceful picketing during a strike.

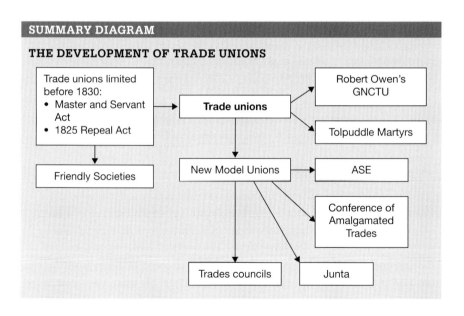

SUMMARY DIAGRAM

THE DEVELOPMENT OF TRADE UNIONS

3 Trade union activity 1866–85

1866–7: A crisis for trade unions

1866–7 was a turning point for trade unions, since it brought a series of challenges which challenged their role in society, leading to a Royal Commission, structural changes to unions and legislation which established their role (see Table 10.7, below).

Table 10.7 Trade union challenges

Issue	Affect on trade union activity
Economic depression: an economic downturn during the years 1866–7	In previous decades, anti-union sentiment had been mild as the economy was booming and it was easier for employers to negotiate than lose profits. In hard times, however, employers took a tougher line with unions, including accusing them of threatening Britain's ability to compete with cheaper foreign labour
Sheffield outrages 1866. A series of acts of violence were committed by union members from Sheffield in the 1860s. This culminated in workers blowing up the house of a strike-breaker with gunpowder	The national newspapers, supported by employers, expressed horror at the scale of violence carried out by members of the Sheffield unions. A special commission was set up to investigate, which offered a pardon to anyone making a full confession. As a result, it heard reports of assaults, sabotage and even the murder of an employer who hired too many apprentices instead of skilled workers. The reputation of trade unions nationally was damaged
Hornby v. *Close* 1867. The Boilermakers' Union took a branch treasurer to court for stealing £24 from union funds. The court ruled that unions were not protected by the Friendly Societies Act	The court ruling effectively questioned the legal status of all unions. The grounds for the decision was that since they existed to interfere with trade, unions were illegal and therefore did not benefit from legal protection for their funds. It also worried members of larger unions, since it meant that the funds they paid into were no longer protected under law

The Royal Commission

In response to the reports from Sheffield and questions raised in the *Hornby* v. *Close* case (see Table 10.7, above), the Conservative government created a Royal Commission which investigated the rules and organisation of trade unions. Essentially, it was to question whether the law needed changing on their existence and operation. The eleven-strong panel of commissioners investigated from 1867 until its report was published in 1869. The trade union response to the report is summarised in Table 10.8 (see page 223).

The commission reports

The commission published two reports, a majority report and then a minority report, in 1869. The majority report recommended that:

Table 10.8 The trade union response to the Royal Commission report investigating union activity

Responses	Consequences
• The Junta responded by working with the government • The Junta worked to present a moderate, non-militant attitude. For example, the secretary of the ASE said 'We believe that all strikes are a complete waste of money' • The Junta pressured the government to include union members on the commission. The government compromised by letting them nominate one commissioner – it selected a barrister sympathetic to the cause • Applegarth and other union representatives were called to give evidence as witnesses and experts • The Junta pushed to allow unions to register as Friendly Societies	• Smaller, local unions opposed to the Junta aimed to register as Friendly Societies • George Potter organised a new Conference of Trades for all unions not in the Junta's Conference of Amalgamated Trades. Thirty unions and nine trades councils sent delegates • The Conference of Trades won the right to send a member to attend the Royal Commission hearings but he was kicked out soon afterwards for a verbal and public attack against the commission • This meant that the Junta, despite not representing all unions, was able to dominate the Royal Commission on behalf of all unions

- Unions should be legalised and allowed to register with the registrar of Friendly Societies.

- The registrar should be able to veto any clauses in union rules which were 'objectionable', a vague term that was to include clauses about employment of apprentices, use of machinery or introduction of piecework.

- Unions should be required to separate their funds for striking from funds for benefits.

The minority report was more favourable, adding recommendations that:

- Unions should be legalised, and the criminal parts of the 1825 repeal of the Combination Acts should themselves be repealed.

- The registrar should not be able to reject unions unless their rules were incomplete or fraudulent.

- Unions should have full protection as Friendly Societies.

ONLINE EXTRAS WWW
Pearson Edexcel

Get to grips with the development of trade unions by completing Worksheet 38 at **www.hoddereducation. co.uk/accesstohistory/extras**

The foundation of the Trades Union Congress

One other key event of note was the creation of the TUC in 1868. This was a national union that emerged from the period of fluctuation for the unions, and is simultaneously a result of the events that led to the Royal Commission as well as a factor in the positive reports of the commission.

The TUC was originally formed by Sam Nicholson in Manchester as a conference for trade unionists to present papers on topics for concern. He had seen a similar model by the National Social Science Association, and had been impressed by the Conference of Trades formed in London by Potter. Thirty-four delegates attended, of whom only two (including Potter) were from London. The London Trades Council declined to send a member, neither were the Junta or the New Model Unions involved. Quickly, the structure changed from presentations of papers into a forum to discuss matters of concern and it was decided to hold an annual meeting.

ONLINE EXTRAS
AQA
WWW

Get to grips with the reasons for the legal establishment of trade unions by 1876 by completing Worksheet 38 at **www.hoddereducation. co.uk/accesstohistory/extras**

A second meeting was held in Birmingham in 1869, with 40 delegates representing about 250,000 union members, and then a third meeting was held in London 1871. The delay was deliberate; they wanted to hear the government's new legislation before meeting. When it became clear that the legislation was not sufficient for the demands of the union, Potter and the Junta put aside their differences to support the demand for further legislation. See Table 10.9 (below).

Table 10.9 The impact of the Royal Commission's report on trade unionism

Result	Consequence
A change in public attitude	The public took a less negative view of unions, seeing many parts of their work as beneficial and positive. This is evident in the media; newspapers which had previously taken the side of employers, such as *The Times, Spectator* and *Pall Mall Gazette*, reported on an engineering strike in Newcastle upon Tyne in support of the strikers, describing their demand for a nine-hour day as 'perfectly reasonable'. In the 1874 election, about ten working-class unionists stood independently for election, and although none won a seat, they won many votes
	Not all views changed – there was still middle-class opposition, and in 1872, five leaders of London gas stoker unions who went on strike and caused a blackout were sentenced to a year of hard labour
New legislation	A series of laws were passed which overall improved the position of unions:
	• Trade Unions' Funds Protection Act 1869: a temporary measure that protected unions' funds
	• The Trade Union Act 1871: allowed unions to register as Friendly Societies, gaining protection and legal recognition. Not all unions were covered
	• The Criminal Law Amendment Act 1871: restricted union activity by confirming older laws against picketing, threats and intimidation, and allowed strikes to be judged as criminal conspiracies
	• The Conspiracy and Protection of Property Act 1875: reversed the 1871 Act, removing criminal legislation relating to trade unions and allowing peaceful picketing
	• The Employers and Workmen Act 1875: abolished the 1823 Master and Servant Act, meaning that in breach of contract cases, employers and workers had equal standing
	• The Trade Union Act Amendment Act 1876: extended the 1871 Act to cover all unions
Trade unions became more influential as a political pressure group	With confirmed legal status and protected funds, unions gained membership and support. They were able to apply more pressure, primarily through the TUC's parliamentary committee. Although Gladstone refused to support union demands as a matter of principle, Disraeli's Conservatives were willing to consider reform. In the 1874 election, the trade unions did not favour a party. Instead, they gave questionnaires to candidates in many constituencies and supported whichever gave the most positive responses. As a result, many MPs were more favourable to the unions. In addition, two trade unionists who stood for the Liberal Party were elected. They were the first so-called Lib–Lab MPs, who stood for Liberals but also labour, working-class interests. This would develop into the foundation of the Labour Party
The TUC became the figurehead of the trade union movement	As a result of joining forces to push for legislation that would put into place the commission's minority report, the Junta and Potter put aside their differences. This brought together New Model Unions and older local unions behind the TUC and its parliamentary committee

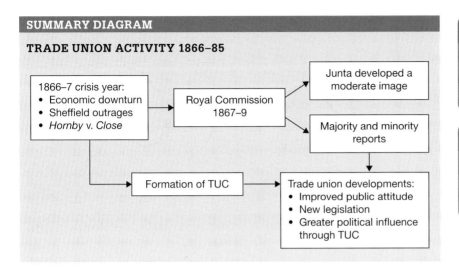

SUMMARY DIAGRAM

TRADE UNION ACTIVITY 1866–85

- 1866–7 crisis year:
  - Economic downturn
  - Sheffield outrages
  - *Hornby* v. *Close*

→ Royal Commission 1867–9 →

→ Junta developed a moderate image

→ Majority and minority reports

→ Trade union developments:
  - Improved public attitude
  - New legislation
  - Greater political influence through TUC

← Formation of TUC ←

ONLINE EXTRAS WWW
AQA
Get to grips with the big themes of the period by completing Worksheet 39 at **www.hoddereducation. co.uk/accesstohistory/extras**

ONLINE EXTRAS WWW
Pearson Edexcel
Develop your analysis of the living conditions of the poor by completing Worksheet 39 at **www.hoddereducation. co.uk/accesstohistory/extras**

5 Key debate

▪ *Had living conditions in Britain improved between 1793 and 1885?*

Despite the fact that it might seem a relatively easy evaluation to make – were people's lives better or not? – the conclusion depends on the measure that is used. It also depends on whether the measure of the change is based on solely statistical evidence or whether qualitative, anecdotal evidence is considered.

The optimist viewpoint

Historians taking the optimist view have argued that the standard of living improved over the period. The main evidence for this is statistical, in the form of records of wages during the period (see Figure 10.1, page 225).

A look at the statistics in Figure 10.1 (see page 225) shows that from 1790, the wages generally increased, while the price of grain overall decreased. Crucially, the relative value of wages was consistently higher than the price of grain from 1816 onwards, and especially in the years 1860–80. Therefore, in simple terms it could be argued that economically workers were better off since they now, on average, had more spending power than previously.

Optimist historians also focus on evidence of changes in food. They point out that the impact of the agricultural modernisation of the eighteenth century meant more effective food production, which meant that there was both greater quantity and variety in diet available to consumers from the 1780s onwards. They have also pointed out the decreasing mortality rates which contributed to population growth.

Figure 10.1 Average wage and price of grain movements. The value for 1790 = 100. Data based on research by B.R. Mitchell and R. Deane (1962) and P. Deane and W.A. Cole (1969). This graph uses a scale which is based on a relative value. It has no units, so the number does not mean a specific value like pounds (£s), tonnes or miles. Instead the start point value is given as 100; in this case, the wages and price of grain in 1790 start at 100. Then the change is shown as how far the value moves up or down compared to the start point of 100.

Similarly, from the introduction of personal data in the 1841 census, it seems that life expectancy increased between 1841 and 1891 from 40.2 to 44.1 years for males and from 42.2 to 47.8 years for females.

? INTERPRETATION QUESTION

How do Extracts 1–3 judge the changes in the living standards of ordinary British people between 1783 and 1885 differently? Which interpretation do you find most convincing, based on your study of the period?

ONLINE EXTRAS
AQA **WWW**

Learn how to write structured answers by completing Worksheet 40 at **www.hoddereducation. co.uk/accesstohistory/extras**

EXTRACT 1

Adapted from Peter Lindhart and Jeffrey Linderson, 'English Workers' Living Standards During the Industrial Revolution: A New Look', *The Economic History Review*, 1983, pp. 12–13.

It seems reasonable to conclude that the average worker was much better off in any decade from the 1830s on than in any decade before 1820. Time and again the unemployment issue has brought discussion of trends in workers' living standards to a halt: lacking national unemployment data before 1851, how can the real wage series be trusted as indicators of annual earnings? Into this empirical vacuum [Marxist historian Eric] Hobsbawm has injected fragmentary hints about unemployment in the industrial north, suggesting that the depression of 1841–3 was 'almost certainly the worst of the century'. Yet no conceivable level of unemployment could have cancelled the near doubling of full-time wages and left the workers of the 1840s with less than their grandfathers had had.

The pessimist viewpoint

Pessimist historians have focused on the flaws in the optimist argument. One issue is that the whole basis for the economic statistics from this period is flawed. Record keeping was not based on a precise system, and often historians are forced to make estimations and guesses to fill gaps, or combine statistics from different areas to make complete sets of data.

One key piece of evidence is census data, recorded every ten years from 1801. However, this was carried out using a very inexact method, and until 1841 did not record personal details. Historians also point out that often statistical evidence presents a simplified view of the country, which hides significant differences between regions of the country or job types. For example, a cotton mill worker in Lancashire may well have had a very different financial experience from an agricultural labourer from Norfolk. Similarly, a major factor for the living conditions of the poorest in society was the provision of poor relief, and this could vary enormously from areas which strictly imposed the workhouse regime to areas like Todmorden which avoided providing a workhouse for many years and continued with outdoor relief.

Historian Keith Snell (1985) argues that although wages did increase, this is misleading. This only reflects male wages, and the labour reforms of the nineteenth century increasingly regulated the working hours of children and women; therefore, Snell argues that despite the increased wages, the overall household income would have been reduced and therefore living standards would be less improved than simple wage statistics imply.

Pessimist historians also argue that comparing wages to average grain prices is misleading, since there could be spikes in price. For example, as Table 10.10 (see below) shows, the average change in grain price hides the enormous difference in the price that grain could reach. Since grain was a staple, pessimists see this as evidence of negative conditions.

Table 10.10 The average and peak prices of grain in Britain between 1780 and 1829

Years	Average price of an imperial quarter of grain	Highest recorded price of an imperial quarter of grain
1780–9	46s. 1d.	54s. 3d.
1790–9	57s. 7d.	78s. 7d.
1800–9	84s. 8d.	119s. 6d.
1810–19	91s. 5d.	126s. 6d.
1820–9	59s. 10d.	68s. 6d.

Source: based on calculations by B.R. Mitchell and R. Deane (1962).

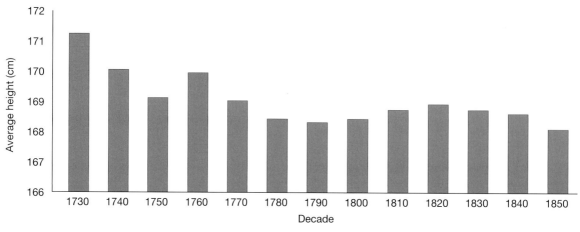

Figure 10.2 Average height of British soldiers 1730–1850. Data from John Komlos, 'Shrinking in a Growing Economy? The Mystery of Physical Stature during the Industrial Revolution', *Journal of Economic History*, Vol. 58, No. 3, pp. 779–802 (1998).

Pessimist historians have also looked at other areas, such as the impact of urban conditions on health. John Komlos (1998) used military recruitment records to show the impact of urbanisation on the height of military recruits, from which he inferred a negative impact on the state of national health (see Figure 10.2, above).

EXTRACT 2

Adapted from Simon Szreter and Graham Mooney, 'Urbanization, Mortality, and the Standard of Living Debate: New Estimates of the Expectation of Life at Birth in Nineteenth-century British Cities', *Economic History Review*, 1998, p. 110.

Most of the work of the previous generation of scholarship on the standard of living debate had produced, by the early 1970s, an 'optimistic' consensus that the standard of living debate was all over by the 1810s, or by the 1820s at the latest. However, the new household budget evidence, along with urban life expectancy data, leads to an entirely different conclusion. The evidence indicates that, notwithstanding probable rises in male real wage rates, during the second quarter of the nineteenth century there was a serious deterioration in the standard of living of the growing proportion of the population recruited into the urban industrial workforce; and furthermore, that this trend of deterioration, although halted in the late 1850s and 1860s, was not significantly reversed until as late as the 1870s and 1880s.

ONLINE EXTRAS
AQA **WWW**

Practise your extract analysis skills by completing Worksheet 41 at **www. hoddereducation.co.uk/ accesstohistory/extras**

The Marxist viewpoint

Socialist historians have taken a pessimistic view of the change, but focused more on the impact of the social conditions of the population than on arguments about positive economic changes. Marxists such as Eric Hobsbawm have considered:

- the loss of quality of peaceful, rural life to enclosure and urbanisation
- the poor urban living conditions endured by many workers
- the harsh conditions in industrial environments
- the growing demand for political representation as well as social reform which was shown in protests, marches and riots shows a level of dissatisfaction among the working population.

ONLINE EXTRAS
AQA **WWW**
Practise your extract analysis skills by completing Worksheet 42 at **www. hoddereducation.co.uk/ accesstohistory/extras**

EXTRACT 3

Adapted from Eric Hobsbawm, *The Age of Revolution 1789–1848*, Abacus, 1962, pp. 297–8.

Science had never been more triumphant; knowledge had never been more widespread. No doubt these triumphs had their dark side, though these were not so readily to be summarised in statistical tables. How was one to find quantitative expression for the fact, which few today deny, that the Industrial Revolution created the ugliest world in which man had ever lived, as the grim and stinking, fog-bound black streets of Manchester already testified? Or by uprooting men and women in unprecedented numbers and depriving them of the certainties of the ages, probably the unhappiest in the world? Nobody could deny that there was poverty of the most shocking kind. Many held that it was even increasing and deepening.

CHAPTER SUMMARY

In 1832, conditions in the 'dark Satanic mills' of Britain were severe, and there was a growing public awareness of these issues. Ideas about self-help conflicted with moral arguments about improving conditions. After a slow start, with the 1833 Factory Act which extended pre-1832 legislation, it became more accepted that the government had a duty to engage with the conditions of workers, and a number of pieces of legislation were passed from 1844 which improved conditions in the workplace for many workers. More importantly, the idea of factory inspections became more accepted, though not necessarily effective.

As well as government legislation, workers themselves took action. From a slow start in the 1830s, New Model Unions formed in the 1850s. These large unions were able to wield greater pressure through organisations such as the Junta and the TUC, as well as trades councils. The government was forced to pay attention, and by the 1870s, the legal rights of trade unions were being established through legislation. Workers had finally found a legally recognised political voice.

The changes in the period contributed to the improvement in living conditions in the period, although how this is measured and interpreted is debated by historians.

Refresher questions

Use these questions to remind yourself of the key material covered in this chapter.

1 Describe the Ten Hour Movement.

2 What did the 1833 and 1844 Factory Acts achieve?

3 Why was the 1878 Factory Act, the 'Consolidation Act', important?

4 What problems did trade unions face in the 1830s?

5 What were Friendly Societies?

6 Why was the GNCTU a significant development, and why did it fail?

7 What were the New Model Unions?

8 What were the Junta and trades councils?

9 Why were the 1869 reports of the Royal Commission into the trade unions important in the development of workers' unions?

10 How was the position of trade unions in 1885 different from that in the 1830s?

Question practice: AQA A level

Essay questions

1 How effective were trade unions in representing the grievances of workers in the period 1832–85?

EXAM HINT You will need to avoid a descriptive approach and focus on analysing how effective trade unions were. You may wish to adopt a chronological approach – but ensure that the focus is on analysis rather than on describing events.

2 How effective was government legislation in improving working conditions in the period 1832–85?

EXAM HINT You will need to avoid a descriptive approach. Even if you adopt a chronological plan, analyse how much government legislation actually affected working conditions – and for whom.

Interpretation question

1 Using your understanding of the historical context, assess how convincing the arguments in Extracts 1 (page 226), 2 (page 228) and 3 (page 229) are in relation to living conditions in Britain, 1793–1885.

EXAM HINT Analyse the content of each extract in turn. Try to identify the main argument together with any subsidiary ones, and then use your contextual knowledge to assess how convincing each extract is. There is no requirement for an overall conclusion on all three extracts.

Question practice: OCR A level

Source questions

1 Using Sources 1–4 below and page 232 in their historical context, assess how far they support the view that the government was interested in improving working conditions in the 1830s.

> **EXAM HINT** Group the sources according to whether or not they support the view in the question. Each source should be explained in relation to the question, its provenance evaluated and contextual knowledge used to test the view of the source. A judgement about each source in relation to the question should be reached, allowing an overall judgement about whether the sources support the view that the government was interested in improving working conditions in the 1830s.

SOURCE 1

From John Fielden, *The Curse of the Factory System*, 1836. Fielden was an MP.

Here, then, is the 'curse' of our factory-system; as improvements in machinery have gone on, the 'avarice of masters' has prompted many to exact more labour from their hands than they were fitted by nature to perform… Since Lord Althorp's Act was passed, in 1833, we have reduced the time of adults to sixty-seven and a half hours a week, and that of children under thirteen years of age to forty-eight hours in the week, though to do this latter has, I must admit, subjected us to much inconvenience, but the elder hands to more, inasmuch as the relief given to the child is in some measure imposed on the adult. The increased speed given to machinery within the last thirty years, has, in very many instances, doubled the labour of both.

SOURCE 2

From an 1839 report by Leonard Horner, the senior factory inspector for the government, to the home secretary, Lord Russell.

Matters are very much in the same state, as regards obedience to the Factory Act, as I have reported them to be for some time past; that is, the main provisions are fairly observed in the majority of instances, and it has been necessary to resort to prosecution in many others; I have no expectation that there will be much change for the better … I particularly allude to the offence of employing children twelve hours a day who are under thirteen years of age. But the culpability is fully as chargeable upon the parents of those children, … as it is upon the masters of the factories. In a visit to a mill near Bury on the 23rd of November last, I noticed … a father, in the receipt of good wages and in regular employment, who had been knowingly working his own child twelve hours a day … from the time when she was little more than nine years old.

ONLINE EXTRAS OCR WWW

Practise your source analysis skills by completing Worksheet 38 at www. hoddereducation.co.uk/ accesstohistory/extras

ONLINE EXTRAS OCR WWW

Practise your source analysis skills by completing Worksheet 39 at www. hoddereducation.co.uk/ accesstohistory/extras

ONLINE EXTRAS OCR WWW

Practise your source analysis skills by completing Worksheet 40 at www. hoddereducation.co.uk/ accesstohistory/extras

SOURCE 3

A letter of complaint from union representatives to Lord Melbourne, home secretary, after he refused to meet with them in 1830.

My Lord,

The cool & very degrading manner in which … [we] were received at Court this day CAN NEVER be effaced from our memories … We have been most miserably disappointed (the great & useless expense & serious loss of time being a minor consideration) but we at the same time most unanimously state our conviction that [other visitors] would have been received with more attention and would not have been so unceremoniously dismissed (after being very uselessly detained in the wet and cold for upwards of two hours) with the cheerless and heartless message that 'there was no answer'.

Your Lordships humble Servants
52 Influential Members of a body of 40,000 Artisans

SOURCE 4

George Loveless, one of the Tolpuddle Martyrs, was persuaded in 1837 to write a memoir of his experiences. This was published as a pamphlet entitled *Victims of Whiggery*. It was used by the unions and the Chartist movement, and Loveless was invited to speak at a Chartist convention in 1839.

As to the trial, I need mention but little; the whole proceedings were characterised by a shameful disregard of justice and decency … I shall not soon forget [the judge's] address to the jury in summing up the evidence: among other things, he told them, that if such Societies were allowed to exist, it would ruin masters, cause a stagnation in trade, destroy property, – and if they should not find us guilty, he was certain they would forfeit the opinion of the Grand Jury. I thought to myself, there is no danger but we shall be found guilty, as we have a special jury for the purpose, selected from among those who are most unfriendly towards us – the Grand Jury, landowners, the Petty Jury, land-renters.

Question practice: Pearson Edexcel A level

Essay questions

1 How far did working conditions change between 1833 and 1870?

EXAM HINT Note the changes brought by successive Mines and Factories Acts, which reduced the hours of employment for women and children. However, health and safety legislation was limited and ineffective.

2 How significant were New Model Unions in representing the demands of workers in the years 1850–70?

EXAM HINT Examine the extent to which New Unions preferred negotiations to strike action, and the extent of their success. Point out that they neglected the interests of poorer unskilled workers.

3 How far was the government's response to trade unions the main factor affecting the development of labour laws in the period 1830 to 1870?

EXAM HINT Compare the impact of the government response on labour laws, such as the Royal Commission report that led to new legislation, with other factors such as the development of trade union organisation and tactics, and improvements in public opinions of trade unions.

Exam focus: AQA

Essay guidance

At both AS and A level for AQA Component 1: Breadth Study: 1F Industrialisation and the people: Britain, c1783–1885, you will need to answer an essay question in the exam. Each essay question is marked out of 25:

■ for the AS exam, Section B: answer **one** essay question from a choice of two

■ for the A level exam, Section B: answer **two** essay questions from a choice of three.

There are several question stems which all have the same basic requirement: to analyse and reach a conclusion, based on the evidence you provide.

The AS questions give a quotation and then ask whether you agree or disagree with this view. Almost inevitably, your answer will be a mixture of both. The task for A level has the same basic requirement for analysis, but the demands are more extensive. Detailed essays with accurate deployment of dates and own knowledge are more likely to do well than vague or generalised essays.

Both mark schemes for AS and A level emphasise the need to analyse and evaluate the key features related to the periods studied. The key feature of the highest level is sustained analysis: analysis that unites the whole of the essay. Below is a summary of the mark schemes but it is always worth checking the full version on the AQA website (www.aqa.org.uk).

Essay questions for Paper 1 (Breadth Studies) will relate directly or indirectly to one of the six key issues listed at the beginning of the syllabus:

■ How was Britain governed and how did democracy and political organisations change and develop?

■ What pressures did governments face and how did they respond to these?

■ How and with what results did the economy develop and change?

■ How and with what results did society and social policy develop?

Level	AS level	A level
1	Extremely limited or irrelevant information. Unsupported, vague or generalist comments (1–5)	Extremely limited or irrelevant information. Unsupported, vague or generalist comments (1–5)
2	Descriptive or partial, failing to grasp full demands of question. Limited in scope (6–10)	Descriptive or partial, failing to grasp full demands of question. Limited in scope (6–10)
3	Some understanding and the answer is adequately organised. Information showing understanding of some key features (11–15)	Understanding of question and a range of largely accurate information showing an awareness of key issues and features, but lacking in precise detail. Some balance established (11–15)
4	Understanding shown, with range of largely accurate information showing an awareness of some of the key issues and features (16–20)	Good understanding of question. Well-organised and effectively communicated, with a range of clear and specific supporting information showing a good understanding of key features and issues, with some conceptual awareness (16–20)
5	Good understanding. Well-organised and effectively communicated. A range of clear information showing a good understanding and some conceptual awareness leading to a substantiated judgement (21–25)	Very good understanding of the full demands of question. Well-organised and effectively delivered, with well-selected, precise supporting information. Fully analytical, with a balanced argument and well-substantiated judgement (21–25)

- How important were ideas and ideology?
- How important was the role of individuals and groups and how were they affected by developments?

Writing an essay: tips from examiners' reports

Focus and structure

- Be sure what the question is asking and plan what the paragraphs should be about.

- Especially with Paper 1 breadth essay questions, it is important that the whole of the time period in the question is considered. Essay titles in breadth essay questions will cover at least twenty years. Do not just focus on the beginning or the end of the period. A response that fails to cover the full date range set in the question will struggle to reach the higher levels.

- Your introduction to the essay should be focused and outline the overall argument of the essay. It is not the place to talk about different definitions of what it meant by democracy, for example. Make sure you clearly state what your opinion is and why you think that.

- Be sure that each paragraph highlights the structure of the answer, for example the opening sentence should be analytical and not descriptive.

- Make sure that the introductory sentence of each paragraph relates directly to the focus of the question.

- Avoiding writing a narrative (an account of what happened). Simply listing events and telling the story will result in a low-level mark.

Use detail

- Make sure that you show detailed knowledge – but only as part of an explanation being made in relation to the question. No knowledge should be standalone; it should be used in context.

- For every piece of detailed knowledge think 'so what?' Why have you added this piece of information? What role is it playing in advancing your argument?

Explanatory analysis and evaluation

- Consider what words and phrases to use in an answer to strengthen the explanation. A good place to start is to use adjective qualifiers (words that precede an adjective that increase or decreases the quality signified by the word they modify).

Use of primary sources and references to historians

- Primary sources can be referred to in your answer in order to add substance to an explanation.

- The views of historians can also be used *but* do not parade knowledge about several historians who do not always agree with each other unless you are actively using their views to augment your own argument. Extensive historiography is not wanted. Indeed, an answer can be in the top level and make no mention of historians whatsoever.

Balance

- Your answer must be a balanced response. This does not mean giving two alternative viewpoints and sitting on the fence or in the middle – you will need to consider a variety of factors and make a judgement. You will need to explain why the alternative view or factors are not as important or valid as the one you are advancing.

Argument and counter-argument

- Think of how arguments can be juxtaposed as part of a balancing act to give contrasting views.

- Think how best to 'resolve' contradictory arguments.

Relative significance and evaluation

- Think how best to reach a judgement when trying to assess the relative importance of various factors, and their possible interrelationship.

Planning an essay

Practice question 1

To what extent was the British government responsible for minimising the impact of radical protest between 1783 and 1812?

This question requires you to analyse the reasons why radical protest had little impact in the period 1783–1812. You must discuss:

- How the government response to radical protest minimised its impact (your primary focus).
- The other factors that reduced the impact of radical protest (your secondary focus).

A clear structure makes for a much more effective essay and is crucial for achieving the highest marks. In addition to an introduction and conclusion, you need three or four paragraphs to structure this question effectively. In each paragraph you will deal with one factor. One of these *must* be the factor in the question. If you don't address the factor (in this case the government's response) you aren't answering the question and will only score a low level.

A very basic plan for this question might look like this:

- Paragraph 1: the government's response to radical protest and why it minimised the impact of demands for reform.
- Paragraph 2: the impact of the counter-reform movement, such as 'Church and King' groups, on radical protest.
- Paragraph 3: the divisions within the radical protest movement which weakened its ability to act effectively as a united force.

It is a good idea to cover the factor named in the question first, so that you don't run out of time and forget to do it. Then cover the others in what you think is their order of importance, or in the order that appears logical in terms of the sequence of paragraphs.

The introduction

Maintaining focus is vital. One way to do this from the beginning of your essay is to use the words in the question to help write your argument. The first sentence of your answer to question 1, for example, could look like this:

> The radical protest movement had limited impact in the period 1783-1812 partly because of the government's response to its activities.

This opening sentence provides a clear focus on the demands of the question, although it could, of course, be written in a more exciting style. Then go on to outline the argument of the essay – anticipating the conclusion. The rest of the essay should flow from these opening statements because you have indicated a clear sense of direction.

Focus throughout the essay

Structuring your essay well will help with keeping the focus of your essay on the question. To maintain a focus on the wording in question 1, you could begin your first main paragraph with the response of the British government.

> The response of the British government was one very important factor in limiting the impact of radical protest.

- This sentence begins with a clear point that refers to the primary focus of the question (the impact of the radical protest movement) while linking it to a factor (the response of the British government).
- You could then have a paragraph for each of your other factors.
- It will be important to make sure that each paragraph focuses on analysis and includes relevant details that are used as part of the argument.
- You may wish to number your factors. This helps to make your structure clear and helps you to maintain focus. However, this can make the essay appear to be concerned with a list, and not encourage links between paragraphs.

Deploying detail

As well as focus and structure, your essay will be judged on the extent to which it includes accurate detail. There are several different kinds of evidence you could use that might be described as detailed. These include correct dates, names of relevant people, statistics and events. You can also make your essays more detailed by using the correct technical vocabulary. For example, for sample question 1 you could use terms such as *habeas corpus* and 'Church and King' groups.

You might also be able to use specific primary sources, including brief quotations, and also references to the views of particular historians who support your arguments. However, the quotations and arguments of historians must be relevant. There is no point in learning historians' quotes and squeezing them in somewhere just because you have learnt them. This will not gain you marks – they need to relate to your argument.

Analysis and explanation

'Analysis' covers a variety of high-level skills including explanation and evaluation; in essence, it means breaking down something complex into smaller parts. A clear structure which breaks down a complex question into a series of paragraphs is the first step towards writing an analytical essay.

The purpose of explanation is to account for why something happened, or why something is true or false. An explanatory statement requires two parts: a *claim* and a *justification*.

For example, for practice question 1, you might want to argue that one important reason was the use of legislation to make it hard for radical protestors to meet and discuss their ideas. Once you have made your point, and supported it with relevant detail, you can then explain how this answers the question. For example, you could conclude your paragraph like this:

The government's use of legislation to prevent public meetings was important[1] because it limited the ability of influential speakers to influence audiences[2], and for the movement to build a large and united following, which minimised the impact of the radical protest movement in challenging the government[3].

1 Claim: the first part of this sentence is the claim while the second part justifies the claim.

2 Relationship. 'Because' is a very important word to use when writing an explanation, as it shows the relationship between the claim and the justification.

3 Justification.

Evaluation

Evaluation means considering the importance of two or more different factors, weighing them against each other, and reaching a judgement. This is a good skill to use at the end of an essay because the conclusion should reach a judgement which answers the question. Ideally this will have been anticipated in the introductory paragraph, thus ensuring that the essay has a clear sense of direction from beginning to end.

For example, your conclusion to question 1 might read:

Clearly[1], the response of the government meant that the radical protest movement was vulnerable to arrest and unable to organise regular public meetings. However[2], the widespread counter-reform movement and the fundamental divisions within the movement also meant that there was little potential for the movement to form a strong and united force for reform in that period. Therefore[3], government opposition prevented the radical protest movement having any impact.

1 Clearly.   2 However.   3 Therefore.

Words like 'however' and 'therefore' are helpful to contrast the importance of the different factors.

Complex essay writing: argument and counter-argument

Essays that develop a good argument are more likely to reach the highest levels. This is because argumentative essays are much more likely to develop sustained analysis. As you know, your essays are judged on the extent to which they analyse.

After setting up an argument in your introduction, you should develop it throughout the essay. One way of doing this is to adopt an argument–counter-argument structure. A counter-argument is one that disagrees with the main argument of the essay. This is a good way of evaluating the importance of the different factors that you discuss. Essays of this type will develop an argument in one paragraph and then set out an opposing argument in another paragraph. Sometimes this will include juxtaposing the differing views of historians on a topic.

Good essays will analyse the key issues. They will probably have a clear piece of analysis at the end of each paragraph. While this analysis might be good, it will generally relate only to the issue discussed in that paragraph.

Excellent essays will be analytical throughout. As well as the analysis of each factor discussed above, there will be an overall analysis. This will run throughout the essay and can be achieved through developing a clear, relevant and coherent argument.

A good way of achieving sustained analysis is to consider which factor is most important.

Here is an example of an introduction that sets out an argument for question 1:

The radical protest movement faced strong opposition from the British government that limited it from having any significant impact[1]. However, this was not the only reason for the failure of the movement. The movement was working against a popular counter-reform attitude from the general public, as well as being divided by fundamental class differences and a lack of central leadership, and this further reduced any potential impact[2]. But the most important reason why the radical protest movement had little impact was the combination of government opposition and popular opinion, especially during the Revolutionary War, which hindered any real national movement for reform[3].

1 The introduction begins with a claim.
2 The introduction continues with another reason.
3 Concludes with an outline of an argument of the most important reason.

- This introduction focuses on the question and sets out the key factors that the essay will develop.

- It introduces an argument about which factor was most significant.

- However, it also sets out an argument that can then be developed throughout each paragraph, and is rounded off with an overall judgement in the conclusion.

Complex essay writing: resolution and relative significance

Having written an essay that explains argument and counter-arguments, you should then resolve the tension between the argument and the counter-argument in your conclusion. It is important that the writing is precise and summarises the arguments made in the main body of the essay. You need to reach a supported overall judgement. One very appropriate way to do this is by evaluating the relative significance of different factors, in the light of valid criteria. Relative significance means how important one factor is compared to another.

The best essays will always make a judgement about which was most important based on valid criteria. These can be very simple – and will depend on the topic and the exact question.

The following criteria are often useful:

- Duration: which factor was important for the longest amount of time?

- Scope: which factor affected the most people?

- Effectiveness: which factor achieved most?

- Impact: which factor led to the most fundamental change?

For example, you could compare the factors in terms of their duration and their impact.

A conclusion that follows this advice should be capable of reaching a high level (if written, in full, with appropriate details) because it reaches an overall judgement that is supported through evaluating the relative significance of different factors in the light of valid criteria.

Having written an introduction and the main body of an essay for question 1, a concluding paragraph that aims to meet the exacting criteria for reaching a complex judgement could look like this:

Thus, the reasons for the radical movement having little impact were complex with several interrelated factors. Failure was not inevitable, but the conditions in Britain in the years 1783–1812 made reform unlikely. The government response to radical protest, both through legislation which hindered public meetings and suppressed the publication of radical ideas, combined with the government use of reactionary propaganda, made it difficult for the radicals to make any progress. However, the social context allowed the government to do this, since the majority of the voting population, as well as the middle classes, feared reform in the face of revolutionary activity on the Continent. Therefore, there was little effective opposition to the government response. This crucial and insurmountable problem for the radicals was exacerbated by the fact that the movement was divided on class lines and lacked leadership. With no clear unified goal there was little way that the movement could hope to overcome the challenge of government opposition such as was made possible in later decades, such as 1830, where protesters had clearer political goals.

Interpretations guidance

Section A of the examination for AQA Component 1: Breadth Study: 1F Industrialisation and the people: Britain, c1783–1885 contains extracts (of approximately 120–150 words) from the work of historians. This section tests your ability to analyse and evaluate different historical interpretations. Therefore, you must focus on the interpretations outlined in the extracts. The advice given here is for both the AS and the A level exams.

- AS exam: you will be given two extracts and asked which is the more convincing interpretation (25 marks).

- A level exam: you will be given three extracts and will be asked how convincing each of the arguments in the extracts are in relation to a specified topic (30 marks).

An interpretation is a particular view on a topic of history held by a particular author or authors. Interpretations of an event can vary, for example, depending on how much weight a historian gives to a particular factor and largely ignores another one. For example, on Pitt's effectiveness as a leader, or on the relative significance of the legislation of Gladstone and Disraeli.

Interpretations can also be heavily conditioned by events and situations that influence the writer. For example, judging the merits of Gladstone's reforms will lead to different responses: someone writing from a Liberal background may see Gladstone as largely successful, whereas someone writing from an Irish nationalist background may see his policies as very flawed.

The interpretations that you will be given will be largely from recent or fairly recent historians, and they may, of course, have been influenced by events in the period in which they were writing.

When looking at historians' arguments you will need to consider the following questions:

- What is the main argument/interpretation that the historian is putting across?
- How good is the argument?
- What factors does the historian consider?
- What evidence does the historian use?
- What subsidiary arguments does the historian make?

Interpretations and evidence

The extracts will contain a mixture of interpretations and evidence. The mark scheme rewards answers that focus on the *interpretations* offered by the extracts much more highly than answers that focus on the *information or evidence* mentioned in the extracts. Therefore, it is important to identify the interpretations. The main interpretation could be anywhere – it might not be the first line that you read. It could be towards the end of the extract or just an overall feeling.

- *Interpretations* are a specific kind of argument. They tend to make claims such as 'Gladstone's Liberal government made significant improvements to social conditions'.

- *Information or evidence* tends to consist of specific details. For example: 'Gladstone's government passed legislation which extended education to children nationally, leading to increased literacy'.

- *Arguments and counter-arguments*: sometimes in an extract you will find an interpretation which is then balanced in the same paragraph with a counter-argument. You will need to decide with which your knowledge is most in sympathy.

Fact and opinion

It is important to be able to identify the difference between a fact and an opinion. For example, a weak candidate will write 'the historian says Gladstone's government passed the Forster Education Act in 1870. I know that this is true.' However, the task is not to assess how accurate the historian is but how convincing the argument is.

The importance of planning

At AS level you are allowed 45 minutes for this question. At A level you are allowed one hour. It is the planning stage that is vital in order to write a good answer. You should allow at least a quarter of that time to read the extracts and plan an answer. If you start writing too soon, it is likely that you will waste time trying to summarise the *content* of each extract. Do this in your planning stage – and then think how you will *use* the content to answer the question.

Analysing interpretations: AS (two extracts)

The same skills are needed for AS and A level for this question. The advice starts with AS simply because it only involves two extracts rather than three.

With reference to these extracts and your understanding of the historical context, which of these two extracts provides the more convincing interpretation of political change in the years 1867–85? (25 marks)

Extracts A and B are used for the AS question. Extracts A, B and C are used for the A level question.

EXTRACT A

Adapted from H.C.G. Matthew, 'The Liberal Age (1851–1914)' in Kenneth O. Morgan, editor, *The Oxford Illustrated History of Britain*, Oxford University Press, 1984, pp. 497 and 499.

By increasing the electorate, the Reform Acts of 1867 and 1884 presented parties with a much larger, though by no means universal, body of voters. Accustomed to losing, the Conservatives began to win. Their target was the boroughs: to obtain political power they had to enlarge their base from the counties to the expanding towns and suburbs. This they did with considerable success in the 1870s and 1880s, by linking an aristocratic and Anglican party with the aspirations of the expanding middle and lower middle classes in the great cities. Disraeli advocated a policy of social reform, supposedly of particular appeal to such members of the working classes as had recently become voters. The early years of the Conservative government of 1874–80 were marked by a burst of social reforms. They affected middle-class perhaps more than working-class interests and because the social measures were permissive rather than compulsory their effect was more limited than might have been expected.

EXTRACT B

Adapted from Annette Mayer, *The Growth of Democracy in Britain*, Hodder Education, 1999, pp. 59, 66 and 69.

After 1868, both the Liberals and the Conservatives engaged in a review of party policies. This analysis of ideas was clearly driven by motives of pragmatism and self-interest. Both parties realised the enormous potential of support created by the process of democratic reform. The second major impact of political reform was the need to restructure party organisations. As patronage declined, so voting behaviour became less predictable. The most obvious method of attracting votes and increasing support was to build up local associations which would encourage grass-root involvement in politics. Through these associations, politics came to the people, men and women, subtly disguised in the form of popular entertainment: tea dances, excursions, summer fetes, cricket matches and garden parties. Political education would be a feature of the entertainment, but it was never permitted to detract from social enjoyment.

EXTRACT C

Adapted from Clive Behagg, *Labour and Reform: Working-class Movements 1815–1914*, Hodder Education, 2000, pp. 95–6.

Gladstone's biographer argues that: 'the third Reform Bill moved the country almost all the way towards political democracy'. This is not a very accurate appreciation of a political system that, despite the changes, represented only a small proportion of society and which remained heavily distorted against the interests of labour. Women were still not enfranchised and parliamentary motions to give them the vote were rejected in every parliamentary session between 1870 and 1885. Under the 1884 Act plural voting continued, and, needless to say, plural voters were not generally working-class voters. There were a variety of restrictions that disenfranchised many working-class men. Nor, we should remember, was this an unfortunate by-product of badly devised legislation. It had been accepted in 1867 and 1884 that residential qualifications and voter registration were useful devices to restrict working-class participation. The political system appeared democratic yet, in practice, it was heavily distorted against the working community.

Analysing Extract A

From the extract:

- The electorate was vastly increased, and led to the Conservatives holding a stronger political position.

- The Conservative Party was very successful at linking aristocratic and Anglican support with middle-class support as a consequence of the changing electorate.

- The need to win over the electorate led to the Conservatives following a programme of reform, though the laws they passed had limited effect as they were more permissive than compulsory.

Assessing the extent to which the arguments are convincing:

- Deploying knowledge to corroborate that the electorate was extended in 1867 and 1884.

- Deploying knowledge to highlight the limitations to the extension of the franchise, and also limitations of Conservative dominance in the 1860s and 1870s when the Liberals were in power.

- Supporting the claim about Disraeli's focus on appealing to the working-class voters with examples of legislation that he used.

- The extract focuses on the impact of political change in relation to the Conservative Party but omits to consider the wider implications of these political changes, which are mentioned in Extract B.

- The extract deals with the working classes broadly, without distinguishing between groups that were enfranchised and those that were not.

Analysing Extract B

From the extract:

- The main impact of political change was for both Liberals and Conservatives to review their party policies with a view to self-interest and gaining political support.

- Political change involved reforming the party structure in order to control voter behaviour and gain votes.

- The general public became more involved in political parties at grass-roots level, including social events like sports matches and fetes.

Assessing the extent to which the arguments are convincing:

- Deploying knowledge of the Liberals and Conservatives changing the focus of their policies to win votes (and agreeing with Extract A).

- Deploying knowledge to support the claim about the changes to party structure, for example addressing the new party structures that were created.

- Juxtaposing the popular events which built grass-roots support against the groups that were excluded from politics even after 1885 to evaluate the scale of impact.

Comparing the analysis of each extract should give the direction of an overall conclusion and judgement about which of the extracts is more convincing. In this case it may be that Extract B is more convincing because it does try to present a balanced view which addresses both main political parties and changing voter behaviour.

The mark scheme for AS

The mark scheme builds up from Level 1 to Level 5, in the same way as it does for essays:

■ Do not waste time simply describing or paraphrasing the content of each extract. Simply copying out long quotations of an interpretation doesn't demonstrate a high level of understanding and won't gain you any marks.

■ Make sure that when you include your knowledge it is being used to advance the analysis of the extracts – not as knowledge in its own right. Always think 'so what?' What job is the addition of your knowledge doing? How is that knowledge advancing your answer? When deploying information always think how it helps in evaluating the interpretation.

■ The top two levels of the mark scheme refer to 'supported conclusion' (Level 4) and 'well-substantiated conclusion' (Level 5):

  □ For Level 4, a 'supported conclusion' means finishing your answer with a judgement that is backed up with some accurate evidence drawn from the source(s) and your knowledge.

  □ For Level 5, a 'well-substantiated conclusion' means finishing your answer with a judgement which is very well supported with evidence, and, where relevant, reaches a complex conclusion that reflects a wide variety of evidence.

Writing the answer for AS

There is no one correct way! However, the principles are clear. In particular, contextual knowledge

should be used *only* to back up an argument. None of your knowledge should be standalone – all your knowledge should be used in context.

For each extract in turn:

■ Explain the evidence in the extract, backed up with your own contextual knowledge, for the political changes that occurred in the period 1867–85.

■ Explain the points in the extract where you have evidence that contradicts the idea of political change.

Then write a conclusion that reaches a judgement on which is more convincing as an interpretation. You might build in some element of comparison during the answer, or it might be developed in the final paragraph only.

Analysing interpretations: A level (three extracts)

For the AQA A level exam, Section A gives you three extracts (see pages 240–1), followed by a single question.

Using your understanding of the historical context, assess how convincing the arguments in each of these three extracts are in relation to political change in the period 1867–85. (30 marks)

An analysis of Extracts A and B has already been provided for the AS question (see page 240).

Analysing Extract C

From the extract:

■ By 1885, there had been limited change to the electorate since only a minority of the population was represented.

■ Despite a larger electorate, plural voting still benefited the wealthiest members of society.

■ The limitations to political change were not an oversight, but a deliberate intention to restrict numbers of working-class voters.

Assessing the extent to which the arguments are convincing:

- Deploying knowledge to corroborate the extent of change to the electorate.
- Deploying knowledge to explain the intentions of the political parties in limiting the electorate.
- The extract minimises the extent of political change and suggests more continuity than change by portraying the actual change as artificial and limited.

Writing the answer for A level

First, make sure that you have the focus of the question clear – in this case, the focus is on political change 1867–85 and how convincing the extracts are on that subject. Then you can investigate the three extracts to see how convincing they are.

You need to analyse each of the three extracts in turn. A suggestion is to have a large piece of paper divided into nine blocks.

Extract's main arguments	Knowledge to corroborate	Knowledge to contradict or modify
A		
B		
C		

- In the first column, list the main argument and any subsidiary arguments each uses.
- In the second column, list what you know that can corroborate the arguments.
- In the third column, list what might contradict or modify (you might find that you partly agree, but with reservations) the arguments.
- You may find, of course, that some of your knowledge is relevant more than once.

Hints from examiners' reports: how to write a 'good answer'

There is no one correct way to organise an answer. It is the overall argument(s) that you are being judged on.

- Briefly refer to the focus of the question.
- For each extract in turn, set out the main argument and any subsidiary ones, corroborating and contradictory evidence.
- Do this by treating each argument (or group of arguments) in turn.
- Refer to the content of an extract directly – perhaps by a brief quotation – but do not copy out whole sections.
- The argument that has been summarised should be related to the focus of the question, not simply a summary of the extract.
- Your own knowledge must only be used to support or refute an argument in the extract, not presented as a separate entity.
- Do *not* wander into provenance or value. You are only concerned with the content of each extract. You do not need to know anything about the historian or schools of history (for example Marxist, post-revisionist and so on). Evaluate the extract, not the historian!
- Do *not* attempt to analyse the extract by focusing on what is not there. Focus on what you are given to analyse.
- Make comparisons between the extracts if this is helpful. The mark scheme does not explicitly give credit for doing this, but a successful cross-reference may well show the extent of your understanding of each extract and add to the weight of your argument. Bear in mind, this is a high-level skill so only do this if you feel particularly confident with this approach.
- Write a brief judgement at the end of the analysis on each extract. Do not write an introduction or an overall conclusion saying which was most convincing.
- This is not an exercise in English literature, so do not stray into focusing on tone or particular use of emotive language. If the historian comes across as angry, for example, this does not make the argument any less or more convincing.

The mark scheme for A level

For each of the three extracts, the mark scheme makes it clear that a good answer will:

- Identify the arguments presented in each extract.

- Assess the extent to which the arguments are convincing, using your own knowledge.

- Take every opportunity to make a balanced answer wherever this is appropriate, by corroborating and contradicting the arguments in each extract. An unbalanced answer will be that the interpretation is completely convincing or, conversely, completely unconvincing.

The mark scheme progresses upwards like this:

- Level 1: general comments about the three extracts or accurate understanding of one extract.

- Level 2: some accurate comments on the interpretations in at least two of the three extracts, but with limited comments or with description.

- Level 3: some supported comments on the interpretations, putting them in their historical context. Some analysis of the content of the extracts, but little attempt to evaluate them.

- Level 4: good understanding of the interpretations provided in the extracts, with knowledge to give a good analysis and some evaluation.

- Level 5: very good understanding and strong historical awareness to analyse and evaluate.

Notice that there is no reference in the A level mark scheme to *comparing* the extracts or reaching a judgement about the most convincing.

Exam focus: OCR

Essay guidance

The assessment of OCR Unit Y110: From Pitt to Peel 1783–1853 means you will answer **one** essay question and **one** source question.

For OCR A level History, the skills required to achieve a high grade for Unit Group 1 are made very clear in the mark scheme, which emphasises that the answer must:

- focus on the demands of the question
- be supported by accurate and relevant factual knowledge
- be analytical and logical
- reach a supported judgement about the issue in the question.

There are a number of skills that you will need to develop to reach the higher levels in the marking bands:

- understand the wording of the question
- plan an answer to the question set
- write a focused opening paragraph
- avoid irrelevance and description
- write analytically
- write a conclusion which reaches a supported judgement based on the argument in the main body of the essay.

These skills will be developed in the section below, but are further developed in the 'Period Study' chapters of the *OCR A level History* series (British Period Studies and Enquiries).

Understanding the wording of the question

To stay focused on the question set, it is important to read the question carefully and focus on the key words and phrases. Unless you directly address the demands of the question you will not score highly. Remember that in questions where there is a named factor you must write a good analytical paragraph about the given factor, even if you argue that it was not the most important.

Types of AS and A level questions you might find in the exams	The factors and issues you would need to consider in answering them
1 Assess the reasons why the radical reform programme failed to achieve change by 1812	Weigh up the relative importance of a range of factors as to why radical protesters did not achieve change by 1812. This is developed below and a range of issues that might be discussed is outlined
2 To what extent did Whig action lead to the passing of the 1832 Reform Act?	Weigh up the relative importance of a range of factors, including comparing the importance of Whig action with other factors such as popular pressure, the impact of the Catholic Emancipation and the division of the Tory Party
3 'Pitt's blue water strategy was the most important reason for the victory over France in the Napoleonic Wars.' How far do you agree?	Weigh up the relative importance of a range of factors, including comparing the importance of Pitt's blue water strategy with other issues to reach a balanced judgement. This strategy might be compared with the use of coalitions, the Peninsular Campaign and perhaps Pitt's Economic policies which allowed Britain to stay in the war
4 How successful was Pitt at reforming the political administration?	This question requires you to make a judgement about Pitt's success in changing the political administration. Instead of thinking about factors, you would need to think about issues such as: • Pitt's development of a cabinet government • His efforts to reduce government corruption • Reorganisation of staffing and financing of government departments • Pitt's attempts to streamline military funding • His handling of the East India Company

Planning an answer

Many plans simply list dates and events: this should be avoided as it encourages a descriptive or narrative answer, rather than an analytical answer. The plan should be an outline of your argument; this means you need to think carefully about the issues you intend to discuss and their relative importance before you start writing your answer. It should therefore be a list of the factors or issues you are going to discuss and a comment on their relative importance.

For question 1 in the table, your plan might look something like this:

- Pitt's repressive policies: link to specific actions, such as suspending *habeas corpus* and imposing the Stamp Tax.
- Lack of leadership: there was no unifying control over the reform movement.
- Class division: the aims of the working and middle classes were different.
- Counter-reformist movement: groups such as the 'Church and King' organisations.
- Fear of radical ideas: the reformist movement after 1789 became associated with the violent actions in Revolutionary France.
- Government propaganda: use of magazines like *The Oracle* to portray radicals as traitors.

The opening paragraph

Many students spend time 'setting the scene'; the opening paragraph becomes little more than an introduction to the topic – this should be avoided. Instead, make it clear what your argument is going to be. Offer your view about the issue in the question – what was the most important reason for failure of the radical movement to achieve change by 1812 – and then introduce the other issues you intend to discuss. In the plan it is suggested that government actions were the most important factor. This should be made clear in the opening paragraph, with a brief comment as to why – perhaps that the legislation passed made it impossible for the radicals to organise effective meetings or publish their ideas. However, although government actions were the most important factor, it is worth just briefly mentioning the other factors that you intend to discuss and giving a brief comment as to your view about their relative importance. This will give the examiner a clear overview of your essay, rather than it being a mystery tour where the argument becomes clear only at the end. You should also refer to any important issues that the question raises. For example:

> There are a number of reasons why the radicals failed to achieve reform by 1812, including government action, lack of leadership and a counter-reform movement[1]. However, the most important reason was government action, particularly through passing harsh legislation[2]. This was effective in preventing the radicals from meeting in large numbers or publishing their ideas to gain support[3]. Although not as important, the other factors were important as they prevented the radicals from winning widespread popularity and ensured that the movement was divided, rather than a united force that could challenge the government[4].

1 The student is aware that there were a number of important reasons.

2 The student offers a clear view as to what they consider to be the most important reason – a thesis is offered.

3 There is a brief justification to support the thesis.

4 Some of the factors and their relative importance are briefly stated.

Avoid irrelevance and description

Hopefully, the plan will stop you from simply writing all you know about why the radicals did not achieve change and force you to weigh up the role of a range of factors. Similarly, it should also help prevent you from simply writing about or describing the ideas of the radicals or actions that Pitt's government took, rather than explaining why the radicals did not achieve reform. You will not lose marks if you do that, but neither will you gain any credit, and you will waste valuable time.

Look at the paragraph below written in answer to the question: 'Assess the reasons why the radical reform programme failed to achieve change by 1812.'

Pitt's government took actions that stopped the radicals from achieving reform[1]. Pitt's government suspended the right of habeas corpus in 1794 and used this to arrest the leaders of the National Convention. Also in 1795, the government passed the 'Two Acts' which were very harsh against radicals[2]. Pitt's government passed the Seditious Meetings Act in 1799 which made it difficult for the radical reformers to be effective at demanding change[3]. The actions of Pitt's government were therefore a very important reason why the radical reformers failed to achieve reform by 1812[4].

1 The answer acknowledges that government action prevented change.

2 The answer describes what happens but does not explain how this contributed to the lack of change.

3 The descriptive approach continues with, at best, a hint that it prevented the radicals achieving change, but it is still not linked to why this stopped change.

4 The response asserts that it was a major cause, but this has not been shown.

There is no real explanation as to how the actions of the government prevented the radicals from being able to pressure the government for change or gain widespread support to be a serious political force, which would be needed to reach Level 3, and certainly no evidence of either evaluation or judgement, which would be needed for the higher levels.

Write analytically

This is perhaps the hardest, but most important skill you need to develop. An analytical approach can be helped by ensuring that the opening sentence of each paragraph introduces an idea, which directly answers the question and is not just a piece of factual information. In a very strong answer it should be possible to simply read the opening sentences of all the paragraphs and know what argument is being put forward.

If we focus on the question on the failure of the radical reform programme, the following are possible sentences with which to start paragraphs:

- Fear of revolutionary ideas became an important factor once the French Revolution broke out in 1789, but from 1783 to 1789 it was not an important factor. …

- Divisions among the reformers, particularly on class lines, ensured that in the long run they were less likely to be successful. …

- The lack of central leadership was important because it meant that the reformers were not a unified political force. …

- Government propaganda capitalised on existing fear of revolutionary ideas and meant that many wealthy and middle-class individuals feared even the more moderate ideas of the reformers. …

You would then go on to discuss both sides of the argument raised by the opening sentence, using relevant knowledge about the issue to support each side of the argument. The final sentence of the paragraph would reach a judgement on the role played by the factor you are discussing in the lack of change by 1812. This approach would ensure that the final sentence of each paragraph links back to the actual question you are answering. If you can do this for each paragraph you will have a series of mini-essays, which discuss a factor and reach a conclusion or judgement about the importance of that factor or issue. For example:

Fear of revolutionary ideas became an important factor once the French Revolution broke out in 1789, but from 1783 to 1789 it was not an important factor[1]. Through the 1780s, the Society for Constitutional Information was seen as simply a talking shop and ignored by many. However, following the outbreak of revolution in France, British radicalism became increasingly extreme with an increase of violent uprisings, such as in Sheffield in 1791 with a three-day protest in which workers chanted 'no king'. This led to fear of violence such as had taken place with the fall of the Bastille in France. In

1792, the Reeves' Association was formed which expressed a genuinely popular opinion against revolutionary ideas. What had been previously considered a novel if foolish ideal was now seen as a dangerous threat to British society and the increased popular opposition strengthened the government position to refuse to consider political reform[2].

1 The sentence puts forward a clear view that fear of revolutionary ideas was only important after 1789.

2 The claim that it was important after 1789 is developed and some evidence is provided to support the argument.

The paragraph above explains the impact of fear of revolutionary ideas on popular opinion but explaining the impact will take you only to Level 3 or 4, depending on how well developed and how well supported your explanation is. At this level answers will produce a list of reasons as to why no change was achieved. Answers that are not developed or are poorly explained will be placed in Level 3, while those that are well developed will reach Level 4. The quality of the answer above, if repeated in other paragraphs, would certainly reach Level 4.

In order to reach Levels 5 and 6 there needs to be clear evidence of the evaluation of factors – how important the factors were in preventing change. The paragraph above does start to move towards that as it argues that the fear of revolutionary change was important, but only after 1789. The paragraph also provides some support for that claim and it is this that turns an assertion that it was important into a judgement and takes the response to the higher levels.

At Level 5, the judgement is likely to be present only in the conclusion, as shown in the example below. However, responses that reach Level 6 will make a judgement about the importance of each factor as they explain their role, so that there will be a series of interim judgements which are then pulled together in an overall conclusion.

Questions for practice

Write six opening sentences for answers to the following questions:

- 'The Whigs offered little serious opposition to Pitt 1783–1806.' How far do you agree?

- Assess the reasons why the 1832 Reform Act was passed.

- How accurate is to call Lord Liverpool's government 1812–27 'Liberal'?

- How far had Whig and Tory attitudes to constitutional reform changed between 1783 and 1832?

The conclusion

The conclusion provides the opportunity to bring together all the interim judgements to reach an overall judgement about the question. Using the interim judgements will ensure that your conclusion is based on the argument in the main body of the essay and does not offer a different view. For the essay answering question 1 (see page 245), you can decide what was the most important factor in the failure to achieve radical change by 1812, but for questions 2 and 3 you will need to comment on the importance of the named factor – Whig action or blue water strategy – as well as explain why you think a different factor is more important, if that has been your line of argument. Or, if you think the named factor is the most important, you would need to explain why that was more important than the other factors or issues you have discussed.

Consider the following conclusion to question 3: 'To what extent was Pitt's blue water strategy the most important reason for the victory over France in the Napoleonic Wars?'

Although the blue water strategy helped Britain to keep open its trade and maintain its international economic power while weakening France without resorting to a land conflict, it was not sufficient to win victory without engaging in the Peninsular Campaign[1]. After all, while the blue water strategy kept Britain strong enough to fund the coalition allies and keep France occupied facing enemies who relied on British money, it was only enough to maintain a stalemate which potentially could have dragged on. Therefore, the blue water strategy, economic strength and use of coalitions created a position from which Britain could attack France. But it was not until the British government used this situation to launch the Peninsular Campaign, which led to a series of victories on land, that France was defeated. It was therefore the Peninsular Campaign that was responsible for the ultimate victory, but the combination of other factors including the blue water strategy that made this tactic possible[2].

1 This is a strong conclusion because it considers the importance of the named factor – blue water strategy – but weighs that up against a range of other factors to reach an overall judgement.

2 It is also able to show links between the other factors to reach a balanced judgement, which brings in a range of issues, showing the interplay between them.

Sources guidance

OCR Unit Y110: From Pitt to Peel 1783–1853 is assessed through an essay and a source-based or enquiry question. There is no choice for the enquiry question. You will answer one question using four sources.

Answering the A level question

The skills needed to answer this question are made very clear by the mark scheme, which emphasises that the answer must:

- focus on the question
- evaluate the sources using *both* provenance and relevant contextual knowledge
- use detailed and accurate knowledge
- reach a supported analysis of the sources in relation to the question.

There are a number of skills that you need to develop if you are to reach the higher levels in the marking bands:

- You have to *interpret* the evidence. You need to link it to the issue in the question and decide what the evidence is saying about that issue.

- You need to consider *how useful* the evidence is. This involves thinking carefully about a range of issues concerning the provenance of the source; you might think about who wrote it, why it was written, whether the person who wrote it would be in a position to know and how typical it might be.

- You need to apply relevant contextual knowledge to the source to judge the validity of the source and its view; you therefore need a good knowledge of the topic in the question.

- You need to link your material to the issue in the question and not write a general essay about the topic.

These skills are illustrated in the guidance to answering the questions below, but are further developed in the 'Enquiry Study' chapters of the *OCR A level History* series (British Period Studies and Enquiries).

Practice question

A level

1 Using all the sources in their historical context, assess how far they support the view that the government was interested in improving working conditions in the 1830s.

SOURCE A

From John Fielden, *The Curse of the Factory System*, 1836. Fielden was an MP.

Here, then, is the 'curse' of our factory-system; as improvements in machinery have gone on, the 'avarice of masters' has prompted many to exact more labour from their hands than they were fitted by nature to perform ... Since Lord Althorp's Act was passed, in 1833, we have reduced the time of adults to sixty-seven and a half hours a week, and that of children under thirteen years of age to forty-eight hours in the week, though to do this latter has, I must admit, subjected us to much inconvenience, but the elder hands to more, inasmuch as the relief given to the child is in some measure imposed on the adult. The increased speed given to machinery within the last thirty years, has, in very many instances, doubled the labour of both.

SOURCE B

From an 1839 report by Leonard Horner, the senior factory inspector for the government, to the home secretary, Lord Russell.

Matters are very much in the same state, as regards obedience to the Factory Act, as I have reported them to be for some time past; that is, the main provisions are fairly observed in the majority of instances, and it has been necessary to resort to prosecution in many others; I have no expectation that there will be much change for the better ... I particularly allude to the offence of employing children twelve hours a day who are under thirteen years of age.

But the culpability is fully as chargeable upon the parents of those children, ... as it is upon the masters of the factories. In a visit to a mill near Bury on the 23rd of November last, I noticed ... a father, in the receipt of good wages and in regular employment, who had been knowingly working his own child twelve hours a day... from the time when she was little more than nine years old.

SOURCE C

A letter of complaint from union representatives to Lord Melbourne, home secretary, after he refused to meet them in 1830.

My Lord,

The cool & very degrading manner in which ... [we] were received at Court this day CAN NEVER be effaced from our memories ... We have been most miserably disappointed (the great & useless expense & serious loss of time being a minor consideration) but we at the same time most unanimously state our conviction that [other visitors] would have been received with more attention and would not have been so unceremoniously dismissed (after being very uselessly detained in the wet and cold for upwards of two hours) with the cheerless and heartless message that 'there was no answer'.

Your Lordships humble Servants
52 Influential Members of a body of 40,000 Artisans

SOURCE D

George Loveless, one of the Tolpuddle Martyrs, was persuaded in 1837 to write a memoir of his experiences. This was published as a pamphlet entitled *Victims of Whiggery*. It was used by the unions and the Chartist movement, and Loveless was invited to speak at a Chartist convention in 1839.

As to the trial, I need mention but little; the whole proceedings were characterised by a shameful disregard of justice and decency ... I shall not soon forget [the judge's] address to the jury in summing up the evidence: among other things, he told them, that if such Societies were allowed to exist, it would ruin masters, cause a stagnation in trade, destroy property, – and if they should not find us guilty, he was certain they would forfeit the opinion of the Grand Jury. I thought to myself, there is no danger but we shall be found guilty, as we have a special jury for the purpose, selected from among those who are most unfriendly towards us – the Grand Jury, landowners, the Petty Jury, land-renters.

Answering the A level question

The question will be worded as follows: 'Using these three sources/four sources in their historical context, assess how far they support the view that ... .'

■ Keep a good focus on the question and do not drift off into describing everything the sources say.

■ Evaluate the sources, that is, say how valid the evidence they give is. You can do this by looking at their *provenance*, that is, what they are, who wrote them, under what circumstances and why. You can also do this by looking at what they say about the issue and testing it against your own knowledge.

■ You have to keep a balance. You should not write an essay on the topic in the question just by using your own knowledge, but you should not just explain what the sources say about the issue either. You need to apply some knowledge to all the sources to answer the question.

In planning your answer to this question it might be helpful to construct a chart similar to the one overleaf:.

Source	View about the issue in the question	Evidence from the source	Provenance	Knowledge that supports the source	Knowledge that challenges the source	Judgement
A						
B						
C						
D						

- In the second column, you decide whether the source supports or challenges the view in the question, and in the third column you should enter evidence from the source that supports your view.

- The next column considers the provenance, which may affect the reliability of the source.

- The next two columns bring in your knowledge to support or challenge the view in the source.

- The final column brings all this together to make a judgement about the source in terms of supporting or challenging the view in the question.

If you complete this chart it should provide you with the material you need to answer the question. Although the mark scheme does not require you to group the sources, it might be more sensible to deal with all the sources that support the view in the question together and those that challenge the view together before reaching an overall judgement. However, remember some sources may have parts that both support and challenge the view in the question!

An opening paragraph to the question using all the sources could start as follows:

Sources A and B both suggest that the government had an interest in improving working conditions, by consideration of the legislation passed, but with limited actual impact. For example Source B, from an inspector appointed by the government to observe conditions, puts forward the view that 'the main provisions [of government action] are fairly observed in the majority of instances' but that he had 'no expectation that there will be much change for the better'[1]. However, Sources C and D suggest that the government had little real interest in improving working conditions, as Source C is a complaint from union representatives that they had been refused access to speak to a government minister, and Source D gives the account of the Tolpuddle Martyrs, where the government allowed men protesting their working conditions to be given an unbalanced trial 'characterised by a shameful disregard of justice and decency' and be sentenced to transportation[2].

1 The answer deals with the two sources that support the view in the question that the government had an interest in improving working conditions and provides a brief quotation from one of the sources to support the claim.

2 The answer now considers the view of the other two sources and offers the alternative view that the government had little interest in working conditions. This view is also supported by a brief quotation from Source D.

The opening paragraph could be developed further by indicating an overall answer to the question. This could be worded 'Overall, the sources support more the view that …'.

Answers can deal with each source separately and, in considering Source C, an answer might take the following approach:

Source C suggests that the government had little interest in engaging with representatives of the unions who represented workers because it angrily describes being 'unceremoniously dismissed' when they tried to speak to Lord Melbourne[1]. However, the source is a letter of complaint, written anonymously by the representatives of the union, in the hope of Melbourne and by extension the government feel shamed by their treatment of the delegation, so it is likely that the disappointment, cost and frustration are exaggerated when they describe being 'uselessly detained in the wet and cold for upwards of two hours'[2]. This records a single event, however certainly the government of the period tended to see unions as more of a problem than a means to improvement, since these unions were still loosely knit groups and had limited legal right to exist.

These unions were still operating under the limited terms of the 1825 Repeal of the Combination Acts, which gave unions very little leeway to pressure employers[3]. Therefore, this source is limited in suggesting that the government was disinterested in working conditions, as there was little reason for Melbourne to take seriously an unofficial union which had no legal standing, and this does not conclusively prove that they were disinterested in the working conditions. The fact that a Factory Act was passed only three years later suggests that the government may have been more interested in working conditions than in meeting unions[4].

1 The opening sentence outlines the view of the source (C) about the issue in the question and there is a brief explanation as to why it takes that view.

2 The answer considers the purpose of the Source and this raises questions as to its reliability.

3 Although the purpose of the source raises questions about its reliability, own knowledge is applied to confirm the view in the source

4 The answer concludes by linking the Source back to the question and although it acknowledges that the source accurately shows a negative government view of unions, it shows that this should not be taken as conclusive prove on the overall issue in the question. Having considered the provenance and used contextual knowledge the response reaches a judgement about the source in relation to the question. This is vital for the higher levels and should be done for each source.

Answers should treat each source in a similar way and then use the judgements reached about each source individually to reach an overall judgement in a concluding paragraph. The conclusion should be based on the evaluation of the sources and not simply own knowledge, as is seen in the example below.

Although Sources C and D challenge the view that the government was interested in working conditions, by showing that the government was not interested in working with unions and was willing to allow local magistrates to charge anyone protesting about working conditions, the purpose of both these sources raises questions about their reliability, as Source C was complaining to the government about their treatment with a view to making Lord Melbourne regret his actions, while Source D was published to deliberately present the Tolpuddle Trial as an affront to British values and gain

national support[1]. However, Sources A and B suggest that the government did at least have an interest in passing legislation that would have some impact, especially in Source B which shows the use of inspectors to try to assess the effects of the legislation[2]. As the origin of both Sources A and especially B suggests that they are more reliable than Sources C and D, it can therefore be concluded that although the extent of government interest in working conditions was limited, especially where it concerned protest or unions, the government did have an interest in improving working conditions[3].

1 The opening sentence relates to the issue in the question, namely that the government was interested in improving working conditions, and summarises the extent to which the sources support it.

2 The second sentence offers the counter-view.

3 The concluding sentence reaches an overall judgement based on an evaluation of the sources and a very brief reference to own knowledge to support the argument.

If a judgement has been reached about each source based on its provenance and using contextual knowledge, then the conclusion above will ensure that the response reaches the top level.

Common mistakes

■ Forgetting that this is the source element of the paper. Your answer needs to be driven by the sources.

■ Responses that consider *only* the provenance of each source or use *only* contextual knowledge to evaluate. You must use *both* to reach Level 4 and above.

■ Avoid stock comments about provenance such as 'he was there and would therefore know' or 'it is written in a private diary so can be trusted'.

■ Your own knowledge is simply deployed rather than used to evaluate the source. You need to make sure that you link your contextual knowledge to the source to show how the view of the source is either valid or invalid.

■ Judgements are made about the issue rather than the source. In light of the provenance of the source and your contextual knowledge, does the source support the view in the question?

Exam focus: Pearson Edexcel

Overview

Pearson Edexcel's Paper 1, Option 1D: Britain, c1785–c1870: democracy, protest and reform, is assessed by an exam comprising three sections:

- Sections A and B test your knowledge of the period 1785–1870. The questions test your breadth of knowledge of four key themes:
  - The growth of parliamentary democracy, *c.*1785–*c.*1870
  - Industrialisation and protest, *c.*1785–*c.*1870
  - Unionism and cooperation, *c.*1785–*c.*1870
  - Poverty and pauperism, *c.*1785–1870.
- Section C tests your depth of knowledge regarding a key historical debate: What explains the abolition of the slave trade at the end of the period *c.*1785–1807?

Sections A and B

The questions in Sections A and B are essay questions, but their demands are different:

- Section A of the exam paper contains two questions, and you have to complete one. The questions in Section A target a short period of time: they test the breadth of your knowledge by focusing on at least ten years.
- Section B of the exam paper also contains two questions, and you have to complete one. Questions in Section B cover a much broader timespan (at least one third of the period that you have studied). This means you should plan your answer carefully and select material to deploy.

Neither Section A nor B requires you to read or analyse either sources or extracts from the work of historians.

Skills

Questions in Sections A and B require you to deploy a variety of skills. The most important of these focus on the question, selection and deployment of relevant detail, analysis and, at the highest level, prioritisation.

Questions in Sections A and B include a second-order concept. These are:

- cause
- consequence
- change/continuity
- similarity/difference
- significance.

Therefore, the questions will typically begin with one of the following stems:

- How far …
- How accurate is it to say …
- To what extent …
- How significant …
- How successful … .

You should identify the second-order concept in the question and link your answer to that concept.

Dual focus questions

Some questions will have a dual focus, for example:

How far do you agree that the aims and methods of popular protest groups in the years 1820–50 were radically different from those of protest groups in the years 1785–1820?

Your answer should focus only on the two statements in the question: do not attempt to introduce a third. You should ensure a balance of coverage of the two issues.

Section C

Section C of the exam paper is different from Sections A and B. While Sections A and B test your own knowledge, Section C tests both your own knowledge and your ability to analyse and evaluate interpretations of the past in the work of historians. Section C contains two extracts from the work of historians, and there is one compulsory question.

Section C focuses on an interpretation related to the following controversy:

What explains the abolition of the slave trade at the end of the period c.1785–1807?

It looks at the following aspects of the interpretation:

- The importance of humanitarian campaigns and the influence of religion.
- The significance of economic and financial factors.
- The significance of individuals, including Thomas Clarkson, William Wilberforce and Olaudah Equiano.
- The changing political climate, including the fear of slave resistance.

Skills

Section C tests your ability to analyse and evaluate different historical interpretations in the light of your own knowledge. Therefore, it tests a variety of skills, including:

- identifying the interpretation
- writing a well-structured essay
- integrating extracts with own knowledge
- reaching an overall judgement.

The AS level exam

Paper 1

The AS exam tests the same content as the A level exam and is structured in exactly the same way. However, there are differences between the two exams:

Sections A and B

There are three key differences between A level and the AS in Sections A and B.

Wording

The wording of AS level questions will be less complex than the wording of A level questions. For example:

A level question	AS level question
How significant was the Chartist movement in developing tactics for demanding reform?	How far were Liberal governments responsible for legislation to improve the lives of the urban poor between 1850 and 1870?
How far did parliamentary reform groups pose a challenge to the government in the years 1793–1820?	Was government policy the main reason for the passing of parliamentary reform in the years 1830–67?

Focus

Section A questions can focus on a more limited range of concepts at AS than at A level. Specifically, at AS level, Section A questions can only focus on *cause* and *consequences* (including success and failure), whereas A level questions can focus on a wider variety of concepts.

Mark scheme

The A level mark scheme has five levels, whereas the AS level mark scheme has only four. This means that full marks are available at AS for an analytical essay, whereas sustained analysis is necessary for full marks at A level.

Section C

Section C of the AS exam focuses on the same aspects of the same debate: 'What explains the abolition of the slave trade at the end of the period c.1785–1807?' As in the A level exam, you have to answer one compulsory question based on two extracts. The AS level exam is different from the A level exam in the following ways.

The question

The AS level question is worded in a less complex way than the A level question. For example:

A level	AS level
In the light of differing interpretations, how convincing do you find the view that 'the decision to abolish slavery in 1807 was primarily a financial issue'?	Historians have different views about the reasons for the abolition of the slave trade. Analyse and evaluate the extracts and use your knowledge of the issues to explain your answer to the following question.
To explain your answer, analyse and evaluate the material in both extracts, using your own knowledge of the issues.	How far do you agree with the view that economic factors were crucial in the abolition of the slave trade, 1807?

The extracts

At AS, the extracts will be slightly shorter and you may get extracts taken from textbooks as well as the work of historians. In this sense, the extracts at AS level should be slightly easier to read and understand.

The mark scheme

The A level mark scheme has five levels, whereas the AS level mark scheme has only four. This means that full marks are available at AS for an analytical essay, whereas sustained analysis is necessary for full marks at A level.

Essay guidance for Sections A and B

Understanding the question

In order to answer the question successfully you must understand how the question works. Each essay question has three components:

- an invitation to reach a judgement …
- … on a subject from your course of study …
- … and a clearly defined time period.

For example:

How far do you agree that … the breakdown of rural communities was the main consequence of economic change … in the years 1785–1832?

Overall, *all* Section A and B questions ask you to make a judgement about the extent of something, in a specific period. In order to focus on the question,

you must address all three elements. The most common mistakes come from misunderstanding or ignoring one of these three key elements.

Planning your answer

Do not plan a narrative answer; instead you should:

- focus on the exact demands of the question
- note any key terms in the question
- note the timescale in the question.

Do not simply consider one part of the chronology and do not go beyond the dates provided.

All of your examined essays will be judged on how far they focus on the question and the quality of their structure. The better your focus and the clearer your structure, the better your chance of exam success.

Your essay should be made up of three or four paragraphs, each addressing the reasons for political instability. Your essay plan might look something like this:

- paragraph 1: breakdown of rural communities, caused by changes like migration and land enclosure
- paragraph 2: the growth of towns and cities
- paragraph 3: the significance of industrialisation
- paragraph 4: the growth of the industrial elite.

In addition to your three or four main points, you should begin your essay with a clear introduction and end with a conclusion that contains a focused summary of your essay.

Creating a strong introduction

Here is an example introduction in answer to the question above. The commentary reveals how to ensure your essay gets off to a good start.

How far do you agree that the breakdown of rural communities was the main consequence of economic change in the years 1785–1832?

From 1785 to 1832, the British economy underwent rapid changes which resulted in significant consequences[1]. One significant change was that population migration and enclosure led to the breakdown of rural populations. However, there were other significant consequences.

Towns and cities grew rapidly, leading to a more urbanised population. Also industrialisation changed production methods, leading to changes in trade and transport, and the emergence of a new industrial elite[2]. The breakdown of rural populations was significant, but the most important change was the industrialisation of production, since this drove urbanisation, and contributed to a movement for political and social reform with long-lasting consequences[3].

1 The essay starts with a clear focus on the question.

2 The last three sentences introduce the alternative consequences.

3 This sentence indicates that the essay will argue that industrialisation was the most significant consequence of economic change.

Reaching an overall judgement

In addition to focus, structure, the level of relevant detail and analysis, your exam essays will be assessed on how far you reach a supported overall judgement. The clearer and better supported your judgement, the better your mark is likely to be.

The mark scheme distinguishes between five levels of judgement:

Level 1 (low)	No overall judgement
Level 2	Stated overall judgement, but no support
Level 3	Overall judgement is reached, with weak support
Level 4	Overall judgement is reached and supported
Level 5 (high)	Overall judgement is reached and supported by consideration of the relative significance of key factors

As you know, your essays are judged on the extent to which they analyse. The mark scheme distinguishes between five different levels of analysis:

Level 1 (low)	Simplistic or no analysis
Level 2	Limited analysis of key issues
Level 3	Some analysis of key issues
Level 4	Analysis of key issues
Level 5 (high)	Sustained analysis of key issues

The key feature of the highest level is sustained analysis: analysis that unites the whole of the essay.

Below is a sample paragraph for the essay title on page 256. This paragraph highlights the use of relevant detail, analysis and a well-supported judgement.

Economic changes in the period 1785 to 1832 led to a breakdown of rural populations[1]. There were two main changes to agriculture which impacted on rural communities. First, methods of agriculture became modernised. Industrial production made more modern ploughs more cheaply available, and fertiliser made the land more productive. Also, selective breeding during the eighteenth century had made animal husbandry more profitable and more landowners dedicated land to rearing animals, which needs fewer workers, rather than crops. As farming became more effective, there was less need for a large workforce to work the land, and many migrated to seek work in urban communities. The second change that affected communities was enclosure. Between 1760 and 1815, there had been over 1800 acts of enclosure covering 7 million acres of communal land. Poorer farmers, who had provided for their families from common land, could no longer produce enough to survive, and many middle-size farmers were unable to pay the costs associated with enclosing the land. These either migrated to towns or became agricultural labourers, dependent on seasonal work on the land of richer farmers. It is true that the population of rural areas did not decrease during this period, but the migration within the population disrupted local communities and broke ties that had existed for generations. This was a direct consequence of economic change[2]. As wealthy landowners enclosed more land and employed cheap labour from dispossessed farmers, their increased profits could be channelled into further technological developments which continued the process of rural disruption by requiring fewer farmhands. By the early nineteenth century, a single pedigree pig or cow could bring £1000 profit for a landowner, far more than the value of the grain that could be grown using the same land resources. The physical changes to the *rural population were manifested in increased discontent. Although there were minor instances of discontent through the period, the Swing Riots in 1830 show that by the end of the 1820s there was substantial discontent at the economic changes that had occurred since 1785*[3]. *True, the population overall did not decrease as the rate of population increase was faster than the rate of migration to urban areas – by 1831, 33 per cent of families still worked on the land – but the disruption and discontent caused by economic change broke down traditional community relationships in an irreversible change which contributed to demands for future reform.*

1 The paragraph starts with a clear focus on the question and indicates that this paragraph will cover the breakdown of rural communities.

2 The paragraph has analysed the nature of the economic change and the link to disruption in rural communities.

3 This sentence is a good example of detailed substantiation, signalled by relevant facts, dates and statistics.

Interpretation guidance for Section C

Identify the interpretations

Section C is different from Sections A and B. It presents two extracts from the works of historians. You are expected to use the extracts and your own knowledge to examine the views presented in the extracts and reach conclusions in answer to the question.

Questions in Section C are *not* source analysis questions. You must *not* carry out source analysis on the extracts. There is no credit for issues such as provenance or reliability.

Most questions will offer two extracts with sharp disagreements between them. You must consider the extent to which they disagree and attempt to reconcile these disagreements.

Planning your answer

Below are some issues for you to bear in mind when planning your answer:

- Consider the precise demands made by the question and make detailed use of the two extracts.
- Use the two extracts together at some stage:
  - ☐ consider their differences
  - ☐ compare and contrast their arguments
  - ☐ evaluate their merits
  - ☐ remember to devote equal attention to both extracts.

Make careful use of your own knowledge. This should not form a narrative, nor should it simply be tacked on to the points raised by the extracts. Your own knowledge should be used to relate to the issues raised in the extracts.

The following guide may be helpful in framing your answer:

- Analyse and evaluate the points made by the author of the first extract.
- Analyse and evaluate the points made by the author of the second extract.
- Use your own knowledge and the material in the extracts to support the proposition made in the question.
- Use your own knowledge and the material in the extracts to modify or challenge the proposition made in the question.

For the highest levels of attainment, use the two extracts as a set and draw reasoned conclusions on the question.

Strong conclusions

Good answers will end with a strong conclusion. This does not necessarily have to be exhaustive in length, but should offer a clear and reasoned judgement linked back to the analysis of the viewpoint, including the extracts.

Sample answer

Here is a sample Section C question with a worked answer to guide you. Study Extracts 1 and 2 before you answer this question.

Study Extracts 1 and 2. Historians have different views about the reasons for the abolition of the slave trade. Analyse and evaluate the extracts and use your knowledge of the issues to explain your answer to the following question: How far do you agree with the view that the Quaker anti-slavery campaign was dependent on the work of individuals for success? To explain your answer, analyse and evaluate the material in both extracts, using your own knowledge of the issues.

EXTRACT 1

Adapted from Christopher Brown, *Moral Capital, Foundations of British Abolitionism*, University of North Carolina Press, 2006, pp. 432–3.

The Quakers were central to the abolition movement. The Quaker propaganda campaign made a difference but informed opinion, alone, was not enough to make antislavery a vital political issue. The distinctive qualities that helped make Quakers pioneers in the antislavery movement – their separation from church and state, their marginal place in British society – handicapped their campaign. At the time the abolition movement began, polite society still looked down on religious enthusiasm. To introduce religious topics on social occasions showed poor taste and bad manners. The 'take-off' of Quaker abolitionism ultimately depended on the cooperation of allies outside the Society of Friends.

Thomas Clarkson had a decisive impact on the established Quaker campaign. He enlarged its ambitions and improved its prospects. His personality and personal experience helped Clarkson become an opponent of slavery, but the historical moment and his social position allowed him to become an abolitionist. He could build on the progress that others had made, using their knowledge, experience and networks. Others in Britain had cared and did care a great deal about the sins of slaving, but no other individuals gave their lives to the antislavery cause in the way Clarkson did.

EXTRACT 2

Adapted from James Walvin, *Black Ivory*, Wiley-Blackwell, 1993, p. 304.

The campaign which culminated in black freedom began in 1787 when a small group of Quakers launched a public campaign against the British slave trade. They were to be assisted by the effectiveness of their own campaign tactics. The campaign against slavery took place in years when more and more British people found their lives shaped by conditions in the towns. It was there that the nonconformist chapels took root and Baptist and Methodist congregations found a new social and political voice. Abolitionists were assisted by the social changes around them and the effectiveness of their own campaign tactics. At a time when British manufacturers, workers and economic theorists were promoting the virtues of free labour, the concept of owning a worker seemed to make no sense.

Here is an example of a worked answer:

In some ways, both extracts emphasise the role of the Quakers in the abolition campaign. In Extract 1, however, the Quakers are presented as being dependent on the influence of individuals such as Thomas Clarkson, with the suggestion that they would have achieved little without such allies. In contrast, Extract 2 is more positive about the significance of the Quaker campaigning based on the social conditions that they were working in. Both extracts are convincing, however Extract 1 really only addresses the earlier years of the campaign whereas Extract 2 gives a view that is more representative of the overall period to the abolition of slavery[1].

The Quakers were certainly vocal about the abolition of slavery. Extract 1 identifies that the Quakers were 'central to the abolition movement'. This is a reasonable statement, since they were heavily involved with the Abolition Committee, which was at the centre of the abolition movement. However[2], the extract points out that the Quakers were, by the nature of their Nonconformist faith, outsiders. Many conservative

Anglicans were concerned about the influence of Nonconformist Christianity and this, to a degree, handicapped the effectiveness. The extract notes that early in the period, it was considered poor taste to discuss religious topics in public. This leads to the key point in supporting the statement in the question, as the extract then argues that the work of Thomas Clarkson was crucial in making the Quakers' campaigning more acceptable. Clarkson certainly did play a key role in bringing slavery to the attention of people through his reports, which often featured emotive examples such as families being divided, or used props like handcuffs. The extract, while emphasising the importance of Clarkson, does refer to 'allies outside the Society of Friends' and that Clarkson could 'build on the progress that others had made', therefore supporting the wider claim that the Quakers were dependent on the role of individuals to make progress.

In contrast, Extract 2 presents the Quakers as not being reliant on the work of individuals. It fully focuses on the social and economic context of the Quaker campaign. It mentions the 'social changes' that were occurring and the growing strength of the Nonconformist Churches in towns. This was particularly the case in northern, industrial towns where Nonconformist groups including Quakers became more significant. While Extract 1 sees the Quakers as reliant on the work of individuals to make their abolitionist arguments socially acceptable, Extract 2 argues that the mindset of the population was already changing based on economic ideas of free labour, to the degree that 'the concept of owning a worker seemed to make no sense'[3]. This is referring to the growing support for the ideas of free trade, which were supported by Pitt's government from 1783. Supporters of free trade argued that only with international competition and free labour could economic forces reach their potential. This appeared to be supported by the fact that in the late eighteenth century, slavery appeared to be becoming less profitable. British merchants were finding that New World traders were driving prices down by their ability to direct local trade. Therefore, the extract sees the social changes of industrialisation, urbanisation and

free trade ideology as a basis for the Quaker campaign.

It is reasonable to argue that individuals were important to the Quaker campaigns. After all, they had been questioning the morality of slavery since the early eighteenth century, since it conflicted with their beliefs on salvation. In this period, they had not been taken seriously as a political voice. The greater success that they enjoyed only came about after the Abolition Committee formed in 1787. Although this primarily relied on a Quaker network for sharing pamphlets, organising meetings and carrying out petitions, it was crucial that individuals such as Clarkson were involved. While Clarkson provided reports that supported the Quaker campaigning, Granville Sharp was also significant in the legal cases that he was involved in - he had already won cases in 1766 and 1772 before becoming involved with the Quaker campaign[4]. William Wilberforce was also important in leading the movement. Not only was he an Anglican, but he was vocal in his opposition to the French Revolution. This addresses the issue in Extract 1 that the Quaker campaigning was considered impolite, since he was an acceptable, conservative voice for sharing the Quaker viewpoint. Wilberforce had also been involved with the Clapham Sect, an Anglican group of politically conservative and respectable men. This helped to legitimise the Quaker message, which ran in parallel to the Clapham Sect. However, it is of note that this argument in Extract 1 is made in reference to 'polite society'. Therefore, it is perhaps more accurate to emphasise the need for individuals, not in society as a whole, but specifically in persuading the wealthier members of society to pay attention[5].

While Extract 1 reasonably supports the importance of individuals in getting the abolitionist message across to the wealthier parts of society, the argument in Extract 2 about the social changes is more applicable to the middle and working classes. Quakers were more represented in middle-class society, and it was the industrialists who were most drawn to the free trade ideology referred to in the extract. To insist on the need for individuals to reach these parts of society would overlook the strong and growing popular support for abolition – during 1791 alone, the Abolition Committee, which was primarily Quaker and used Quaker networks, was able to send 519 petitions to parliament, which indicates that the Quakers had achieved a substantial level of support.

However, what neither extract really takes into account were other crucial factors that led to the Quaker success. One factor was the role of women. Many Quakers were women and there was a broader abolitionist support among women. One key impact was that women read and even wrote much of the anti-slavery literature produced in the period. This made it socially acceptable to discuss such topics in polite company, which went a long way to breaking down the taboo referred to in Extract 1. Alongside this social change was the rise in shocking accounts which contributed to making abolition a popular topic. For example, in 1783 the case of the slave ship Zong, in which the captain drowned 128 slaves to stop the spread of disease, and then a case in 1796, in which slaves starved to death on a ship where the captain had failed to load enough food, caused enough popular uproar that the Quaker message was more readily accepted by the population, including polite society**[6]**.

Extract 1 is correct to emphasise the importance of individuals such as Clarkson, in making the Quaker message acceptable. However, this is more relevant to the earlier part of the period than to the later part, after which humanitarian concerns and the Abolition Committee had gained respectability in their own right. It is also

more applicable to the impact on the wealthier members of society rather than the population as a whole. In reference to the whole period leading up to the 1807 Abolition Act, Extract 2 carries more weight in seeing the Quaker campaigning in a broader social and economic setting which made slavery less appealing. Further, there were more social changes, for example with the role of women, than were acknowledged in Extract 2. However, since ultimately it was an Anglican, Wilberforce, who proposed the bill which led to the abolition of slavery, it was really the role of individuals that focused a campaign which was made possible by changing social conditions**[7]**.

1 The introduction demonstrates immediate focus on the question, sets out where the extracts stand, and suggests what the essay will argue.

2 Extract 1's statement that the Quakers were central to the movement is evaluated through a specific development by referring to the Abolition Committee.

3 While it is acceptable to deal with the extracts one at a time, reaching the highest levels of attainment requires exploring the two extracts together.

4 Other examples of own knowledge have been used to support and discuss the view from the extracts.

5 The final part of this paragraph is beginning to combine the contrasting ideas by identifying that the view in one extract is really only addressing one section of society.

6 This paragraph raises issues that are relevant to the question but not addressed in the extracts.

7 The conclusion sums up the argument and in the last sentence gives a fresh idea to add weight to that argument.

Timeline

Year	Monarch and prime minister	Domestic events	Foreign events
1783	King George III William Pitt the Younger (Tory)		
1784		Pitt's successful general election	
1786		Sinking fund introduced	
1789			French Revolution
1791		Wilberforce presented first anti-slavery bill to parliament	
1793			France declared war on Britain
1794		Treason Trial of the London Corresponding Society leaders	
1797		Fox declared the end of Whig parliamentary opposition	
1798		Wolf Tone's United Irishmen rebellion	
1799		Combination Act (also 1800)	
1801	Henry Addington (Viscount Sidmouth, Tory)	Act of Union joined Ireland and Britain	
1802			Peace of Amiens signed
1804	William Pitt the Younger (Tory)		
1805			Battle of Trafalgar
1806	William Grenville (Whig)	Foreign Slave Trade Act	
1807	William Cavendish-Bentinck (Duke of Portland, Whig)	Abolition of the Slave Trade Act	
1808			Start of Peninsular Campaigns
1809	Spencer Perceval (Tory)		
1811		Luddite discontent spread	War with USA until 1815
1812	Robert Jenkinson (Lord Liverpool, Tory)		
1814			Capture of Paris
1815		Corn Laws introduced	Congress of Vienna Battle of Waterloo
1819		Peterloo Massacre	
1821			Start of 'Greek question'
1822		Liverpool's cabinet reshuffle	
1824		Combination Acts repealed	
1825		Combination Act repeal legislation amended	
1827	George Canning (Tory) Frederick Robinson (Viscount Goderich, Tory)		
1828	Arthur Wellesley (Duke of Wellington, Tory)	Corn Laws amended with sliding scale	
1829		Catholic Emancipation Act passed	
1830	Charles Grey (Earl Grey, Whig)	First public meeting of Birmingham Political Union First large-scale freight and public railway opened (Manchester to Liverpool) Swing Riots began	

Year	Monarch and prime minister	Domestic events	Foreign events
1832		Reform Act passed	
1834	William Lamb (Viscount Melbourne, Whig) Robert Peel (Conservative)	Poor Law Amendment Act passed Tamworth Manifesto	
1835	William Lamb (Viscount Melbourne, Whig)	Lichfield Compact	
1837	Queen Victoria		
1838		People's Charter published	
1839		First Chartist petition	
1841	Robert Peel (Conservative)		
1842		Second Chartist petition	
1846	John Russell (Whig)	Repeal of the Corn Laws	
1848		Third Chartist petition Public Health Act	
1851		Great Exhibition, London	
1852	Edward Stanley (Earl Derby) (Conservative) George Hamilton-Gordon (Earl Aberdeen, Conservative)		
1853			Crimean War
1855	Henry Temple (Viscount Palmerston, Conservative)		
1857			Indian Rebellion against Britain
1858	Edward Stanley (Earl Derby, Conservative)		
1859	Henry Temple (Viscount Palmerston, Conservative)	Formation of Liberal Party	Second War of Italian unification
1865	John Russell (Whig)		End of American Civil War
1866	Edward Stanley (Earl Derby, Conservative)		
1867		Second Reform Act	
1868	Benjamin Disraeli (Conservative) William Gladstone (Liberal)		
1871		Trade Union Act	
1872		Ballot Act	
1873		Great Depression began	
1874	Benjamin Disraeli (Conservative)		
1875		Public Health Act	
1880	William Gladstone (Liberal)		
1883		Corrupt and Illegal Practices Act	
1884		Third Reform Act	
1885	Robert Cecil (Marquess Salisbury, Conservative)	Redistribution Act	

Glossary of terms

Abdicate   When a monarch resigns from ruling.

Act of Habeas Corpus   An old English law which gave anyone arrested the right to face trial or be released.

Adulteration   Adding cheaper, low-quality ingredients to a food or drug, possibly with dangerous consequences, to reduce the cost or give the appearance that there is more of the product.

Agents provocateurs   Government employees who would join radical organisations to identify the leaders and encourage radical behaviour so people could be arrested.

Amalgamated Society of Engineers (ASE)   A New Model Union of skilled engineers formed in 1851.

American War of Independence   Conflict between American colonists and the British army 1775–83, which resulted in the American colonies forming an independent nation.

Anglo-Zulu War   A six-month invasion in 1879 of Zululand in order to create a South African colonial federation. Although victorious, there were many British losses, such as when 800 British soldiers were killed when Zulu troops destroyed a British column at Isandlwana.

Anti-Bourbon   The French royal family name was Bourbon; anti-Bourbon refers to opponents of the French monarchy.

Anti-Corn Law League   A political movement, formed initially in 1836 and which became a national movement in 1838. It focused on persuading the government to abolish the Corn Laws.

April Uprising   A rebellion in 1876 by Bulgarian nationalists led to reprisals by the Turkish government. Turkish military units, who were Muslim, massacred many Bulgarians, who were primarily Christian. Reports reached Britain of brutal violence and piles of rotting bodies and skulls. Official British estimates suggested 15,000 dead.

Beaconsfieldism   This was the term Gladstone used for the Conservative imperialist foreign policies, which included the Zulu and Afghan Wars. The name was a reference to Disraeli's title of Earl of Beaconsfield.

Bills   A proposal for a law is a bill. When it is passed, it becomes an Act.

Bloody Code   A collection of laws for which the punishments were execution.

Census   An official government collection of population data. In Britain, this has been completed every ten years since 1801.

Chartism   A political movement which demanded political reform such as universal suffrage. Chartists were particularly strong in the north of England. Some of their main tactics were petitions and marches.

Cholera   A water-borne disease which causes severe dehydration and death.

Coaching inns   Businesses which provided food, drink and accommodation to people travelling by coach.

Coalition   An alliance of politicians with differing viewpoints.

Collectivism   The belief that the State should make judgements on the affairs of individuals and ensure that adequate living conditions are provided.

Common land   Land that was often owned by a local landlord, but unfenced and used communally by all.

Conference of Amalgamated Trades   An organisation that formed to represent a number of unions from different industries. It acted as a forum to unite labour organisations.

Congress System   Also known as the Concert of Europe, this was the diplomatic network which protected the *status quo* in subsequent years. It is different from congress diplomacy, which is the principle of using meetings to maintain peace. Both of these are different from the Congress

of Vienna (the meeting in Vienna 1814–15) and the Vienna Settlement (the 1815 agreement on borders and territories).

Constituencies   Voting areas in Britain. In 1783–1870, each one had one or two MPs.

Corn Laws   Legislation introduced in 1815 which kept food prices high to protect landowners' profits. The Corn Laws were unpopular with working people.

Counter-reformist   A person who opposes reform.

Dublin Parliament   From 1264 until 1800, Ireland had its own parliament. From 1692, it met in Dublin.

Dutch East Indies   A Dutch colony in Southeast Asia which is now Indonesia.

East India Company   A private business which controlled trade in Asia, particularly India. It had become almost a government in its own right as it made political decisions, controlled private troops and carried out diplomatic negotiations with other countries.

Enclosure   The act of closing off pieces of common land for private use.

Establishment   The group of people with power.

Evangelical   A term used collectively to describe fundamentalist Christians who adhere to the Gospels in the Bible and have an enthusiasm to spread their beliefs.

Exchequer   The British government's economic department.

Fall of the Bastille   On 14 July 1789, a crowd stormed the Bastille, a medieval fortress in Paris that was used as a political prison. This event is still celebrated annually in France.

Fenian   A member of the Irish Republican Brotherhood, a revolutionary nationalist Irish organisation which sought Irish independence.

Flying shuttle   A powered mechanism which made cloth that was both wider and woven more quickly than was possible with earlier methods, and needed fewer weavers.

Free trade   The belief that the economy should be left alone by the government, without tariffs or restrictions.

French Revolution   Event in 1789 when French radicals overthrew the monarchy and formed a new government. The revolutionary government was based on the radical idea of equal rights for all citizens.

Gentry   Wealthy people below the nobility in social class.

Gold bullion   Bars of gold kept by a bank to guarantee the value of its printed money.

Grand National Consolidated Trades Union (GNCTU)   Robert Owen's attempt to form a national trade union in 1834.

Great Exhibition   A public event at Crystal Palace, London, in 1851 which showcased British industrial and imperial strength.

Holy Alliance   This agreement between Russia, Prussia and Austria was so-called because they agreed to base their relationship on Christian values.

Home Rule   Irish nationalists campaigned in parliament for the right for independent political rule in Ireland.

Humanitarian   Concerned with the well-being of human beings.

Individualism   The belief that individuals should direct their own lives without State interference.

Insolvency   When a person or business does not have the money to cover their bills.

Invisible trade   Financial transactions involving services, such as banking or insurance, not goods.

Irish Repeal Party   A political movement formed in 1830 by Daniel O'Connell. Encouraged by the 1829 Emancipation Act, its demanded the repeal of the Acts of Union that joined Ireland to the UK.

Italian unification   The process of the Italian states overthrowing their Austrian masters and forming a country. In 1859, Sardinia and

France succeeded in forcing Austria out of most of Italy, making unification a possibility.

Junta   An unofficial committee of the secretaries of five influential unions which co-ordinated with each other.

Knobsticks   Strikebreakers; a derogatory term for workers who ignored strike action and continued to work.

Ladies of the bedchamber   Personal attendants to the queen. These were traditionally from noble families.

Laissez-faire   Government policy of leaving an issue alone and not interfering.

Land Plan   Chartist leader Feargus O'Connor organised an investment scheme to buy land, with the idea that shareholders would get enough land to gain the vote. The scheme was badly planned, and it could not provide all shareholders with land. The government investigated it and found that it did not meet the requirements for legal registration. It was shut down in 1851. The whole scheme discredited the Chartist leadership.

Land tenure   The issue of who owns the land and what their rights are.

Liberal Tories   Tory politicians in the 1820s who were more liberal.

Lodging houses   Cheap hostels where a person could pay for a bed.

Majority government   When a government has enough votes in the Commons to pass laws that they propose.

Methodists   A group of Protestant Churches, separate from the Church of England, with fundamentalist beliefs based on a strict reading of the Bible.

Middle passage   The name for the stage of the slave-trading voyages in which slaves were transported across the Atlantic from Africa.

Minority government   When the government controls fewer votes in the Commons than their opponents, making it hard to pass laws that they propose.

National debt   The amount of money that the government of a country has borrowed from banks and money lenders.

New Model Unions   Organisations of smaller unions working together. They developed formalised structures and management.

Nonconformist   A member of a Christian sect that is not Anglican, such as Quakers or Methodists.

Obstructionism   A political tactic of using long speeches to disrupt government business in parliament.

Ottoman Empire   The empire of the country now known as Turkey.

Outdoor relief   Money, food and clothing that was given to people in poverty. It was 'outdoor' in the sense that they received the help without having to enter a workhouse.

Patronage   Offering positions, salaries, pensions or honours to supporters.

Pauper   A person in poverty who needed financial assistance. While some people spent their whole lives as paupers, others who lived close to the poverty line could drift in and out of being a pauper.

Peerage   A title of nobility. From most to least important they are duke, marquess, earl, viscount, baron. Collectively they can be called 'lord'.

Peninsular Campaign   British campaigns against France in Portugal and Spain from 1808 to 1814.

Petition   A political statement signed by supporters and presented to parliament to demand reform.

Philanthropic   The principle of promoting the welfare of others, often through charity to good causes.

Poaching   Hunting animals on land owned by someone else.

Poor relief   Financial support given to those in poverty under the Poor Law.

Protectionism   An economic system for safeguarding domestic production by imposing tariffs and levies on imported goods from foreign countries.

Protestant Ascendency The political, economic and social domination of Ireland by the minority group of landowners and Protestant clergy, all of whom belonged to the Anglican Church.

Quakers Also known as the Religious Society of Friends. A Christian denomination which emphasises personal spiritual experience over ritual and tradition.

Regency Crisis When George III took ill, Pitt's opponents tried to appoint Prince George as regent to rule in his father's place.

Reparations Money paid after a war by the losing side.

Republican A political viewpoint in favour of a government without a monarch.

Revolutionary and Napoleonic Wars Conflict broke out between France and other European nations in 1792, called the Revolutionary War. Britain became involved in 1793. After a brief peace in 1802–3, the war resumed until 1815. This second phase is known as the Napoleonic Wars.

Rotten borough A constituency with very few voters, often fewer than 30, where the landlord could essentially pick the MP they wanted.

Royal Commission A committee formed by the monarch to investigate a specific issue for the government, with the aim of informing future legislation.

Run on the banks This was where protestors who had paper money would go to the London banks and demand the cash equivalent in gold, causing a cash crisis.

Second Anglo-Afghan War A British invasion of Afghanistan between 1878 and 1880 to prevent Russian involvement which would have left British India vulnerable to future invasion. Although victorious, it involved 50,000 British troops.

Self-help A common belief in the mid–nineteenth century that people should help themselves out of poverty through hard work.

Sinecure An honorary position given by the Crown for loyalty. It involved no work but gave an income.

Sinking fund A method of government investment to reduce national debt.

Socialist A person who believes in socialism, the notion that the workers should own the factories in which they work and that society should function cooperatively, rather than the wealthy few controlling the economy.

Spinning mule A powered machine which span threads into yarn for weaving more quickly than older methods, with fewer workers.

Status quo The existing situation.

Swing Riots An outbreak of unrest in 1830 across southern England and East Anglia. Labourers smashed threshing machines and burned workhouses and barns in protest at harsh living conditions and the mechanisation of agriculture.

Tithe War 1830–3 The tithe was an obligatory payment by citizens in Ireland to pay for the upkeep of the Anglican Church. This was resented by Catholics, but after the 1829 Emancipation Act, more organised resistance to paying emerged. The government responded by seizing goods, and this led to outbreaks of violence.

Tolpuddle Martyrs A legal case in 1834, in which six agricultural labourers from the village of Tolpuddle in Dorset were convicted of swearing an oath as members of a labour union, and sentenced to transportation.

Tories Politicians who supported the king and opposed reform.

Trade unions Organisations of workers formed to protect their rights against their employers. One tactic is to organise strikes to demand better conditions or pay.

Trades council A meeting of representatives from different unions with the aim of uniting their demands.

Transportation Some criminals were punished by being sent abroad to serve their sentence. Australia was the main destination from 1787.

Treaty of Nanjing At the end of a war between Britain and China (the Opium War) in 1842, China ceded the rights for British merchants to trade freely at five Chinese ports.

Triangle trade Refers to the British slave trade, a reference to the three stages of the journey (Britain to Africa, to the Americas, to Britain).

Turnpike roads Private roads, set up by private investors, which charged a toll, or fee, for people travelling on them.

Ulster Protestants Protestants in the Ulster region of Ireland who supported British, Protestant control of Ireland.

Ultra Tories Tory politicians in the 1820s who were more conservative.

United Irishmen An Irish republican association which opposed British control of Ireland.

Universal male suffrage The right for all men to vote. (Suffrage is the right to vote, while universal suffrage is the right for men and women to vote.)

Urbanisation The process of towns and cities growing in size and population.

Utilitarianism The belief that the driving force of the individual is to seek pleasure and avoid pain through their own efforts.

Visible trade Financial transactions involving goods and materials.

Whig Politicians who opposed royal power and sought reform.

Workhouse A place where people in poverty could go for financial support. After 1834, these became particularly horrible places that were feared by the poor.

Yeomanry A yeoman was a man owning a small rural area of land, and the yeomanry was a military group made up of these men.

Further reading

General reading

Richard Brown, *Revolution, Radicalism and Reform, England 1780–1846* (Cambridge University Press, 2000)
Covers the broad topics on the nature and impact of protest and radical reform up to 1846

Chris Cook and John Stevenson, *The Longman Handbook of Modern British History 1714–2001* (Longman, 2001)
A collection of data and evidence on the period, including thematic timelines, tables and charts, with all manner of statistical data about the period

Eric Evans, *Parliamentary Reform, c.1770–1918* (Longman Seminar Studies, 2000)
A detailed reference specific to political reform

Eric Evans, *The Forging of the Modern State, Early Industrial Britain 1783–1870* (Longman, 2001)
A thorough account of the period, organised chronologically and thematically

Chapter 2

Christopher Brown, *Moral Capital: Foundations of British Abolitionism* (North Carolina University Press, 2006)
A discussion of the issue of abolition of slavery

Ian Christie, *Wars and Revolutions: Britain, 1760–1815* (Harvard University Press, 1982)
Considers the impact of the revolutionary period on Britain

Richard Cooper, 'William Pitt, Taxation, and the Needs of War.' *Journal of British Studies*, Vol. 22, No. 1, 1982, pp. 94–103
An interesting article assessing the financial policies of Pitt. Available free online with JSTOR

David Eltis and Stanley L. Engerman, 'The Importance of Slavery and the Slave Trade to Industrializing Britain.' *Journal of Economic History*, Vol. 60, No. 1, 2000, pp. 123–44
A discussion of the economic relevance of slavery for Britain. Available free online with JSTOR

William Hague, *William Pitt the Younger* (HarperCollins, 2004)
A well-regarded biography of Pitt which covers all aspects of his period

Jennifer Mori, *Britain in the Age of the French Revolution, 1785–1820* (Routledge, 2000)
An interesting work on Britain during the period of the French Revolution

Chapter 3

Eric Hobsbawm, *The Age of Revolution: Europe, 1789–1848* (Abacus, 2012)
A major historical work which has sections on British society and politics during this period

David Horspool, *The English Rebel: 1000 Years of Troublemaking from the Normans to the Nineties* (Penguin, 2009)
A different angle on radicalism which focuses on radicalism in the period as part of a wider theme

Graham Phythian, *Peterloo: Voices, Sabres and Silence* (The History Press, 2018)
A largely narrative account of Peterloo, interesting for a better knowledge of the event

Paul Weindling, 'Science and Sedition: How Effective Were the Acts Licensing Lectures and Meetings, 1795–1819?' *British Journal for the History of Science*, Vol. 13, No. 2, 1980, pp. 139–53
A review of the government response to radicalism. Available free online with JSTOR

Chapter 4

Roger Knight, *Britain Against Napoleon: The Organisation of Victory, 1793–1815* (Penguin, 2014)
Looks at Britain's role in the Revolutionary and Napoleonic Wars with a focus on the importance of domestic policy

Mike Rapport, *The Napoleonic Wars: A Very Short Introduction* (Oxford University Press, 2013)
A short overview of the Revolutionary and Napoleonic Wars

Chapter 5

John Addy, *The Agrarian Revolution* (Prentice Hall, 1972)
Focuses specifically on agricultural change

Brian Inglis, *Poverty & The Industrial Revolution* (Endeavour Media, 2018)
An overview of industrialisation that is focused on the lives of the poor

Roger Osborne, *Iron, Steam & Money: The Making of the Industrial Revolution* (Pimlico, 2013)
An overview of the process of industrialisation

Chapter 6

Hugh Cunningham, *The Challenge of Democracy, Britain 1832–1918* (Pearson, 2001)
A broad coverage of political change in the period

Annette Mayer, *The Growth of Democracy in Britain* (Hodder Education, 1999)
A detailed A level text on the extension of democracy that focuses on the Reform Acts

Robert Pearce and Roger Stearn, *Government and Reform: Britain 1815–1918* (Hodder Education, 2000)
A wider ranging A level text on political reform

Graham Stewart, *Britannia – 100 Documents That Shaped a Nation* (Atlantic Books, 2010)
A collection and discussion of significant historical documents, including the Tamworth Manifesto and 1832 Reform Act

John Walton, *The Second Reform Act* (Routledge, 1983)
A detailed study of the 1867 Reform Act

Chapter 7

Richard Aldous, *The Lion and the Unicorn: Gladstone vs. Disraeli* (Pimlico, 2007)
An account of the careers and relationship of the two men

Eugenio Biagini, *Gladstone* (Palgrave, 2000)
A comprehensive but accessible study of Gladstone's career

John Walton, *Disraeli* (Routledge, 1990)
The equivalent work on Disraeli

Chapter 8

N. Tonge and M. Quincey, 'Depression and Decline? The British Economy 1870–1900', in *British Social and Economic History 1800–1900. Documents and Debates* (Palgrave, 1980)
A chapter reviewing the state of the economy and the issue of depression from the 1870s

Chapter 9

Alan Kidd, *State, Society and the Poor in Nineteenth Century England* (Palgrave, 1999)
A challenging text on poverty and the response of society in the nineteenth century

Rosemary Rees, *Poverty and Public Health 1848–1948* (Oxford University Press, 2001)
An A level work on social pressure and reform

Chapter 10

A. Harrison and B. Hutchins, *A History of Factory Legislation* (Routledge, 2013)
A challenging but thorough account of the details and significance of the Factory Acts

Keith Laybourn, *A History of British Trade Unionism, c.1770–1990* (Sutton, 1990)
A focused account on the development of trade unions in Britain

Henry Pelling, *A History of British Trade Unionism* (Pelican, 1976)
A second overview of trade union history

Index